Understanding Family Violence

Treating and Preventing Partner, Child, Sibling, and Elder Abuse

Vernon R. Wiehe

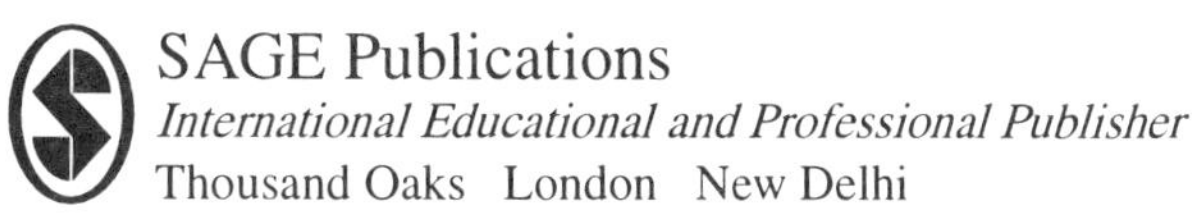
SAGE Publications
International Educational and Professional Publisher
Thousand Oaks London New Delhi

For information:

SAGE Publications, Inc.
2455 Teller Road
Thousand Oaks, California 91320
E-mail: order@sagepub.com

SAGE Publications Ltd.
6 Bonhill Street
London EC2A 4PU
United Kingdom

SAGE Publications India Pvt. Ltd.
M-32 Market
Greater Kailash I
New Delhi 110 048 India

Printed in the United States of America

Library of Congress Cataloging-in-Publication Data

Wiehe, Vernon R.
Understanding family violence: Treating and preventing partner, child, sibling, and elder abuse / by Vernon R. Wiehe.
p. cm.
Includes bibliographical references and index.
ISBN 0-7619-1644-X (cloth: acid-free paper)
ISBN 0-7619-1645-8 (pbk.: acid-free paper)
1. Family violence—United States—Prevention. 2. Family violence—Treatment—United States. 3. Family social work—United States. I. Title.
HV6626.2.W53 1998
362.82′927′0973—ddc21 98-8982

This book is printed on acid-free paper.

98 99 00 01 02 03 10 9 8 7 6 5 4 3 2 1

Acquiring Editor: C. Terry Hendrix
Editorial Assistant: Dale Grenfell
Production Editor: Michèle Lingre/Astrid Virding
Editorial Assistant: Lynn Miyata
Designer/Typesetter: Janelle LeMaster
Copy Editor: Joyce Kuhn
Cover Designer: Candice Harman

UNDERSTANDING FAMILY VIOLENCE

Contents

Preface

Violence in the family is a serious problem. Daily, the media present accounts of partner, child, or elder abuse. Another type of family violence, sibling abuse, shown by research to even be more prevalent than partner and child abuse, is rarely mentioned but often is excused as "normal sibling rivalry" (Straus, Gelles, & Steinmetz, 1980).

The purpose of this book is to acquaint readers with a theoretical understanding of family violence, the various ways the problem is being treated, and how each type of family violence may be prevented. The book is directed to undergraduate and graduate students in fields of study such as psychology, sociology, nursing, social work, family studies, and pastoral counseling. I will collectively refer in the text to these students in these various fields of study as "mental health professionals." Although the book is not intended to be a "how to" guide for clinicians working with perpetrators and victims of family violence, those engaging in an empirically based practice where their interventions flow from their theoretical understanding of the problem will find the book's contents helpful in working with abusive individuals and families.

Heavy emphasis is placed in the book on research because I often find individuals working in the field of family violence who do not have a sound empirical understanding of the problem but, rather, are "flying by the seat of their pants." In some instances, these individuals are attracted to the work because of their own past history of being a victim of abuse from a parent, mate, or sibling. Their knowledge is largely based on their personal experiences, which may not be typical. In other instances, those working in the field are often so overburdened with the demand for services that they cannot keep abreast of the research that is occurring. In still other situations, an understanding of family violence may be based on the portrayal of the problem in the media, which may overdramatize certain aspects of the problem. A sound theoretical understanding based on research must be the foundation of our understanding of the various types of family violence, of our interventions in treating the problem, and of our efforts to prevent it.

Here I digress a bit to discuss the importance of theory in understanding a social problem such as family violence. I liken the use of theory to the function of a magnifying glass. Imagine that you have a piece of paper in front of you with such very small print that when you attempt to read the message on the paper, the paper becomes a blur of ink. However, when you look at the small print through a magnifying glass, the blur of ink begins to take the shape of letters and the combination of letters forms words and the words come together in sentences that present to you a message that you can both read and understand.

Theory acts in a somewhat similar fashion. Human behavior is very complex. Situations of family violence—for example, an adult male sexually abusing a small child—reflect the complexity of human behavior. Unfortunately, when we experience the dissonance of trying to understand a problem, such as child sexual abuse, we often resort to "myths" or stereotypical ways of thinking about the problem that may cause us to incorrectly understand the problem or to inappropriately intervene. A theoretical understanding of the problem based on research can help prevent this from occurring. Thus, a heavy emphasis has been placed on theory in this book.

What is theory? I like to think of theory as a framework, as a foundation for understanding human behavior. In the social sciences we avoid the use of the word *cause* when trying to understand human behavior because of its complexity. Rather than trying to identify what causes, for example, child sexual abuse, we prefer to talk about factors *related* to or *associated* with the problem. Here is where theory enters the picture. Research or the application of scientific methodology enables us to identify factors that may be related to or associated with a problem. Two levels of theory are presented in the text. In the opening chapter, several general theories of aggression are presented because family violence is aggression of one person against another. In subsequent chapters, as the various types of family violence are discussed—child, partner, elder, sibling abuse—more specific theories in the form of factors identified from research that are related to each of these types of abuse are identified.

What purpose do these theories serve? First, theories help in understanding human behavior, or in this instance, the various types of family violence; and second, theories provide clues for intervention and prevention. Remember the example of the magnifying glass. Reading about an incident of an adult male sexually abusing a child may be revolting and disgusting. Your sense of decency and respect for others may cause you to say, "How could someone do this to a small child?" Your response may cause you to lash out in anger against the perpetrator. Viewing this same incident from a theoretical perspective helps you begin to *understand* the incident. Do not confuse understanding the problem with *condoning* the problem. Your attempt to understand the factors contributing to a perpetrator sexually abusing a child does not mean that you approve of the behavior. Thus, the first purpose that theory serves is to enable us to understand complex human behavior. (This understanding changes over time as new research occurs. Thus, it is important for mental health professionals to stay current in their knowledge of family violence by reading journals and attending professional conferences.) The second purpose that theory serves is that as we develop a theoretical understanding of a problem or become aware of factors that are related to or associated with a problem, we begin to receive clues or indicators for ways we can intervene in the problem or prevent the problem from occurring. Let's go back to the sexual abuse perpetrator. Research shows, for example, a factor that is related to some men who sexually abuse children is that they themselves were victims of sexual abuse. This theoretical knowledge suggests that a possible component for the treatment of some sexual abusers may be therapy that gives perpetrators an opportunity to talk about their own victimization, which they in turn are repeating on others.

Four types of family violence are discussed: child, partner, elder, and sibling abuse. Three forms in which each of these types of violence appear in families are presented: physical, emotional, and sexual abuse. Child neglect, while a form of child abuse, is not discussed in this book because it is not considered a form of family violence. Child neglect is an act of omission rather than commission. This is not to deny, however, that child neglect is itself a serious societal problem.

I relied heavily in the chapter on child abuse on an earlier publication titled *Working With Child Abuse and Neglect* (Wiehe, 1996) and in the chapter on sibling abuse on my book, *Sibling Abuse: The Hidden Physical, Emotional, and Sexual Trauma* (Wiehe, 1997b).

Key terms defined throughout the book are shown in boldface to emphasize their importance as relevant elements to incorporate in discussions on family violence in general or on specific types of abuse.

May the book give you a better understanding of family violence as a social problem in society as well as its treatment and prevention. After reading this book, you may even wish to consider working to combat this problem by volunteering in one of the many social service agencies dedicated to helping survivors and preventing others from becoming victims of family violence.

1

Aggression

In the following chapters, various types of family violence are discussed—child, partner, elder, and sibling abuse. A theoretical framework for understanding each of these types of family violence in terms of factors associated with that specific type of abuse is presented. These factors answer the question, "Why would someone abuse another person—a child, a partner, an elderly parent, or a sibling?"

Prior to discussing factors identified in research as associated with each of these types of abuse, several theoretical perspectives from social psychology for understanding aggression in general are presented because aggression underlies each of these types of family violence (Meyer, 1996). The purpose of this chapter is to answer the questions, "Why do people behave aggressively toward each other?" and "How can we understand such behavior?" The theories presented in this chapter serve as a foundation for the more specific theoretical frameworks for understanding each of the various types of family violence presented in the subsequent chapters.

Prior to discussing these theories of aggression, terms used repeatedly throughout this book are defined. These terms are shown in boldface type to emphasize their importance as elements for inclusion in discussions on family violence.

DEFINITION OF TERMS

What is aggression? **Aggression** is generally defined as injurious or destructive behavior of one person directed toward another. The individual who is the target of the behavior does not want to be treated in that way (Meyer, 1996). The term **behavior** refers to physical and verbal acts. Physical acts of aggression may include hitting, punching, slapping, or even the use of weapons. Verbal aggression includes insulting, demeaning, or hurtful comments directed toward another person. As will be discussed in subsequent chapters, verbal aggression, labeled in family violence as **emotional abuse** or **psychological maltreatment,** although leaving no physical evidence can be extremely destructive to a victim's emotional well-being and often underlies physical acts of aggression (Claussen & Crittenden, 1991).

Behavior that is aggressive should be distinguished from behavior that is assertive, even though these two terms are often used interchangeably. A company's marketing strategy or a salesperson's approach to a client is often described as aggressive. "He is an aggressive salesman," someone might say about a successful insurance sales representative. A company's marketing strategy or a salesperson's approach to customers does not represent behavior that intends to be injurious or destructive, that harms, hurts, or destroys another person. Thus, to label this behavior aggressive is inappropriate. Rather, a more appropriate word for describing the company's marketing strategy or a salesperson's approach to customers would be to describe these behaviors as assertive. To be assertive implies stating one's position forcefully, boldly, and with conviction, being persistent and persuasive. Being assertive also includes standing up for one's rights in interpersonal relationships, which is a skill taught in assertiveness training.

Two types of aggression may be identified: **hostile** and **instrumental** (Buss, 1971). This distinction is important for the discussion of child abuse in the next chapter. Hostile aggression is behavior with the intent to harm or injure another person. For example, a parent inappropriately trying to teach a child not to play with fire may light a match and hold the burning match to the child's hand. The parent intends to hurt the child as part of this inappropriate method of discipline.

Instrumental aggression involves behavior that may produce injury, but the intent or motivation of the individual engaging in the behavior is not to hurt or injure another person. Instrumental aggression may be seen, for example, in parental use of corporal punishment. Although a parent may not intend to injure a child when using corporal punishment, during the course of a whipping or beating, bruises may appear, an arm may be sprained, a concussion may occur, or similar injuries may result.

Several other terms used repeatedly in subsequent chapters are defined. The individual engaging in the aggressive behavior is referred to as the **perpetrator.** The person who is the object or target of the aggressive behavior is the **victim.** However, individuals who have been victims of various forms of abuse prefer to call themselves **survivors.** Being a victim implies helplessness. For example, the victim of an automobile accident may be trapped in the wreckage or may be unconscious. The victim needs someone to act as a rescuer. Being a survivor, however, implies persistence and recovery, despite the abuse that has occurred. In subsequent chapters, the term survivor is generally used to refer to the individual who was the target of abuse by a perpetrator; however, at times the term victim is used when referring to the targeted individual while the abuse is occurring.

THEORETICAL PERSPECTIVES OF AGGRESSION

Several theoretical perspectives have been proposed as a way to understand aggression. Those discussed here are (a) aggression as instinct or drive, (b) aggression as a result of frustration, (c) aggression as a learned behavior, and (d) aggression as power and control (patriarchal theory). A general model of aggression that incorporates aspects of all four theories concludes the chapter.

A combination of these theories and model, in addition to theoretical factors specifically associated with each of the types of family violence, are used in subsequent chapters to understand the various types of abuse that occur in families.

Aggression as Instinct or Drive

Sigmund Freud proposed that aggression was an inborn instinct or drive, a self-generating force, as compared to later theorists who felt aggression was a reaction or response to a situation (Crain, 1992; Meyer, 1996). Freud postulated that all human beings have two basic drives: aggressive and sexual (libidinal). The two drives were thought to appear in human behavior in a fused state. The aggressive drive was seen as basically destructive. Thus, it was referred to as **thanatos,** or the **death instinct.** This destructive energy or aggression could be directed toward others or could be turned in on the self. If the latter occurred, a person would engage in self-punitive behaviors or suicide. The aggressive drive, Freud felt, could also be diverted into positive channels, such as in the pursuit of a career or a hobby.

Freud theorized that aggressive and libidinal energy, similar to steam, must be released periodically. Just as steam builds up pressure that needs to be released, so these instinctual energies within the human psyche may be in need of occasional release or expression. Release may occur directly in the display of aggressive behavior or indirectly through socially acceptable ways, such as work, hobbies, competitive games, and sports. This is known as the energistic perspective of Freud's psychosexual theory of the human psyche.

Konrad Lorenz (1966) studied animal behavior and, like Freud, believed that aggression is an instinct; however, he viewed aggression as necessary for the survival of a species. Lorenz emphasized that most animals show aggression in keeping with Darwin's principle that only the fittest of a species survive (Ridley, 1987). However, animals generally inhibit their aggression against their own species, except for dominance, territory, or mates, so that the species can continue to exist. Lorenz suggested that these inhibitions did not evolve in the human species. With the invention of weapons and without inhibitions against directing aggression toward other humans, the human species is placed in a position of potential self-destruction. Thus, humans must find ways to drain off or sublimate this aggressive energy or instinct (Penrod, 1986). Although Lorenz's views have been subjected to extensive criticism, the fact remains that human beings are capable of engaging in aggressive behavior toward other humans.

Social psychologists disagree with the instinctual theory of aggression primarily on the basis that there is no empirical evidence to substantiate aggression as a drive. Circular reasoning is used to explain aggressive behavior. For example, the question "Why do birds flock together?" may prompt someone to answer that birds have an instinct or drive to flock together. If confronted for evidence to substantiate this behavior, someone may reply, "Just look at birds, they are flocking together" (Meyer, 1996). Such circular reasoning is often used to support Freud's instinctual theory of aggression in the absence of empirical evidence. The fact that people display aggressive behavior is used as proof that aggression is an inborn behavior in human beings.

The instinctual theory of aggression is also criticized on the basis that if this were a universal trait in all human beings, then all humans would display aggression. Anthropologists report, however, that there are cultures whose members do not display aggressive behavior. For example, the Philippine Tasady tribe does not have a word for war (Eibl-Eibesfeldt, 1979; Nance, 1975). Also, the Iroquois Indians were known to be a very peaceful and nonaggressive tribe. It was only after they were attacked by White settlers that the Iroquois engaged in warfare in self-defense (Hornstein, 1976).

This is not to deny, however, that there is a relationship between aggression and biological influences. Complex neural systems in the brain when stimulated electrically or chemically can promote aggressive behavior. Similar effects are noted with certain types of head injuries. Head injury victims may react with rage distinct from ordinary anger (Miller, 1994; Rosenbaum et al., 1994; Warnken, Rosenbaum, Fletcher, Hoge, & Adelman, 1994). Their rage may be sudden and unpredictable, like a storm of overwhelming fury triggered by some trivial stimulus. For example, Rosenbaum et al. (1994) evaluated for past history of head injury 53 partner-abusive men, 45 maritally satisfied men, and 32 maritally discordant, nonviolent men. The researchers found that a head injury was a significant predictor of being a batterer. Similarly, in a study involving 57 normal controls and 278 veterans who had suffered penetrating head injuries during their military service in Vietnam, the veterans with head injuries had significantly higher scores on aggression/violence scales than their non-head-injury counterparts (Grafman, Schwab, Warden, & Pridget, 1996).

Biochemical changes can also influence aggression, as seen in the effect of alcohol and drugs on the brain. Alcohol and drugs may lower restraints against aggression, causing an individual to behave aggressively (Bushman, 1993; Flanzer, 1993; Gustafson, 1994; Parker, 1993; Rivers, 1994; White, Brick, & Hansell, 1993). As discussed in later chapters, substance abuse is a significant factor in child abuse (Chaffin, Kelleher, & Hollenberg, 1996; Murphy et al., 1991; Peterson, Gable, & Saldana, 1996), partner abuse (Conner & Ackerley, 1994; Fagan, Barnett, & Patton, 1988; Roberts, 1988), and elder abuse (Anetzberger, Korbin, & Austin, 1994; Conlin, 1995; Pittaway, Westhues, & Peressini, 1995).

Research also has shown that lead residues from lead-based paints can act as a brain poison that interferes with a person's ability to restrain impulses. A recent study of 301 boys from the Pittsburgh inner city found that boys with above-normal lead values in their bones were more likely to engage in aggressive acts and delinquent behaviors than boys with less lead in their bones (Needleman, 1996). This study controlled for various social and family factors that previously were linked to delinquent behavior, including socioeconomic status and child-rearing factors.

Genetic differences also can impact on aggressiveness. Differences in temperament can be observed shortly after birth, even among siblings in the same family. These traits may endure into adulthood (DiLalla & Gottesman, 1991; Rushton, Fulker, Neale, Nias, & Eysenck, 1986; Thomas & Chess, 1977).

Psychobiologists and evolutionary psychologists are currently studying the biological basis for aggression or violence. These studies view aggression in relationship to levels of the neurotransmitter serotonin (Wright, 1995). Research has documented a relationship between serotonin levels and impaired impulse control, violent outbursts, and increased aggressiveness (Conroy, 1993; Linnoila, Virkkunen, George, & Higley, 1993; Roy & Linnoila, 1989). The relationship of serotonin levels and aggressiveness seems especially pronounced in men who abuse alcohol (Linnoila & Virkkunen, 1992; Virkkunen & Linnoila, 1990). The study of serotonin levels in humans has been preceded by research on serotonin levels in vervet monkeys. A hierarchy of status exists among male monkeys. It was found that monkeys with the highest ranking have the highest serotonin levels and those with a low ranking have the lowest levels and are most violent (Raleigh, McGuire, Brammer, & Pollack, 1991). Evolutionary psychologists do not, however, rule out the influence of environment. The social environment in an evolutionary sense may biologically shape individuals. If further research shows a relationship between low serotonin levels and aggression, then aggression may possibly be controlled through pharmacological treatment (Hankoff, 1990).

In summary, although there is little empirical support for the theory of aggression being a biological drive, as hypothesized by Freud, there is a biological basis for aggression, as seen in genetic differences relative to aggression and the effect on the brain of head injuries, lead poisoning, and the use of drugs and alcohol.

Aggression as a Result of Frustration

The theory that aggression may result from frustration was first proposed by Dollard and his associates (Dollard, Doob, Miller, Mowere, & Sears, 1939) and subsequently has undergone empirical testing (Carlson, Marcus-Newhall, & Miller, 1990; Dill & Anderson, 1995). This theory suggests that aggression stems from frustration resulting from a person experiencing blockage or interference in attaining a goal. The greater the motivation is to achieve the goal, the greater is the frustration. Frustration can build up until it is released on the source of the frustration or displaced on another object or person. For example, an unemployed father frustrated by his inability to find work to support his family may physically or verbally lash out at his spouse and children.

Social psychologists distinguish between types of frustration that may provoke an aggressive response. If the frustration is perceived as unintended, caused by circumstances beyond anyone's control, accidental, or justified, there is less chance that an aggressive response will occur, as compared to frustration that is perceived as intentional (Dill & Anderson, 1995; Dyck & Rule, 1978; Freedman, Sears, & Carlsmith, 1981; Kulik & Brown, 1979). For example, John is planning on meeting Joe for a movie. John waits outside the theater, but his friend does not appear. He is frustrated over what is happening. Sirens are heard, and a short time later, John hears someone saying there has been an accident on the freeway that has blocked traffic. John begins to understand why his friend has not appeared at the theater. Apparently, Joe is caught in a traffic jam; his absence is not intentional. John's frustration begins to dissipate.

The same scenario may be repeated under difference circumstances. This time there is no traffic accident. When John returns home, he calls Joe and learns that Joe decided not to meet John because he thought the movie would not be very good. John's frustration of waiting for his friend coupled with the friend's intention of not showing up and letting John wait provokes an angry response in John. John's anger is evident in the conversation he has with Joe and his resolve never again to go anywhere with him. Thus, the attribution or understanding of the circumstances surrounding the frustration is a key determinant regarding the nature of a person's response to the frustration.

The relationship between frustration and aggression was demonstrated in a study involving a room full of toys to which a group of children was exposed but not allowed to enter. After a period of time, the children were allowed to enter the room and play with the toys. A similar group of children was given immediate access to the toys without having to wait. Those children who were frustrated in attaining their goal of wanting to play with the toys by not being allowed initially to do so demonstrated aggressive behaviors when they played with the toys by smashing them and in general being very destructive, whereas the children who were allowed immediate access to the toys did not display such behavior (Barker, Dembo, & Lewin, 1941). Thus, a linkage between frustration and aggression was observed in the first group of children, but aggression was not evident in the second group experiencing no frustration.

Similarly, an experiment was designed using 34 college students in which their attainment of an expected gratification was either blocked in an unjustified manner, blocked in a justified manner, or not blocked at all (Dill & Anderson, 1995). The degree of hostile aggression directed at the source of the frustration was measured under each condition. Unjustified frustration produced more hostile aggression than justified frustration, but even justified frustration produced more hostile aggression than no frustration at all.

Frustration at the societal level also can stimulate aggressive behavior. Economic depression—namely, the loss of jobs and the inability to purchase necessary items—can produce various forms of aggressive behavior. For example, researchers found a strong relationship between the price of cotton and the number of lynchings that occurred in the South between 1882 and 1930 (Hovland & Sears, 1940; Mintz, 1946). When cotton prices were depressed, the number of lynchings increased. The decline in cotton prices could be interpreted as producing frustration in cotton farmers. Not being able to ventilate their anger against the source of their frustration, they displaced their anger onto African Americans in the form of lynchings (Sampson, 1991).

As will be discussed more fully in the chapter on child abuse, research shows that parents who are under stress due to physical, emotional, and financial problems—factors that may be conceptualized as stress and frustration—are at risk for engaging in the physical and emotional abuse of their children (Burrell, Thompson, & Sexton, 1994; Garbarino & Vondra, 1987; Whipple & Webster-Stratton, 1991).

In the years since 1939 when Dollard and his associates proposed the frustration-aggression theory, social psychologists have conducted numerous laboratory experiments to test this theory. The results provide varying levels of empirical support. The lack of strong empirical support for the original frustration-aggression hypothesis has led to modifications of the theory. Berkowitz (1978) suggested that two prerequisites are necessary for frustration to be expressed in aggression; namely, a readiness to act aggressively and external cues that trigger the expression of aggression (Penrod, 1986). Frustration can produce an emotional state that can easily result in an aggressive response, but there must be a readiness to act in this manner. Also, external aversive stimuli rather than only frustration can increase the likelihood of aggressive behavior. Frustration in such situations is referred to by social psychologists as a state of arousal and can be stimulated by aversive factors such as physiological arousal, verbal and physical attack, uncomfortable temperatures, especially heat, and the use of drugs or alcohol.

External conditions also can affect the relationship between frustration and aggression. This has been shown in studies known as "the weapons effect" (Berkowitz & LePage, 1967). Researchers found that the presence or availability of weapons could prompt or "prime" individuals to act aggressively. Students participated in an experiment involving the giving and receiving of mild electrical shocks. Research participants sat at various tables. Some tables had nothing on them except the shock machine's telegraph key. Other tables contained neutral objects, such as badminton rackets and shuttlecocks. A third group of tables contained a shotgun and a revolver. Persons sitting at the tables with weapons increased the number and length of the shocks they gave others as compared to those persons sitting at the tables on which no objects were placed or at tables containing neutral objects. The researchers concluded that the presence of weapons or external aggressive cues suggested to the study participants that aggression was appropriate. Replication of this research has generally supported the original findings of Berkowitz and LePage (1967; Anderson, Anderson, & Deuser, 1996; Frodi, 1975; Leyens & Parke, 1975; Page & Scheidt, 1971; Turner, Layton, & Simons, 1975; Turner, Simons, Berkowitz, & Frodi, 1977). These studies have implications for the relationship between the availability of guns and homicides, often occurring in the context of family violence in American society (Kleck & Patterson, 1993; Loftin, McDowall, Wiersema, & Cottey, 1991; Zuckerman, 1996).

Guns are readily available in American society and may be a significant factor contributing to interpersonal and family violence. Approximately 200 million guns are in private hands in the United States. The impact from the availability of guns can be seen in comparison figures for the United States and other countries relative to the number of people who are murdered with the use of a gun: "In 1992 handguns were used to murder 13 people in Australia; 33 people in Great Britain; 60 people in Japan; 128 in Canada; and more than 13,000 in the United States" (Williams, 1997, p. A19). A portion of these individuals in the United States who were murdered by guns may have lost their lives in the context of family violence as weapons are often used in physical abuse.

Social psychologists conclude that the frustration-aggression hypothesis remains tentative and that multiple factors may be associated with the expression of aggressive behavior. Critics of the frustration aggression theory point out that frustration does tend to lead to aggression in some circumstances but not always (Berkowitz, 1969). The unemployed worker, referred to earlier, may chose to look for other types of employment or relocate where employment is available, rather than lash out at his spouse and children. Also, theorists suggest that a broader term than frustration should be used as the source of aggression because aggression can be elicited or instigated by other factors, such as the character and perceived intent of the instigator, personality factors and life experiences of the frustrated individual, and environmental conditions (Raven & Rubin, 1983).

Aggression as a Learned Behavior

A third theory of aggression suggests that aggressive behavior is learned from observing others being aggressive (Bandura, 1977; Felson, 1992). This is known as **social learning theory,** and the process on which the theory is based is referred to as **modeling,** or, in colloquial terms, "monkey see, monkey do." This imitation process was initially demonstrated in a study involving 3- to 5-year-olds, some of whom observed an adult behaving aggressively toward a large plastic doll known as a Bobo doll and who later imitated that behavior in their interactions with the doll. The youngsters in the study who had not observed the adult's aggressive behavior did not behave aggressively toward the doll when they played with it (Bandura, Ross, & Ross, 1963).

Research indicates that persons serving as models who are rewarded for their aggressive behavior are more likely to be imitated than models who are not rewarded (Bandura, 1965; Walters & Willows, 1968). When a behavior is rewarded, an individual is more likely to repeat that behavior, or conversely, when a behavior is punished, an individual is more likely to avoid the behavior. Also, individuals tend to imitate or model the behavior of others they regard as important, powerful, or successful (Freedman et al., 1981). These factors may in part explain the powerful effect that television and movie personalities have on viewers when behaving aggressively in the roles they are playing and then often being rewarded rather than punished for that behavior (Paik & Comstock, 1994).

Parents serve as important role models for children through their behavior toward each other and through the way they interact with their children (Bjorkqvist & Osterman, 1992). As discussed in the chapter on partner abuse, children who witness abusive behavior between their parents are likely to model this behavior in their interactions with siblings and peers (Henning, Leitenberg, Coffey, Bennett, & Jankowski, 1997; Spaccarelli, Sandler, & Roosa, 1994; Wiehe, 1997b). Parental aggressive behavior toward children in the form of corporal punishment presents to children an example or model that spanking in the form of hitting or slapping are methods of problem solving. Children punished in this manner have been shown to model this physically aggressive behavior in their relationships with others (Weiss, Dodge, Bates, & Pettit, 1992).

Modeling or imitating behavior can also occur as the result of children watching aggressive behavior on television or in videos or movies. The National Institute of Mental Health has reviewed extensive research on the relationship between television and aggressive behavior. Researchers at the Institute have concluded, based on laboratory experiments and field studies, that violence on television does lead to aggressive behavior by children and teenagers who watch such programs. Television violence is as strongly correlated in magnitude with aggressive behavior as compared to any other behavioral variable that has been measured (National Institute of Mental Health, 1982). The effects of television, movies, and videos on aggressive behavior can occur in several ways: (a) Constant and repeated exposure to violence in the media may **instigate** aggressive behavior in the viewer, depending upon the strength of the cue and the readiness of the observer to behave in that manner; (b) repeated exposure in media programming may have a **disinhibiting** effect in that a viewer may more readily engage in aggressive acts modeling his or her behavior after what was seen on the television or movie screen; and (c) long-term exposure to violence in the media may have a **desensitizing** effect in that the violence may alter a viewer's sense of reality, the result being that the viewer neither reacts any longer with revulsion at the violence nor perceives the violence as behavior to be avoided (Eron, 1980a; Eron & Huesmann, 1985; Huston et al., 1992).

Listening to rap music in which the lyrics degrade women and portray women wanting forced sex may facilitate sexually aggressive behavior in listeners. In a study conducted by Barongan and Hall (1995), 27 men listened to misogynous rap music and the same number of men listened to neutral rap music. The misogynous rap music, in which the lyrics were clearly discernible, contained frequent references to both sex and violence, referring to women as "bitches" and "ho's" and suggesting that women enjoyed coercive sex. After listening to the music, the study participants viewed neutral, sexually violent, and assaultive film vignettes and were asked to choose one of the vignettes to show to a female confederate participating in the research. A significantly greater proportion of the men who listened to misogynous rap music showed a sexually aggressive film as compared to the men who heard neutral rap music. The researchers felt this finding suggested that misogynous music may facilitate sexually aggressive behavior in listeners. The data support earlier research showing a relationship between cognitive distortions and sexually aggressive behavior (Hall & Hirschman, 1991).

The modeling effect of television, videos, and movies can be understood from the perspective that the viewer visually is brought into the violence occurring on the screen; however, studies show that even printed media can produce a modeling effect when graphic accounts of violent behavior are reported. For example, national suicide levels increased following newspaper accounts of suicides (Phillips, 1974). Likewise, a statistically significant rise in the number of homicides was found to occur several days after heavyweight fights (Phillips & Hensley, 1984).

The modeling of self-destructive aggressive behavior can be seen recently in the death of several young people who modeled the behavior of a young man in the movie *The Program.* The movie character, a college football hero, following a dare from peers to prove that he had nerves of steel, laid down in the middle of a busy highway as cars and trucks sped past in the dark. Unlike the movie hero, who survived, several adolescents were killed instantly when they modeled the stunt and were struck by traffic (Hinds, 1993).

Aggressive computer games may also instigate aggressive behavior in players. Irwin and Gross (1995) studied 60 second-grade boys, ages 7 and 8 years, who played two Nintendo games. One was an aggressive game involving two martial arts heroes who faced ruthless street gangs and aggressively worked their way through various obstacles in order to rescue a friend. The second game was nonaggressive, requiring the player to race a motorcycle against time over various obstacles with no opportunity for a collision with other motorcycles. The researchers found increased physical aggression in the boys who had played the aggressive game. These youngsters were observed modeling the physically aggressive behaviors of the video game characters in their play with peers. They also displayed verbal aggression by describing their behavior as they acted out what they had observed (Irwin & Gross, 1995).

Aggression as Power and Control (Patriarchal Theory)

Aggression can also be understood from the theoretical perspective of patriarchal theory, which focuses on the power and control that males exert over females or the subordinate position in society in which men place women. This can be seen at the societal level as males occupy positions of power and control in the corporate world, in government, in religious organizations, and in society in general. Just as males dominate females at the societal level, so too does this occur in the context of the home and family (Dobash & Dobash, 1979; Freeman, 1995; Lott, 1994). The socialization of children in keeping with the patriarchal theory begins early in their development, with boys being encouraged to assume an active, aggressive position in life and girls a more passive, nonassertive role (Byer & Shainberg, 1994; Carroll & Wolpe, 1996; Hyde, 1994; Lott, 1994; McCammon, Knox, & Schacht, 1993; Ruth, 1995).

Likewise, the display of aggression is often gender related in terms of males aggressing against females or males exerting power and control over females through physical, emotional, or sexual abuse (Koss, 1992; Roberts, 1996b; Walker, 1994; Wiehe & Richards, 1995). The patriarchal theory of aggression focuses on the concepts of **structural** and **personal** power (Waldby, Clancy, Emetchi, & Summerfield, 1989).

Structural or institutionalized power is defined as the power granted by society to individuals and groups. Individuals and groups use structural power to dominate and control others through variables such as gender, race, income, and religion. For example, men control women, Caucasians dominate

African Americans, and the rich control the poor. Groups of persons with little or no structural power, such as women, African Americans, and the poor, are victims of the misuse of this power through exploitation and aggression by those holding structural power—namely, men, Caucasians, and the rich. The misuse of structural power can be seen, for example, in child sexual abuse. Waldby et al. (1989) write,

> Child abuse represents a misuse of the power that society "legitimately" accords to males and to adults. As this structural power of males and adults exists, there also exists the *potential* for every man to misuse his power over women (e.g. rape) and for every adult to misuse his/her power over children (e.g. sexual assault). As well as this potential, there exists the *option* for abuse, as society actually legitimizes the misuse of power. The legitimizing of the abuse of power is child sexual abuse. It occurs on several fronts. For example, the child who disclosed to adults, who she hopes will protect her from abuse, is often not believed. Society reinforces this situation by perpetuating some of the myths about child sexual abuse. Secondly, the legal system allows for relative ease of removal of the child survivor from the family, yet poses difficulty in removing the offender, thus reinforcing the blame on the child and granting the right to continue offending on the male/adult. Thirdly, society provides limited punishments for sex offenders; imprisonment for those few offenders who are found guilty by the criminal justice system; and the public shaming for those even fewer offenders who become newsworthy for a day. On the whole, most offenders are not punished by society. (pp. 102-103)

The abuse of structural power can be checked through the enhancement of personal power. **Personal** power is defined as inner strength, the desire and drive within individuals to attain mastery of their lives and to achieve desired personal goals. The abuse of personal power can be seen in the control of others for personal gain with little thought to their physical or emotional needs, such as occurs in child and partner abuse. Perpetrators thwart children and partners from reaching their full human potential by victimizing them, which creates problems in their psychosocial functioning. A proper use of personal power should assure all individuals the right to develop to their full human potential.

The feminist perspective of aggression focuses on the power and control of males over females. This theoretical perspective has implications for understanding, treating, and preventing the various types of family violence and for fostering sociopolitical change. An understanding of any type of family violence—child, partner, elder, sibling abuse—must include an analysis of the problem from the perspective of the patriarchal theory: namely, that aggression is an expression of power and control of the perpetrator over the victim and in most instances is gender related (Gelles, 1993; Petrik, Petrik, & Subotnik, 1994; Waldby et al., 1989).

A General Model of Aggression

Raven and Rubin (1983) reviewed the literature on hostile aggression over the past 40 years and produced a model for understanding how aggression occurs that incorporates aspects of the theories previously discussed (see Figure 1.1).

Frustration/Instigation

The model begins with the box on the far left of the figure identified as "Frustration/Instigation"—namely, what potentially spurs on or stirs up the aggression. The form and degree of instigation is an important

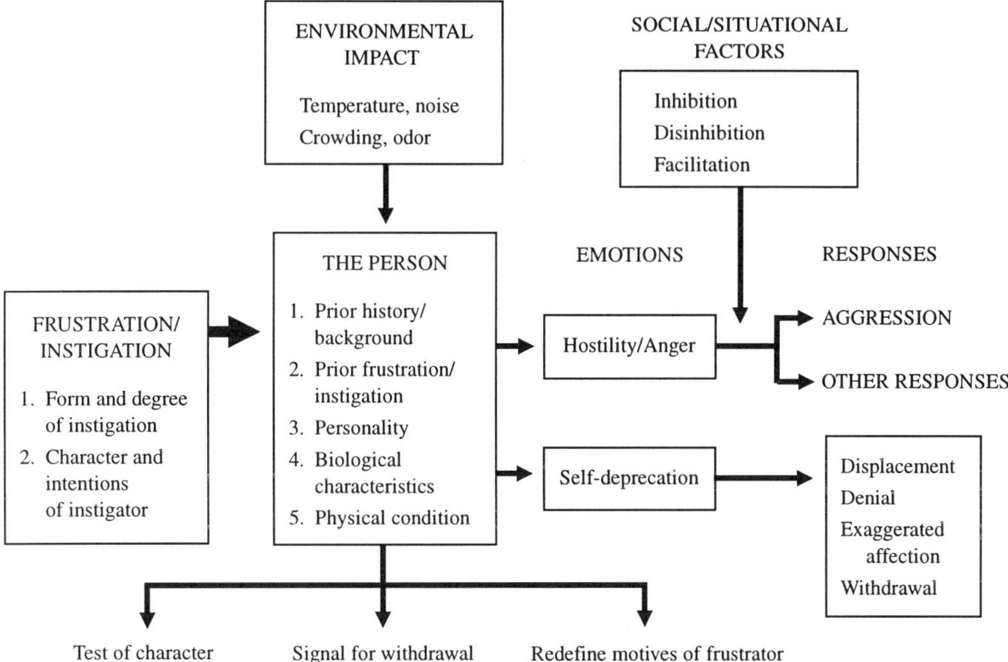

Figure 1.1 A General Model of Aggression
SOURCE: Adapted from *Social Psychology* (2nd ed., p. 275), by B. Raven and J. Rubin, New York: John Wiley. Copyright © 1983 by John Wiley & Sons, Inc. Used with permission.

factor. As discussed earlier, the greater the frustration or instigation, the more likely the greater the aggressive response. Several studies support this hypothesis. For example, in an experiment where two participants could each decide how much to shock the other, persons would give more shock if their own shock level was high (O'Leary & Dengerink, 1973; Taylor, 1967). Also, the goal-gradient hypothesis suggests that the closer a person is to achieving a goal, the greater that person's motivation to attain that goal and the greater the frustration if attainment is not possible (Raven & Rubin, 1983). The reaction of frustration was observed when someone would step in front of people who were in line at banks, restaurants, and ticket counters (Harris, 1974). Persons at the front of the line or who were about to attain their desired goal of completing the transaction for which they had been standing in line were more likely to respond aggressively than those further back in line. A polite response of the experimenters in the form of excusing their behavior for stepping in front of someone reduced but did not eliminate the aggressive response of those in line.

The character and intentions of the instigator are also factors in the frustration or instigation of aggression. Experimenters frustrated people participating in their research. When these individuals were later given a choice of more than one person against whom to express aggression, they tended to displace their aggression on the experimenter who frustrated them and whom they did not like (Berkowitz, 1965; Berkowitz & Geen, 1966; Berkowitz & Green, 1962; Geen & Berkowitz, 1966).

The way that people perceive the intentions of others affects the nature of their response. If they perceive someone as deliberately or intentionally doing something to them, such as cutting in front of them in traffic or in line at a counter, they are more likely to respond aggressively than if someone does something unintentionally or by accident—for example, accidentally stepping on their foot (Ebbesen, Duncan, & Konecni, 1975; Kulik & Brown, 1979; Raven & Rubin, 1983; Taylor & Pisano, 1971). As stated earlier, the polite behavior of the experimenters who excused themselves when stepping in front of others provoked a less aggressive response than those who did not excuse themselves. The former gave a message to those in line who were targets of this behavior that the experimenters' actions were not intentional and thus more acceptable.

The Person Experiencing Frustration/Instigation

A person's response to frustration/instigation or a potentially aggressive situation allows for a variety of responses. A rational human being is involved who is capable of making decisions or choices. The individual who receives the potentially aggressive cue or stimulus must interpret what is happening and in some way respond. Each person is different, as reflected in the variables identified in the box labeled "The Person" in Figure 1.1.

The nature of previous frustration and a person's response may influence later responses to potentially aggressive cues. Also, an individual's exposure to aggression may influence the way that person responds to frustration and potentially aggressive situations. In a study of 875 eight-year-olds, those children who were rated by their classmates as aggressive and hostile were also more likely to be aggressive and hostile at home. The aggressive and hostile males in this study were found to prefer television programs characterized by aggression and violence (Eron & Huesmann, 1985). The researchers found that a circular pattern had developed, in that the aggressive children tended not to associate with their peers because of their unpopularity and therefore spent more time watching television programs that portrayed violent behavior, which they modeled with their own behavior. A follow-up study of the research sample was conducted 10 years later, involving approximately half of the original sample. Those who earlier had been rated as high in aggressive behaviors were still rated as very aggressive. These individuals also tended to rate themselves as very aggressive, rate others similarly, and in general perceived the world as very aggressive. Those rated as aggressive at the age of 8 were three times more likely to have police records when interviewed 10 years later (Raven & Rubin, 1983).

A person's gender may also be a factor in that person's response to frustration/instigation. Although some social psychologists suggest that males tend to be more aggressive than females (Maccoby & Jacklin, 1974), not all studies support this hypothesis (DaGloria & DeRidder, 1979). The way in which males are socialized to be assertive and aggressive may account for the differences noted in aggressive responses between genders (Deaux, 1976; Eron, 1980b; Gross, 1978).

An individual's physical condition can also impact on that person's response to frustration or potentially aggressive situations. As discussed earlier, biochemical changes due to the use of drugs and alcohol, lead poisoning, and closed head injuries may increase aggressive responses.

Environmental Impact

A person's environment may affect a potentially aggressive response. Climate is one such factor. Field and laboratory studies relate high temperatures to high rates of aggression, including violent crimes, partner abuse, and the delivery of electric shocks in laboratory experimental situations (Anderson, 1989; Anderson, Deuser, & DeNeve, 1995). Riots and other forms of violence in large urban communities are more likely to occur during periods of hot weather (Baron & Ransberger, 1978; Carlsmith & Anderson, 1979). Likewise, loud and unpleasant noises may set up an aversive environment that may affect the nature of the person's response to frustration (Donnerstein & Wilson, 1976; Geen & O'Neal, 1969).

Alternative Definitions of a Situation

A person may interpret the potentially aggressive stimulus in various ways. The boxes at the lower middle part of Figure 1.1 identify three possible responses to the stimulus: a test of character, a signal for withdrawal, or a redefinition of the stimulus as not being an aggressive cue. Thus, although a person may experience frustration/instigation, that person may redefine the provocative situation and not necessarily respond aggressively.

Social/Situational Factors

Social or situational factors may also impact on a person experiencing frustration. A person's dominant group may influence that individual's perception of the instigating behavior. A country that is the target of terrorist attacks in which innocent citizens are injured defines this behavior as aggression. That nation's retaliation, which may also harm innocent citizens, is considered less aggressive because the behavior is justified as self-defense. The United States' military operation in Panama in December 1989 was code-named "Just Cause," perhaps to justify the violence that occurred (Leyens & Fraczek, 1984; Sampson, 1991).

Studies were cited earlier that generally supported the "weapons effect"—namely, that the presence of a weapon may present a mental cue to the person seeing the weapon that the weapon is a resource that may be used in a potentially aggressive situation. The high rates of homicide in states where guns are readily available for purchase is cited as support for the fact that weapons can serve as a cue to aggressive behavior (Kleck & Patterson, 1993; Loftin et al., 1991; Raven & Rubin, 1983; Zuckerman, 1996).

The norms of a person's social group also impact on the nature of that person's response to frustration or instigation. The research of Bandura and his associates, referred to earlier, lends support to this hypothesis (Bandura, 1973; Bandura et al., 1963). Children observing their teacher striking a plastic Bobo doll repeated this behavior in their interaction with the doll, as compared to a control group where the teacher played with Tinker Toys rather than hitting the doll. The latter group of children did not display aggressive behavior when playing with the doll. The children observing the teacher striking the Bobo doll were receiving a message from their teacher that behaving aggressively toward the doll was acceptable behavior. Just as aggression may be seen as the acceptable norm of behavior, the observation of others not engaging in aggression in potentially aggressive situations may act as an inhibitor of aggression.

Responses to Frustration or Instigation

Responses to frustration or instigation may be directed to the source of the frustration or displaced to other objects or persons that may serve as a scapegoat.

If the source of the frustration is held in high esteem by the victim or is in a very powerful position, the victim may deny that the instigation ever occurred. Another response, as indicated on the far right-hand side of Figure 1.1, is exaggerated affection for the individual responsible for the frustration or instigation. This response or psychological defense is identified in psychoanalytic theory as "identification with the aggressor" (Freud, 1946). Hostages have been found to respond to their captors in a seemingly affectionate manner, possibly as a defense for the aggressive feelings they actually are experiencing and as a way of forestalling further frustration. This is known as "the Stockholm syndrome" and can be seen in the response of some women to the abuse they receive from their husbands. They do not leave their partner, even after severe beatings (Ferraro & Johnson, 1983).

Another response to frustration or instigation is to withdraw from the situation or become involved in other activities. An important point is that frustration need not necessarily lead to an aggressive response, for alternate responses are possible, based on numerous variables, as shown in this model.

SUMMARY

Four theoretical perspectives on aggression and a model that synthesizes aspects of these various theories were presented. Both biological and social/psychological theoretical perspectives for understanding aggression were discussed.

When aggression is a typical or customary response to provocative situations, and when family members, especially children, repeatedly observe this response, violence tends to become a normative behavior. Thus, children may model this behavior rather than engage in alternative forms of conflict resolution such as problem solving. Aggression, however, is only one of numerous possible responses to a situation that might provoke such behavior.

In the following chapters the way in which aggressive behavior is exhibited in the setting of the family is discussed in terms of child, partner, elder, and sibling abuse.

2

Child Abuse

Mr. and Mrs. Jessup, a young couple in their late 20s, are the parents of two boys, Scott, age 4, and Tim, age 3. Both boys attend nursery school while their parents work. Recently, while a nursery school aide was helping Tim go to the bathroom, she observed red marks and bruises on his buttocks. The nursery school aide showed the marks to Tim's teacher, who concluded that the marks appeared to have been made with a belt. When Tim was asked about the marks, he only replied that they hurt. The teacher recalled that earlier in the day Tim was pulling on his pants and not wanting to sit on a hard chair during storytelling time, making her now realize that perhaps he had been in pain. Later, the teacher asked Scott, Tim's older brother, if Tim had received a whipping recently. Scott said that Tim's father had whipped him because he had lied.

Later in the day when Mrs. Jessup picked the boys up at the nursery school, the teacher told her about the marks that they had observed on Tim's buttocks and Scott's comment about the whipping Tim had received from his dad. The teacher also informed Mrs. Jessup that a report had been made to child protective services in compliance with the law. Mrs. Jessup was very upset that a report had been filed. When the teacher showed Mrs. Jessup the marks on Tim's buttocks, she initially tried to explain them away by saying they probably were scratches from where he was bitten by mosquitoes on a recent camping trip or marks he received from "roughhousing" with his brother.

When Mrs. Jessup realized the teacher was not accepting these excuses, she broke down and began to cry. She described her husband as having some "old-fashioned ideas about punishing kids with a belt." She also admitted that her husband had a "quick temper" that often came out over things the boys did.

An investigation by child protective services revealed the marks had been caused by a whipping Tim had received from his father. An outcome of the investigation was that the parents would attend Parents Anonymous (PA) meetings and a parent education course. Mrs. Jessup seemed relieved that they were going to get help with alternative ways of punishing the boys other than whipping them, which had become an issue between her and her husband. Mr. Jessup expressed some reluctance in attending the PA meetings and parenting course but agreed to do so.

* * *

Merilee, an 8-year-old girl, lives with her mother in a small two-bedroom apartment. Her mother works as a clerk in a large discount store. Recently, Merilee began to have difficulty at school. She appeared withdrawn, unable and unwilling to complete assignments, and seemed to be "lost in her own thoughts," as her teacher described. The teacher referred Merilee to the school guidance counselor. Merilee's mother, when informed of the referral, expressed appreciation to the teacher because she had also noted a change in her daughter's behavior over the past several weeks.

The guidance counselor met with Merilee on three occasions, using storytelling and hand puppets to put Merilee at ease and to assist her in talking about herself. In the third session, Merilee began to cry and spoke about her fear of her mother's boyfriend, Jake. She later revealed that Jake, who recently had begun to live with them, stayed with her after school before her mother returned home from work. She stated that Jake was doing something she didn't like when they watched TV together. "He puts his hands in my panties and wants me to touch his thing." Merilee went on to describe that this behavior had been occurring for the past several weeks and that Jake had told her she shouldn't tell anyone about this. The guidance counselor assured Merilee that it was appropriate and important that she had shared this information with her.

The counselor discussed with Merilee's mother the information she had received from Merilee. A report was filed with child protective services in accord with the state's mandatory reporting laws regarding child sexual abuse.

* * *

Sharon, an attractive but overweight teenager, contacted her high school guidance counselor for help with a problem. She tearfully explained to the counselor that she had recently attempted suicide by taking some pills she had found in the family medicine cabinet. The pills only made her sick to her stomach, which she covered up by telling her family that she had the flu.

While exploring the nature of Sharon's suicide attempt, the counselor learned that Sharon had recently become increasingly depressed over her weight and her family's response to this problem. Her weight was a frequent issue in the home, especially at mealtime or when the family was snacking while watching TV. Recently, her father began to call her "Fats," a name her siblings mimicked. Sharon's response to this verbally abusive behavior was to blame herself for her weight problem, which has resulted in her failing school performance and poor self-esteem.

Sharon accepted the counselor's invitation to join a self-esteem-building group the counselor was leading in the school she was attending.

Child abuse is a serious social problem, which was first brought to the public's attention in 1962 when Dr. C. Henry Kempe and associates published an article in the *Journal of the American Medical Association* in which they placed a label on what they and many pediatricians were observing in their practices—namely, children whose injuries reflected that they had been abused (Kempe, Silverman, Steele, Droegemueller, & Silver, 1962). Kempe et al. called this "battered children syndrome." Extensive research continues today on the causes, treatment, and prevention of child maltreatment not only in the United States but in countries throughout the world.

DEFINITION OF TERMS

Child abuse occurs in three forms: physical, emotional, and sexual. Although all three are discussed individually, they rarely occur in isolation (Ney, Fung, & Wickett, 1994).

Physical Abuse

Physical abuse consists of inflicting injury on a child through hitting, biting, kicking, slapping, and similar means. Injuries may also result from the use of objects such as a belt, stick, rod, or bat. Physical abuse generally involves *willful* acts by adults resulting in injury to the child; however, this type of abuse may also result from parental actions where the intent was not to injure or harm the child. Two types of aggressive acts were defined in the previous chapter: hostile and instrumental. The deliberate infliction of injury on a child, such as hitting the child or throwing the child down the stairs, are examples of hostile aggression. Whipping a child as a form of punishment, where the intent is not to harm the child but harm occurs as a result of the action, is an example of instrumental aggression (Buss, 1971).

A form of physical abuse to which infants are often subject is shaking, which can result in "shaken baby syndrome." An infant may be shaken by a frustrated parent after long periods of crying, especially when the child does not respond to the parent's attempts to console the child. Infants who are shaken are very vulnerable to head injury because of a heavy head and weak neck muscles (Showers, 1992).

Emotional Abuse

Emotional abuse, or psychological maltreatment, is defined as verbal behavior in which an adult attacks a child's self-esteem

- *Rejecting.* Treating a child different from siblings or peers in ways suggesting a dislike for the child; actively refusing to act to help or acknowledge a child's request for help
- *Degrading.* Calling a child "stupid"; labeling as inferior; publicly humiliating a child
- *Terrorizing.* Threatening to hurt physically or forcing a child to observe violence directed toward loved ones; leaving a young child unattended
- *Isolating.* Locking a child in a closet or in a room alone for an extended period of time; refusing to allow interactions or relationships with peers or adults outside the family
- *Corrupting.* Teaching or reinforcing behavior that degrades children who are racially or ethnically different; teaching or reinforcing criminal behavior; providing antisocial and inappropriate models as normal, usual, or appropriate
- *Exploiting.* Keeping a child at home in the role of a servant or surrogate parent in lieu of school attendance; encouraging a child to participate in illegal or dysfunctional behavior
- *Denying Emotional Responsiveness.* Ignoring a child's attempts to interact; mechanistic child handling devoid of hugs, stroking, kisses, and talk

Figure 2.1 Types of Child Emotional Abuse
SOURCE: Brassard and Galardo (1987, p. 128).

and social competence. This form of abuse is seen, for example, in comments made with the intent of ridiculing, insulting, threatening, or belittling a child. Emotional abuse is difficult to document because of the absence of physical evidence often found in physical abuse and sometimes in sexual abuse. Although emotional abuse can occur alone, researchers identify this form of abuse as the core component and major destructive force in all types of child abuse (Brassard & Galardo, 1987; Claussen & Crittenden, 1991).

Emotional abuse generally is conceptualized as occurring between a parent or parent surrogate and a child, yet this type of abuse can also occur at the societal level—for example, when children are victims of prejudice, cultural bias, or gender stereotyping or are living in dangerous or unsafe environments (Ayalon & Van Tassel, 1987; Jones & Jones, 1987; Reschly & Graham-Clay, 1987; Telzrow, 1987).

Figure 2.1 presents various ways in which emotional abuse may occur.

Sexual Abuse

Sexual abuse is defined as an adult's or older child's use of a child for sexual gratification. Sexual abuse may occur on a contact or noncontact basis. Contact forms include sexually touching a child or requesting that a child sexually touch an adult, attempted penetration, intercourse, and sodomy. Noncontact forms include indecent exposure to a child, forcing a child to observe adult sexual behavior, or taking pornographic pictures of a child.

Sexual abuse occurring with a family member (blood relative, relative by marriage, live-in boyfriend) is referred to as **incest,** or **familial abuse.** Sexual abuse by an individual outside the family is known as **extrafamilial abuse.**

TABLE 2.1 National Estimates of Child Abuse and Neglect Reports, 1976-1995

Year	*Estimated Number of Children Reported*	*Estimated Number of Children per 1,000 Population*
1976	669,000	10.1
1977	838,000	12.8
1978	836,000	12.9
1979	988,000	15.4
1980	1,154,000	18.1
1981	1,225,000	19.4
1982	1,262,000	20.1
1983	1,477,000	23.6
1984	1,727,000	27.3
1985	1,928,000	30.6
1986	2,086,000	32.8
1987	2,157,000	34.0
1988	2,265,000	35.0
1989	2,435,000	38.0
1990	2,559,000	40.0
1991	2,684,000	42.0
1992	2,909,000	45.0
1993	2,967,000	45.0
1994	3,074,000	46.0
1995	3,120,000	46.0
1996	3,126,000	47.0

THE EXTENT OF CHILD MALTREATMENT

The National Center on Child Abuse Prevention Research of the National Committee to Prevent Child Abuse (NCPA) has collected data on the extent of child maltreatment in the 50 states and the District of Columbia. A major obstacle, however, in preventing a direct count of the number of children reported and substantiated for various forms of child maltreatment is the wide variation that exists among the states in their data collection procedures. Some states are not able to give a direct count of the number of children reported for maltreatment, others record reports by families or incidents rather than by children, and time periods used for data collection vary among states. To account for these differences, the data reported by the National Center on Child Abuse Prevention Research are adjusted, based on rates of reporting used by the American Association for Protecting Children (AAPC) in 1986 (Wang & Daro, 1997).

As Table 2.1 reflects, the estimated number of children reported for child abuse and neglect rose from 669,000, or at the rate of 10.1 per 1,000 children, in 1976 to

TABLE 2.2 Percentage Reported and Substantiated Cases in 1996 for Child Abuse and Neglect

Type of Abuse	*Reported (%) (n = 25 states)*	*Substantiated (%) (n = 31 states)*
Physical abuse	25	23
Sexual abuse	7	9
Emotional abuse	3	4
Neglect	61	60
Other*	4	4

*Includes cases such as abandonment, educational neglect, dependency, and other situations not specified in data collection instrument.

3,126,000, or 47 per 1,000 children, in 1996. The increase in reporting in part may be due to (a) a heightened awareness about child abuse on the part of the general public and professionals who are mandated by law to report suspected cases of child abuse and (b) more universal methods of data collection at the state level.

Although child neglect is not a focus of this chapter, national data on child abuse frequently include the category of child neglect. Table 2.2 presents a breakdown of the 1996 data on reported and substantiated cases of child abuse by forms of abuse, including the percentage of cases that child neglect comprises.

However, even though a reported incident of child abuse or neglect might not be substantiated for lack of sufficient evidence, this does not necessarily mean that abuse did not occur or that the family could not have used preventive services. All but 15 states, the Virgin Islands, and Guam have a two-tiered substantiated/unsubstantiated way of analyzing child abuse cases. The states that are the exception add an intermediary classification for cases where maltreatment is believed to exist but cannot be substantiated (Report from the Department of Health & Human Services, National Resource Center on Child Abuse and Neglect, 1995, cited in Drake, 1996).

An alternative way of classifying child maltreatment cases other than substantiated/unsubstantiated has been proposed that recognizes that abuse in some situations may have occurred, even though sufficient supportive evidence is lacking, and that the family is in need of services, especially of a supportive and preventive nature. This model classifies cases along two dimensions; harm and level of proof available (i.e., substantiated/unsubstantiated). By adding the dimension of harm, appraisal can be made in maltreatment situations where potential harm may occur because of the accused person's behavior or actions, and thus a case may be substantiated that otherwise would not be. For example, children left unsupervised on the streets or who live in substandard housing may be at high risk for abuse for which preventive interventions may be appropriate, even though under the two dimensions of substantiated/not substantiated, a finding of nonsubstantiation may likely occur (Drake, 1996).

Sexual Abuse

Although the data reported above show the number of reported cases of child sexual abuse, these figures reflect only the tip of the iceberg regarding the extent to which child sexual abuse occurs, because most incidents are never reported. A study to determine the extent to which women had experienced incestuous and extrafamilial sexual abuse as a child was conducted with a representative sample of 930 women, drawn by a marketing and public opinion research company in San Francisco (Russell, 1986). The research defined incestuous abuse as any kind of exploitive sexual contact or attempted contact occurring between relatives, no matter how distant the relationship, before the victim turned 18 years of age. Extrafamilial abuse was defined as unwanted sexual experiences ranging from attempted petting to rape before the victim turned 14 years of age and completed or attempted forcible rape experiences of victims, ages 14 through 17. Trained interviewers conducted in-person interviews with the research participants.

Sixteen percent of the sample (152 women) reported at least one experience of incestuous abuse as defined above before age 18. Twelve percent of these women (108) had already been sexually abused by a relative before reaching 14 years of age. Abuse by a nonrelative was even more prominent, with nearly a third of the sample (31%, or 290 women) reporting at least one sexual abuse experience before reaching age 18. Before these women had reached their 14th birthday, 20% (189) had been sexually abused by a nonrelative. Combining the two categories of incestuous and extrafamilial child sexual abuse, 38% (357) of the 930 women in the sample reported at least one experience of sexual abuse before reaching 18 years of age; 28% (258) identified at least one such experience before the age of 14.

If the findings reflect the prevalence of child sexual abuse in the United States, then 1 woman in 8 is incestuously abused before age 14 and 1 in 6 before age 18. The data also indicate that over 25% of the population of female children have experienced sexual abuse (exploitive sexual contact or attempted sexual contact) before age 14 and over a third by age 18.

In another study to determine rates of sexual abuse, men and women nationwide were surveyed to find out if they had experienced any form of childhood sexual abuse (Finkelhor, Hotaling, Lewis, & Smith, 1990). The Los Angeles Times Poll, a survey research organization, conducted this study by telephone, interviewing a sample of 2,626 men and women, 18 years of age or older. Interviewers obtained sexual abuse information by asking respondents if when a child (age 18 or under) they remembered (a) someone trying to have or succeeding in having any kind of sexual intercourse with them; (b) any kind of experience involving touching, grabbing, kissing, or rubbing up against their body; (c) someone taking nude photographs of them, exhibiting parts of their body to them, or performing a sex act in their presence; or (d) any sexual abuse involving oral sex or sodomy.

Twenty-seven percent of the women and 16% of the men recalled a history of sexual abuse. The median age for sexual abuse was 9.9 years for boys and 9.6 years for girls. Approximately 25% of all recalled victimization occurred before age 8. Boys were more likely to be abused by strangers, girls by family members. Half of the offenders or perpetrators were authority figures in the children's lives.

Revictimization of Children

To what extent are children who were once abused later revictimized? Children maltreated during the 4-year period from 1986 to 1989 were studied for revictimization through analysis of 24,506 records of

TABLE 2.3 Child Abuse and Neglect Fatalities Nationwide, 1992–1996

Year	*1992*	*1993*	*1994*	*1995*	*1996*
Total projected fatalities nationwide	1,129	1,216	1,278	1,248	1,046
Fatalities per 100,000 children	1.73	1.81	1.93	1.86	1.56

substantiated cases of abuse in the Colorado Child Abuse and Neglect Registry. The probability for revictimization was found to be contingent on the child's age, gender, and form of maltreatment. Younger children (0-12 years) were at greater risk of revictimization than adolescents (13-17 years), females were somewhat more at risk for repeated victimization than males, and those physically maltreated were at greater risk than those experiencing emotional or sexual abuse (Fryer & Miyoshi, 1994).

Fatality Following Child Abuse

Being a victim of abuse places a child at risk for fatality. Between 1973 and 1986, 11,085 children born in Washington state were reported to the state child abuse registry. The fatality rate of these children was compared to a group of nonabused children matched on gender, county of birth, and year of birth. The children who had been abused had a threefold greater risk of death than the nonabused group and were almost 20 times more likely than their nonabused counterparts to die from homicide. Those at highest risk were the ones abused prior to one year of age. There were no differences between the two groups by gender. A report of physical abuse carried the greatest risk of subsequent death (Sabotta & Davis, 1992).

According to statistical data compiled in 1996 at the national level on fatalities due to child abuse and neglect, an estimated 1,046 children died that year, representing 1.56 per 100,000 children and based on data from 30 states constituting 67.5% of the U.S. population under 18 years of age (Wang & Daro, 1997). For 19 of these states reporting, 51% of the deaths were due to neglect, 59% to abuse, and 3% due to abuse and neglect. For 16 states reporting, 77% of the deaths were to children under 5 years of age and 45% under 1 year of age. Forty percent of the deaths had prior or current contact with child protective service agencies. Twenty-nine percent of the fatalities occurring between 1991 and 1993 involved parental drug or alcohol abuse. Researchers caution that the data on fatalities may be conservative estimates due to potential misdiagnosis. Also, many states have difficulty acquiring sufficient information from the coroner's office and the judicial system about the particular circumstances surrounding a child's death in order to determine if abuse or neglect may have been a factor (Lung & Daro, 1996; National Resource Center on Child Abuse and Neglect, 1995). Table 2.3 presents the projected number of child abuse and neglect fatalities nationwide from 1992 through 1996.

A study of 3,459 incidents in which a parent killed a child under the age of 18, which was recorded in the Uniform Crime Reports between 1976 and 1985, provides further information on child fatalities due to homicide. Male and female children were at equal risk of being killed in their first week of life. However, males were the victims in approximately 55% of the parent-child homicides from the end of the first week of life to age 15. This percentage of male victims increased to 77% in the 16-18 age group. Mothers were almost always the ones who killed their infants in the first week of life; however, between that first week and the teenage years, mothers and fathers were about equally the perpetrator of the homicide. In the 13-15 age group, fathers committed 63% of all parent-child homicides; this percentage increased to 80% for the 16-18 age group. The causes of death for very young children tended to be personal weapons, asphyxiation, or drowning, but as age increased, the instruments of death were predominantly guns and knives (Kunz & Bahr, 1996).

Interagency child death review teams have emerged in metropolitan areas across the country in response to the increasing awareness of severe violence to children resulting in death. Child death review involves a systematic, multidisciplinary, and multiagency process of coordinating data and resources from the coroner, law enforcement agencies, the courts, child protective services, and health care providers. The teams generally review all coroner cases (unattended death or questionable cause of death) for children 12 years of age and younger (Gellert, Maxwell, Durfee, & Wagner, 1995).

HISTORICAL PERSPECTIVE

Although today society takes for granted its obligation to protect children and assure them opportunities for optimum physical, social, and psychological development, historically this has not always been an accepted principle.

The Historical Role of Children

Children were viewed differently in English and early American society as compared to today. Consequently, many children were victims of abuse. Several reasons are cited for this. First, because many children did not survive childhood due to illnesses that were untreatable, parents often did not become as emotionally attached to their children as they do today (DeMause, 1976). Parents often had large families in the hope that some children would survive into adulthood. Second, children went to work at an early age to provide added income for the family. Following the Industrial Revolution, children in colonial America often were exploited for their labor, with many apprenticed to work in mills, factories, and other industries sometimes as young as 8 years of age (DeMause, 1976; Kadushin & Martin, 1988; Popple & Leighninger, 1996). Third, early American laws, modeled after English poor laws, did not provide special protection to children, who often were warehoused with adults in workhouses or on poor farms without regard for physical, emotional, or mental handicaps. Although indenture in many instances provided an escape from these undesirable institutions, children frequently were set up to be victims of further maltreatment from cruel and thoughtless masters (DeMause, 1976). Finally, religion often reinforced stern and even cruel or abusive parental treatment of children. The theological concept of the inherent corrupt and sinful nature of children, known as original sin, often was used as justification for whippings and beatings with a rod (Greven, 1977).

Court records, anecdotal accounts, and popular folklore literature indicate that the sexual abuse of children also has been prevalent in history. For example, the belief was held in 18th-century England that sex with a child was a cure for venereal disease. Also, 25% of capital rape prosecutions between

1730 and 1789 involved victims younger than age 10 (Simpson, 1988). Domestic servants as well as child laborers in fields and factories often became victims of sexual abuse (Olafson, Corwin, & Summit, 1993). What Freud at one time described as fantasies that his adult female patients were experiencing regarding having sex with their fathers, the basis of his oedipal conflict, may actually have been cases of incestuous abuse (DeMause, 1991).

Societies for the Prevention of Cruelty to Children

Early efforts to combat child abuse are often associated with the story of Mary Ellen. In 1874, Etta Wheeler, a church social worker, heard about 9-year-old Mary Ellen, who was abused and neglected by a couple, Francis and Mary Connolly, to whom she was apprenticed. The story claims that Wheeler, trying to find some legal way to rescue Mary Ellen, appealed to the Society for the Prevention of Cruelty to Animals on the basis that Mary Ellen was at least a member of the animal kingdom. Wheeler was successful in getting Mary Ellen removed from the Connolly home and placed in a new home.

Although this story is used as the basis for the first efforts to combat child maltreatment, criminal cases involving child abuse were recorded in Massachusetts as early as 1655. Historical records indicate that Henry Bergh, who founded the American Society for the Prevention of Cruelty to Animals in 1866, had intervened in 1871 on behalf of an 8-year-old girl, Emily Thompson, who was being physically abused (Lazoritz & Shelman, 1996). However, the Mary Ellen case may represent the beginning of an aggressive effort to combat child abuse, for shortly thereafter the New York Society for the Prevention of Cruelty to Children was formed. Similar societies dedicated to combating child maltreatment were established throughout the United States. These agencies frequently became a division of already existing organizations concerned with the protection of animals (Costin, 1991; Popple & Leighninger, 1996; Watkins, 1990).

As these societies or early child protective service agencies continued to intervene in cases of child abuse, awareness developed that their activities had to be broader than just rescuing children being abused. Thus, the agencies began advocacy efforts on behalf of maltreated children, encouraging states to adopt legislation protecting children from abuse or to strictly enforce already existing legislation.

Federal Legislation

The passage of the Social Security Act in 1935 represented a significant step at the national level in confronting child maltreatment. Although child protective services up to this time were primarily under the auspices of private voluntary agencies, the passage of the Social Security Act provided for federal support of child welfare services in the various states. Despite the provision of these federal funds, private voluntary agencies often continued to provide child protective services where public child welfare services were underdeveloped. Also, local departments of public welfare that assumed responsibility for child protective services often were overwhelmed in meeting the financial needs of the communities they served (Kadushin & Martin, 1988).

In 1935, additional federal legislation benefiting children was passed in the form of Aid to Dependent Children (ADC), later called Aid to Families with Dependent Children (AFDC), and as a result of the welfare reform legislation in 1996 now identified as Temporary Assistance to Needy Families

(TANF). In 1938, the Fair Labor Standards Act was enacted, which restricted child labor. States also enacted laws requiring mandatory schooling of children, thereby keeping them from abuse in the labor market and educating them for wholesome and productive lives (Day, 1996; Jansson, 1997).

Contribution of the Medical Profession

The development of diagnostic x-ray technology in the 1940s made possible the determination of injuries in children resulting from physical abuse, thereby making the detection of physical abuse easier and more accurate. In 1946, John Caffey, a New York pediatrician, published an article in a radiology journal in which he shared his observations on 6 infants who had multiple fractures of long bones and chronic subdural hematomas. Although Caffey wanted to explain these observations from the perspective that they were injuries resulting from convulsive seizures, scurvy, or other skeletal diseases, he had to rule out these causes because of the absence of supporting evidence. He had to conclude that "the fractures appear to be of traumatic origin but the traumatic episodes and the causal mechanism remain obscure" (p. 173). Caffey was obviously suspicious but reluctant and fearful to admit the injuries could have resulted from child abuse.

In 1962, C. Henry Kempe, a professor of pediatrics, and his colleagues published an article in the *Journal of the American Medical Association* in which they labeled the phenomenon Caffey and they observed as "battered children syndrome" (Kempe et al., 1962). This article brought to public awareness the serious problem of child abuse, documented now by physicians observing battered children on a regular basis in their practices. John Demos (1986), a historian, comments on the impact of this article:

> Child abuse evoked an immediate and complex mix of emotions: horror, shame, fascination, disgust. Dr. Kempe and his co-authors noted that physicians themselves experienced "great difficulty . . . in believing that parents could have attacked their children" and often attempted "to obliterate such suspicions from their minds, even in the face of obvious circumstantial evidence." In a sense the problem had long been consigned to a netherworld of things felt but not seen, known but not acknowledged. The "Battered Child" essay was like a shroud torn suddenly aside. Onlookers reacted with shock, but also perhaps with a kind of relief. The horror was in the open now, and it would not easily be shut up again. (p. 69)

Federal Child Abuse Legislation

In January 1974, Congress passed legislation designed to have a significant impact on child maltreatment: the Child Abuse Prevention and Treatment Act (Public Law 93-247). This law imposed stringent requirements that states had to meet if they wished to secure federal funding for child maltreatment problems. These requirements included the passage of child abuse and neglect laws; procedures for reporting child abuse, including immunity from prosecution of persons doing the reporting; procedures for investigating and adjudicating reported cases; confidentiality of records; the training of personnel; and the appointment in judicial proceedings of guardians ad litem for children who were victims of maltreatment.

The Child Abuse Prevention and Treatment Act also provided financial assistance to public and private agencies for demonstration projects that would identify, treat, and prevent child abuse and neglect. The law established the National Center on Child Abuse and Neglect, which assumed a leadership role in coordinating research on child abuse and the National Clearinghouse on Child Abuse and Neglect Information, which became a major informational resource for professionals and concerned citizens interested in child maltreatment.

Subsequent legislation amended the Child Abuse Prevention and Treatment Act of 1974 and provided additional legislation relative to the welfare of children. The Adoption Assistance and Child Welfare Act (Public Law 96-272), passed by Congress in 1980, had a specific impact on the problem of child abuse. This legislation prescribed that state social service agencies direct their family services to (a) prevent unnecessary substitute placements, (b) offer rehabilitation and reunification services to restore families whose children are in substitute care, and (c) assure permanent plans for children who cannot be reunited with their parents.

This legislation mandated a new approach to child welfare services—namely, a family-focused or family-based approach. This approach to the delivery of social services has become known as family-based services, the goal of which is to ensure that every effort is made to maintain the family as a functioning unit. Family-based services are designed to provide maximum services to a family at a time of crisis, such as a report of child maltreatment, in order to prevent the breakup of the family. This service delivery approach focuses on families rather than on individuals. Services in this context are intended to strengthen and maintain the family and to prevent family dissolution through foster home placement or the termination of parental rights. This is important in child maltreatment cases where historically children were often removed from an abusive home rather than efforts being made to eliminate the dysfunctional behavior and retain the family unit. However, this approach to service delivery has also been criticized for jeopardizing the safety of children in instances where children have remained in the home and abuse once again occurred despite the intervention of protective services.

Role of Voluntary Agencies and Allied Professions in Combating Child Abuse

Although publicly supported child protective service agencies assume the bulk of responsibility in intervening in reported cases of child abuse, voluntary or private agencies also work aggressively in the treatment and prevention of this social problem. For example, in 1970, Parents Anonymous (PA) was established by a parent with abuse problems and a licensed clinical social worker to meet the need for services for families where child abuse was a problem (Fritz, 1989). The National Committee to Prevent Child Abuse (NCPCA) was established in 1972 and currently works through its statewide chapters toward the prevention of child maltreatment. The Child Welfare League of America (CWLA) is a national standard-setting organization for child welfare agencies and accredits agencies meeting these standards, including child protective service agencies. The American Association for Protecting Children (AAPC), the children's division of the American Humane Association, provides comprehensive training in the fundamentals of child protective service work to child protective service personnel. The American Public Welfare Association (APWA) is concerned with developing and advocating effective public policies directed to improving the lives of low-income individuals and families and has set standards for public protective service agencies. Many of these organizations actively lobby for legislation at the federal level that provides protection to children from physical, emotional, and sexual abuse.

Concern for the prevention and treatment of child abuse has assumed in recent years a multidisciplinary, corporate, and international perspective. The American Professional Society on the Abuse of Children (APSAC) and the International Society for the Prevention of Child Abuse and Neglect (ISPCAN) are examples of interdisciplinary associations of professionals within the United States and throughout the world working together in child abuse prevention and treatment through supporting research, education, and advocacy on behalf of abused children and societal conditions associated with abuse.

Professional associations other than those directly concerned with social services have aggressively confronted child abuse from their own disciplinary perspectives. For example, the American Academy of Pediatrics, a professional association for certified pediatricians, educates its membership in the identification, investigation, and treatment of child abuse and supports legislation at the state and federal levels on the treatment and prevention of this social problem. The American Bar Association has established the Center on Children and the Law, which addresses child maltreatment and related legal matters by educating attorneys, judges, and other professionals involved in court proceedings affecting children. Lawyers prosecuting child maltreatment cases can receive assistance through the National Center for Prosecution of Child Abuse. This organization publishes an authoritative manual, *Investigation and Prosecution of Child Abuse*, that is used by many child abuse prosecutors,

A number of business corporations at the local, regional, and national levels provide financial support to voluntary agencies in their efforts at treating and preventing child abuse. Personnel from these corporations also assume leadership positions on the agencies' boards of directors.

UNDERSTANDING CHILD PHYSICAL ABUSE

In Chapter 1, several general theories of aggression were discussed. These theories provide a basic foundation for understanding family violence. More specific theories for understanding child abuse are presented here in terms of factors identified in research to be associated with the physical, emotional, and sexual abuse of children. These factors are organized into three categories: individual-related factors, family-related factors, and social- and cultural-related factors. In some instances, factors associated with one category may also relate to other categories.

Individual-Related Factors

Intergenerational theory. This is one of the most frequently cited theories for understanding child abuse. The theory suggests that children who are victims of physical abuse grow up to abuse their children in turn when they become parents. This theory is based largely on self-reports from abusive parents rather than on data from rigorous empirical studies (Baldwin & Oliver, 1975; Conger, Burgess, & Barrett, 1979; Elmer, 1960; Green, Gaines, & Sandgrund, 1974; Johnson & Morse, 1968; Nurse, 1964; Oliver & Taylor, 1971; Paulson & Chaleff, 1973; Silver, Dublin, & Lourie, 1969). Although being abused as a child may put one at risk for abusing children (Bagley, Wood, & Young, 1994), adults abused as children may also resolve not to treat their children in the way they were treated by confronting the fact of their abuse and learning new parenting skills to avoid engaging in abusive behavior (Egeland & Susman-Stillman,

1996; Kaufman & Zigler, 1987; Wiehe, 1992).

Unrealistic expectations. Child abuse may occur because parents hold unrealistic expectations of their children, which the latter are unable to attain. Unrealistic expectations may include premature toilet training, cessation of crying, and achievements in school and extracurricular activities (Bavolek, 1989; Berg, 1976; Clark, 1975; Kravitz & Driscoll, 1983). Unrealistic parental self-expectations may also set up abusive situations. For example, a parent may assume continuous responsibility for child care without the use of baby-sitters or day care. This parental self-expectation may prevent a mother from pursuing a career or seeking normal respite from the stress associated with child care, thereby placing her at risk to be abusive.

Stress. Inadequate financial resources, marital problems, and negative life experiences may create stress on parents that may in turn impact on their parenting abilities and put them at risk to be physically abusive to a child (Burrell et al., 1994; Chan, 1994; Hawkins & Duncan, 1985; Rodriguez & Green, 1997; Whipple & Webster-Stratton, 1991). Research shows, for example, that listening to long hours of infant crying can produce high levels of stress in parents (Tyson & Sobschak, 1994).

Parenting abilities. Inadequate parenting knowledge and skills are associated with the physical abuse of children. For example, poor problem-solving skills were found to discriminate between samples of abusive and nonabusive mothers. Abusive parents demonstrated a narrow or limited repertoire of responses to problems commonly encountered in their child-rearing experiences, such as in the area of discipline (Azar, Robinson, Hekimian, & Twentyman, 1984). Parental frustration and the inability to effectively cope with child-rearing problems may result in the use of severe forms of corporal punishment as a way of maintaining control of the child (Reid, Taplin, & Lorber, 1981). Inadequate preparation for parenting roles in terms of knowledge and attitudes about children's development was found to be a strong predictor of abuse potential for adolescent mothers (Dukewich, Borkowski, & Whitman, 1996).

Role reversal. Role reversal occurs when children are expected to be sensitive to and responsible for the happiness and emotional well-being of the parents, a role expectation of parents toward children (Ackley, 1977; Bavolek, 1984; Steele, 1975). Parental role reversal may result from emotional deprivation that adults experienced early in their own lives for which they attempt to compensate by turning to their children. When these needs are not met by their children, parents may resort to physical or emotional abuse.

Empathy. Research suggests a positive relationship between empathy and certain prosocial behaviors that parenting requires such as being understanding, being able to give comfort, being helpful and cooperative (Frodi & Lamb, 1980; Hoffman, 1978; Hogan, 1979); valuing the welfare of another and perceiving the other to be in need (Batson, Turk, Shaw, & Klein, 1995); being flexible (Downs & Jenkins, 1993); and showing sensitivity to another's needs (Ainsworth, Blehar, Waters, & Wall, 1978; Belsky, Rovine, & Taylor, 1984; Egeland & Farber, 1984). A parental lack of empathy for a child's physical and emotional needs may also be a source of physically abusive behavior. Research shows that abusive mothers are less empathic toward their children than nonabusive mothers (LeTourneau, 1981; Milner, Halsey, & Fultz, 1995; Wiehe, 1987). Studies identify the ability to empathize as a moderating or controlling variable in exhibiting aggression. Participants in psychological experiments were asked to administer an electrical shock to a person in another room. Individuals scoring high on an empathy measurement were unable to do so (Feshbach, 1964; Feshbach & Feshbach, 1969; Mehrabian & Epstein, 1972). It was as if they were saying to themselves, "How would I feel if someone were doing this to me?" Likewise, empathic parents may avoid physically abusive behavior, such as hitting a child, because they are able to identify with how they would feel if they were the child. Nonempathic mothers are often provoked to anger by their infants' crying, culminating at times in these mothers abusing infants by violently shaking them. Empathic mothers identify with their children's discomfort and attempt to meet their needs (Frodi, 1981; Frodi & Lamb, 1980). Other variables may also relate to the absence of empathy in physically abusive mothers, such as depression and sadness (Marino, 1992; Milner et al., 1995), stress (Rosenstein, 1995), and the manner in which parents cognitively process information about their children's behavior (Berkowitz, 1990; Milner, 1993).

Substance abuse. While not a cause of child abuse, research has demonstrated a significant relationship between substance abuse and physical child abuse (Behling, 1979; Chaffin et al., 1996; Famularo, Kinscherff, & Fenton, 1992; Famularo, Stone, Barnum, & Wharton, 1986; Murphy et al., 1991; Peterson et al., 1996). In a review of 190 randomly selected records from the caseload of a large juvenile court, researchers found that 67% of the cases involved parents who could be classified as substance abusers. Alcohol abuse was significantly related to physical abuse and cocaine abuse to sexual abuse (Famularo et al., 1992).

A study of children born to mothers who used drugs during pregnancy showed that these children were at a higher risk of subsequent abuse than were children from the general population. Over a 5-year period, children born at an urban medical center whose mothers used drugs during their pregnancy were identified using results of toxicology screens from birth and maternal records. Evidence of child maltreatment was obtained from the State Central Registry of Abuse and Neglect. Of the 513 children exposed in utero to drugs, 155 (30.2%) were reported as abused, and 102 (19.9%) of these had substantiated reports. The rate of abuse was two to three times that of children living in the same geographic, high-abuse-risk area of the city in which the research occurred (Jaudes, Ekwo, & Voorhis, 1995). Parental substance abuse also is a significant predictor of child maltreatment re-reports (Wolock & Magura, 1996).

Relationship to the child. Mothers' boyfriends are responsible for substantially more child abuse than other nonparental caregivers, even though they perform relatively little child care. Several reasons are suggested for this finding. Mothers' boyfriends tend to use more physical coercion than other caregivers, possibly because their social role lacks legitimate authority. Also, violent outbursts by a boyfriend against his girlfriend's child or children appear to be associated with either the boyfriend siding with the mother against the child or he perceiving that the mother and child are against him (Margolin, 1992).

Mother's age. Is the age of the mother, especially those who are teenagers, a significant factor associated with the physical abuse of a child? The age of the mother at the time of the child's birth rather than at the time the abuse occurred was significantly related to child abuse in a sample of nearly 2,000 abusive mothers. Her immaturity, lack of education, and low income place her at risk for not being able to handle the stress of parenthood (Connelly & Straus, 1992). As stated earlier, for adolescent mothers, their lack of knowledge and their attitudes about children's development were strong predictors for potential abuse (Dukewich et al., 1996). However, contradictory findings were found in an analysis of 23,764 maltreatment reports in Illinois in 1988 and all parents in Illinois with children in out-of-home care on February 28, 1990 ($n = 8{,}535$) (Massat, 1995). Adolescent parents were not overrepresented among maltreating parents or among parents of children in out-of-home care. The research contends that the statement that teenage mothers are more frequently abusive than their older counterparts is a myth that has two destructive effects: First, programs for adolescent parents may be deemed successful in preventing abuse when in fact teenage parents are no more likely than older parents to abuse their children, and second, valuable resources are spent on programs preventing abuse in adolescent parents when this is not an issue. These funds could more profitably be spent on programs for teenage parents focusing on health care, nutrition, child care, and educational/vocational opportunities for young women with children.

Family-Related Factors

Loss of control. Some parents physically abuse a child as a futile last effort to gain control of the child (Patterson, 1982). Parents who experience loss of control of a child feel they are being manipulated and controlled by the child, resulting in feelings of hostility and frustration. An escalating cycle can occur as the parent attempts to gain control but in frustration and anger eventually lashes out against the child in the form of physical abuse (Lorber, Felton, & Reid, 1984; Patterson, 1982; Reid et al., 1981).

Family composition. Gender, age of children, and family size also are factors associated with child physical abuse. Although the National Incidence and Prevalence Studies of Child Abuse and Neglect (National Center on Child Abuse and Neglect, 1988a, 1988b) reported that female children experience more abuse overall than male children; this is due largely to sexual abuse being included in the definition of abuse and the fact that females are sexually abused at four times the rate of males. Research on physical abuse, however, indicates that more males than females are abused (Wolfner & Gelles, 1993). The risk of death resulting from physical abuse is greatest in children under 1 year of age. Children from large families with four or more children are more endangered and experience more physical abuse than children from smaller families (Coulton, Korbin, Su, & Chow, 1995; National Center on Child Abuse and Neglect, 1988a, 1988b).

Social- and Cultural-Related Factors

Poverty. Children from low-income families are at greater risk for physical abuse than children not living in poverty (Dattalo, 1995; Krishnan & Morrison, 1995; Kruttschnitt, McLeod, & Dornfeld, 1994; National Center on Child Abuse and Neglect, 1988a, 1988b). An analysis of 77 communities within the Chicago metropolitan area revealed that child maltreatment rates were related to indicators of socioeconomic and demographic well-being for these neighborhoods and for the subunits within them. High-risk areas for child abuse were characterized by social disorganization and a lack of social coherence in contrast to low-risk areas that gave evidence of a stronger social fabric (Garbarino & Kostelny, 1992). Similarly, in a study involving census and administrative agency data for 177 urban census tracts, researchers found that children living in neighborhoods characterized by poverty were at highest risk for maltreatment (Coulton et al., 1995). Economic distress frequently occurred in these areas because women were earning substantially less than men due to gender discrimination. Poverty limited the mothers' access to educational, recreational, and day-care resources for their children, which could have increased stress associated with the mothers' physical abuse of their children (Garbarino, 1976). Although there is a relationship between poverty and child abuse and neglect, other factors associated may be involved, such as the ability to delay gratification, educational achievement, lack of impulsivity, ability to control anger, good communication skills, good psychological adjustment, and freedom from severe chemical dependency (Drake & Pandey, 1996). Undesirable economic change is also associated with increased rates of child abuse. Financial difficulties resulting from high job loss in two geographic areas in California were found over a 30-month period to be associated with increases in child abuse (Steinberg, Catalano, & Dooley, 1981).

Social isolation. The physical abuse of children is associated with parents not having access to supportive services and social networks and the absence of resources in very small communities and in rural areas (Coohey, 1996). Families living in rural and isolated areas may not have access to supportive services such as day care nor are extended family members (adult siblings, parents) available to provide support and respite from parenting responsibilities. Also, families living in small communities and rural areas where supportive services are not available may not be able to access such services in nearby metropolitan areas (Hawkins & Duncan, 1985).

Values. Cultural and religious values may support the use of corporal punishment, such as whipping or beating a child with a rod, which may be regarded as physically abusive behavior. Biblical texts, if taken literally, are often used to advocate corporal punishment of children (Proverbs 13:24, 19:18, 22:15; Hebrews 12:5-10). This is especially true in fundamentalist churches that subscribe to a literal view of the Bible (King James version), and where clergy are not educated. For example, the text of Proverbs 13:14, "He who spares the rod hates his son, but he who loves him is careful to discipline," is often shortened to the proverbial "Spare the rod and spoil the child." However, biblical scholars point out that this text is very different from the proverb, as reflected in translations other than the King James version. The proverb makes a direct causal link between not using the rod and its effect on the child—namely, spoiling the child. The biblical text, however, refers to the attitudes of the caregiver and makes no reference to the effect of the punishment on the child. Rather, it appeals to providing love and careful discipline, which means to teach or guide the child. Finally, the rod probably refers to a shepherd's staff used to guide the sheep, not to beat them (Carey, 1994).

Theological doctrine may view children as inherently corrupt and sinful, from which the deduction may be made that children are in need of severe discipline in order to correct that state (Greven, 1977). These views again are most prominently seen in the Bible Belt or southern part of the United States (Flynn, 1994). In a sample of 881 members of religious denominations classified as literal or nonliteral believers in the Bible, persons who were members of churches subscribing to a literal belief in the Bible preferred the use of corporal punishment over alternative methods of discipline (Wiehe, 1990).

FACTORS ASSOCIATED WITH EMOTIONAL ABUSE

Again, research is cited according to the categories of individual-related, family-related, and social- and cultural-related factors.

Individual-Related Factors

Emotional abuse, defined earlier, as a distinct type of child abuse, frequently is a component in both physical and sexual abuse (Claussen & Crittenden, 1991; Hart & Brassard, 1987). Thus, factors associated with these forms of abuse may also be applicable in understanding the emotional abuse of children.

Parents who repress emotions such as pain, joy, and anger may encourage children to do likewise and thus be unresponsive to their emotional needs (Brassard & Galardo, 1987; Miller, 1983). Cultural factors may encourage this parental behavior. Children may respond by feeling unloved and unwanted. This parental behavior may be identified as emotional abuse.

Family-Related Factors

Children often become the scapegoats for problems occurring in the marital relationship in that parents blame them for marital conflicts, such as attributing family financial problems to expenses associated with raising children or by projecting personal dislikes and frustrations on a child who resembles a spouse (Garbarino & Vondra, 1987). Such behavior is emotionally abusive for children because they are unjustly made to feel responsible for their parents' problems or are made to feel that it would be better if they didn't exist.

Psychological maltreatment may be seen in parental communication consisting primarily of aversive interchanges that emphasize what a child is doing wrong and the absence of prosocial communication where a child is verbally rewarded for good behavior. Aversive parental communication may reinforce in a child negative behaviors such as whining, pestering, and misbehaving as ways to gain parental attention, even though in a cyclical fashion the attention prompts further emotional abuse. The aversive nature of the parents' communication with a child also impacts negatively on the child's self-esteem and self-worth (Patterson, 1982).

A child's failure to meet parental expectations that may be unreasonably high or inappropriate to a child's abilities impacts on the child's self-concept, self-esteem, and self-confidence (Bateson, 1972; Bavolek, 1984; Garbarino & Vondra, 1987). Inappropriate expectations frequently occur when parents compare one child with siblings who have different abilities and talents. Unrealistic and inappropriate expectations also may result when parents lack knowledge of child developmental stages and accompanying cognitive and social skills. Parents may resort to psychological pressures that can be emotionally abusive in an attempt to coerce the child to comply with their inappropriate expectations (Burgess & Conger, 1977; Patterson, 1979).

Parents sometimes resort to emotionally abusive behavior under the disguise that they are trying to motivate a child to make some type of behavioral change. For example, parents may resort to name-calling when a child is obese, careless about personal hygiene, or doesn't keep his or her room neat. Such emotionally abusive behavior does not motivate the child to make the desired changes but is very destructive to the child's self-esteem (Wiehe, 1997b).

Social- and Cultural-Related Factors

Parents may be so overwhelmed with problems and stress in their lives that they fail to be sensitive to and meet the emotional needs of their children. This may result in children feeling rejected and unwanted. Stress factors associated with this form of emotional abuse may include too large a family, inadequate financial resources, and parental drug and alcohol abuse as well as a general climate in the family in which there is an absence of emotional support among family members (Garbarino & Vondra, 1987). In some instances, parents may be reflecting traditional ethnic or cultural values in the way they were raised by their parents.

Treating children differentially on a gender basis may result in emotional abuse. Parental beliefs and expectations about gender-appropriate behavior may influence the way parents treat their children, with the result that the latter are not allowed to develop to their full potential (Telzrow, 1987). Parents may be reinforced in these beliefs and practices by religious and cultural values as well as by the differential way in which genders are portrayed in the public media (Downs & Gowan, 1980; Mamay & Simpson, 1981).

FACTORS ASSOCIATED WITH CHILD SEXUAL ABUSE

Although it is commonly held that sexual abuse occurs in only lower socioeconomic families, the literature on sexual abuse does not support this assumption. Research does not identify any known social class of children particularly at risk for experiencing this social problem (Finkelhor, 1993).

Prior to discussing factors identified in research as associated with child sexual abuse, five aspects important for understanding this social problem are discussed: the perpetrators of sexual abuse, the context in which sexual abuse occurs, adults' belief of children's reports of sexual abuse, the sexual/nonsexual components of sexual abuse, and the psychopathology of perpetrators.

The Perpetrators of Sexual Abuse

Strangers or known perpetrators. The media frequently portray child sexual abuse as occurring in the context of a child being lured away from his or her parents on a playground or in a supermarket and subsequently being molested by a stranger. An "urban legend" has developed, repeated on television talk shows and on the Internet, that reports an anonymous young girl being kidnapped by a stranger from a mall, Disneyworld, or Disneyland, having her head shaved, dressed in other clothes, and used for sexual purposes (Best, 1990; Gelles, 1996). Sexual abuse by strangers occurs far less frequently than by relatives and acquaintances. Studies report that 75% to 80% of the offenders are related or known to the victim (Finkelhor, 1979; Finkelhor et al., 1990; MacFarlane et al., 1986; Tsai & Wagner, 1978). The perpetrator may be the father, stepparent, boyfriend, grandfather, uncle, brother, neighbor, teacher, scout leader, member of the clergy, or similar individuals. Here, the perpetrator is referred to as male because men represent approximately 95% of those who sexually abuse girls and 80% of those abusing boys (Finkelhor, 1984a; Harper, 1993; Lawson, 1993). This is not meant to imply, however, that sexual abuse perpetrators are always male.

Sexual abuse perpetrated by women. Sexual abuse of children by women, especially mothers against sons and daughters, is increasingly receiving attention in the research literature (Adshead, Howett, & Mason, 1994; Kaufman, Wallace, Johnson, & Reeder, 1996; Miletski, 1995; Roys & Timms, 1995; Rudin, Zalewski, & Bodmer-Turner, 1995). The survivors of sexual abuse by women feel betrayed by the male stereotyping that occurs in people's minds, in laws, and in the literature about sexual abuse in which perpetrators are portrayed only as males: "For most Americans, disengaging male images from sex crimes is like imagining boats without water, a failure to deal with reality" (Rosencrans, 1997, p. 19).

The false assumption is made that since females do not have penises they cannot perpetrate sexual abuse. However, women can be sexual without a penis. A survey was conducted involving 93 volunteer, adult women across the nation, who self-reported sexual abuse by their mothers primarily but not exclusively during their childhood (Rosencrans, 1997). Respondents to the research reported experiencing various types of sexual abuse from their mothers including daily enemas, fondling, oral stimulation, and the insertion of fingers and objects into the victim's body. Sexual abuse also occurred through the victim being forced to fondle the mother-perpetrator and being forced to watch the mother engaging in sexual activity. In a very small subsample of 9 boys sexually abused by their mothers, a frequent form of the sexual abuse was the perpetrator masturbating the victim (Rosencrans, 1997).

Sexual abuse perpetrated by women especially against their sons and daughters rarely gets reported to social service, mental health, or criminal justice agencies (Johnson & Shrier, 1987). Sexual abuse by mothers often is not reported because the victim falsely assumes the activity is in the context of the mother's caretaker role and fears exposing the family to public shame and embarrassment. Also, the child victim may be reluctant to report a mother's abuse because she may be the only "family" the victim has (Miletski, 1995). Victims often do not conceptualize what they experienced as abuse until years later in adulthood, frequently in relation to therapy sought for problems in living. The sexual abuse of prepubescent and pubescent young males by adult women is often excused as "teaching" a boy how to be a man sexually. Consequently, the young male victim may regard the abuse as positive or engage in self-blame (Miletski, 1995). Also, underreporting of female sexual offenders occurs because there usually is the absence of physical evidence such as semen and pubic hair (Rosecrans, 1997; Rudin et al., 1995). Female perpetrators are reluctant to admit to the sexual abuse in which they engage with their children lest they be perceived as extremely deviant, and professionals tend to dismiss such reports because of their lack of knowledge about this type of abuse (Miletski, 1995).

Victimization by a female perpetrator can have results as devastating as victimization by a male perpetrator, including self-blame, low self-esteem, problems in sexual functioning ranging from the avoidance of sex to sexual compulsivity, and substance abuse (Rosencrans, 1997).

Context in Which Sexual Abuse Occurs

Because most perpetrators of sexual abuse are known to the victim, the context in which this form of abuse occurs involves the victim implicitly trusting the perpetrator. This trust may be based on the loving relationship between the two persons, such as a grandfather and his granddaughter. The relationship may also be one of authority—for example, a scoutmaster and a scout. This violation of trust impacts significantly on the victim's ability to trust others in the future, as discussed later in the effects of sexual abuse on survivors.

Sexual abuse occurs in the context of enticement and subsequent entrapment. The perpetrator may entice and then entrap the victim by indicating that the latter is someone special and that the sexual activity will be a mutually held secret between them. This context may be reinforced by the offender giving the victim gifts such as candy, special favors, or privileges and attention. In other instances, as frequently occurs in sexual abuse between siblings, threat of physical injury is used by the perpetrator to force the victim to comply with his wishes (Wiehe, 1997b). Thus, the victim becomes entrapped in the desire to please the perpetrator, whom the victim trusts or respects, or the victim feels compelled to comply for the sake of his or her own safety (Summit, 1983). The outcome of this scenario, as frequently seen in adults who were sexually abused as children, is self-blame for allowing oneself to become entrapped. However, in reality there may have been no choice but to comply because the victim did not understand what was happening or was operating under a threat.

Disbelief of Sexual Abuse Reports

Another important aspect of child sexual abuse is the disbelief and blame that children often experience when reporting their sexual victimization to a parent or another adult. When the abuser is a person the victim knows, the tendency exists among adults receiving the report to disbelieve it. A mother's denial of a child's report of sexual victimization may be linked to her own past victimization that she continues to defend against and deny.

Although popular media at times give the impression that a large percentage of child abuse reports are unfounded, clinical observations and empirical data do not support this impression (Goodwin, Sahd, & Rada, 1982; Peters, 1976; Sorensen & Snow, 1991). In a study of 576 child sexual abuse reports made to the Denver Department of Social Services (Jones & McGraw, 1987), 70% of these reports were reliable, 22% were considered suspicious but unsubstantiated, and 8% were fictitious. Fictitious reports were examined in detail from a clinical perspective. No distinctive feature clearly distinguished fictitious from reliable reports. For example, an absence of emotion in describing an abusive incident, at times perceived as an indicator of fictitious reporting, was found to be indicative of earlier abuse the victim had experienced and the victim's repression of emotional reactions to the earlier victimization. Jones and McGraw (1987) concluded that fictitious allegations are unusual and that sexual abuse reports, even when appearing on the surface as suspicious, should be carefully investigated.

In their study of children's disclosure of intrafamilial sexual abuse, Sirles and Franke (1989) found that mothers were most likely to believe their children's reports of sexual abuse if the offender was a member of their extended family, such as a grandfather, an uncle, or a cousin, as opposed to a husband or boyfriend. Mothers believed their children in 92% of these situations. Belief decreased to 85% if the offender was the biological father. Only 56% of the mothers believed the reports if the offender was a stepfather or live-in partner. Several reasons may account for the latter. In blended families or where the mother is bringing a boyfriend into the home, the children may not accept the new person. The mother senses the resentment and assumes that the sexual abuse report is the child's attempt to get rid of the stepfather or friend. Also, after an earlier failed marriage or relationship, the high emotional investment a mother has in a relationship with a new husband or live-in partner may account for her unwillingness to believe her child's report of sexual abuse by this person.

In Sirles and Franke's study, the age of the child was an important factor in whether or not the report of the abuse was believed. If the child was of preschool age (2-5 years), 95% of the mothers believed the child's report of abuse. For children of latency age (6-11 years), 82% of their mothers believed them. If the child was a teenager (12-17 years), belief occurred in only 64% of the cases. The researchers offer several reasons that account for the age factor. Mothers may tend to believe sexual abuse reports from very young children because youngsters lack sexual experience and the ability to make up details about sexual exploitation. Also, younger children are more attached to their mothers who consequently may be more willing to believe them than older children. Conversely, teenagers are less attached to their mothers, possess sexual information enabling them to falsify a sexual abuse report, and may even be known by the parents to be sexually active.

In a similar study by Heriot (1996), mothers had difficulty believing their children when the abuse involved intercourse or oral sex as compared to being touched or fondled. Seemingly, the seriousness of the abuse contributed to the mother not being able to believe the daughter. Also, the research found that mothers had difficulty believing teenagers' reports of sexual abuse because of anger resulting from other problems the teenagers were presenting.

Research also shows that the attitude of a child's caregiver is an important factor in a child disclosing sexual abuse. Children with caregivers willing even to consider the possibility of abuse were over three-and-a-half times more likely to disclose their abuse than those whose caregivers did not take such an open stance (Lawson & Chaffin, 1992).

Parental disbelief of sexual abuse reports may affect a child in various ways. Summit (1983) categorized the typical ways in which female children who are victims of sexual assault by adults known to them respond to their abuse. He identifies these responses as "child sexual abuse accommodation syndrome." Five components comprise this syndrome: secrecy, helplessness, entrapment and accommodation, delayed and unconvincing disclosure, and retraction. The first two components describe the victim's vulnerable position. As indicated earlier, the perpetrator approaches the victim in the context of secrecy. Frequently, the young victim is helpless. The child may have been instructed to obey adults, may have been threatened by the perpetrator, and may not have been taught how to attempt to prevent victimization. The remaining three components describe a sequential process occurring for the victim. Following entrapment and submission to the sexual abuse, the child may wait a while before telling anyone. For example, one young girl reported her sexual victimization by a visiting uncle from a distant city 1 year later when her parents announced that he was returning for another visit. When disclosure is made, it may not be convincing, and individuals close to the victim may disbelieve or blame the victim. The perpetrator may respond to confrontations about the alleged abuse by engaging in excessive denial or by attempting to shift responsibility for the sexual misconduct to the victim or to someone else. The victim accommodates to the pressures and consequences experienced in the disclosure process and, as a way of retreating, denies that the abuse really occurred.

Researchers studying 630 cases of alleged child sexual abuse concluded that disclosure is a process, not an event. The authors felt that their data did not support the common assumption that most abused children are capable of immediate active disclosure of their sexual victimization. Children comprising the research sample were not able to provide a coherent, detailed account of their sexual victimization in an initial investigative interview. In some instances, children disclosed the sexual abuse in a very tentative manner, subsequently recanted the disclosure, and only later reaffirmed the original report of their victimization (Gonzalez, Waterman, Kelly, McCord, & Oliveri, 1993).

Disclosure of sexual victimization may occur in a very covert way with the result that the parents may not recognize the intent of the child's message. In the later chapter on sibling abuse, an adult survivor of sexual abuse tells how she was sexually abused by her brother when she was a small child. The abuse would occur when her parents would go away for the evening and her older brother would be her baby-sitter. The victim would go into the parent's room when they were getting dressed to leave and ask, "Do you really have to go out tonight?" The parents were unaware that their daughter was trying to tell them that she was being sexually abused by her brother. She couldn't come out and tell them because her brother had threatened to harm her if she told her parents. Thus, a child's disclosure of sexual abuse may occur in bits and pieces or incrementally, depending upon circumstances such as relationship of the victim to the person to whom the reporting is being done and tacit permission that the victim receives from this individual (Petronio, Reeder, Hecht, & Ros-Mendoza, 1996).

Sexual/Nonsexual Components

Both sexual and nonsexual components comprise a sexual offender's behavior. The sexual component, seen in the touching, caressing, sexual arousal, and orgasm experienced by the perpetrator, may be a primary or secondary factor in the abuse. The nonsexual component may include power, control, an expression of anger, dominance over the victim, or the fulfillment of identification and affiliation needs (Groth, 1979).

Psychopathology of Perpetrators

Historically, theories about child sexual abuse have focused on the offender's psychopathology—namely, that perpetrators of child sexual abuse were a small group of highly deviant individuals and that their psychopathology was the cause of the abuse. This view was based on the samples of perpetrators studied, which were primarily incarcerated offenders (Finkelhor, 1984a). However, incarcerated offenders represent only a small fraction of individuals who sexually abuse children. Those incarcerated may not be representative of adults engaging in this behavior who otherwise are functioning normally in society.

Sexual abuse perpetrators incarcerated for their offense hardly represent the general population of perpetrators because only a small number of perpetrators are ever brought to court for their offense. In a national sample of adult men and women, 27% of the women and 16% of the men reported a history of childhood sexual abuse. Nearly half of these men and a third of the women never disclosed their abuse. Thus, probably only a very small percentage of the perpetrators were prosecuted or even incarcerated (Finkelhor et al., 1990). In a survey of 930 women in the San Francisco area, 648 cases of child sexual abuse before the age of 18 were found. Only 5%, or 30 cases (4 cases of incestuous abuse and 26 cases of extrafamilial child sexual abuse), were reported to the police. Only 7 of these 30 cases were known to result in convictions (Russell, 1986).

Thus, sexual abuse does not involve only a small, extremely deviant subgroup of the population. Rather, sexual interest in children may be far more common than generally thought. In a survey of 193 male undergraduate students regarding their sexual interest in children, 21% of the respondents reported sexual attraction to some small children. Of these, 9% described having sexual fantasies involving children, 5% admitted to having masturbated to such fantasies, and 7% indicated some inclination to have sex with a child if they could avoid being caught (Briere & Runtz, 1989b). In another study of 318 university students, 4.7% of males and 4.2% of females reported some hypothetical likelihood of having sex with a child if no one would find out about it and they would not be punished (Briere, Henschel, & Smiljanich, 1992). In a later study involving 180 female and 99 male university students, Smiljanich and Briere (1996) found a much higher sexual interest among males (22.2%) as compared to females (2.8%) and found males' attraction to children to be associated with lower self-esteem, greater sexual conflicts, more sexual impulsivity, greater use of pornography depicting consenting adult sex, and more self-reported difficulty in attracting age-appropriate sexual partners. Finkelhor (1984a) suggests that adult sexual interest in children may be stimulated in part by child pornography and the sexualization of children as seen in films, advertising, and child beauty pageants where children assume miniature adult roles.

FOUR PRECONDITIONS OF CHILD SEXUAL ABUSE

Finkelhor (1984a) presents a theoretical model for understanding child sexual abuse that includes individual and social/cultural factors. This model, identified as Four Preconditions for Sexual Abuse, suggests that multiple factors are associated with child sexual abuse. The model places into an organizing framework earlier theories on the subject (Lukianowicz, 1972; Lystad, 1975; Tierney & Corwin, 1983). Finkelhor (1984a) states,

> Most approaches (theories) have tended to emphasize a few factors such as deviant patterns of sexual arousal or psychosexual immaturity. However, there is a large range of behaviors that needs to be explained. It includes the man who spends his whole life fixated on ten-year-old boys, or the man who after many years of heterosexual fidelity to his wife is possessed by a strong impulse to caress his granddaughter's genitals, or the man who persuades his girlfriend to help bring a child into their bed in order to "experience something new," or the adolescent, preoccupied with his lack of sexual experience, who forces his younger sister to have sex with him, or the father who promiscuously fondles all his daughters and all the friends they bring home. To explain all this diversity, a multifactor model that matches a variety of explanations to a variety of different kinds of abusers is needed. (p. 36)

Finkelhor's model is based on four preconditions that must be met before abuse can occur. The model may be generalized to different types of sexual abuse within the context of intra- and extrafamilial abuse. Both psychological and sociological factors are incorporated into the model.

Precondition I: Motivation to Sexually Abuse

There are reasons why adults are sexually interested in children. Finkelhor (1984a) identifies three: emotional congruence, sexual arousal, and blockage.

Emotional congruence suggests that an adult may find relating to a child emotionally gratifying. The emphasis here is on emotional rather than sexual gratification. As stated earlier, child sexual abuse may involve nonsexual as well as sexual components. Some adults are emotionally more comfortable relating to a child than to peers because of their poor self-esteem, poor self-worth, or arrested psychological development (Groth, Hobson, & Gary, 1982). Sexual involvement with a child may meet other emotional needs by providing the perpetrator with a sense of power, control, and security that he cannot achieve with peers (Finkelhor, 1984a). The source of this need for power and control, according to feminist perspectives of psychosocial development, stems from male socialization. Men are socialized to be dominant and in control and women to be submissive and passive (Russell, 1986). Research from an attachment theoretical perspective shows that sexual abuse perpetrators often remain aloof from close or intimate relationships. They feel anger toward others, especially toward women from whom they anticipate rejection. Thus, they may turn to children to meet their sexual needs (Hudson & Ward, 1997).

The second reason motivating an adult to sexually abuse a child is the adult's *sexual arousal* concerning children. Research cited earlier suggested that adult male sexual interest in children may be more widespread than generally thought (Briere et al., 1992; Briere & Runtz, 1989b; Smiljanich & Briere, 1996). Why this arousal is evident or stronger in some adults as compared to others remains largely unexplained. Possible reasons include the sexualization of small children in the media, an offender's history of sexual traumatization as a child, and biological factors such as hormonal levels or chromosomal composition (Finkelhor, 1984a).

Blockage refers to adults' inability to have emotional and sexual needs met in relationships with other adults. Blockage may result from earlier unsuccessful attempts at sexual gratification with adults. For example, a male may experience impotence in an adult sexual relationship or rejection from a mate, with the result that sexual activity with another adult represents discomfort and frustration. Consequently, the adult male may turn to a child with whom he can be in control and be assured of sexual success. Blockage also may result when a marital relationship is unsatisfactory and sexual gratification is sought from an easily accessible individual such as a daughter (Finkelhor, 1984a; Meiselman, 1978). Feminist theory, however, is critical of the latter explanation because it assumes a role of sexual subservience on the part of women. An underlying assumption in this explanation is that a woman is expected to meet her mate's sexual demands without regard for her own wishes. If she fails to do so, the consequence is that her mate may transfer his sexual interests to a daughter, and if this occurs, she is in part to blame (Driver, 1989).

Precondition II: Overcoming Internal Inhibitors

Internal inhibitions may be absent or must be overcome by the perpetrator for child sexual abuse to occur. Factors cited for a breakdown in inhibition include substance abuse, found in a large number of child sexual abuse cases (Chaffin et al., 1996); psychosis, found relatively rarely (Marshall & Norgard, 1983); and poor impulse control (Groth et al., 1982).

Feminist theories add that inhibitions against sexual abuse are lowered when society blames the victim rather than the perpetrator. Blaming the victim provides offend-

	Level of Explanation	
	Individual	*Social/Cultural*
Precondition I: Factors Related to Motivation to Sexually Abuse		
Emotional congruence	Arrested emotional development Need to feel powerful and controlling Re-enactment of childhood trauma to undo the hurt Narcissistic identification with self as a young child	Masculine requirement to be dominant and powerful in sexual relationships
Sexual arousal	Childhood sexual experience that was traumatic or strongly conditioning Modeling of sexual interest in children by someone else Misattribution of arousal cues Biologic abnormality	Child pornography Erotic portrayal of children in advertising Male tendency to sexualize all emotional needs
Blockage	Oedipal conflict Castration anxiety Fear of adult females Traumatic sexual experience with adult Inadequate social skills Marital problems	Repressive norms about masturbation and extramarital sex
Precondition II: Factors Predisposing to Overcoming Internal Inhibitors	Alcohol Psychosis Impulse disorder Senility Failure of incest inhibition mechanism in family dynamics	Social toleration of sexual interest in children Weak criminal sanctions against offenders Ideology of patriarchal prerogatives for fathers Social toleration for deviance committed while intoxicated Child pornography Male inability to identify with needs of children
Precondition III: Factors Predisposing to Overcoming External Inhibitors	Mother who is absent or ill Mother who is not close to or protective of child Mother who is dominated or abused by father Social isolation of family Unusual opportunities to be alone with child Lack of supervision of child Unusual sleeping or rooming conditions	Lack of social supports for mother Barriers to women's equality Erosion of social networks Ideology of family sanctity
Precondition IV: Factors Predisposing to Overcoming Child's Resistance	Child who is emotionally insecure or deprived Child who lacks knowledge about sexual abuse Situation of unusual trust between child and offender Coercion	Unavailability of sex education for children Social powerlessness of children

Figure 2.2 Preconditions for Sexual Abuse

SOURCE: Used with the permission of The Free Press, a Division of Simon & Schuster, from *Child Sexual Abuse: New Theory and Research* (p. 54) by David Finkelhor. Copyright © 1984 by David Finkelhor.

ers justification for their behavior (Rush, 1980). The view that a man's home is his castle or private domain to do as he wishes may be interpreted by some males as including intrafamilial sexual abuse (Finkelhor, 1984a; Rush, 1980).

Precondition III: Overcoming External Inhibitors

External inhibitors outside the perpetrator and child victim must be overcome for sexual abuse to occur (Finkelhor, 1984a). An important external force is the supervision a child receives that protects the child from possible sexual victimization. If such protection (external inhibitor) is not provided, the likelihood increases that the child will be sexually exploited. For example, when parents are physically or psychologically absent (e.g., divorce or illness), the likelihood of sexual abuse occurring increases (Kaufman, Peck, & Tagiuri, 1954; Maisch, 1973). Social and physical isolation of families or the absence of privacy in sleeping and bathing arrangements may also increase a victim's vulnerability (Fleming, Mullen, & Bammer, 1997; Summit & Kryso, 1978; Wiehe, 1997b). Children are at risk for sexual abuse if their mother is mentally ill or the child has no one in whom to confide (Fleming et al., 1997).

Precondition IV: Overcoming the Resistance of the Child Victim

The potential perpetrator must in some way influence, undermine, or overcome a child's possible resistance to sexual abuse. A child's emotional insecurity or affectional deprivation, possibly stemming from psychological maltreatment, may make the child vulnerable to attention and affection from a potential perpetrator. Lack of sexual information may increase a child's likelihood of succumbing to a perpetrator's sexual advances. Trust in and respect for the perpetrator, such as the trust a child holds for a close family member or the respect a student has for a teacher, also may lower a child's resistance to sexual abuse. Finally, threats of physical harm from the perpetrator may break down a child's resistance to sexual victimization (Finkelhor, 1984a; Summit, 1983; Wiehe, 1997b).

FEMINIST PERSPECTIVES ON CHILD SEXUAL ABUSE

The feminist perspective on child sexual abuse asserts that this social problem stems from several factors, one of which is the inequality in society between men and women, the latter including children (Birns & Meyer, 1993). Men are socialized to be dominant, to have power and control over women including the expression of their sexuality. The sexualization of children in child pornography or in child beauty pageants where very young girls pose in postures and attire typical of adult models gives a message to some adult males that children are appropriate sex objects (Wurtele & Miller-Perrin, 1992).

Feminist literature criticizes the association often made between the dysfunctional family and child sexual abuse. Emphasizing the role of the dysfunctional family as a causative factor in child sexual abuse supports the traditional family hierarchy in which males control and dominate females, as noted in the expression "the male is the head of the house." Dysfunctional family theory implies that sexual abuse may occur when family members do not assume expected, traditional roles. For example, as stated earlier, a wife is unjustly blamed for not fulfilling an expected role of providing her husband sexual gratification when he turns to the daughter for fulfillment of this need.

An emphasis on the dysfunctional family also may inappropriately shift the therapeutic focus in working with sexual abuse offenders and victims from incest as the primary issue to dysfunctional relationships. This shift in treatment focus may be dangerous because the restoration of traditionally expected family roles becomes the primary focus of treatment and the sexual abuse becomes a secondary issue. The restoration of traditionally expected family roles may openly or covertly include reinforcing male domination and manipulation of females rather than redistributing power among family members irrespective of gender (Driver, 1989; Waldby et al., 1989). Thus, the feminist approach to child abuse treatment involves expansion from a narrow perspective focusing primarily on the perpetrator or offender to include the creation of broader cultural change in society where men and women are seen as equals.

RESPONDING TO CHILD ABUSE

How do cases of child abuse become known to the authorities? What happens when a family is reported for child abuse? Although differences occur across states in the way the courts and social services are organized, a similar process is followed in the initial intervention in child abuse cases (see Figure 2.3).

The Report

Intervention begins when an allegation of child abuse is reported to a child protective service agency. Child protective service agencies are usually administered as part of a larger tax-supported social service agency identified by different titles in different states, such as the Department of Human Services, the Department for Social Services, or Child and Youth Services. A report of alleged child abuse also may be made by calling a local or statewide 24-hour toll-free hot line generally listed in the front pages of telephone directories.

States have adopted mandatory child abuse reporting statutes in compliance with the federal Child Abuse Prevention and Treatment Act that provide civil and criminal immunity to persons making a "good faith" report of child abuse. These statutes also mandate that certain professionals such as physicians, nurses and other allied health professionals, social workers, teachers, and law enforcement officials must report cases of child abuse of which they become aware in their professional duties. Physicians are an important source of reporting suspected cases of child abuse because they are often one of the first persons to see the abused child (Warner & Hansen, 1994). Two exceptions to the professionals mandated to report are attorneys who have client privilege and in some states clergy with penitent privilege. The grounds for making such reports are usually based on the person having "reasonable cause to believe" or "reasonable suspicion" that a child is being abused.

Although mandatory reporting of child abuse is required, research shows that many mental health professionals do not report cases of child abuse, especially in families with whom they are engaged in treatment (Attias & Goodwin, 1985; Finkelhor & Zellman, 1991; Kalichman & Craig, 1991; Kalichman, Craig, & Follingstad, 1989; Swoboda, Elwork, Sales, & Levine, 1978). Some mental health professionals feel that confidentiality is essential to the treatment of clients and that if they report an incident of abuse revealed in an interview their therapist-patient relationship is severely compromised. In some instances, mental health professionals will encourage the family to

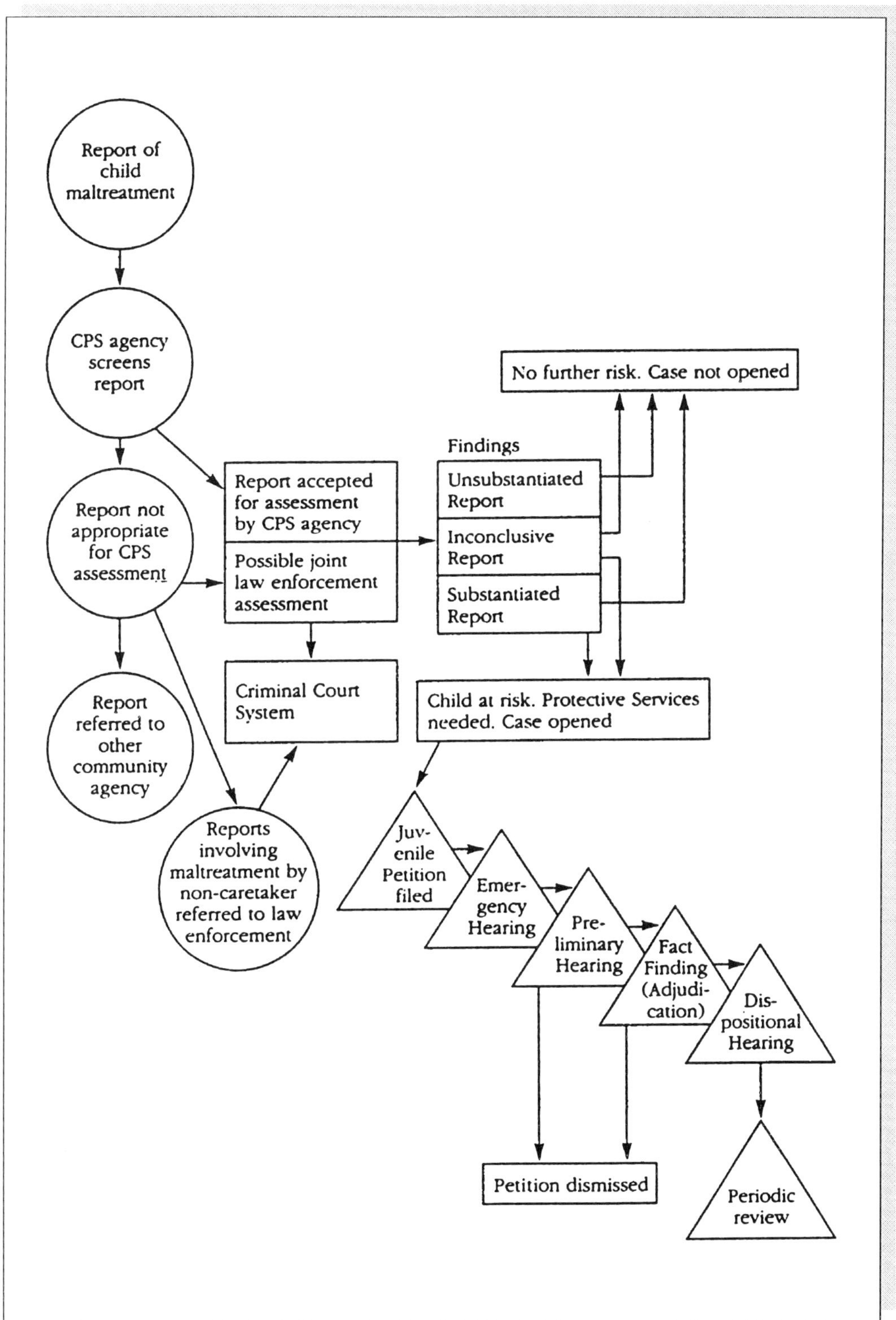

Figure 2.3 The Path of Intervention
SOURCE: Reprinted from *Working With Child Abuse and Neglect: A Primer* (Figure 5.1, p. 84) by Vernon R. Wiehe, Thousand Oaks, CA: Sage. Copyright © 1996 by Sage Publications, Inc. Used with permission.

- All mandated reporters are expected to have a complete understanding of their state laws regarding requirements to report suspected child abuse.
- Standard informed consent procedures may be developed by treatment professionals that clearly detail the conditions under which confidentiality is limited.
- Clients are informed of a report before it is filed unless doing so would endanger the welfare of the child or children.
- Thorough and detailed records should be kept of information released in mandated reports.
- Coordinated systems for managing reports among the diverse members of interdisciplinary treatment teams increase the efficiency of reporting.
- Cases of suspected child abuse that do not appear required to be reported should be discussed with a colleague in order to achieve objective reliability in reporting decisions.

Figure 2.4 Reporting Child Abuse
SOURCE: Kalichman, Brosig, and Kalichman (1994, pp. 39-41).

report the abuse; however, most state laws do not exempt mental health professionals from reporting in these instances (Crenshaw, Bartell, & Lichtenberg, 1994; Smith & Meyer, 1984).

In a study of 1,196 professionals (general and family practitioners, pediatricians, child psychiatrists, clinical psychologists, social workers, public school principals, and heads of child care centers), three case characteristics—previous abuse, severity of abuse, and recantation—were found to be powerful predictors of professionals' likelihood of reporting abuse (physical and sexual abuse and neglect). A history of previous abuse led to judgments of greater seriousness and increased the likelihood of reporting. When the alleged victim recanted a report of abuse when questioned by an authority figure, professionals were less likely to intend to report. Respondents also were more likely to report abuse for younger children, for children from poorer families, and when the perpetrators in a child neglect vignette were lazy or angry. Figure 2.4 presents guidelines for professionals relative to the reporting of child abuse perpetrators who may be in treatment but reoffend.

Intake

Intake is the first phase on the path of intervention in child maltreatment. Upon receipt of a call alleging child maltreatment, the case is screened to determine if the report falls within the legislatively mandated mission of the agency (Wells, Stein, Fluke, & Downing, 1989). For example, if the alleged perpetrator is not in a caregiving role but sexually abuses a child, such as exposing himself to a child playing in the park, the case is referred to the police. If the report, for example, involves a teacher or doctor having observed marks on the child's body indicative of having been slapped or whipped, child protective services proceeds with the case. In the latter case, criminal prosecution may also be pursued in serious cases.

Assessment

If as a result of the intake process a report of child abuse is determined appropriate for child protective services intervention, an initial assessment or investigation occurs. The purpose of the assessment is to gather information and to determine on the basis of this information if child maltreatment has occurred, the likelihood that it might happen again, who maltreated the child, and what action should occur as a result. The assessment should include a holistic view of family functioning including both strengths and weaknesses. If sexual abuse or serious injury occurred, the police are involved in the investigation. Law enforcement's primary role is to conduct a criminal investigation.

Many communities have established child advocacy centers that allow for multiagency and interdisciplinary professional involvement both in the assessment phase and subsequently in treatment. These centers provide a regional location where representatives from child protective services, law enforcement, and the state attorney's office can come together to interview the parties involved. Trauma to the child is reduced by conducting a single interview in a joint session or a videotaped interview rather than conducting separate interviews to meet each agency's and professional's need, even though various professionals may require different emphases in their interviews (Hibbard & Hartman, 1993).

When assessing sexual abuse allegations, a medical examination serves as an important resource. The physical exam will determine if there is physical injury or the presence of venereal disease. If penetration is alleged to have occurred, a doctor may be able to detect some physical signs of trauma. With the assistance of a process called colposcopy, the physician may be able to photograph and preserve medical evidence (Berkowitz, 1987; McCann, Voris, Simon, & Wells, 1990; Woodling & Heger, 1986).

The maintenance of confidentiality is important throughout the process of working with cases of alleged child abuse. Most states have specific guidelines regarding the release of any information gained as a result of an investigation. Thus, social workers often are not at liberty to discuss with the media and others information about alleged cases of child maltreatment.

Involving the Criminal or Civil Court Systems

The courts serve an important role in the investigation or determination of whether or not maltreatment has occurred and in the implementation of interventions with an abusive family.

Criminal court involvement. The criminal court becomes involved in child maltreatment cases when a criminal charge is filed alleging that a crime in the penal code has been committed. The criminal court's purpose is to determine the alleged perpetrator's guilt or innocence. Civil or juvenile court action in an alleged child abuse case is not to determine guilt or innocence but to make a determination as to whether a child has been abused, known as a "finding of dependency." When the court makes such a finding, the child is brought under the court's jurisdiction and orders can be issued to protect the child. Law enforcement agencies and the District Attorney's office have primary involvement in criminal court actions.

Juvenile court involvement. The juvenile court system is generally engaged after the report has been investigated and the need for ongoing protective services has been identified. A protective service worker may at this point petition the juvenile court if the family is resistant to participating in the treatment plan. The child protective service worker will be extensively involved in juvenile court proceedings. The court then may order the family into compliance with the plan. Without this order, the provision of services to the family is voluntary. The point at which the juvenile court is involved will vary depending on the severity of the abuse and the goals of the case. If a child is at imminent risk of harm and there is a need to remove the child from the home to prevent further harm, an early and immediate decision to involve the court may be made in the assessment phase.

Preliminary hearing. The preliminary hearing is the first step in the juvenile hearing process, resulting from an emergency custody order referred to above or a juvenile court petition. At this hearing, all parties are advised of their rights, and if the allegations in the petition are sufficient, the case is set over for an adjudicatory hearing. The child in a maltreatment case being heard in the juvenile court is represented by a guardian ad litem or the child's attorney. Others involved in the case also may be represented by attorneys. The need for the guardian ad litem is based on the adversarial roles of the other attorneys involved in a case. For example, a petition is generally filed at the request of the child protective service worker who has alleged child maltreatment by the caretaker. Generally, the petitioner's interests are presented by a state or county attorney, operating in a quasi-prosecutorial role, who provides proof of the allegation rather than serving as an independent representative of the child. The family also may be represented by independent counsel operating in a defense attorney capacity. Therefore, the guardian ad litem's role is to act independently of the other attorneys and to represent what is perceived as the best interests of the child. In this role, the guardian ad litem may review agency records, interview the child, call and cross-examine witnesses, and make recommendations to the court. Research shows that guardians ad litem most frequently report information concerning the child's physical safety, the interaction between the parent(s) and the child, and personality characterististics of the parent(s) (Goldman et al., 1993).

Children may also be assisted in juvenile court by CASA volunteers (court-appointed special advocates), who are trained laypersons. Although the role of these volunteers differs in various communities, in general their duties include serving as or working closely with the guardian ad litem by gathering information through interviewing the child and the child's family in the home and assisting the family with transportation and other needs as the case moves through the court system. The CASA volunteer also may monitor the home following an assessment and prior to periodic reviews (Courter, 1996; Duquette & Ramsey, 1986). The CASA volunteer program is being used in many communities throughout the United States. In 1977, there was one program with 110 volunteers who served 498 children. Today, there are over 650 CASA volunteer programs, with 38,000 volunteers serving approximately 130,000 children. Approximately 25% of the children under court jurisdiction are served by a CASA volunteer. In half of the 650 programs, the CASA volunteer also serves as the guardian ad litem (Litzelfelner & Petr, 1997).

Adjudicatory hearing. The adjudication follows the preliminary hearing. The purpose of the adjudicatory hearing is for the state to provide evidence to prove the facts of the petition. The petitioner or state bears the burden of proof in providing evidence that the child was maltreated. Two different outcomes may result from an adjudicatory hearing. If there is inadequate evidence to support the petition, the case is dismissed. This dismissal also results in closure of the ongoing child protective service case because there are no legal grounds to continue the case. If the evidence supports the petition, the court issues a true finding on the petition. When a true finding is issued, the court will move to the dispositional phase of the process. This phase can be held as part of the adjudicatory hearing or in some states in a required separate hearing. This dispositional hearing represents the court's efforts to resolve a case after issuing a finding by attempting to provide interventions or treatment that will ensure the child's safety from further maltreatment while strengthening the family unit. Dispositional options to the family may include ordering the family to comply with specific treatment recommendations, removing the perpetrator from the home, or ordering the child's removal. The decision for removal is the most serious dispositional option.

Periodic review. The next step in the process is the review. These reviews are scheduled periodically, such as every 6 months, to assess the family's progress. Modification in court orders may be made depending on the family's progress. For example, if the court had ordered that a physically abusive parent have no contact with the child, that order may be amended to allow supervised visits as the parent progresses in treatment. If a family fulfills the goals identified in the treatment plan and the child appears to be in no further danger for maltreatment, the case is closed.

Removing a Child From the Home

The decision to remove a child from the home is a very serious one and is always reviewed by the court system, although some states allow for the child to be removed before court review. If the latter occurs, then the court must be petitioned within a specific number of hours. In the majority of states, however, the child protective service worker must first seek approval from the court before a child can be removed from the home. Most states require a hearing within a few days of the order's issuance to remove a child. This hearing, called the emergency or protective custody hearing, gives due process to the parties involved by hearing testimony to determine if there is probable cause to continue the child's emergency placement. This hearing may also serve as a preliminary hearing. The decision to remove a child may be made at this stage or following adjudication.

The Adoption Assistance and Child Welfare Act, passed by Congress in 1980, stipulates that if states want federal supplementary funds for child welfare services and foster care maintenance they must have a federally approved comprehensive plan for the substitute care of children removed from the family home. The law also stipulates that states have to show that in each case of a child being removed from the home "reasonable efforts" have been made to prevent or eliminate the need for the child's removal and that every effort is being made for the child possibly to be returned home. This aspect of the law is enforced through federal audits of state social service agencies. The law also regulates "permanency planning" for children or the need for agencies to find a permanent and stable home for a child rather than to allow the child to remain indefinitely in foster care. Cases are periodically reviewed to prevent the latter from occurring.

Several options are available to an agency in terms of permanency planning. Returning the child home remains the plan as long as it appears that the family is amiable to and capable of successful completion of the treatment plan. If the child is in late adolescence and reunification is not possible, the plan may be to keep the child in permanent substitute care and to assist in the development of independent living skills. Placement with a relative may also be an option and is generally a first priority within the first hours and days of protective custody. If such placement is not available and the family is unable to provide a safe home, adoptive placement is considered. Before adoption can occur, all persons with parental rights to the child must have those rights terminated. This action, referred to as a termination of parental rights, involves the initiation of a new court action.

EFFECTS OF ABUSE ON THE VICTIMS

Numerous studies have been done on the effects of physical, emotional, or sexual abuse on the victims shortly after the abuse has occurred as well as later in the survivors' adult lives. The results of these studies are reviewed.

Effects of Physical and Emotional Abuse

The psychological functioning of a sample of children with case histories of at least 2 years of physical and emotional parental abuse (average age 10.3 years) was compared with a group of nonmaltreated children (average age 9.4 years). The children were matched on socioeconomic characteristics and were from the same geographical communities. The abused children showed greater feelings of sadness and lower self-esteem and self-worth. Their lack of control over what had happened in their lives generated in the survivors a sense of helplessness toward life in general or more specifically about themselves, others, and the world (Cerezo & Frias, 1994).

School-age and adolescent children who were physically abused were compared to a sample of children not abused. The abused children exhibited pervasive and severe academic and socioemotional problems, even when socioeconomic status was controlled in the two groups. The school functioning of the adolescent children was so poor that they were at high risk of dropping out of school. The abused children also showed more behavioral problems in the classroom than their nonabused counterparts. Demonstrations of anger, distractibility, anxiety, and lack of self-control made it virtually impossible for the abused children to achieve in school despite the excellence of their educational program (Kurtz, Gaudin, Wodarski, & Howing, 1993).

Similarly, research shows that child abuse represents a significant risk factor for poor long-term intellectual and academic outcomes. Childhood victims of abuse showed lower levels of intellectual ability and academic achievement attained in young adulthood compared to matched controls (Perez & Widom, 1994; Wodarski, Kurtz, Gaudin, & Howing, 1990). These effects of childhood victimization on intellectual and academic functioning even extend into adulthood due to the cumulative nature of intellectual/academic dysfunctioning; namely, children get further and further behind in the educational process as their age propels them into higher grades but their intellectual functioning is not at a comparable level. Thus, in discouragement and sometimes simply out of embarrassment, children will avoid attending school or drop out of school when legally able to do so. Although these effects are often thought to be associated with the lower socioeconomic status of the families in which abuse was occurring, when socioeconomic status of families was controlled in the research, the differences in intellectual and academic functioning remained between the abused and nonabused samples. The reasons for these effects are not clear; however, it is suggested that early childhood abuse (and neglect) may lead to consequences that have a negative effect on subsequent cognitive and intellectual development. Certain forms of physical abuse, such as battering, may lead to developmental retardation, which can affect cognitive development (Perez & Widom, 1994).

A positive association has been found between physical abuse in the form of frequent corporal punishment and psychological distress and depression in a sample of nearly 2,000 children, ages 10-16 (Turner & Finkelhor, 1996). Although psychological distress was found to be greatest at higher frequencies of corporal punishment (more than 10 times a year), the association was also found for low (1-2 times per year) and moderate (3-10 times per year) groups. Other studies have found similar relationships between children being punished corporally and later experiencing psychological distress (Holmes & Robins, 1988; Straus, 1994; Straus & Kaufman-Kantor, 1994).

In a study of 3,346 American parents with a child under age 18 living at home, researchers found that 63% reported one or more instances of verbal aggression, such as swearing and insulting the child. Children who experienced frequent verbal aggression from their parents that could be classified as emotional abuse, showed higher rates of physical aggression, delinquency, and interpersonal problems than other children when measured on the Conflict Tactic Scales, an instrument used frequently in studies of family violence. The findings held true for preschool, elementary school, and high school children and for males and females (Vissing, Straus, Gelles, & Harrop, 1991).

Effects of Sexual Abuse

Rejection/Psychological Distress

Disclosing to others that one has been sexually abused can result in hostile and rejecting responses from significant individuals in the victim's life. The process of disclosure can undermine the supportive relationship the victim may have with these individuals and place the disclosing victim in a socially isolated situation. A worsening of psychiatric symptomatology can occur at the time of disclosure for adult psychiatric patients (McNulty & Wardle, 1995).

The discovery or disclosure of extrafamilial sexual abuse can traumatize the entire family system. Mothers of sexually abused children, in comparison to those of nonabused children, experienced greater overall emotional distress, poorer family functioning, and lower satisfaction in their parenting role. Fathers of sexually abused children had similar reactions but not to the extent of the mothers' (Manion et al., 1996).

Depression and Suicide

Children who have been sexually abused have been shown to be more lonely, have higher rates of depression, make more suicide attempts and have more suicidal ideation than nonabused children (Feinauer, Callahan, & Hilton, 1996; Gibson & Hartshorne, 1996; Goodwin, 1981; Peters & Range, 1995; Smucker, Craighead, Craighead, & Green, 1986). In a study of sexually abused children seen for a psychological evaluation at a university clinic, researchers found that 37% of the sample had thought about suicide but indicated they would not do it, and 5% reported they wanted to kill themselves (Wozencraft, Wagner, & Pellegrin, 1991). Similarly, in a study of 266 college students, both women and men in the sample who had been sexually abused were more suicidal even as adults as compared to their counterparts who had not experienced sexual abuse. Women reported similar degrees of suicidality as men, but they demonstrated greater survival and coping strategies and more fear of suicide than men. Those whose sexual abuse involved touching were more suicidal and felt less able to cope. Adults whose sexual abuse was exploitive but involved no touching (i.e., unwanted sexual invitations or suggestions, unwanted exposure to others' genitals via exhibitionism) were not significantly different from nonabused adults. The researchers felt the experience of being touched in a sexual way appeared to be more damaging than other kinds of unwanted sexual experiences in terms of suicidality and coping (Peters & Range, 1995). High rates of attempted suicide also have been found in samples of adults who were sexually abused by a sibling when they were growing up (Wiehe, 1997b).

Children who have been sexually abused often initially respond to their molestation by being depressed. The depression experienced by these children may be the beginning of mental health problems as these children grow into adulthood (Koverola, Pound, Heger, & Lytle, 1993).

Psychological Problems

A study of 93 prepubertal children evaluated for sexual abuse and a comparison group of 80 nonabused children matched on age, gender, and race were given the Child Behavior Checklist (CBCL). The sexually abused children had significantly more behavioral problems than the comparison group. These included depression, aggression, sleep and somatic complaints, hyperactivity, and sexual problems (Dubowitz, Black, Harrington, & Verschoore, 1993).

In a study of 750 males, ages 18-27, 117 had experienced one or more unwanted sexual contacts as a child. Approximately 50% recalled experiencing multiple events of sexual abuse. The survivors were shown to have higher rates of current or recent depression, anxiety, suicidal feelings, and behavioral problems. Those sexually abused also demonstrated sexual interest in or actual behavior involving minors when compared to their counterparts who had not experienced multiple incidents of sexual abuse as a youngster (Bagley et al., 1994).

High rates of posttraumatic stress disorder (PTSD) have been found in samples of sexually abused children and adult survivors of sexual abuse (Deblinger, McLeer, Atkins, Ralphe, & Foa, 1989; Greenwald & Leitenberg, 1990; Rodriguez, Kemp, Ryan, & Foy, 1997; Rodriguez, Ryan, Rowan, & Foy, 1996; Rowan, Foy, Rodriguez, & Ryan, 1994). The symptoms experienced by these survivors are similar to those experienced by Vietnam veterans and may include sleep disturbances, anxiety, and depression, which negatively impact on their daily psychosocial functioning and for which many seek professional help (McNew & Abell, 1995).

Dissociation is a problem often resulting from childhood sexual abuse (Gelinas, 1983; Goodwin, 1985; Herman, Russell, & Trocki, 1986; Young, 1992). Victims will dissociate themselves from the trauma occurring to them in sexual abuse and deny the feelings that accompany the trauma as well as the trauma itself. Multiple personality disorder, a dissociative disorder, is also seen in some sexual abuse survivors.

Ethnic differences were found to account for circumstances of sexual abuse in males, ages 13-18, and the impact of the abuse on their psychological functioning. Latino males were more likely to have been sexually abused by an extended family member, to have experienced more genital fondling, and be exposed to more sexually abusive behaviors. African American young males by contrast were more likely to be abused by an immediate family member and had higher anger scores than Latino males. No differences were noted between the two groups on depression scores (Moisan, Sanders-Phillips, & Moisan, 1997).

Substance Abuse

The effects of sexual abuse in terms of multiple substance abuse can already be seen in young children. A survey was administered to 122,824 public school children in Grades 6, 9, and 12. Substance-user groups were created based on the frequency of use and the number of different substances used. Physical and sexual abuse were associated with an increased likelihood of the use of alcohol, marijuana, and almost all other drugs for both males and females in the grades surveyed. Those students reporting both physical and sexual abuse used multiple substances at the highest rates. The victims of abuse also reported initiating the use of substances at a much earlier age than their nonabused peers (Harrison, Fulkerson, & Beebe, 1997).

Adult women sexually abused as a child often are found as adults to be drug and alcohol abusers (Boyd, Blow, & Orgain, 1993; Boyd, Guthrie, Pohl, Whitmarsh, & Henderson, 1994). In their sample of 35 alcoholic women and a comparison group of nonalcoholics, Covington and Kohen (1984) found that 34% of the alcoholics as compared to 16% of the nonalcoholics had experienced sexual abuse from a relative as a child.

A relationship between childhood abuse and adult alcoholism was found to be a problem for women but not for men. In a group of 117 women attending Alcoholics Anonymous who responded to a self-administered questionnaire, nearly 25% had a childhood incest experience (Widom, Ireland, & Glynn, 1995). Other research shows, however, that childhood sexual abuse can impact on males. In a study of men admitted for treatment of alcoholism to the Alcohol Rehabilitation Department at Camp Pendleton Naval Hospital, 30% admitted having been sexually victimized during childhood (Johanek, 1988).

In a study of 60 recovering chemically dependent women living in a long-term treatment facility, 68% had been recipients of unwanted sexual contacts from perpetrators such as uncles, brothers, fathers, family friends, neighborhood boys, and strangers (Teets, 1995).

The relationship between childhood sexual abuse and later substance abuse problems may occur because drugs and alcohol are used to relieve the painful memories associated with the abuse that reoccur periodically for the survivor (see Figure 2.5). Based on the relationship between being sexually abused and later drug/alcohol abuse, treatment for substance abuse should be a significant component of treatment for adult sexual abuse survivors (Simmons, Sack, & Miller, 1996).

Eating Disorders

Research shows a relationship between being sexually abused as a child and eating disorders in adolescence and later in life (Hernandez, 1995; Kern & Hastings, 1995; Wonderlich et al., 1996). Being sexually abused can lead to self-denigratory beliefs that in turn lead to emotional instability. Sexual abuse survivors frequently exhibited behavior characteristic of anorexia and bulimia to reduce these feelings (Lacey, 1990; Miller, McCluskey-Fawcett, & Irving, 1993; Waller, 1994). In one study, 72 young adult women identified as having a high probability of suffering from bulimia nervosa were compared with 72 matched controls who did not display bulimic symptoms. Both groups were given measures to determine if sexual abuse had occurred in their past. The women diagnosed as bulimic were found to have significantly greater rates of self-reported sexual abuse after the age of 12 with an adult relative as the perpetrator. Nonsignificant but high rates of sexual

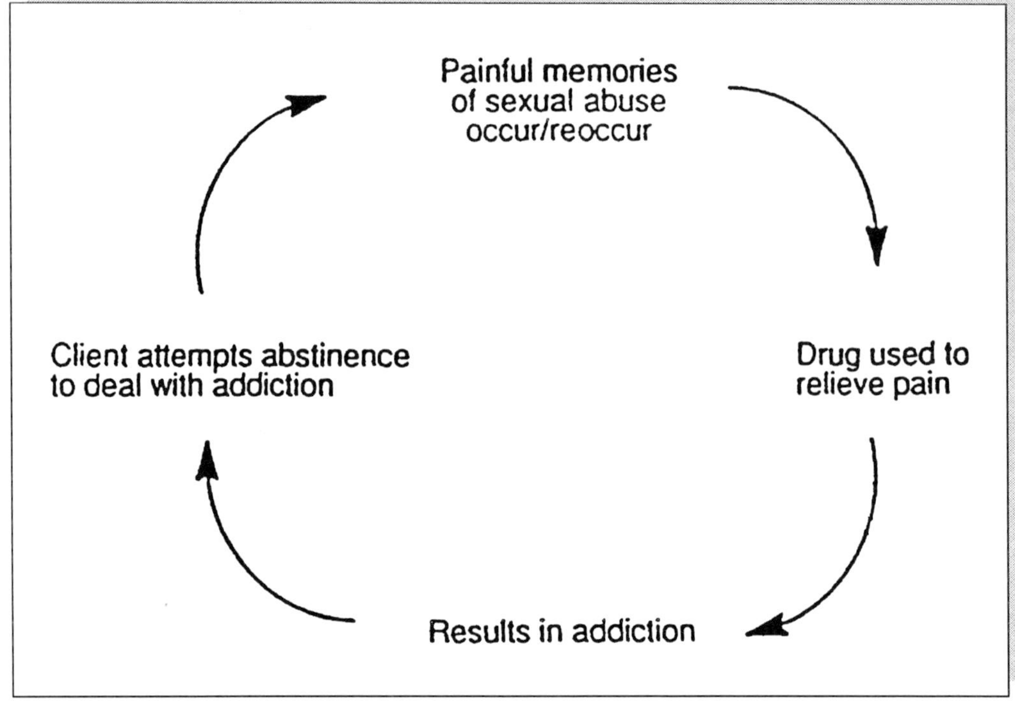

Figure 2.5 Sexual-Substance Abuse Cycle
SOURCE: Reprinted from "Sexual Abuse and Chemical Dependency: Implications for Women in Recovery," by K. Simmons, T. Sack, and G. Miller, 1996, in *Women & Therapy,* Vol. 19, pp. 17-30. Copyright © 1996, The Haworth Press. Reprinted by permission of the publisher.

abuse prior to age 12 were also found for this group (Miller et al., 1993).

Problems in Intimate Relationships

Women sexually abused as children have been found to have problems forming intimate relationships with others. Using a random sample of 737 women currently involved in a significant-partner relationship, those who experienced various forms of abuse earlier in life were contrasted with those not abused. Victims of childhood sexual abuse showed greater difficulty in establishing interpersonal relationships compared to their counterparts who had experienced no abuse (Feinauer et al., 1996). Other studies have found similar results (Briere & Runtz, 1989a; Browne & Finkelhor, 1986; Busby, Glenn, Steggell, & Adamson, 1993). The adult sexual abuse survivors' problems in forming intimate relationships may stem from the depression, avoidance behaviors, and borderline personality disorders (Feinauer et al., 1996).

Difficulty in intimate relationships may also be seen in terms of problems in sexual functioning. In a study of 359 married adult women who sought sex therapy with their spouses, researchers found that childhood sexual abuse significantly discriminated between women with and without a diagnosed sexual dysfunction. Sexual abuse involving penetration was specifically associated with adult sexual dysfunction (Sarwer & Durlak, 1996). These findings support earlier studies with similar results (Bagley & Ramsay, 1986; Briere & Runtz, 1987; Kinzl, Traweger, & Biebl, 1995).

Health Problems

Having been abused as a child can have long-term health consequences for a woman. In a study of 668 highly educated middle-class women being seen in a gynecological practice, comparisons were made between those who reported a history of physical, emotional, or sexual abuse on a self-administered, anonymous questionnaire and those not reporting having been abused. The abused women (19.8% of the sample) reported significantly more hospitalizations for illnesses, a greater number of physical and psychological problems, and lower ratings of their overall health. The researchers found that the greater the number of childhood abuses, the poorer the woman's adult health and the more likely that she would experience abuse as an adult. Divorce also occurred more frequently in the abused group (Moeller, Bachmann, & Moeller, 1993).

Research also shows that childhood and adult sexual victimization is often found in the history of women seeking medical assistance for chronic pain (Alston & Lenhoff, 1995; Walker et al., 1995).

Parenting Problems

Being a victim of sexual abuse, especially father-daughter incest, can affect the survivor's parenting ability. In a study of women with a history of father-daughter incest as children and comparison groups of women whose fathers were alcoholic but were not sexually abusive and women who had not experienced sexual abuse as children, researchers found the women with a history of father-daughter sexual abuse exhibited difficulties in adequately parenting their children. These mothers felt less confident and less emotionally controlled as parents as compared to their counterparts. There were similarities with the mothers who had alcoholic fathers. It should be noted that alcohol was a significant problem in many of the families where father-daughter incest had occurred, as has been found in other studies (Herman, 1981; Russell, 1986). Mothers who were childhood incest victims reported feeling a lack of confidence in their parenting responsibilities and seemed overwhelmed by the demands of parenting, especially relative to promoting autonomy in their children. Notable also were problems associated with parental consistency, organization, the appropriate assignment of responsibilities to their children, and the ability to parent in a firm, sure but sensitive manner (Cole, Woolger, Power, & Smith, 1992; Maccoby & Martin, 1983).

TREATING CHILD ABUSE

This section addresses two issues related to treating chld abuse: interventions based on a differential diagnosis and how the treatment of child abuse differs from treatment in general.

Differential Diagnosis

Earlier, numerous factors in the form of individual, family, and sociocultural factors were identified from research as being related to the various forms of child maltreatment. A proper assessment of child maltreatment, whether physical, emotional, or sexual, requires that a mental health professional view the maltreatment from these multiple perspectives. Professionals working with abusive parents may be tempted to (a) assume that the abuse stems from the fact that the parents were probably abused as children or (b) place a psychiatric diagnostic label on the case; however, such action fails to take into account the multiple factors that may be associated with the abuse affecting the individual parents, the family as a social system, and the larger social context in which they live. Appraising a case of child maltreatment from a multifactor perspective is termed *differential diagnosis.*

Based on the identification of the various factors relating to the maltreatment and possibly even the interaction of these factors with each other, an approach to treatment or a treatment plan must be created for that individual case of child abuse. The resources the professional uses will be based on the availability of such resources in the community, the mental health professional's own expertise in implementing various types of treatment, and the mandate or mission of the agency in which the professional works, which allows for ongoing treatment or referral to other treatment resources.

Differences Between Generic and Child Abuse Treatment

The treatment of child abuse differs in several ways from other types of counseling or psychotherapy, referred to as generic treatment (Gil, 1996). First, working with individuals and families where child abuse is occurring requires that the therapist engage in an immediate and prompt appraisal of the abuse and make an assertive intervention, especially if the child is at risk for further abuse. In generic treatment, the therapist can gradually diagnose clients' problems and intervene over time as a psychosocial appraisal occurs of the presenting problem(s). Second, in child abuse the therapy must be focused on the abuse that has occurred and the resolution of factors associated with this maladaptive behavior. Generic therapy allows for numerous side issues to be introduced in therapy and related interventions to occur as an understanding of the problem unfolds. Third, the treatment of child abuse is often mandatory in nature, thus introducing into the treatment relationship variables, such as hostility, feelings of helplessness, and client resistance, that might not appear in generic therapy. Fourth, therapy in child abuse generally occurs within an interdisciplinary context requiring the therapist to consult with medical, criminal justice, and school personnel involved in the case and to use community resources of which the therapist must be knowledgeable. The involvement of professionals from other agencies and disciplines requires that the therapist be sensitive to confidentiality issues. Fifth, countertransference issues become heightened for a therapist in child abuse cases who must frequently make recommendations around issues such as a family's readiness to have their children returned to them and the likelihood that they may abuse again. These decisions must be based on the therapist's best professional skills in assessment, diagnosis, and treatment; however, doubt regarding such decisions may always linger for the therapist. Therapists may "alternately feel controlling and helpless, optimistic and hopeless, competent and incompetent, confident and frightened, angry and calm, elated and sad" (Gil, 1996, p. 14).

Treating Physical and Emotional Child Abuse

Community resources, such as day care centers, family counseling agencies, and child guidance clinics, useful resources in treating a range of problems in living, are also used in treating physical and emotional child abuse. Although the literature on the treatment of physical and emotional child abuse focuses primarily on the treatment of the parents, a greater emphasis is now being placed on treating the child victims immediately following the occurrence of the abuse (Graziano & Mills, 1992). Several resources specifically directed at treating physically and psychologically abusive families are discussed.

Parents Anonymous (PA)

This program, operated primarily by parents who once were abusive to their children, is available in many communities throughout the United States (Bornman & Lieber, 1984; Fritz, 1989; Lieber, 1983). PA groups are based on a self-help model and meet once a week for 2 hours in a free meeting place, such as a church basement, YM/YWCA, or community center. The group leader is a parent, generally an individual who in the past experienced problems in parenting and was helped through PA or similar resources. Each PA group also has a sponsor, a volunteer professional who acts as a resource and consultant to the group. Both serve as positive authority figures for group members. They represent individuals who care and are concerned about the best interests of the group participants as the latter struggle on a daily basis with the stresses of parenting.

Group participants at PA meetings give identifying demographic information about themselves and their families; however, they may remain anonymous by using only first names. Group members generally trade telephone numbers in case they need to contact someone between meetings if they experience a crisis in their parenting. Participation with other parents in the weekly meetings and the sharing of phone numbers result in the group becoming like an extended family or support system, thereby breaking down the social isolation that often characterizes abusive families.

An open and accepting climate pervades PA meetings, with some members quietly listening while others discuss parenting problems encountered during the past week. The agenda of meetings is generally open, with participants determining topics for discussion based on their individual parenting needs.

Although there is an absence of research using rigorous research designs to evaluate the effectiveness of PA groups, client satisfaction scales completed by participants reveal that group members find participation in the program helpful in learning effective nonabusive parenting skills (National PA office, personal communication, June 12, 1997). Information on Parents Anonymous can be obtained by contacting the national office at 675 W. Foothill Blvd., Suite 220, Claremont, CA 91711; telephone (909) 621-6184.

Parent Education Courses

These courses are offered in many communities under a variety of auspices, such as through adult education programs, child abuse councils, and community mental health agencies. Three examples of parent education courses are Systematic Training for Effective Parenting (STEP), Parent Effectiveness Training (P.E.T.), and the Nurturing Program.

Systematic Training for Effective Parenting (STEP). This program consists of nine sessions, each of which lasts between 90 minutes and 2 hours. Each session includes discussion of a chapter from *The Parent's Handbook,* a video or audio presentation, and practice of the parenting skill learned. The sessions focus on helping parents understand children and effectively communicate with them. An emphasis is also placed on alternative methods of discipline other than corporal punishment. The use of natural and logical consequences is taught as a method of discipline that develops personal responsibility in children. Parents are encouraged to apply at home with their children what they learn in the sessions. Also available is a program designed specifically for parents of teenagers, known as STEP/teen, that assists parents in communicating with teenagers through listening, expressing feelings, and developing responsibility and using methods of discipline appropriate to this age group. Information on STEP programs is available from American Guidance Service, Publishers' Building, P.O. Box 99, Circle Pines, MN 55014-1796; telephone 1-800-247-5053.

Parent Effectiveness Training (P.E.T.). This program has been extensively field tested and evaluated since its founding by Dr. Thomas Gordon in 1962. P.E.T. is led by an instructor trained in the program at a 5-day workshop. The program focuses on teaching parenting skills and especially emphasizes effective disciplinary methods other than corporal punishment. P.E.T. is both a preventive program for parents of very young children who have not yet developed problems and a means of helping parents with older children change undesirable behaviors and overcome problems they are having at home or at school. The program recognizes different parental/caregiver situations including stepparents, single parents, foster parents, and parents with different ethnic backgrounds and varying amounts of formal education. P.E.T. requires 24 hours of training, implemented in 3-hour sessions over a period of 8 weeks. A trained instructor may provide individual instruction to a person or couple or meet with participants in a group setting of 5 to 10 persons, which enables the instructor to personalize the course to the specific needs of the participants. Information on P.E.T. is available from Gordon Training International, 531 Stevens Avenue, Solana Beach, CA 92075-2093; telephone 1-800-628-1197.

The Nurturing Program. This is a parent education course for parents and their children, ages 2-12. The program, designed to modify inappropriate parenting patterns, involves parents and their children on two levels of learning: the cognitive level, by learning new knowledge and skills and the affective level, by experiencing positive healthy human interactions. The focus is on four parenting behaviors shown by research to be associated with child physical and psychological abuse: inappropriate developmental expectations of children, reversing parent-child roles, lack of empathic awareness of children's needs, and strong parental belief in the use of corporal punishment. Parents and their children meet in separate sessions at the same time for 2.5 hours each week for 15 consecutive weeks. Weekly sessions for parents and children are based on specific learning goals and objectives. Children meet in small age-oriented groups (2-4 years, 5-8 years, 9-12 years), learning nurturing and interaction skills. Parents and children participate together at the end of their sessions in a snack activity to share learning experiences. The program uses training manuals, filmstrips, and audiocassettes for teaching parents new skills in behavior management. Information on the Nurturing Program is available from Family Development Resources, Inc., 3160 Pinebrook Road, Park City, UT 84098; telephone (801) 649-5822.

Parent education courses have been shown to be an effective way for parents to learn new parenting skills (Barth, Blythe, Schinke, & Schilling, 1983; Campbell & Sutton, 1983; Dembo, Sweitzer, & Lauritzen, 1985; Schulman, Lorion, Kupst, & Schwarcz, 1991). Although positive results have been shown to occur from the use of parent education programs with abusive parents, studies evaluating the effectiveness of this intervention present research methodological problems, among them no random assignment to treatment and comparison or control groups, failure to match groups, no control of experimenter bias, and an insufficient number of participants in the research design (Todres & Bunston, 1993). A serious problem when evaluating the effectiveness of these groups with parents adjudicated for child abuse and mandated to attend such groups is the desire of the parents to present themselves in a favorable light, especially if their children have been removed from the home. In-home behavioral observations, similar to the methodology used by Patterson (1982), is one way to avoid this bias. Also, parent education evaluative studies generally fail to conduct long-term follow-up evaluations to determine if the immediate effect of the parent education course endures over time when parents return to the routines of daily parenting and the stresses accompanying this role. In-home coaching by professionals associated with the parent education course may facilitate both the transfer of skills learned in group sessions to the home setting and the endurance of these skills over time (Goldstein, Keller, & Erne, 1985).

Family-Based Services

The Homebuilders Program is an example of an intensive family preservation program within the larger treatment model known as family-based services. As the name implies, services are provided to the family as a social system, often in the context of the family's home and at an intensive level. The goal of the Homebuilders Program is to work intensively for a brief period of time (4-6 weeks) with a family to avoid placement of the children outside the home. The unit of intervention is a family that has maltreated a child and is at high risk for doing so again, and the treatment setting is the home. Therapists carry a very small caseload of two families at a time and work from 10 to 20 hours a week with each family, providing multidimensional services including crisis intervention, family therapy, advocacy, life skills training, and concrete assistance in meeting housing, food, clothing, and other needs (Bath & Haapala, 1993).

A less intensive and more continuous supportive program is provided by individuals with a knowledge of parenting who regularly meet with the abusive parent(s) at home. Services offered in the privacy of the family's home can be an effective approach to working with abusive parents who generally are not likely to seek treatment for themselves because of low motivation, transportation and child care problems, or the stigma of having been abusive. Home visits may be weekly or less frequent, depending on the needs of the parents. During the visit, the person with parenting knowledge can observe firsthand the home situation and stresses under which the parents are operating and thus work in a very concrete way with the parents on problems in parenting that may be occurring. The visits also allow for the introduction of other social and medical services the family may need (Wasik & Roberts, 1994).

Information on family-based services can be obtained from the National Association for Family-Based Services, 1513 Stoney Point Road, NW, Cedar Rapids, IA 52405; telephone (319) 396-4829.

Stress Management

Research shows that stress management training can be helpful for parents at risk of abusing a child because of high amounts of stress. In laboratory experiments in which an infant crying was simulated for long periods of time, researchers found mothers' anxiety was reduced after stress management training. The use of biofeedback was found especially helpful for mothers in controlling stress (Tyson & Sobschak, 1994).

Treating Sexual Abuse Victims

Treatment Issues

There are several reactions that a sexually abused child may have. First, the victim may experience a loss of trust toward other persons. This loss may be especially evident in intrafamilial abuse where the perpetrator was loved and trusted by the victim. Second, an altered body image may result if the child feels damaged or permanently impaired, often from physical trauma accompanying the sexual abuse. Third, the child may feel guilty and responsible for the abuse even though realistically the victim had few alternatives other than to acquiesce to the perpetrator's demands. These feelings may be especially pronounced in older children who experienced some autonomic sexual pleasure with the abuse. Fourth, the victim may need assistance in self-protection from further sexual abuse. Fifth, anger, depression, and at times self-destructive behavior may result from the sexual abuse.

Individual Therapy

Individual therapy for the child victim without involvement of the child's family generally is not recommended (Friedrich, 1990). Sexually abused children often come from dysfunctional families with many preexistent problems. If treatment focuses on the child victim and ignores the family's multiple problems, there is little likelihood that the child's individual therapy will be effective. Individual treatment, however, may appropriately be used when the family is involved in treatment simultaneously. In these situations, behavior change occurring with significant others in the family can support the changes the child may be making (Friedrich, 1990).

When a child victim is treated individually while the family is simultaneously seeking help, treatment generally focuses on the child's perception of the trauma and its impact. The therapist may encourage the child to retell what happened and thereby attempt to understand the victimization from the child's perspective and how the child perceives the trauma's impact on his or her life. The therapist's task then is to help the child reexamine the trauma from a reality perspective, correcting inappropriate conclusions involving guilt, self-blame, and responsibility for the abuse (Friedrich, 1990).

Play therapy is a technique often used in working with sexually abused children. Dolls, toys, stories, drawings, and other means of play may be used to help children talk about their sexual victimization and its impact on their lives. For example, drawings have been shown to help a child retrieve a past traumatic experience when used as an associative tool for accessing and assessing such experiences (Burgess & Hartman, 1993; Kendall-Tackett, 1992). Play therapy assists a child in discussing frightening and threatening information and perceptions about the traumatic event. The technique is also a means through which the therapist can communicate with the child alternative solutions to conflicts the child may be experiencing resulting from the victimization (Marvasti, 1989).

When using storytelling, a therapist may begin a story about a small child, similar in age to the child in treatment, in which a scary event occurs. The therapist may ask the child to complete the story in order to determine how the child would handle a scary event symbolic of the sexual abuse that has occurred. Hand puppets or small rubber figures of people that can be bent into various positions are often used as characters in storytelling. The figures may be children (representing peers and siblings), older persons (symbolic of parents, grandparents, and other adult family members), a police officer (representing persons in authority such as the police, judges, attorneys, and social workers), and a witch or robber (perpetrator). Anatomically correct dolls also are used to aid children in talking about sexual abuse that may be embarrassing and shameful to them (Cohn, 1991; Everson & Boat, 1994).

Group Therapy

Group therapy is regarded as the treatment of choice for latency age and adolescent sexual abuse victims and in some instances even for younger children (Berliner & Ernst, 1984; Friedrich, 1995; Friedrich, Berliner, Urquiza, & Beilke, 1988; Lanktree & Briere, 1995; McGain & McKinzey, 1995; Nelki & Watters, 1989; Steward, Farquhar, Dicharry, Glick, & Martin, 1986). Group treatment can be less intensive and the group environment less threatening than individual treatment. Also, the group provides participants a supportive feeling, counteracting the social isolation and alienation that children often experience as a result of their sexual victimization. Finally, as a sense of trust develops in the group, victims may be able to talk about the experiences of other group members, which frequently they cannot do for themselves. Eventually, however, they may feel comfortable examining their own victimization and its impact on their psychosocial functioning. However, group therapy may be too intense for some sexual abuse victims, especially early in the treatment process (Friedrich, 1990). In these instances, group treatment may be deferred until after the initial disclosure/crisis is resolved and the victim has had the benefit of individual crisis intervention therapy.

Various issues may be discussed in group therapy depending on the gender and age composition of the group and whether a structured or nonstructured approach is being used. Common issues are participants' victimization, including their feelings of anger, guilt, shame, helplessness, and self-blame; individual and family problems associated with the victimization; peer relationships; and the need for victims to develop a sense of mastery and competence in their lives, especially relative to sexuality issues (Friedrich, 1990; Lindon & Norse, 1994; Nelki & Watters, 1989; Steward et al., 1986).

The literature presents various group treatment models (Fowler, Burns, & Roehl, 1983; Mandell & Damon, 1989; Schiffer, 1984). For example, one agency treating sexual abuse victims uses a nine-session model, with the various sessions focusing on specific subjects relative to sexual victimization such as touching, secrets, guilt, anger, and responsibility (Nelki & Watters, 1989). Children's groups run parallel to a parents' or caregivers' group. The final session is a joint meeting of children, caregivers, and the therapists from both groups.

Corder, Haizlip, and DeBoer (1990) describe a structured, time-limited treatment group for sexually abused children, ages 6-8. Techniques used in the group help children explore their reactions to their victimization and develop coping skills. These techniques include specially designed coloring books, therapeutic board games, drawings, and storytelling.

The Adolescent Sexual Abuse Treatment Program in Northampton, Massachusetts, involves groups of 7 adolescents ranging in age from 13 to 18 who meet together 90 minutes each week for 20 weeks (Homstead & Werthamer, 1989). A 4-week interlude following completion of the 20-week program allows members to leave or to continue in another 20-week cycle with another group. Participants must agree to four rules when joining the group: confidentiality, respect and support of others, freedom regarding verbally participating in sessions or remaining silent, and promptness in attending sessions. The therapist uses creative and flexible approaches to treatment that are based on participants' needs. For example, participants may be encouraged to keep journals to record reactions to their victimization. Sexual abuse education, an important feature of these groups, breaks down myths about sexual abuse, provides correct information, and increases participants' awareness of the various stages of the healing process. Co-therapists lead the groups. The use of two adults as group leaders provides group members the opportunity to observe and model the effective way two adults can interact, disagree, and accomplish tasks. This is a corrective experience for many of the group participants, who come from families where parents interact dysfunctionally with each other.

A group treatment program used in a group home setting that has been evaluated and has shown positive effects on the participants is the SAY Group, a 20-week closed-enrollment group that employs a cognitive-behavioral approach (Sinclair et al., 1995). The program is described as follows:

> The SAY Group treatment process can be roughly divided into three phases: familiarization, working, and termination. The familiarization phase takes place in the first 5 weeks of treatment and lays the foundation for the working phase. Human sexuality, the effects of victimization, and rules for participation are emphasized. The working phase is the second treatment stage, lasting from week 5 to week 15 of SAY Group. During the working phase, youth disclose victimization memories, including their affective, cognitive, and behavioral reactions. During the termination phase in the final 5 weeks of SAY Group, youth review their progress and are encouraged to set goals for continued improvement. In all phases of SAY Group, therapy is facilitated through the use of *The SAY Book* (Collins & Collins, 1989). *The SAY Book* contains exercises for youth to complete between and within sessions that address issues such as depression, betrayal, self-image, anger, and so on.
>
> A primary objective of SAY Group is to help youth reduce the effects of sexual abuse and to change their self-concept from that of a victim to that of a survivor. Therapeutic disclosure and processing of victimization memories are central components of treatment. SAY Group does not employ the more confrontive techniques sometimes associated with a PTSD-oriented treatment (e.g., implosion or flooding). Rather, participants are gradually moved toward disclosing their abuse experiences and their effects by means of developing trust and rapport within the group, utilizing education materials and nonconfrontive group pressure, and applying normalizing and reframing techniques. A key therapeutic goal is to help group members modulate their experience of both internal and external abuse-related stimuli. (Sinclair et al., 1995, pp. 536-537)

An evaluation of the effectiveness of the SAY Group was done by having 43 participants complete pre- and posttest measurements and having evaluative information also completed by their group-home caregivers. The group participants and their caregivers reported significant decreases in PTSD symptoms and internalizing behaviors, such as low self-esteem and self-destructive behavior, anxiety, somatic complaints and fears. The group participants also reported a significant decline in aggressive behavior and overall problem behavior. A control or comparison group, however, was not used in the evaluative research to rule out the possibility that the changes in improvement may have been due to concurrent individual therapy or other factors (Sinclair et al., 1995).

Family Therapy

Treating the entire family as a unit can be highly effective in working with families where sexual abuse has occurred, even though this treatment modality poses problems for the therapist. The entire family often does not welcome the therapist's intervention and presence. Thus, family treatment may require a process of constant reengagement with family members. Initially, family members may not be seen together as a group but individual family members may be involved in treatment, then mother and daughter together, and finally other siblings. The offender father in intrafamilial sexual abuse generally is not introduced into family sessions until after he has taken responsibility for his actions, which may occur in the latter stages of his individual therapy.

An important issue in family treatment of intrafamilial abuse is enhancing the mother's competence to function effectively in the family, especially if the offender father has been removed from the home. The safety of the child victim is an important task facing the mother, especially if the father, though removed from the home, retains visiting rights to the child victim. Dysfunctional parent-child relationships also are significant issues in family therapy with sexually abusive families.

While reunification may be a goal for some families, a precondition for reestablishing the family is the perpetrator taking responsibility for his behavior. Treatment involving the entire family is especially important after reunification occurs in order to prevent the family from reestablishing former dysfunctional patterns of behavior and to help the family examine alternative modes of interaction and problem solving (Friedrich, 1990, 1995).

Victim-Offender Communication

Communication between the victim and the offender is a controversial and emotionally charged issue in the treatment of sexual abuse victims. Controversy surrounding this aspect of treatment focuses on the concern that revictimization can occur when communication takes place before the victim is ready to confront the offender (Cameron, 1994). Revictimization can happen in very subtle ways, such as when the offender uses language that is not sensitive to the victim's guilt and self-blame or when nonverbal language (body postures, facial expressions, affect) do not support the offender's verbalizations (Yokley & McGuire, 1990).

Communication between victims and offenders can be classified according to different levels of intensity (direct and indirect) and the nature of the communication (personal and nonpersonal). Direct communication implies face-to-face contact between the victim and the offender, generally in the presence of a therapist, in individual or group therapy settings. Indirect communication may occur through letters, videotape recordings, or the telephone. Personal communication implies that the victim and the offender communicate with each other. Nonpersonal communication suggests that the victim and the offender may not be known to each other—for example, an offender may appear before a treatment group of victims, even though the offender may not have sexually abused any of the group participants (Yokley, 1990).

Advocates for victim-offender communication indicate that the technique can effectively be used in sexual abuse treatment when a victim's safety, needs, and rights are kept paramount. Communication between a victim and an offender may be beneficial in four ways: A victim may be reassured of the reality of the abuse rather than denial when the offender communicates an admission of the offense; the victim may experience relief from guilt and self-blame when the offender communicates acknowledgment of full responsibility for the offense, including coercion and manipulation of the victim; the victim is provided an opportunity to directly express to the perpetrator anger for the abuse and its impact on the victim's life; and a sense of power, self-control, and mastery of life events can result for the victim when an offender communicates responsibility for the offense (Yokley, 1990; Yokley & McGuire, 1990).

TREATMENT OF ADULT SURVIVORS

Although some adult survivors of childhood sexual abuse engage in denial and suppression of the painful memories associated with their victimization, increasingly survivors are seeking help for the effects of their childhood sexual victimization because (a) this social problem has been more openly discussed and (b) treatment resources have become available (Leitenberg, Greenwald, & Cado, 1992). The problems for which adult survivors seek professional help include depression, somatic complaints, the inability to maintain effective interpersonal relationships, sexual dysfunction, and substance abuse (Kinzl et al., 1995; Lowery, 1987).

National Self-Help Organizations

Several national organizations have established chapters throughout the United States to treat adult survivors of childhood sexual abuse. For example, VOICES in Action, Inc. (Victims of Incest Can Emerge Survivors) is a national organization of incest and child sexual abuse survivors dedicated to prevention and recovery through networking, support, and education. The organization sponsors *The Chorus,* a bimonthly newsletter that features articles on resources and referrals for incest victims and on legal and recovery issues. National and regional conferences offer workshops dealing with a variety of issues for incest survivors and professionals working with survivors. Further information can be obtained from their national office: VOICES, P.O. Box 148309, Chicago, IL 60614; telephone 1-800-786-4238.

Similarly, Survivors of Incest Anonymous, Inc. has chapters throughout the United States and sponsors self-help groups for men and women 18 years of age or older. Treatment is based on the 12-step Alcoholics Anonymous model. Further information can be obtained from Survivors of Incest Anonymous, Inc., P.O. Box 21817, Baltimore, MD 21222-6817; telephone (410) 282-3400.

Parents United, Daughters and Sons United, and Adults Molested as Children United also are national organizations with chapters throughout the United States providing guided self-help for sexually abusive parents and child/adult survivors of sexual abuse. Information may be obtained from Parents United, 615 15th Street, Modesto, CA 95354; telephone (209) 572-3446.

Group Therapy

Group treatment is frequently the treatment of choice for adult survivors of sexual abuse (Alexander, Neimeyer, & Follette, 1991). Groups for adult childhood sexual abuse survivors generally follow a self-help or peer-group treatment model. The group provides a milieu or environment wherein adults can support one another as they awaken to the reality of their childhood sexual abuse; examine the dysfunctional ways they have coped with this trauma; and learn new, more effective coping mechanisms. Treatment issues in these groups generally focus on participants' memories and emotions associated with the trauma, problems in interpersonal relationships such as the inability to trust others based on the violation of trust participants experienced, and anger toward the perpetrator (Bear & Dimock, 1988; Blake-White & Kline, 1985). Another important treatment issue for adult survivors, besides the abuse itself, is the nonsupportive parenting and high family stress the victim experienced as a child. These factors are central issues in the symptoms of depression and low self-esteem that adult survivors of childhood sexual abuse frequently exhibit (Wind & Silvern, 1994).

Group therapy also has effectively been used with gay and lesbian survivors of childhood sexual abuse and their partners. Groups frequently are created for only these survivors, who often do not feel comfortable participating in groups for heterosexual individuals (Reid, Mathews, & Liss, 1995).

Five stages of recovery frequently occur in adult survivor treatment groups: acknowledging the reality of the abuse rather than continuing to deny it; overcoming secondary responses to the abuse, such as fear, anger, guilt, or a sense of being overwhelmed or out of control; forgiving oneself and thereby stopping self-punishment for the abuse; identifying and implementing effective coping behaviors to deal with the trauma; and relinquishing the identity of being a victim of abuse and moving on in life (Sgroi, 1989b, 1989c).

Being an adult sexual abuse survivor also has implications for their marital partners. In a study of 20 male partners of sexual abuse survivors, several factors were noted. First, the partners of survivors were concerned about how they could get their own needs met in their marital relationship vis-à-vis the needs of their partner. The men knew their partner was hurting badly and were open to that emotional pain; however, they had needs of their own that they were fearful of expressing, for doing so might provoke a negative response from their partner. This predicament often left them with feelings of anger, guilt, and shame. Second, the men expressed difficulties with closeness, especially when their partners withdrew or distanced themselves based on a fear of closeness resulting from the abuse. Third, there was an absence of spontaneity in the relationship. The sexual abuse survivor often did not respond in a predictable manner, leaving the male partner confused and "walking on eggs." Finally, the lack of or infrequency of sexual intercourse, as well as the survivor's response to the partner's interest, was a frequent complaint of the men. Supportive therapy groups organized for partners of sexual abuse survivors can serve as a safe place where they work through the problems encountered with their sexually abused partner and receive support from other persons experiencing the same problems (Chauncey, 1994).

MEGAN'S LAW

In mid-October 1994, 7-year-old Megan Konka was raped and murdered by a twice-convicted child molester living in her neighborhood. Residents of Hamilton Township, New Jersey, where the crime occurred, were outraged that this convicted child molester was living with two other sex offenders in their community. As a result of public outcry over this incident, the State of New Jersey in late October 1994 passed the Sexual Offender Registration Act, which became commonly known as Megan's Law. In subsequent months, more than 30 states passed similar legislation. Courts in several states, however, later ruled such laws unconstitutional (Smith, 1995).

In May 1996, President Clinton signed the federal counterpart of Megan's Law, known as the Jacob Wetterline Crimes Against Children and Sexually Violent

Offender Registration Act, although the law still is commonly referred to as "Megan's Law." This legislation enables the federal government to leverage states to comply with the provisions of the law by denying federal funds ordinarily allocated to states. By August 1996, all 50 states had established a statewide sex offender registry, and most have some form of community notification law. Two components typically are found in the laws passed by the states. First, persons convicted of a sex offense, including rape, sexual assault, and child molestation, are required to register their addresses annually with state and local authorities upon being released from prison. High-risk offenders are required to register their address with local authorities every 90 days. Violent sex offenders are also required to continue registering for their entire life, and nonviolent offenders must do so for 10 years. The second component is a notification provision that allows for at least some public disclosure of the registry information. In some states, citizens can call a 900 number to access a state's database to find out if any paroled sex offenders are living in their community. Others states require that a written request be made to a state office for that purpose.

Some states have created an evaluation system known as the risk assessment scale by which convicted sex offenders are divided into three categories: low, medium, and high risk. The scale includes the type and frequency of assaults, the victim's age, and the offender's history of drug use and response to therapy. This assessment is used to dictate terms by which each type of offender must register with community law enforcement officials.

In late August 1996, President Clinton also signed into law a measure creating a $2 million computer database that will track more than 250,000 people either wanted for sex crimes or who have a criminal record for such offenses. This national database, to be created by the Department of Justice, should be fully operational by 1999 and will be available only to law enforcement authorities ("Megan's Laws," 1996).

Differing views are held by attorneys, mental health professionals, and the general public regarding this legislation. The registration of sex offenders provides children protection from being victimized; however, offenders who have been in therapy and wish to return to a normal life believe that such legislation violates their constitutional right to privacy, subjects them to a harsher penalty than was mandated by the law in effect when the crime was committed, ignores gains they may have made in therapy that will help them in not abusing again, and amounts to being punished twice for the same crime. Some officials are concerned that the registration of sex offenders and the availability of this information to the general public will encourage acts of vigilantism, ostracism, loss of jobs or homes, and public shame toward ex-convicts. In some communities, ex-offenders have been harassed, evicted, fired from jobs, and in one incidence, burned out by frightened neighbors (Bernstein, 1995; Davis, 1996).

TREATMENT OF OFFENDERS

Sexual abuse offenders are generally typed as "regressed" or "fixated" (Groth, 1979). Although these types are not always clearly and discretely differentiated, the distinction is useful as a framework for assessing the motivation for the offense and for determining what treatment approach is most likely effectively to deter further offenses. Some researchers suggest that instead of delineating two distinct types of sex offenders all should be viewed along a continuum, with regressed and fixated as the bipolar positions (Simon, Sales, Kaszniak, & Kahn, 1992).

Intrafamilial sexual abuse perpetrators generally are identified as regressed offenders. The regressed offender has maintained a sexual relationship with an age-mate but under personal or family stress may turn to a daughter to meet his intimacy and emotional needs and/or to punish his estranged wife. The child serves as a substitute or surrogate mate for the perpetrator. The prognosis for regressed offenders' treatment generally is positive.

The fixated offender, or pedophile, has a well-established preference for children. The fixated offender sees the child as an equal. Fixated offenders may sexually relate to adult females and even in some instances marry; however, these relationships are generally initiated by the other partner and may be a response to social pressures or to provide access to children (Groth, 1979). Fixated offenders often have multiple victims and may be involved in the publication and distribution of child pornography. Treatment prognosis for these perpetrators is poor. Intensive treatment must occur during incarceration and after release to avoid recidivism. Without treatment, incarceration is little more than a revolving door to continued crimes against children.

Three approaches to offender treatment—pharmacological, behavior modification, and psychotherapy (Groth & Oliveri, 1989; Sgroi, 1989a)—are employed in community and prison-based programs and may be used individually or together.

Pharmacological treatment is used with perpetrators who do not want to engage in sexually abusive behavior but are unable to control it (Groth & Oliveri, 1989). Drugs such as Depo-Provera (medroxyprogesterone acetate) lower testosterone levels and in turn decrease unwanted sexual fantasies and sexually aggressive behaviors. This treatment strategy requires careful medical supervision because negative side effects can occur, such as a lowered sperm count or damaged sperm, breast development, diabetes, and hypertension (Meyer, Walker, Emory, & Smith, 1985). A disadvantage in using pharmacological treatment is that the offender relies on the drug as an external control and fails to learn internal controls for his sexually abusive behavior.

Treatment using behavior modification focuses on the offender's sexual arousal patterns. The offender's reaction to various sexual and nonsexual stimuli is measured with a penile plethysmograph, a device attached to the penis that records changes in penile erection. The relative magnitude of the response reflects the amount of sexual interest the individual has in a particular stimulus (Becker & Quinsey, 1993). Emphasis in treatment is placed on helping the offender gain greater control over dysfunctional behaviors in response to sexual stimuli (Sgroi, 1989a).

The use of psychotherapy in a treatment program is helpful with offenders' understanding how past life experiences influence their sexually abusive behavior. To accomplish this, perpetrators must recognize, admit, and accept responsibility for the abuse; recognize the antecedents to their abusive behavior; and then use this awareness as a way to control it. Although individual psychotherapy may be used, group psychotherapy is generally more effective (Knopp, 1984).

Social learning theory often provides the theoretical basis for the group treatment of sex offenders. The Barnert Hospital Mental Health Clinic, Juvenile Sexual Behavior Program (JSBP), an outpatient program in Paterson, New Jersey, is one example of such a treatment program for juvenile offenders between the ages of 13 and 18 (Sermabeikian & Martinez, 1994). The JSBP views sexual deviance as behavior that was learned, observed, or experienced by the offender. The rationale for the intervention is to treat, disrupt, and prevent the sexually abusive behavior before it becomes chronic or compulsive. This year-long group treatment program has the following specific goals: personal responsibility for one's sexual behavior, improvement in the ability to make better decisions, increased acceptance of societal rules and persons in authority, a shift from exploitative to nonexploitative use of power and control in relationships, development of healthy sexuality in peer relationships, increased awareness of the interpersonal issues of adolescence and adulthood, an increase in control over impulsive behavior, improvement in communication and assertive expression of feelings and needs, a decrease in distorted cognitions regarding relationships and sexuality, and an increased awareness of the thoughts, feelings, and behaviors that lead to abusive behavior (Sermabeikian & Martinez, 1994, pp. 971-972).

The group is co-led by a male and a female therapist who model prosocial and nonabusive behaviors between males and females. The group members also serve as models for each other when they display prosocial behaviors and do not follow previously held belief systems that supported their sexual offense. The group process involves a series of progressive components. The first stage focuses on the disclosure of the sexual offense and confronting offenders' denial or attempts at minimizing the offense and its consequences. The next step involves group members examining cognitive distortions and irrational thinking that supports the sexually offending behavior. From this phase of treatment the adolescent offenders should develop the ability to use judgment and self-observation before acting on impulses and engaging in dysfunctional behavior. Emphasis in this phase of treatment is also put on an empathic understanding of the effect of the offense on the victim. The final phases of treatment are aimed at helping offenders develop knowledge and skills more effectively to cope with a range of life situations they will face as they proceed through adolescence and become adults (Sermabeikian & Martinez, 1994).

Treating sexual offenders can impact on therapists, who besides hearing details in therapy sessions of violent fantasies and horrifying interpersonal sex crimes, often struggle with the effectiveness of their interventions relative to whether or not the offender will again engage in sexual maltreatment (Blanchard, 1995; Edmunds, 1997). Also, whereas society holds a view of vengeance toward sexual abuse offenders, successful treatment requires an empathic and understanding approach on the part of the therapist to the offender.

In a study of 98 therapists treating sexual abusers, therapists reported painful, disturbing, and repulsive visual images of sexual assaults reported by their clients, some decrease in their own sexual interest/activity since working with offenders, concern for their personal safety, and heightened anxiety regarding the safety of their own children or grandchildren (Jackson, Holzman, Barnard, & Paradis, 1997).

TREATMENT ISSUES RELATIVE TO RACE AND CULTURE

Mental health professionals often treat clients of different racial and cultural backgrounds when working with child abuse victims, survivors, or perpetrators. An insensitivity to issues of race and culture can be a barrier to effective understanding of abuse and to the therapist's successful intervention in the problem. Being sensitive to racial and cultural issues, however, does not mean condoning abuse.

The influence of race in the presenting problem often is overlooked by White therapists (Robinson, 1989). Racism may not only affect clients' development of the problem but also place constraints on what they are able to do about the problem. Discussing the impact of race on treatment, Robinson (1989) states,

> Whether the goals of intervention include change in behavioral patterns, intrapsychic restructuring, environmental changes, or change in interpersonal relationships, the presence of racist behaviors may contribute to difficulty in problem resolution. This realization allows the clinician to help the client acknowledge the complexity of the situation and clearly delineate the goals of treatment and the potential impact of planned interventions. Initiating a frontal attack on racist policies or behaviors usually is not appropriate or effective. It is extremely important for the clinician to have some ideas regarding the racial factors influencing a problem and attendant implications for the alternatives that the clinician considers as interventions. The clinician accrues this knowledge base as a result of an awareness of the community in which he or she practices. The clinician's affirmation of the contextual reality of the client tends to increase the intensity of the treatment alliance and the client's availability to consider his or her own contribution to problem maintenance. (p. 326)

Multiracial and multicultural analysis teams can help mental health professionals develop sensitivity to issues of race and culture (Garbarino & Ebata, 1983). These teams may periodically review agency cases or be available to the staff on a consultative basis. When individuals representing racial and cultural groups are not involved in helping the staff consider racial and cultural issues relative to clients in their caseloads, stereotyping can occur that often mistakenly is assumed to be sensitivity.

Mental health professionals must engage in self-examination regarding their covert and overt racist attitudes that would impede them from working effectively with clients of differing racial and cultural backgrounds. This introspection can occur—the example given here is for Caucasian therapists working with African American clients—by asking the following questions (Robinson, 1989):

- What is the history of my experience with African Americans (positive, negative, and neutral events and their outcomes)?
- What did my family of origin teach me regarding African Americans relative to the following areas: intelligence and intellectual capacity and potential, cleanliness of person and environment, hierarchical status vis-à-vis White people, truthfulness versus deceitfulness, sexual potency and restraint, sex-role functioning in family interaction, personal worth and respect, inclination toward hostility, and the handling of aggression, such as attacking others or fighting?
- How have these teachings affected me over time? What have I done about these teachings?
- What is my personal style for dealing with diversity and conflict?
- How do I exercise authority and relate to the authority of others?
- How do I react in situations in which I observe African Americans being subjected to racist behaviors and ideology?
- What is the pervasive attitude in the agency regarding African American clients?

When treating African American clients or members of other racial and ethnic groups, Caucasian mental health professionals must

	African American	*Asian American*	*Latino*	*Native American*
Cultural Values	Independence Respect for authority Obedience Racial identity	Self-control Social courtesy Emotional maturity Respect for elders	Family loyalty Interpersonal connectedness Mutual respect Self-respect	Centrality of family Sharing Harmony Humility
Common Parenting Practices/Beliefs	Strict discipline Communal parenting	Parental control Strict discipline Negotiation of conflict Parent as teacher	Permissive discipline Communal parenting	Permissive discipline Communal parenting Shame as discipline

Figure 2.6 Cultural Values and Common Parenting Practices/Beliefs in Four Ethnic Minority Groups
SOURCE: Adapted from "Cultural Diversity: A Wake-Up Call for Parent Training" (p. 197) by R. Forehand and B. Kotchick, 1996, in *Behavior Therapy,* Vol. 27, pp. 187-206. Copyright © 1996 by the Association for Advancement of Behavior Therapy. Used by permission of the publisher.

be sensitive to their mistrust issues and the potential effect these may have on the helping relationship. Research indicates that when African Americans who are mistrustful of Whites are assigned a White counselor, they tend to have diminished expectations for treatment and may find it difficult to discuss personal information, such as sexual behavior, that may be very relevant to child maltreatment. Mistrust of Caucasians may stem from childhood socialization, from personal life experiences, or from parents' contacts with Whites in the criminal justice, legal, and social services systems (Watkins, Terrell, Miller, & Terrell, 1989). Developing a sensitivity to racial and cultural issues will prevent mental health professionals from immediately viewing clients' behavior as psychopathological or indicative of resistance and the absence of motivation (Boyd-Franklin, 1989; Logan, Freeman, & McRoy, 1990; McGoldrick, Giordano, & Pearce, 1996; Proctor & Davis, 1994).

Mental health professionals must be sensitive to differing cultural values that impact on parenting practices and beliefs of minority groups when assessing families for child abuse, when working in a therapy role with individuals or families of ethnic or minority groups or even when leading parent education groups. Figure 2.6 identifies differing cultural values of four ethnic minority groups and the way these values may impact on parenting practices and beliefs.

PREVENTING CHILD ABUSE

The word *prevent* implies "to come before"—namely, to take action against what could potentially become a problem. This is often referred to in the field of mental health as primary prevention (Bloom, 1995).

The goal of primary prevention programs in child maltreatment is to prevent child abuse from occurring. The enactment of various public policies at the national and state levels relevant to children's health and welfare may be viewed as primary prevention. An example of this may be seen in nationwide efforts for states to adopt legislation prohibiting the use of corporal punishment in schools.

Prevention Educational Programs

Specific educational programs that mental health agencies or communities sponsor are examples of primary prevention. One such program aimed at parents of newborn infants in an Ohio county is the "Don't Shake the Baby" project. The goal of the program is to educate parents about a form of child abuse that occurs when a parent shakes a baby, generally out of frustration because of extended periods of crying. Shaking a child can result in head trauma that leads to blindness, disability, and even death. A packet containing information on this syndrome and ways to prevent it is given to new mothers in the hospital at the time birth certificate information is collected. Among new parents responding to an evaluative follow-up, 75% indicated they had read the material and found the information helpful (Showers, 1992).

A child's elementary school years provide an opportune time when preventive educational programs can be implemented, especially those to prevent child sexual abuse. Child abuse councils in many communities sponsor programs that teach children to "own" their bodies and to discriminate between good touches and secret touches. These programs also emphasize "empowerment" by teaching children that they have a right to privacy, the right to say no to hugs and touches they do not wish, the right to question adult authority when used in the context of sexual abuse, and the right to run, scream, and seek help when they are in potentially abusive situations.

Programs aimed at educating children about sexual abuse have been shown to be effective on a short-term basis in terms of participants retaining the knowledge gained. Determining if these programs in fact prevent child abuse when a child later is confronted with a potentially abusive situations presents research methodological problems; however, the assumption is made that participants will make a connection between the information learned in a preventive education program and the situation facing them.

An example of the effectiveness of an educational sexual abuse prevention program involved 400 children from Grades 1, 3, and 6 who participated in a program called Touching, which used a play that the children saw. Following the program, the children were tested in four groups. Half of the sample participated in the prevention program; the half who were on a waiting list served as the control group. Half of each group was pretested and the other half was not so, as to determine if pretesting had any effects on the posttest scores. The children who participated in the prevention program scored significantly higher than the control group on an instrument measuring the impact of the program. All participants retained their knowledge when retesting was done 5 months later. As the children increased in age, their retention of the material increased (Tutty, 1992).

Children from Grades 3, 4, and 5 at public and parochial schools participated in a child abuse prevention program titled KIDS ON THE BLOCK that used puppets and skits. (Information on this program is available from 3983-C Gerwig Place, Columbia, MD 21046.) In this study, which used a quasi-experimental design, 413 children who participated in the program were compared with 383 who did not participate. A specially constructed questionnaire measured four dimensions of child abuse: a general understanding of child abuse, the ability to discriminate between normal punishment and physical abuse, knowing the difference between appropriate and inappropriate touch, and the proper response to physical and sexual abuse. Although the mean scores on the pretest were almost the same, statistically different scores were obtained on the posttest, with the group receiving the instruction demonstrating a marked improvement in their understanding of child abuse (Dhooper & Schneider, 1995).

Some people, however, express concern that children exposed to educational programs aimed at preventing child sexual abuse may experience emotional or behavioral problems. Concern also is expressed that the information may frighten young children or that they may misinterpret appropriate touching and expressions of affection as aversive. Studies evaluating the impact of primary prevention programs do not support these ill effects (Finkelhor & Dziuba-Leatherman, 1995; Miltenberger & Thiesse-Duffy, 1988; Nibert, Cooper, & Ford, 1989).

The argument often is heard that parents rather than the school want to take responsibility for educating their children about sex, including the prevention of sexual abuse. Research shows, however, that parents are not knowledgeable about the extent and prevalence of child sexual abuse and thus cannot effectively accomplish this task. Several studies document this.

For example, 51 mothers and 50 fathers of preschool and day-care-center children (n = 111) overwhelmingly rated themselves or their spouse as the preferred person to educate their children about sexual abuse. The parents were interviewed about the topics that should be covered in such a discussion and when such preventive education should occur. Although the parents had good intentions in wanting to handle sexual abuse prevention education themselves, the children would have received inaccurate or partial information and missed some of the most essential information about preventing sexual abuse. The researchers concluded that parents clearly need assistance, intervention, and realistic training to learn about sexual abuse and how to teach their children about this social problem (Elrod & Rubin, 1993).

Primary prevention efforts against child sexual exploitation must begin early in a child's life; however a study shows that only 29% of 521 parents of children, ages 6-14, in the Boston metropolitan area discussed sexual abuse with their child (Finkelhor, 1984b). Only 22% mentioned possible abuse by a family member. Most of the parents believed that the optimal age for discussing sexual abuse with a child was around 9. Unfortunately, by that age many children already have been victimized. Also, parents mistakenly assumed that all potential perpetrators would be strangers rather than family members.

In a similar study in which 20 sexually abused girls, ages 10-15, were interviewed, the data revealed they had been provided with little or no sex education or information about sexual abuse (Gilgun, 1986) by neither their parents nor their schools. The girls' abuse was described as occurring in a knowledge vacuum, for not only did these victims not understand what was happening, they lacked even an adequate vocabulary to discuss what had happened. Gilgun concluded that information about sexuality and child sexual abuse must begin at an early age. The provision of this information is not a one-time event but a process that occurs over a period of time relative to a child's psychosexual developmental stages.

Other Preventive Strategies

The use of public service announcements providing guidelines or suggestions for good parenting is another example of primary child abuse prevention. Parenting courses offered by high schools or through community education programs aimed at strengthening anticipated or current parenting roles also may help to prevent child abuse.

The availability of day care services, a resource providing parents respite from stress associated with parenting, may be regarded as an example of primary prevention or, if child maltreatment already has occurred, as a way of helping prevent recidivism of the problem. Stress is a significant factor associated with the occurrence of child physical or emotional abuse. Day care is a valuable resource for reducing parental stress related to factors such as family size, physical or mental illness, lack of financial resources, physical or psychological absence of a mate, and social isolation. Child care programs also provide children at risk for abuse the opportunity to learn and develop social skills that they may not otherwise acquire at home (Cohn, 1983).

Telephone hot lines on which individuals can remain anonymous but seek help at times of crisis or high stress can prevent child maltreatment from occurring by helping the parent or parent surrogate calm down, examine alternative ways to view and respond to a problem occurring with a child, and provide the caller emotional support through the crisis.

Finally, programs aimed at high-risk parents serve as preventive efforts against child maltreatment. Examples are prenatal support programs sponsored by hospitals and public health clinics for expectant parents. Program goals include preparing participants for parenting roles and enhancing bonding between parents and children.

SUMMARY

The seriousness of child abuse in American society directed national attention to combating this type of family violence with the passage in 1974 of the Child Abuse Prevention and Treatment Act. Child maltreatment, whether it be in the form of physical, emotional, or sexual abuse, is a multifaceted problem, the understanding of which requires identifying individual, family, and social- and cultural-related factors. Numerous treatment resources have been developed to help victims and survivors cope with the effects of the abuse on their lives. One of the most effective treatment modalities is group treatment that enables members to share their experiences with others in the group and to receive support from them as they learn better ways of coping with the effects of their childhood abuse. Abuse survivors often have problems with interpersonal relationships, substance abuse, depression, and psychosocial functioning in general. Educational programs aimed at children and adults have effectively been used to prevent child abuse.

SUGGESTED READING

Journals

Aggression and Violent Behavior

Child Abuse & Neglect

Journal of Child Sexual Abuse

Journal of Emotional Abuse

Journal of Family Violence

Journal of Interpersonal Violence

Books

Briere, J., Berliner, L., Bulkley, J., Jenny, C., & Reid, T. (Eds.). (1996). *The APSAC handbook on child maltreatment.* Thousand Oaks, CA: Sage.

Edmunds, S. (1997). *Impact: Working with sexual abusers.* Brandon, VT: Safer Society Press.

Filip, J., Schene, P., & McDaniel, N. (Eds.). (1991). *Helping in child protective services: A casework handbook.* Englewood, CO: American Association for Protecting Children.

Friedrich, W. (1990). *Psychotherapy of sexually abused children and their families.* New York: Norton.

Friedrich, W. (1995). *Psychotherapy with sexually abused boys: An integrated approach.* Thousand Oaks, CA: Sage.

3

Partner Abuse

Mr. and Mrs. W, both age 42, have been married for 8 years. They reside in a large metropolitan community located in a western state. Mr. W has been employed as a foreman in a large lumber business that sells building materials to local contractors. He has been steadily employed by this company for the past 18 years, having worked his way up from being a yard hand to foreman. Mrs. W works part-time as a cashier at a local supermarket. Mr. W has two children from his previous marriage, 16-year-old twins, who live with his former wife but for whom he is financially responsible. Mrs. W has a 10-year-old son from her previous marriage who lives with them along with the couple's 6-year-old daughter.

Mrs. W contacted the shelter for abused women in her community after her husband returned home from work one evening, began arguing with her, and eventually hit her several times in the face with the back of his hand. When Mrs. W called the shelter, she learned space was available for her and her two children. She immediately drove to the shelter, using her own car as transportation. She brought with her the two children and a suitcase she had packed.

Mrs. W reported to the intake worker who interviewed her that her husband had fallen asleep on the couch, which enabled her and the children to leave. She seemed very apologetic for contacting the shelter and guilty for leaving her home. Mrs. W told the intake worker that her husband often stopped after work to "have a few drinks with the boys," but on this particular occasion he was very drunk and belligerent. Mr. W hit his wife across the face after she confronted him about his drinking bouts, which had become more frequent during the past months.

Mr. W had been cleaning his shotgun the previous evening in preparation for the hunting season. After he hit Mrs. W, he stated he was going to put the shotgun together and blow her head off. Mrs. W described her husband as having a violent temper. On one occasion he shot the family dog after it had wet on the living room carpet. Mrs. W also told the shelter social worker that her husband had been abusive toward the children by hitting them with a wooden rod when they failed to meet his expectations. Mrs. W reported that her husband had slapped her on numerous occasions, but she excused his behavior on the basis of stress he was under at work or that he had been drinking.

Mrs. W and the two children spent three evenings at the shelter. The shelter intake worker instructed Mrs. W, when she initially inquired about the availability of space, not to disclose the location of the shelter to her husband; however, she could leave a phone number for him to reach her. Mr. W immediately began calling the shelter trying to convince his wife to return home. Mrs. W had numerous long, tearful telephone conversations with her husband. The two children, who continued to attend school while living at the shelter, seemed relaxed and relieved to be there. Mrs. W's son was heard to say in reference to Mr. W that he hoped his Mom would "kick the mean guy" out of the house. Despite the shelter social worker and other residents discouraging her from returning to her husband, Mrs. W. was determined to do so after a few days when she felt her husband had "cooled off." She gave the staff and residents at the shelter the impression she somehow deserved her husband's rage because she pushed him too hard about his drinking. Early on the morning of the fourth day of her stay, Mrs. W packed her suitcase, announcing that she was taking the children to school and returning to her husband where she belonged.

* * *

Mr. and Mrs. T are 19 and 20 years of age, respectively. They moved to a large metropolitan area in Florida from a rural area in a nearby southern state after Mr. T could not find work as a welder, an occupation he learned in trade school. Mrs. T had recently miscarried following complications from an unexpected pregnancy. She had quit her job as a waitress in a small cafe because of the medical problems she was having with the pregnancy. The couple were living in a substandard mobile home they had rented in a poorly maintained mobile home park.

One evening after Mr. T. returned home from work, the couple began to argue about finances, which were extremely tight. A large bill had come in the mail that day for a complete layette Mrs. T had ordered from a catalog for the baby. Mr. T became very angry when he learned it was not possible to return the merchandise. During the course of the argument, Mr. T pushed his wife backwards, causing her to fall over a coffee table. When she was lying on the floor, Mr. T kicked her in the groin. She received a cut above her eye, had bruises on her arms and legs, and her blouse was torn. Mrs. T immediately ran to the bedroom, locked herself in the room, and called the police while Mr. T attempted to break down the bedroom door.

When the police arrived, Mr. T was arrested for assault based on Mrs. T's injuries, her torn clothing, and the broken table. Mr. T was jailed, and the following day a hearing was held in Domestic Relations Court. Because this was Mr. T's first offense, he was given the opportunity at the hearing to participate in a 15-week diversion treatment program for male batterers sponsored by the local county attorney's office. A social worker at the court met with Mrs. T and referred her to a program for spouse abuse victims sponsored by the YWCA. Mrs. T asked that her husband be allowed to return home; however, a forcible detainer was placed in effect that stated that if any violence occurred on the part of Mr. T, he would immediately be arrested and jailed.

Mr. T attended the diversion treatment program. Although initially he denied responsibility for his behavior, as the sessions progressed he assumed responsibility for his violent behavior toward his wife. During an exit interview after the final group session, the group leader recommended to Mr. T, and later shared the same with Mrs. T, that the couple should seek further counseling at a local family counseling agency. The couple contacted the agency and were being seen in individual and joint interviews at the time of the 1-month follow-up after the conclusion of the diversion treatment sessions.

DEFINITION OF TERMS

Partner abuse, also referred to as domestic violence, generally is defined as the abuse of a wife by her husband or the abuse of a woman by a male companion with whom she is cohabiting. As discussed later, domestic violence can also occur when a male is assaulted by his female partner or between two individuals of the same sex who are living together as a couple. Because most perpetrators of partner abuse are males in heterosexual relationships and the literature on domestic violence is focused largely on heterosexual couples, this chapter uses masculine pronouns to refer to the perpetrator and feminine pronouns to refer to the victim.

Throughout this chapter, the terms **partner** and **couple** refer to those in a relationship where violence is occurring. The couple may be married, but, as discussed later, partner abuse is more likely to occur in cohabiting couples than in married partners.

Partner abuse generally occurs in the form of physical, emotional, or sexual (marital rape) abuse. **Physical abuse** is defined as hitting, slapping, kicking, throwing the spouse to the floor or ground, or assault involving the use of a weapon such as a knife, broom handle or other household objects, or a gun. **Emotional or psychological abuse** may include the use of ridicule, insults, accusations, infidelity, and ignoring the partner, all of which result in an erosion of the victim's self-esteem and self-worth. Emotional abuse also can occur when the perpetrator puts his partner in the position of having to gain his favor through her compliant behavior, similar to a small child who has misbehaved. A perpetrator who deliberately isolates a partner from friends, family, and neighbors inflicts another form of emotional abuse. Emotional abuse can also involve the withholding of economic support, sometimes identified as economic abuse. This may occur through the perpetrator maintaining tight control of economic resources, such as the family checkbook, cash, and the car. The expectation that the woman in the relationship is responsible for all housekeeping and child-rearing tasks with little or no assistance from her partner, sometimes identified as domestic exploitation, may be considered another form of emotional abuse. **Sexual abuse** occurs in the marital relationship when the perpetrator demands sexual activity without the woman's consent, referred to as marital rape. The male assumes that it is his right and privilege to have sex whenever he wishes and in any form he desires, regardless of her feelings.

Although the three primary forms of partner abuse—physical, emotional, and sexual—are identified and defined individually, research indicates that all three types may occur sequentially or concurrently and that emotional abuse may underlie physical and sexual abuse. For example, physical abuse often occurs as a result of emotional abuse in instances where a partner does not fulfill the servitude role expected by her mate. Researchers have found that battering often takes place in clusters; for example, sexual abuse may occur with the perpetrator demanding sexual intercourse against his partner's wishes while at the same time emotionally abusing her by making degrading comments about her sexuality and by calling her names (Aguilar & Nightingale, 1994).

MARITAL RAPE

Marital rape is defined as any sexual activity by a married or cohabiting partner that is performed or caused to be performed without the consent of the other partner. This includes fondling, oral sex, anal sex, intercourse, or any other unwanted or forced sexual activity. Included in the definition is sexually degrading practices that a perpetrator wants to engage in against his partner's wishes, such as inserting objects into the rectum or vagina. Also, a woman's being forced to engage in sexual intercourse immediately following discharge from a hospital after giving birth may be considered marital rape (Campbell, 1989).

The various types of marital rape have been classified into three categories: *force-only rapes,* defined as perpetrators using as much force as necessary to coerce their partners into sex; *battering rapes,* where beatings accompany forced sex; and *sadistic rapes,* where the assaults also involve torture and bondage (Finkelhor & Yllö, 1985). The essence of the definition of marital rape is that the sexual activity is not mutually agreed on by both partners. The commonly accepted legal definition of rape refers to sexual intercourse by a man with a woman who is not his wife and without her consent. This definition, unfortunately, denies the possibility of the occurrence of marital rape.

Historically, legal exemption was made in British Common Law and carried over into American legal practices that as part of the marriage contract a husband was entitled to sexual relations with his wife (Augustine, 1990-1991; Russell, 1990). Sir Matthew Hale (1609-1676), a British jurist, is credited with interpreting the English law for married women as the basis for exempting a husband from the charge of rape (Hale, 1736/1991). He asserted that the implied or irrevocable consent inherent in the marriage contract in which the wife willingly gives herself to her husband negates the possibility of marital rape. This means that she may not refuse him any sexual favor that he desires. Other factors have tended to negate the concept of marital rape. For example, tradition has protected the privacy of the marital relationship, and what occurred between partners in the bedroom was regarded as no one else's business. Historically, women were viewed as chattel or property of the husband, so consequently he could do with her what he wished. Also, the contention was made that because a man and woman are united into one legal body in marriage a man cannot be found guilty of raping himself. This concept was revoked by the passage of the Married Woman's Property Act in the 1800s, when the identities of the husband and wife were legally separated (Barshis, 1983; Wiehe & Richards, 1995).

Since the early 1970s, with the growth of the feminist movement, laws supporting the expectation that men are entitled to sex with their wives have come under attack. In 1993, marital rape became a crime in every state. As of 1996, however, 33 states grant some exemptions to husbands (Laura X, National Clearinghouse on Marital & Date Rape, personal communication, May 22, 1997). In many states today, a husband can be prosecuted for raping his wife even when he is living with her. However, the tendency still exists not to identify forced sex in the context of the marital relationship as rape and to regard martial rape as far less serious than stranger and acquaintance rape (Adams, 1993; Sullivan & Mosher, 1990).

Sex-role and religious views affect attitudes toward marital rape. In a mail survey to which 267 persons responded (43% female, 57% male), the data indicated that those persons subscribing to traditional patriarchal views of society in which the male is dominant in a relationship and subscribing to traditional Judeo-Christian beliefs tended to support forced marital intercourse (Jeffords, 1984). Confusion and even disagreement with the concept of marital rape continues to persist, as seen in a study on the subject involving 1,300 persons in Texas who responded to a questionnaire about marital rape. Researchers found that 35% of the respondents favored legal recourse for a woman raped by her partner, but 65% did not believe a wife had the right to accuse her husband of rape (Jeffords & Dull, 1982). However, biblical passages and other ancient religious texts, often used to place women in subjugation to men, must be interpreted today in terms of cultural, psychological, sociological, and historical information at the time these texts were written (Yllö & LeClerc, 1988).

Marital rape can be understood from a feminist theoretical perspective. A social structure defined by a hierarchy in which the male is strong, virile, and superior is identified as patriarchy. The woman is viewed as weak, inferior, and needing the protection, care, and attention of the male (Wiehe & Richards, 1995). In a patriarchal family structure, women are subjugated to men, and men may likely subscribe to the ideology of *machismo,* defined as an "organized system of ideas forming a worldview that chauvinistically exalts male dominance by assuming masculinity, virility, and physicality to be the ideal essences of real men who are seen as adversarial warriors competing for scarce resources (including women as chattel) in a dangerous world" (Sullivan & Mosher, 1990, pp. 275-276). A survey of 146 college men found that men subscribing to this ideology were more accepting of marital rape than stranger rape and were less opposed to sexual violence than their nonmacho counterparts (Sullivan & Mosher, 1990).

Researchers estimate that there are 2 million instances of marital rape per year in the United States and that this is the most prevalent form of rape, outnumbering both stranger and acquaintance rape (Bidwell & White, 1986; Russell, 1990). In a sample of 930 women in the San Francisco area, 14% of all women who had ever been married had been raped by their spouse at least once during the marriage, with one third reporting a one-time occurrence only, one third reporting 2 to 20 incidents, and one third reporting more than 20 incidents (Russell, 1990). In a sample of 326 women, 10% who were living with a partner indicated that physical force or the threat of force was used in order to have sex with them. More sexual assaults by husbands (10%) were reported as compared to assaults by strangers (3%) (Finkelhor & Yllö, 1985). It is assumed that in stranger rape the number of reported rapes represents only the tip of the iceberg compared to the actual number of incidents. With marital rape, the reporting is likely even more limited due to the absence of a clear definition of marital rape and the fact that many women feel they "owe" their husbands sex on demand (Frieze, 1983).

Marital rape crosses all socioeconomic boundaries, ages, races, ethnic backgrounds, educational levels, and lengths of marriage (Russell, 1990). Frequently, the first incident of rape occurs in the first year of marriage. Marital rape victims who seek services through public clinics and counseling agencies, however, often are of lower socioeconomic status. Upper-class women may seek help through private therapists and thus not become part of research samples or may not report their rape based on a cost/benefit ratio of the cost of the victim reporting and exposing herself and her husband, as compared to the benefits of remaining in the marriage and the financial and social rewards associated with the marriage (Yegidis, 1988).

As discussed later, alcohol or drug usage is a contributing factor to marital rape, although it is not the cause of the problem or an excuse for violent sexual behavior (Barnard, 1990; Frieze, 1983).

A previous history of physical, emotional, or sexual abuse is shown by research to be associated with marital rape. Three times as many individuals who had experienced incest in their childhood later were victims of marital rape (Russell, 1990). In a study of 40 marital rape survivors, researchers found that 68% of them had experienced emotional abuse, 35% physical abuse, 53% sexual abuse, and only 18% no abuse at all in their childhood (the percentages do not total 100% because survivors identified more than one type of abuse). Although marital rape also is more likely to occur in a spousal relationship where emotional and physical abuse is occurring, it can also happen in marriages where there is little violence (Browne, 1993; Russell, 1990).

How do women respond to marital rape? Some attempt to minimize the risk of being raped by actively resisting, avoiding their partner, or attempting to placate him (Mills, 1985). However, when marital rape occurs, it can have serious effects on the survivors. Long-term effects of marital rape include negative feelings toward men; low self-esteem; feelings of fear, anxiety, guilt, embarrassment, and outrage; changes in behaviors, including an increase in drinking and a refusal to consider remarriage; and depression (Bergen, 1996; Bidwell & White, 1986; Frieze, 1983; Russell, 1990; Wiehe & Richards, 1995). Research shows that in many instances, survivors of marital rape seem to experience more serious effects than victims of stranger rape (Whatley, 1993).

Russell (1990), who has studied marital rape, urges that because of the extent of the problem, its serious effects, and the fact that historically marital rape has been ignored, it should not be subsumed under the rubric of partner abuse but be considered as a social problem in its own right. In some instances, community agencies dealing with victims of stranger rape are reluctant to provide services to marital rape victims because they see the problem as being outside the scope of their services or feel that serving marital rape victims is not within the constraints imposed by funding agencies (Bergen, 1996).

PARTNER ABUSE IN GAY AND LESBIAN RELATIONSHIPS

Just as physical, emotional, or sexual abuse between partners occurs in heterosexual relationships, so also these forms of abuse occur between partners in same-sex relationships. The physical abuse is similar to what occurs in heterosexual relationships (hitting, slapping, the use of a weapon), but emotional abuse frequently occurs in the form of "outing," by threatening to disclose a partner's homosexuality to family, friends, or employers (Elliot, 1996). Sexual abuse in same-sex relationships may include any nonconsenual sexual act (rape) or demeaning language, such as minimizing a partner's feelings about sex, withholding sex, or making humiliating remarks about the partner's body or sexual performance (Elliot, 1996).

Estimates for the percentage of gay male couples where abuse is occurring range between 10.9% (330,000 incidents) and 20% (650,000 incidents) (Island & Letellier, 1991). In a sample of over 1,000 lesbians, partner abuse was found to occur in 17% of these relationships (Loulan, 1987). Other researchers have found even higher rates (Lie, Schlitt, Bush, Montagne, & Reyes, 1991). The rate of partner abuse in same-sex relationships, often reported as higher than in heterosexual relationships, may in fact be approximately thc same because prevalence rate are difficult to determine in same-sex relationships where researchers must rely on nonrandom, self-selected samples (Renzetti, 1992).

Three factors were found to be associated with battering that occurred in lesbian relationships (Renzetti, 1992) and in gay relationships: dependency versus autonomy, jealousy, and the balance of power. Dependency involves a phenomenon also occurring in heterosexual relationships—namely, the balancing of the need for attachment, closeness, or intimacy with one's partner while at the same time maintaining a sense of autonomy or independence, referred to as a *fusion* issue. This may be especially significant for gay and lesbian relationships where an absence of social validation and support is found for these couples outside of the gay and lesbian communities which causes couples to turn more intensively to each other (Lockhart, White, Causby, & Isaac, 1994; Renzetti, 1992):

> In response to the negativism and hostility of heterosexual society, lesbian couples may attempt to insulate themselves by nurturing their relationships as relatively "closed systems" (Krestan & Bepko, 1980). This fosters emotional intensity and closeness in the relationship, but may simultaneously generate insecurity by disallowing separateness or autonomy for the partners (Lindebaum, 1985). Consequently, says McCandlish (1982), "each partner will tend to treat as rejection any attempts by the other to have separate friends, be emotionally distant, or have a different world view" (p.77). This is the problem that Lindebaum (1985) calls *fusion* and Pearlman (1989) refers to as merging. (Renzetti, 1992, pp. 29-30)

Jealousy, which may be a factor stemming from dependency, has been found to be a frequently cited source of conflict or strain in gay and lesbian relationships (Berzon, 1989; Renzetti, 1992; Tanner, 1978). Jealously, which may be bound with envy, may be more pronounced in same-sex partnerships than in heterosexual relationships. This may be due to the fact that an external admirer of one partner, being the same sex as both partners, may provoke jealously and envy in the other partner because this attention is not also being shown to him or her (Renzetti, 1992). The jealousy may exacerbate extreme possessiveness, as evidenced in extensive questioning and even restriction of a partner's freedom similar to the behavior abused women suffer from their jealous male perpetrators. When comparing what couples argue about in samples of gay, lesbian, and heterosexual couples, research has found that gay and lesbian couples have more conflict over distrust. The source of the conflict, resulting in jealousy and resentment for gay and lesbian couples, was previous lovers who still remained in the social support networks of these couples as compared to previous lovers for heterosexual couples where contact could more easily be terminated (Kurdek, 1994).

Balance of power refers to the ability to influence others and to get others to do what one wants whether they want to do it or not. Who maintains the power in a relationship is often associated with the individual who brings the most resources to the relationship (Renzetti, 1992). Although heterosexual couples often divide responsibilities in the home along traditional gender-stereotypic roles—for example, women doing the cooking and cleaning and men maintaining the lawn and exterior of the house—the fulfillment of these responsibilities can become a source of conflict for same-sex partners where equality of power is often a significant issue.

Additional issues are also found to be associated with same-sex partner abuse. One such issue is substance abuse. Research shows a higher level of substance abuse within the gay and lesbian population as compared to the general population (Farley, 1996). Although not a cause of battering, the presence of HIV infection in gay males can be a stress factor contributing to abusive behavior that may erupt in the relationship (Letellier, 1996).

A significant problem for gay and lesbian couples where partner abuse is occurring is the absence of resources for help, especially for couples living in small towns and rural areas. These couples experience isolation and have little hope of asking for legal protection or psychosocial help because of the lack of civil rights protection in many states and the absence of resources (Elliot, 1996). An important issue relative to preventing violence in gay and lesbian relationships is recognizing the problem and confronting the denial often associated with same-sex partner violence (Hamberger, 1996). Also, establishing community networks of gay and lesbian community organizations with existing domestic violence programs in the heterosexual communities can provide treatment to victims of violence and prevent the same from occurring (Hamberger, 1996).

BATTERED HUSBANDS

The issue of husbands being abused or battered by their wives is a controversial topic. A 1977 article titled "The Battered Husband Syndrome" stirred great controversy when it appeared, which still continues (George, 1994; Steinmetz, 1977-1978). Although some research reports statistical data showing that women are as abusive toward their male partners as men are toward their female partners (Straus, 1993), the data generally are criticized on the basis that the figures inflate female-toward-male aggression by including moderate aggressive behavior such as pushing and shoving. By contrast, the rates of abusive behavior of males toward females generally only include more severe aggressive acts such as slapping, hitting, and knocking the victim down (Dobash, Dobash, Wilson, & Daly, 1992; Gelles, 1974; Kurz, 1993; Straus et al., 1980). The nature of these injuries makes them more serious and more visible. Also, women are more likely to engage in violent behavior out of retaliation or self-defense (Straus,

1980). According to FBI statistics, men are nearly 2.4 times more likely to kill their mate than women are to kill their male partner (Close, 1994).

The argument is made that the rates of abuse should not be an issue in determining whether or not husband battering is a social problem but, rather, the way in which social problems or deviance are recognized in society (Lucal, 1995). Factors important to an issue becoming a social problem recognized by society include the organization of a social movement around an issue and the attention that social scientists or mass media give to the problem. Neither of these is occurring with regard to battered husbands. More important, "gender images of women and men . . . have been the most detrimental to the construction of battered husbands as a social problem. Because men do not make good victims, it has been difficult to present them as likely to be abused (especially compared to women, the elderly, and children)" (Lucal, 1995, p. 108). Traditional sociocultural role prescriptions for men indicate that they should be in control in the marital relationship, and when males are experiencing abuse from their wives, they are reluctant to report such abuse or to seek help. Agencies dealing with the victimization of women through partner abuse by providing individual counseling, group therapy, and support groups focus on female victims and find it difficult to incorporate males in their treatment programs. This is not, however, to deny that there are husbands who experience battering from their wives.

INCIDENCE OF ABUSE

As with any form of family violence, the number of reported incidents of abuse represents only a portion of the actual number of assaults occurring between partners, for abuse occurs in families of all socioeconomic, racial, and religious backgrounds.

Recent Concern for Partner Abuse

Concern for the abuse or battering of partners has been relatively recent even though this social problem has always existed. The content of articles in *Journal of Marriage and the Family,* a prominent journal focusing on issues related to marital and family living, were reviewed from 1939 to 1969 (O'Brien, 1971). Not even one article was found that focused on violence in the family. This is not to suggest that family violence or domestic abuse was not occurring but, rather, that it was overlooked due to the false principle that what happened behind the closed doors of the family home was the family's private business. Also, there was a reluctance on the part of professionals as well as nonprofessionals to admit that violence was occurring in the family home, in many instances in a large percentage of homes of various socioeconomic levels. Fortunately, however, since the publication of the O'Brien article's review in 1971, partner abuse has received extensive media attention resulting in the enactment of laws providing for the prosecution of perpetrators, greater protection of victims, and the mandatory reporting of incidents by professionals who have knowledge that such abuse is occurring.

General Statistical Information

Estimates regarding the number of women who are abused range widely. This is due in part to differences in the meaning ascribed to the term *intimate violence*, the title under which data are collected, of which partner abuse is a part as well as the limited nature of reporting for this type of family violence. Many incidents of violence against domestic partners are never reported because of the private nature of the incident, the perceived stigma associated with the event, and the feeling that no purpose will be served in reporting it.

A discrepancy exists between the number of reported and actual incidents of abuse. The National Crime Survey, sponsored by the Bureau of Justice Statistics, annually collects information on criminal victimization, regardless of whether or not the incident was reported to the police. The data are collected through a national survey of 50,000 households and 100,000 individuals, age 12 and older. The survey has found that nearly half (48%) of all incidents of domestic violence against women are not reported to the police. Thus, statistics gathered from police reports on women assaulted or "reported incidents" should be multiplied by 2 to get a more accurate picture of this type of violence. The National Crime Survey has found that once a woman has been victimized by domestic violence, her risk of being revictimized is high: In a 6-month period following the initial victimization, 32% were revictimized (Bureau of Justice Statistics, 1984, 1995).

It is estimated that over 2 million women are annually abused by a partner and that 50% of all women will be victims of battering at some time in their life (Walker, 1979, 1994). Women in the 19-29 age group and those in families with incomes below $10,000 are more likely than other women to be victims of violence by partners and intimate acquaintances (Bureau of Justice Statistics, 1995). Even though statistical data show that the victims generally are of minority and low socioeconomic background with several small children and no job skills, many battered women also are from middle and upper socioeconomic backgrounds where "the power of their wealth is in the hands of their husbands" (Walker, 1979, p. 19). Battered women come from all socioeconomic strata, age groups, races, ethnic, and religious backgrounds. Statistics may reflect more women from lower socioeconomic levels seeking services relative to their abuse. The absence of financial resources causes these women to seek help from public agencies and therefore to become a part of the statistics for partner abuse. Middle- and upper-income women have financial resources available to them, thus making it unnecessary to have to turn to public agencies. Also, they may be more protective of the family's status in the community and of their husband's profession and thus do not seek help or will terminate the marriage through the use of a private attorney. Therefore, unless their abuse comes to the attention of the police and the courts, middle- and upper-income women are often not included in statistical information on partner abuse.

Reports of domestic violence primarily come from local police departments responding to such calls. However, many police departments fail to report the same kinds of calls and arrests, thereby making statewide statistical data meaningless. Also, those departments reporting such calls use assorted definitions, making comparisons impossible. Unfortunately, the absence of accurate statistical data on domestic violence makes it difficult to establish public policy and programs for combating this social problem.

The National Coalition Against Domestic Violence (1995), a nonprofit membership organization committed to ending violence against women and children, estimates that there are at least 4 million reported incidents of domestic violence against women every year. In the United States, a woman is more likely to be assaulted, injured, raped, or killed by a male partner than by any other type of assailant. Between 15% and 25% of pregnant women are battered. Data suggest that higher levels of marital violence are found among military men compared to their civilian counterparts (Cronin, 1995).

Violence becomes a normal way of problem solving for many couples, as shown from samples of battered women drawn from clinical practices and shelters. Violence for these couples often increases in frequency and severity over time (Pagelow, 1981; Walker, 1984). Women drawn from clinical and shelter samples, however, are not necessarily representative of battered women in general because many women never seek the help of counselors or shelters. The differences in these two groups of women, for example, can be seen in their reported annual frequency of abusive incidents. Women in shelter samples reported a frequency of 65 to 68 assaults per year, which is 11 times greater than the average frequency of 6 times per year from women participating in the 1985 National Violence Survey (Straus, 1990).

Partner abuse may begin prior to a couple's actual marriage when they are courting. Researchers studied 625 couples for incidents of violence. The couples were recruited at City Hall in Buffalo, New York, when they were completing their application for a marriage license. None of the couples had been married before, and the males were between the ages of 18 and 29. When the couples were asked to report the frequency with which husbands engaged in marital violence, 36% of the couples indicated as least one episode of husband-to-wife premarital aggression in the form of pushing, grabbing, shoving, or slapping. When a social status score was calculated for the couples, using the Hollingshead (1975) Four Factor Index of Social Status, working- and middle-class husbands' rates for moderate aggression were found to be twice that of upper-class husbands. Working- and middle-class wives reported approximately three to four times more moderate aggression by husbands than did upper-class wives. Higher rates of marital violence were observed among unemployed husbands. Over half (59%) of the women participating in the research reported that they had cohabited with their partner prior to marriage (McLaughlin, Leonard, & Senchak, 1992). Men who engage in violence during courtship share some of the same characteristics with men who batter in marriage (Ryan, 1995). Thus, violent behavior in the dating relationship may be expected to carry over into the marital relationship.

Little attention is paid in statistical data to the number of women killed by intimate partners, which is known as femicide. In a study of the number of females, age 16 and over, who were killed by male intimate partners during 1980, 1981, and 1982, rates of femicide ranged from 2.3 per million in Iowa to 16.2 per million in Alabama. Approximately 4 women were killed every day during the years cited above. The mean age of victims was 35, with the number of killings declining with each subsequent age category. Although Caucasian women constituted the majority of the sample (60.4%), African American women were disproportionately represented at 37.1% of all the victims. The majority of the killings occurred in the context of a domestic dispute (Stout, 1991).

Abuse in Cohabiting Couples

Violence occurs more frequently in cohabiting couples than in married or dating couples. In a study of 526 dating couples at a large midwestern university and a national probability sample of 5,005 married and 237 cohabiting couples, the cohabiting couples had a higher rate of assault than dating and married couples, even when age, education, and occupational status were controlled (Stets & Straus, 1989). Other research has found that the percentage of couples reporting abuse is between one and a half and two times greater among cohabiting couples than among married couples (Ellis

& Dekeseredy, 1989). This may be due to cohabiting couples being more socially isolated from their families, who can act as monitors of violent behavior. Also, issues of autonomy and control may be more pronounced in cohabiting couples. Some researchers suggest that highly dependent men in cohabiting relationships use violence in an attempt to maintain dependence or commitment from a woman in a context where stability and interdependency symbolized by a marriage license is not available (Ellis & Dekeseredy, 1989). Finally, the cost of risking violent behavior as a problem-solving mechanism may be greater for married couples than for cohabiting couples from the perspectives of material, social, psychological, and religious investment in the relationship.

Abuse Among Elderly Women

Most studies on victims of domestic abuse use samples of women in their 20s and 30s because these age groups have the highest reported rates (Seaver, 1996). A forgotten yet highly vulnerable group of abused women are those over age 50, especially very frail elderly women (Aronson, Thornewell, & Williams, 1995). These women are often included as victims of physical abuse under the category of elder abuse, but actually their victimization more appropriately falls under partner abuse. However, their abuse is often not accurately perceived, and consequently they are not adequately served by partner abuse or elder abuse programs. A feature distinguishing older women abused by their partners from younger women is that the older women frequently have fewer financial resources than younger abused women because they were excluded from paid employment in the Depression years, may have worked only briefly during World War II as replacements for men called into military service, later held low-paying jobs with few benefits such as health insurance and pensions, or remained at home to care for children and other family members (Seaver, 1996). Also, rates of disability may be high among elderly abused women. The factor of disability and the absence of financial resources tend to prevent elderly abuse victims from leaving their abusive mate.

One example of an intervention with older abused women is found in Milwaukee, Wisconsin, under the auspices of the Milwaukee Women's Center, where a shelter has been established for battered elderly women. Other services available to this group include a weekly support group, volunteer mentors, and case management. Women were referred to the program by a crisis line they called as well as by community elder abuse agencies, hospitals, and social service agencies. The shelter is located on the ground floor, making it easily accessible for elderly women who have difficulty climbing stairs. Women who have used the shelter range in age from 53 to 90, are mostly Caucasian, and have moderate to low income. The majority of the women, however, contrary to many elderly abused women, were not dependent on their abusers for care but more likely other persons were dependent on them, such as spouses and adult children. As with younger abused women, there is no common profile of older women suffering abuse from their partners, other than living with an abusive mate. Although older abused women stereotypically are viewed as confirmed in their status as an abused wife over many years of living with an abusive mate, the Milwaukee program found that the women who have participated in the program have responded enthusiastically to the idea that they deserve more peaceful lives and have carefully weighed and followed through on alternative options available to them (Seaver, 1996).

Battered Women Who Kill Their Perpetrators

Estimates of women who are battered by their partners range from 2 to 4 million, with approximately 750 of these incidents resulting in the victim killing her perpetrator (Trafford, 1991). Research indicates that a battered woman often kills her perpetrator when the latter is intoxicated or forces the woman to have sex, including types of sex she does not wish to engage in, or when the woman or a close relative is threatened to be killed by the perpetrator (Browne, 1987; Walker, 1984). Women who kill their perpetrators face charges of murder or manslaughter and questioning from prosecutors regarding why they just didn't leave the abuser. The question is often raised as to the validity of the woman's complaint that her husband was abusing her. And while an abused woman's attorney will plead self-defense, the victim is often revictimized through the court proceedings.

Roberts (1996a) studied a sample of 105 women incarcerated in a New Jersey correctional facility for killing their partners and who were serving sentences ranging from 3 years to life. This sample was compared to a sample of battered women similar in age, race, and occupational background randomly selected from two large suburban police departments and two battered women's shelters. Three significant findings came from the study. First, 60% of the women who killed their partners had never graduated from high school, were living in cohabiting relationships, had received emergency medical treatment because of the seriousness of their injuries, had a history of assault by men other than their abusive partner, and had a substance abuse problem. Second, the lives of those comprising the prison sample had been in imminent danger, with some women even knowing the time and method by which they would be killed by their partner. Third, the majority of the prison sample had in the past attempted suicide as a self-destructive method of coping with their abuse. Roberts (1996a) suggested that killing their partner was likely the only means of escape left for these women after their failed suicide attempt.

UNDERSTANDING PARTNER ABUSE

Partner abuse can be understood from various theoretical perspectives. One of these is social learning theory, which maintains that violence is a learned response, as discussed in Chapter 1. The perpetrator may have learned this dysfunctional response from witnessing violence in his family of origin or from the attitude prevalent in society expressed often in the media that males have a right to dominate females.

Another perspective is that of attachment theory (Carden, 1994). The perpetrator may not be able to maintain a relationship of trust and mutuality with his partner because of deficiencies in attachment to significant parental figures that he experienced as a child. This may result in feelings of anger, anxiety, and grief over the failures of these earlier relationships that are carried over and expressed toward his partner in their marriage.

Two more widely held theoretical ways of viewing partner abuse, which include aspects of social learning and attachment theory, are the feminist and systems perspectives (Bograd, 1994; Carden, 1994; Golden & Frank, 1994; Hansen, 1994; Sprenkle, 1994; Stevens, 1994). They are often presented in opposing positions, and each has different implications for the treatment of partner abuse, as discussed later in the chapter.

Feminist Perspective

The feminist perspective asserts that partner abuse is the result of male domination and exploitation of women. The central issue is that of *power,* which rests in the hands of men, and the function of this power is to *control* women, identified in the literature as patriarchy (Hester, Kelly, & Radford, 1996).

The inequality of men and women has a long history. For example, a Roman marriage law in 753 B.C. stated that a woman should be joined to her husband in marriage and share in all his possessions; however, sharing was defined as the woman being ruled over by her husband and she conforming to his wishes and demands (Martin, 1981).

The societal attitude that men should have power and control over women was evident in British Common Law, which later influenced American law. The abuse of women in 19th-century England was a common phenomenon. John Stuart Mill (1806-1873) attacked this practice and became a champion of women's rights in the publication of what was regarded in his day as an extremely controversial essay titled "The Subjection of Women." British Common Law attempted to control the extent to which men could beat their wives by imposing the "rule of the thumb," which stated that the instrument a man used for beating his wife could be "a rod not thicker than his thumb." Although this rule was intended to protect women from severe beatings, it in essence gave men license to beat their wives.

In early American history, several states adopted laws prescribing the extent to which punishment could be meted out to men who beat their wives; however, in some instances, such as in Pennsylvania, an attempt to pass a law in 1886 forbidding wife beating failed to pass the legislature. As late as 1910, the Supreme Court ruled in a case that a wife did not have cause for action on an assault and battery charge against her husband. The Court felt such a ruling would open the doors of the courts to accusations of all sorts of one partner against the other and bring into public notice complaints for assault, slander, and libel (Langley & Levy, 1977).

Inequality between men and women is still prevalent in American society, as seen, for example, in the economic and political arenas where men dominate in commerce and in the formulation of public policy, and women are relatively powerless. The powerless status of women is also seen in the workplace in terms of comparable worth, whereby males and females may do work requiring comparable skills and responsibility under similar working conditions, but women will not necessarily receive equal pay (Bellak, 1982).

The need for power and control stems in part from the way in which men are socialized as young boys. Parents often treat male children in a more physical manner, as seen in "rough-house playing," and female children in a more gentle manner. Boys are offered "masculine" toys such as guns and trucks, whereas girls are encouraged to play with dolls, engage in more passive games, or mimic in their play housekeeping and child caregiving activities, assuming the latter will be their primary role later in life (Zastrow & Kirst-Ashman, 1997). Boys are often encouraged to suppress emotions, not to cry when injured, and to present a strong, tough exterior, for being caring, empathic, and sensitive to their own and others' emotions are viewed as feminine traits.

The way young males are socialized may relate to the aggression they later exhibit as adults toward women. When men are socialized as small boys to reject what are perceived as feminine attributes (e.g., being caring, empathic, and sensitive), the likelihood increases that they will also reject intimacy and emotional connections when

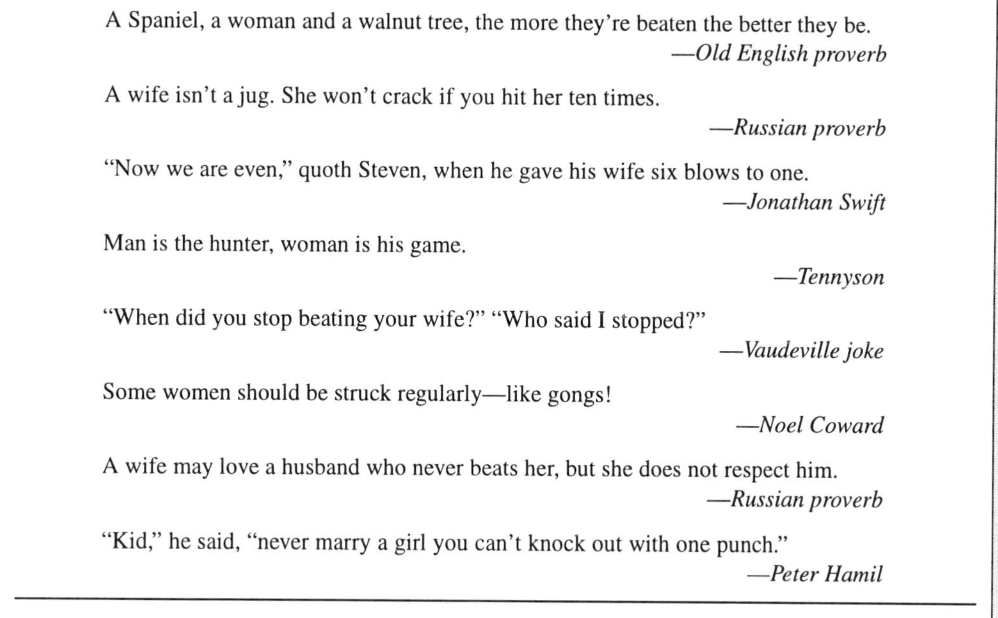
A Spaniel, a woman and a walnut tree, the more they're beaten the better they be.
—*Old English proverb*

A wife isn't a jug. She won't crack if you hit her ten times.
—*Russian proverb*

"Now we are even," quoth Steven, when he gave his wife six blows to one.
—*Jonathan Swift*

Man is the hunter, woman is his game.
—*Tennyson*

"When did you stop beating your wife?" "Who said I stopped?"
—*Vaudeville joke*

Some women should be struck regularly—like gongs!
—*Noel Coward*

A wife may love a husband who never beats her, but she does not respect him.
—*Russian proverb*

"Kid," he said, "never marry a girl you can't knock out with one punch."
—*Peter Hamil*

Figure 3.1 Literature Quotations Reflecting the Power and Control of Men Over Women
SOURCE: Levy and Langley (1977).

adults, such as with their partners. With a reduction in sensitivity to their partner's feelings and emotions, their likelihood of acting out aggressive impulses increases, as occurs in partner abuse (Lisak & Ivan, 1995).

The issue of men dominating and controlling women is played out in many areas of society, as can be seen in quotations from literature. Langley and Levy (1977) begin each chapter of their book, *Wife Beating: The Silent Crisis,* with a quotation from literature reflecting the subordination of women by men. These quotations are compiled in Figure 3.1.

As indicated earlier, the socialization of men to be in control and the absence of power on the part of women influences relationships between the genders not only in corporate board rooms, legislatures, some religious organizations, and other societal institutions but also in the marital relationship. Just as men feel they must exert power and control over women in the world of commerce, so feminist theory states that men feel they must dominate and control women in all aspects of the marital relationship. Physical and emotional abuse is used by some males to maintain their position of power in the spousal relationship. Sex on demand, or marital rape, is seen as appropriate behavior by some males.

Figure 3.2 depicts the way perpetrators use power and control in the abuse of their partner.

Systems Perspective

The systems perspective of partner abuse focuses on the setting in which abuse occurs—namely, the family or marital dyad. The family or marital couple is seen as a social system. All persons in the system are viewed as in some way influencing or con-

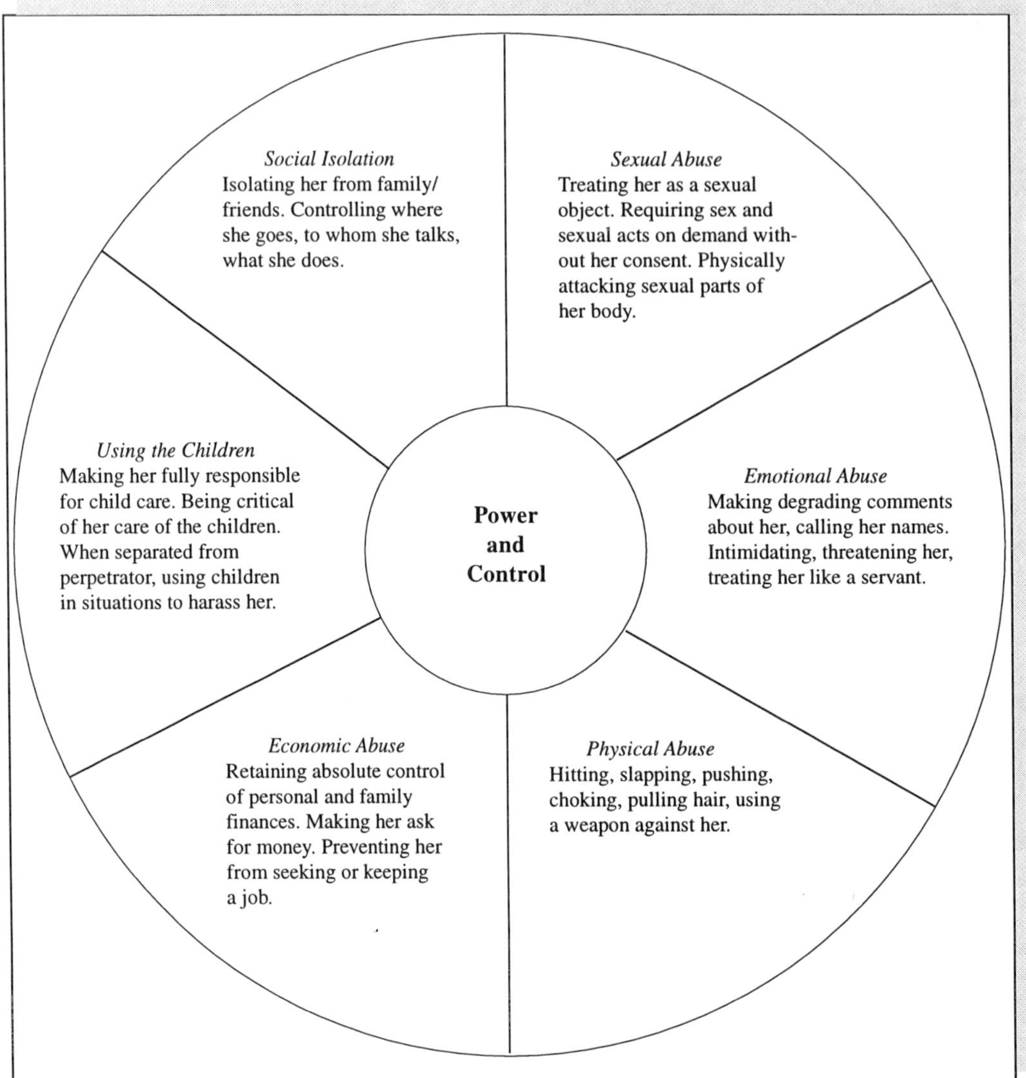

Figure 3.2 Power and Control in Partner Abuse
SOURCE: Adapted from diagram from Lexington (Kentucky) Spouse Abuse Center.

tributing to the abuse that occurs and in turn are affected by the abuse (Giles-Sims, 1983; McKeel & Sporakowski, 1993). Factors influencing the social system that may contribute to the abusive behavior occurring between the husband and wife may include substance abuse, stress, ineffective communication patterns, having been a victim of violence, and poor impulse control (Finkelhor & Dziuba-Leatherman, 1994; Flanzer, 1993; Hutchison, Hirschel, & Pesackis, 1994; Langhinrichsen-Rohling, Smutzler, & Vivian, 1994; Smith, 1990; Yegidis, 1992). The family as a social system is part of a larger sociocultural system. Factors within the larger sociocultural system may in turn affect the family social system, such as economic changes in the form of loss of employment or socially established gender roles (Giles-Sims, 1983). Although social systems such as a family are relatively stable over time, they must adjust to changes occurring for members within the system as well as changes coming from outside the system. Such changes may create stress for the family that in turn may be evidenced in abusive behavior among family members. Giles-Sims (1983) writes, "System theory focuses on the processes that occur, and the interrelationships between events, people, or other elements of the system. The presence and level of a pattern of behavior such as wife battering results from ongoing patterns of interaction within the system" (p. 18).

The systems perspective, however, does not place blame on either partner in the marital dyad or on other members of the family system. Rather, each member of the social system is analyzed in terms of his or her contribution to the violence and the way in which the violence affects that person. A basic principle of this theoretical perspective is that regardless of the behavior or contribution of any member of the social system to the problem, *no one merits or deserves to be abused.*

Research indicates that marital violence may be an outgrowth of conflict between both partners to which each actively contributes, although not necessarily to the same extent, that escalates into violence. Wives report that their husbands engage in more psychological coercion and aggression than they do as the conflict escalates into physical violence (Cascardi & Vivian, 1995; Deschner, 1984; Neidig & Friedman, 1984).

The violent context of society may also be a systemic factor contributing to the abuse that occurs in a marital relationship. In Chapter 1, the effects of children viewing violence on television and in videos or movies were discussed. Constant and repeated exposure to violence may instigate aggressive behavior in the viewer, may have a disinhibiting effect, or may desensitize the viewer's sense of reality as to the serious consequences of the violence (Eron & Huesmann, 1985; Leyens, Camino, Parke, & Berkowitz, 1975; Paik & Comstock, 1994; Phillips, 1983). A study of admissions to hospital emergency rooms following a professional football game found that the number of women being treated for injuries resulting from assault by a male partner increased not after watching a favorite team lose but, rather, after a team victory (White, Katz, & Scarborough, 1992). The researchers hypothesized that admissions to emrgency rooms rose after a team won because the male viewing a professional football team's successful use of violence in winning the game identified with that domination and transferred it to his surroundings. Also, ongoing accounts of national sports figures engaging in domestic violence might prompt some men to emulate that behavior at home with their own partners.

The system's perspective for understanding partner abuse suggests the use of conjoint therapy—namely, the husband and wife together—at some stage in the treatment process. Opposition to both conjoint therapy and the systems theoretical perspective of partner abuse is evident in this comment:

> Social workers who are aware of abuse in a relationship and who agree to see the couple together collude in another way with a set of damaging insinuations that further imperil women. Although the very act of working with a couple in which there is an abusive partner implies that the problem is in the relationship, it is not (Dobash & Dobash, 1992). Abusive men are solely responsible for their abusive behavior (Thorn-Finch, 1992). Conversely, the victim of assaultive behavior has no part in the attacks against her. No matter how provocative or inappropriate the woman's behavior, it neither justifies nor excuses the man's abuse (Jones & Schechter, 1992). (Golden & Frank, 1994, p. 636)

The systems view of partner abuse has raised much controversy in the field of family violence, as can be seen, for example, in the debate following the appearance of an article in a national social work journal describing partner abuse as a "two-way street" (McNeely & Robinson-Simpson, 1987). The assertion is made that the violence in which women engage follows after battering incidents perpetrated by the male partner. The female's violence is in self-defense, which can hardly be characterized as mutual battering (Saunders, 1988). However, this argument fails to address the issue regarding how other factors in the couple's social system may impact on their interactions. It must be repeated again that no matter what contribution a partner or other factors may make to a couple's relationship, no one deserves to be abused. Violent behavior is the sole responsibility of the individual perpetrating that behavior. Criticism has also been raised about the systemic model in that laypersons and even some mental health professionals confuse correlates to the abuse with the causes of abuse. Verbal aggression on the part of a wife may be a *correlate* to an abusive incident with a partner, but the verbal aggression is not a *cause* of the abuse (Carden, 1994; Jacobson, 1994; Sprenkle, 1994). Again, a basic principle must be that the male abuser is personally responsible for his abusive behavior and for his failure to respond to marital tensions in a nonviolent manner. Finally, the systems perspective of partner abuse is criticized for allowing the perpetrator to avoid assuming full responsibility for his abusive behavior but covertly shift part of the blame on his partner.

THE CYCLE OF VIOLENCE

Walker (1979, 1994), based on her research with battered women, proposed that male battering can be understood as occurring in a cycle consisting of three phases or stages. The three phases continue to repeat themselves over time and may become more intense and frequent unless the couple separates or seeks professional help. The various stages may occur over different lengths of time (see Figure 3.3). Knowledge of these three phases is important in understanding (a) why women remain in abusive relationships and (b) the treatment and prevention of partner abuse, issues discussed later.

Phase 1 of the violence cycle is the *tension-building stage*, in which the perpetrator engages in minor abusive incidents with his partner. His wife attempts to "keep peace" in the family or diffuse the situation by denying the seriousness of the incidents or by blaming herself or some external factor for in some way provoking the abuse. The wife's behavior demonstrates her belief that she is capable of controlling the violence for her husband. The initial tension-building phase may last for weeks, months, or years.

Phase 2 of the cycle is the *acute battering incident,* in which an external event impacting on the couple or something that the perpetrator is experiencing may provoke loss of control. The battering incident may be relatively brief, lasting less than an hour, or it may go on for several hours. The wife may be severely injured as a result of her husband's rage. She may call the police, but if the police are not trained in handling domestic violence calls they may ineffectively intervene. For example, male police officers responding to these calls may identify with the husband or may merely attempt to calm down both parties and then leave only to have the violence erupt more severely later due to the husband's anger that his wife called the police.

This second phase represents a critical period for the wife if she wishes the cycle of violence to be broken. She must leave the home and seek shelter elsewhere or, where laws provide such action, have the husband

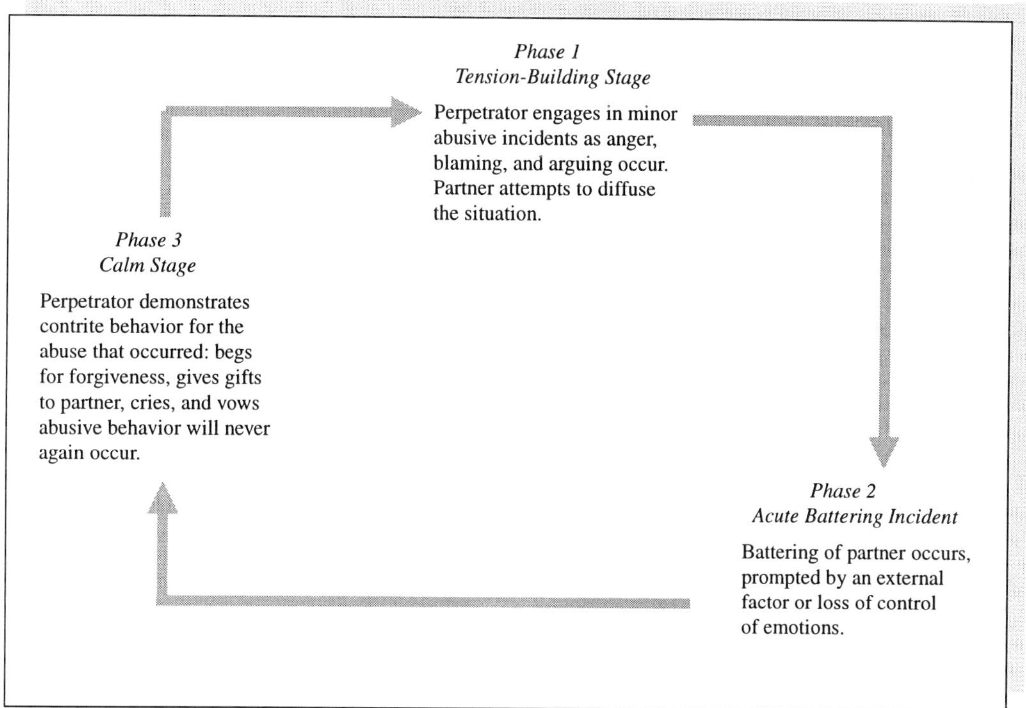

Figure 3.3 The Cycle of Violence
SOURCE: Walker (1979, 1984).

removed from the home. An alternative solution to breaking the cycle is for the couple to seek professional help for their marriage.

Following the turmoil of Phase 2 is the calm period, Phase 3, identified as *kindness and contrite, loving behavior.* This stage is also known as the honeymoon phase. The victim may be physically injured as a result of Phase 2 and most certainly be emotionally upset. When the husband realizes the results of his assault, he engages in kindness and contrite behaviors, such as begging for forgiveness and promising that the abuse will never again happen. The perpetrator may shower his wife with flowers and gifts as tokens of his repentance, and the couple may engage in passionate sexual relations. If they have not sought professional help or if the victim has not separated herself from the husband in Phase 2 but allows herself to become a partner with the perpetrator in this final phase, her victimization becomes complete. She is caught in the cycle, for the cycle eventually will repeat itself beginning with the initial phase. Despite the perpetrator's promises that such abusive behavior will never again occur, the couple gradually over a period of time slips back into Phase 1 as life goes on, disagreements arise, and tensions build. The cycle of violence is about to be repeated (Dutton, 1995; Walker, 1979, 1994). Some women say this "contrite" period becomes shorter and shorter after repeated incidents of battering, and some say it never exists for them.

EFFECTS OF ABUSE ON THE VICTIM

At the most obvious level, being the victim of abuse is destructive to one's self-esteem and self-image. Research on this subject provides information on other effects as well.

Economic Impact

Being a victim of partner abuse has a significant impact on the woman's employment status, as was found in a study of 123 women attending support groups for battered women (Shepard & Pence, 1988). The results indicated the victims' work performance was seriously affected by the presence of physical abuse. Over 50% reported having been absent from work as a result of being physically abused. An even greater percentage indicated they had been late for work or had to leave work early, and 25% reported losing a job partly because of being abused. Many in the sample stated that their husbands discouraged them from working or going to school; for others, the damage to their self-esteem from the abuse lowered their confidence in finding employment. In some instances, the abuser harassed the victim on the job, which created difficulty for her in maintaining her employment. The results of this research relate to an important question discussed later: Why do women remain in abusive relationships? Because many women abused by their partners are not economically independent, their victimization often interferes with their ability to secure or maintain employment that would facilitate leaving their abusive relationship.

Physical Impact

The physical impact of the abuse that women receive from partners is evident in visits made to emergency rooms and private physicians for treatment of their injuries, which may include bruises and welts on the face, lips, mouth, and other areas of the body as well as fractures to limbs and the skull, nose, or facial structure (Campbell, Pliska, Taylor, & Sheridan, 1994; McLeer & Anwar, 1989; Veltkamp & Miller, 1990). In a survey of 33 battered women seeking counseling/support services from a community agency, 31% were so severely battered that they suffered concussions or required surgery (Cascardi & O'Leary, 1992). The impact of their victimization also can create physical problems for the victims in terms of a general deterioration of their physical condition. For example, psychological abuse was found to relate to more frequent visits abused women made to a physician (Marshall, 1996).

Women who have been battered by their partners often find it difficult to secure medical insurance. A congressional survey in 1994 found that 50% of the largest insurance companies refused to insure battered women because they were perceived as being involved in high-risk lifestyles and consequently too costly to insure (Zorza, 1994). Although the battered woman is the victim of a crime, she is basically being punished for her victimization when she cannot get health insurance and then revictimized by, in essence, being blamed for the abuse she experiences from her husband. An additional outcome of this policy of insurance companies is that it places the victim's life in danger. If the abusive husband is the source of the insurance for the spouse and her children and if she cannot get insurance for herself, she cannot risk leaving the marital relationship even though it is abusive. Thus, the inability to purchase health insurance becomes another factor that keeps women from leaving abusive relationships (Shen, 1995).

Psychological Impact

Fear of closeness. Comparisons were made of the psychological impact of being a victim of partner abuse, marital rape, and stranger rape (Shields & Hanneke, 1992). The results indicated that such victims had pronounced difficulties in feeling close to another person and being able to trust others. Victims also demonstrated a fear of being taken advantage of by others. "Being controlled" was a frequent phrase used by battered women to describe their relationship to their partner. The data indicated that the effects of the abuse were quite similar to those that victims of stranger rape experienced in terms of their psychological response, despite the difference that stranger rape involved sexual victimization and the battering was nonsexual.

Posttraumatic stress disorder.

Research indicates that battered women are significantly at risk for developing posttraumatic stress disorder (Houskamp & Foy, 1991; Kemp, Green, Hovanitz, & Rawlings, 1995; Lawrence & Foy, 1993). Posttraumatic stress disorder (PTSD) is described in the fourth edition of the American Psychiatric Association's (1994) *Diagnostic and Statistical Manual of Mental Disorders* as follows:

> The essential feature of Posttraumatic Stress Disorder is the development of characteristic symptoms following exposure to an extreme traumatic stressor involving direct personal experience of an event that involves actual or threatened death or serious injury, or other threat to one's physical integrity. . . . The person's response to the event must involve intense fear, helplessness, or horror. . . . The characteristic symptoms resulting from the exposure to extreme trauma include persistent reexperiencing of the traumatic event, persistent avoidance of stimuli associated with the trauma and numbing of general responsiveness, and persistent symptoms of increased arousal. (p. 424)

In a study comparing 179 battered women and 48 nonbattered but verbally abused women, the battered women with PTSD were compared to their non-PTSD counterparts. The research revealed that the battered women with PTSD had experienced more physical and verbal abuse, more injuries, more forced sex, and a greater sense of threat than their non-PTSD counterparts. Although there may be a tendency to associate PTSD only with individuals who have experienced extreme physical and sexual abuse, yet the study revealed that 63% of the verbally abused women met the criteria for PTSD. The data identified predictors of the extent of PTSD in the victims—for example, the use of disengagement coping strategies like wishful thinking that the abuse would stop; having experienced negative life events, especially childhood abuse; and the lack of perceived social support (Kemp et al., 1995).

Depression and anxiety. The psychological effects of battering may also include symptoms similar to PTSD, such as anxiety, depression, a reexperiencing of the traumatic event, feelings of helplessness, and sleep and appetite disturbances (Lawrence & Foy, 1993). In a sample of 33 battered women, 52% suffered from severe levels of depressive symptomatology. As the number, form, and subsequent consequences of physically aggressive acts experienced from their perpetrators increased or worsened, the women's depressive symptoms increased and their self-esteem decreased (Cascardi & O'Leary, 1992).

Several correlates of depressive symptoms have been found in battered women (Sato & Heiby, 1992). These include realistically assessing their battering relationship, engaging in self-blame, having experienced previous losses (home, earnings, security, self-respect), and having a history of depression. Although victim self-blame is a theme often found in various types of interpersonal violence, it is important to note that Cascardi and O'Leary's (1992) sample of women did not blame themselves for the battering they were experiencing from their partners. This is supportive of similar earlier findings (Holtzworth-Munroe, 1988; Miller & Porter, 1983). Researchers suggest that the attribution of blame may shift over time, with women blaming themselves when the abuse begins, but as the frequency and severity of the abuse increases with time they begin to place the blame on the perpetrator (Cascardi & O'Leary, 1992).

Low self-esteem. In a study of the effects of battering on victims' self-esteem, researchers found that battered women experienced lower self-esteem than their nonbattered counterparts. Differences were noted in the impact of battering on the women in terms of when the abuse occurred and the type of abuse experienced. Those women who had been battered within the past year had significantly lower levels of self-esteem than those who had not experienced battering for over a year. The researchers felt that the victim distancing herself from her perpetrator may have a positive impact on her self-esteem over time. However, the research did not control for the fact that these women may initially have had higher levels of self-esteem. Other factors such as counseling and support from family and friends may have contributed to the differences. Regarding the type of abuse, women in the battered group who had experienced emotional abuse of a controlling nature appeared to have suffered the greatest impact on their self-esteem (Aguilar & Nightingale, 1994).

Impact on sexuality. Being victimized by an abusive partner impacts also on the woman's sexuality, even though the abuse was not sexual in nature. When a demographically matched sample of abused and nonabused women in distressed marriages were compared, the physically abused women reported significantly lower levels of intimacy and compatibility in their marriages. Also, when the abused women were compared to nonabused women in distressed marriages, the former rated themselves as having a lower degree of sexual assertiveness, arousability, and satisfaction even though they reported a greater frequency of sexual intercourse than did the nonabused women (Apt & Hulbert, 1993).

IMPACT OF THE ABUSE ON CHILDREN

An estimated 3.3 million children in the United States each year witness an incident of physical conflict between their parents (Carlson, 1994, cited in Henning, Leitenberg, Coffey, Turner, & Bennett, 1996). Prior to reviewing research on the impact of spousal violence on children, note must be made of the fact that children being raised in homes where partner abuse is occurring are often themselves victims of abuse. Thus, the violence the parents display toward each other in the marital relationship may also extend to the parent-child relationship. Straus et al. (1980) found in their nationwide study of violence in American families that husbands and wives who were abusive to each other were also most likely to be abusive to their children.

Research shows that women in battering relationships are concerned about their children witnessing the violent behavior between the parents. Hilton (1992) interviewed 20 battered women about their concerns for their children and how these concerns affected their decision to leave the perpetrator. It was found that 55% of these women's children had witnessed the spousal violence and 90% were indirect victims in that the children were threatened by the perpetrator, were used to convey insults and ridicule to their mothers, or their mothers were assaulted while pregnant or holding infants. Over half (55%) of the women left their partners because of the risks to the children.

In a sample of 300 women who were victims of spousal violence and who sought refuge at a shelter for battered women, information given by the abused wives revealed that 40% reported that their mate physically abused the children living in their household (Suh & Abel, 1990). The nature of the physical abuse the children experienced included bruises, broken bones, broken noses, and other injuries. The data also indicated that men in their 20s and 30s showed a greater probability of being child abusers. The perpetrator's use of alcohol correlated significantly with the likelihood that he would abuse his children as well as his wife.

Other studies indicate that between 45% and 70% of battered women in shelters report the presence of some form of child abuse in their families. Even by conservative estimates, child abuse is 15 times more likely to occur in families where partner abuse is present (Stacey & Shupe, 1983; Stark & Flitcraft, 1988).

What effects might living in a home where parents are engaging in violent behavior toward each other have on the children? Children ranging in age from 4 to 12 who witnessed parental violence, some of whom had been abused themselves, were compared to a group of children of similar economic background who had not witnessed family violence (Hughes, Parkinson, & Vargo, 1989). Problem behaviors, anxiety levels, and depressive symptoms of the children were assessed using parent and child self-report measures. The children who witnessed violence, regardless of whether or not they had been abused, and who were 6 to 12 years of age, were reported by their mothers to have the greatest adjustment difficulties. Most of these children, however, did not report themselves to be distressed, with the exception of the oldest group (10-12 years of age) who admitted to significantly high levels of anxiety. The high levels of distress shown by the children who had both witnessed violence and were abused may be an example of "cumulative stressors" (Rutter, 1978, 1980). Namely, the risk of children experiencing emotional problems cumulates or increases dramatically with the presence of two or more stressors (witnessing violence and being a victim), also referred to also as a "double whammy" effect (Hughes et al., 1989).

Besides the emotional stress associated with witnessing parental violence, these children experience frequent parental household moves, parental alcohol problems, and parental divorce that place them at greater risk for psychosocial problems (Spaccarelli et al., 1994).

There may be a relationship between children witnessing marital discord and the existence of behavioral problems (Gottman & Katz, 1989; Hughes & Barad, 1983; Johnson & Lobitz, 1974; McCloskey, Figueredo, & Koss, 1995; Oltmanns, Broderick, & O'Leary, 1977; Silvern & Kaersvang, 1989). As many as one third of children exposed to violent behavior between their parents were found to have problems in their own psychosocial functioning. The problems included a poor self-concept, anxiety disorders, truancy, and the display of aggressive behavior (Hilberman & Munson, 1978; Levine, 1975). These problems may continue for the children as they grow into adulthood. Those adults who witnessed interparental physical conflicts before the age of 16 continued to exhibit higher levels of psychological distress and lower levels of social adjustment compared to their adult counterparts who did not witness interparental conflicts as children (Henning et al., 1996).

As was discussed in Chapter 1, social learning theory suggests that children who witness violence between their parents may model this behavior in their relationship with siblings and peers. Behavioral problems were found in boys but not in girls of families where the parents were engaged in overt hostility toward each other. The researchers suggest that fathers may be more protective of their daughters than their sons and so refrain from aggressive behavior toward the mother in front of daughters. An alternate explanation may be that, although children of both genders witness aggressive behavior between their parents, girls may be better able to handle the discordant behavior than boys (Porter & O'Leary, 1980). Witnessing parental or spousal violence may lead children to feel that conflict is resolved through violence, that interactions in families naturally contain violence, and that violence is a method of stress reduction and problem solving (Jaffe, Wilson, & Wolfe, 1986).

Although witnessing parents engaging in abusive behavior toward each other may affect the children, researchers caution that a one-to-one causative relationship should not be established between children of mothers abused by their partners and children's subsequent behavior/personality problems (Rosenbaum & O'Leary, 1981a). Other factors may enter into the relationship that negate this causative relationship. For example, even though a mother is abused by her mate, she may still effectively parent her children and provide them opportunities for positive emotional growth.

Therapy is suggested for children who witness spousal violence. Several methods of working with children in groups who have witnessed spousal violence are being used in counseling and mental health centers. One method involves placing children in a psychoeducational treatment program according to their age and accompanying developmental stage—for example, preschool children (ages 3-5), school age (ages 6-8), latency age (ages 8-10), young adolescents (ages 11-13), and adolescents (ages 13-16) (Ragg, 1991; Ragg & Webb, 1992). Another approach to treating these children involves working with them in sibling groups, including sibling groups from different families despite age differences. The sibling relationship is often most intense in times of stress, and siblings tend to trust and rely on each other because they have shared experiences in common (Frey-Angel, 1989). A third program, most often led by a male-female team of therapists who may at the same time be working with the children's parents in adult groups, meets once a week for a 10-week period (Grusznski, Brink, & Edleson, 1988). The group opens with an activity, and then two major topics generally are discussed. Significant issues covered in the group sessions include confronting the false belief children often have that somehow they are responsible for their parents' fighting, coping with feelings of shame and isolation as a result of their parents' conflicts, dealing with personal safety when parents are fighting, and nonviolent means for problem solving.

Evaluation of a 10-week group treatment program for children, ages 8-13, who had witnessed parental violence revealed they, as compared to those in the nonparticipant control group, showed significant changes from pre- to posttest scores on their attitudes and responses to anger and a sense of responsibility for the parents and for the violence occurring (Wagar & Rodway, 1995). The latter variable related to a phenomenon the clinicians had noted in some children who witnessed parental violence in that these children assumed the role of "scapegoat," or self-attribution of blame, for the violence occurring in their parents' relationship. Children's teachers, therapists, and the group leaders also noted the following changes in the children who participated in the treatment group: increased self-confidence, increased expression of feelings, and refusal to intervene when their parents fought with each other.

RESPONSE PATTERNS OF ABUSED WOMEN

Questions often are raised regarding why abused women continue to remain in an abusive relationship or why they return to their mates after an abusive incident. These are actually victim-blaming questions similar to asking a domestic abuse victim what she did that provoked her partner's abusive behavior. The predicament, however, in which victims often find themselves must be analyzed to understand the victim's situation and the implications of the problem for the creation of supportive services and social policies that will help the victim in separating from her perpetrator or will prevent the perpetrator from having access to his victim.

Early literature attempting to understand the response patterns of abused women to their perpetrators suggested that the victims were masochistic and psychologically found pleasure in their abuse. Also, the rationale was proposed that these women had a deep-seated psychological need for abusive mates (Saul, 1972; Snell, Rosenwald, & Robey, 1964). These studies, using a psychoanalytic theoretical perspective, were based on isolated case studies and viewed the problem of partner abuse from an intrapsychic perspective. This very narrow perspective failed to take into account social, cultural, and situational variables (public policy) that often keep the victim locked in the abusive relationship.

Later studies, however, taking into account these and other variables (e.g., economic, psychological) have corrected this initial response to the question of why women remain in or return to abusive marital relationships. The cycle of violence presented earlier suggests that unless the battered woman leaves the relationship or the couple seeks professional help at Phase 2, the acute battering incident, the cycle of violence will be repeated. The woman becomes enmeshed in the relationship and will be revictimized at a later time.

Recently, the issue has been raised regarding whether or not it is always wise for an abused wife to leave her mate following an abusive incident. Although civil protection orders are available to prevent further contact of the perpetrator with his victim, as many as 60% of the women seeking such legal protection experienced physical or psychological abuse in the year after the order was issued (Keilitz, 1994). Civil protection orders require women to terminate their relationship with their abuser, which may put them at greater risk to be abused and even killed (Hart, 1988; Mills, 1996). Lenore Walker (1994), an authority on spouse abuse with extensive experience in working with victims, writes,

> Even today, many therapists still believe that the abuse will stop if they can only get their client to leave the abusive man. Research demonstrates, however, that leaving does not stop the violence. Instead, it continues, often escalating at the time of separation to life-threatening proportions. . . . An important point regarding battered women, moreover, is that they may actually be physically safer staying with the abuser, over whom they still have some influence, rather than being alone and unprotected without the ability to calm him down. Many men who batter women stalk and harass them. They do not let the women go. (p. 55)

Although the victim's future safety may depend on her leaving the abusive relationship immediately following the occurrence of battering, this action does not occur easily but is done at some cost to the victim and her family. Part of the control that the perpetrator forces on his victim is isolation from family and friends who could assist or support her in separating from the abusive partner. Also, although battered women's shelters established in many communities provide an opportunity for abused partners to leave their abusive mates, not all communities, especially sparsely populated or rural areas, have such shelters. Even shelters located in large urban areas often cannot meet the demand for their services.

If a woman leaves her abusive mate, she must have the financial means to support herself and her children. Frequently, women with children are not financially independent and so must rely on their husband's income for their own and their children's support. Although states are increasingly adopting legislation that enforces child support payments, in many communities strict enforcement of court orders requiring husbands to provide financial support for spouses and children does not occur, thereby placing women in severe financial jeopardy if they were to leave their abusive husbands. Also, the alienation that occurs when the husband is forced to leave the home or when the wife and children leave frequently creates a hostile climate in which the husband refuses to provide financial support. Court procedures for mandating financial support often take time thereby creating a situation in which the battered spouse is at risk of losing her place of residence and being placed in an irreversible financial situation. Applying for welfare is not a desirable option for many abused women because of their assets that prevent eligibility, the small amount of money received if they are eligible, and the stigma that is associated with receiving welfare funds. The lack of job skills also may prevent the abuse victim from being able to adequately provide for herself and her children. Finally, separating from the husband may result in social alienation from other family members and friends.

Three models and other related research that aid in understanding the response patterns of women toward the abuse they are experiencing are presented under the names of the authors: Pfouts (1978), Ferraro and Johnson (1983), and Walker (1979).

Pfouts Model

Pfouts (1978) categorized various responses of wives to their abuse using the benefits-costs ratio suggested by social exchange theory. That theory, originally formulated by Thibaut and Kelley (1959), suggests that a person's behavior depends on the interaction of satisfaction experienced in a present situation as compared to the perceived satisfaction that will occur in available alternatives. The benefits-costs ratio thus is an important component in a victim's decision to remain in the abusive relationship or to seek other alternatives. This model suggests that an abused wife either consciously or unconsciously makes a two-step decision regarding the abusive situation in which she is involved. She must decide first if the benefits or satisfaction of her current marriage (income, family, friends, home) outweigh the costs of the marriage in terms of the abuse, its pain and suffering to her, and the implications for her children who witness the abusive behavior. Based on the outcome of this decision, she must then decide how the abusive incidents as well as her life situation in general rate in comparison to viable alternatives available to her. As indicated earlier, the alternatives of removing the husband from the home or she and the children leaving entail costs of their own—namely, attempting to secure child support payments, finding housing in the latter case, and losing social supports provided by relatives and friends.

Comparative Economic, Social and Psychological Payoffs of Nonviolent Alternatives for the Wife	*Economic, Social, and Psychological Payoffs of the Abusive Marriage for the Wife*	
	Payoffs of Marriage: Low	*Payoffs of Marriage: High*
Payoffs of alternatives: lower than abusive marriage	I. *The Self-Punishing Response* The wife blames herself for being trapped in a violent marriage in which she can neither change her husband's behavior nor find nonviolent alternatives for herself and her children.	II. *The Aggressive Response* The wife responds to violence with violence, sometimes against her husband but more often against her children, or she takes her anger into another violent relationship.
Payoffs of alternatives: higher than abusive marriage	III. *The Early Disengagement* Because she has viable alternatives, the wife either moves quickly out of the marriage or forces the husband to give up the abusive behavior.	IV. *The Reluctant Mid-Life Disengagement Response* Because she has devoted many years to "saving" the marriage, the wife moves reluctantly into a nonviolent alternative when she finally becomes convinced that the abuse is too high a price for her and her children.

Figure 3.4 Factors Determining the Coping Responses of Abused Wives
SOURCE: From "Violent Families: Coping Responses of Abused Wives" (Table 1) by J. Pfouts, 1978, in *Child Welfare,* Vol. 57, pp. 101-111. Copyright © 1978 Child Welfare League of America. Used with permission.

Figure 3.4 identifies four potential coping responses for abused wives based on this two-step benefits-costs analysis: self-punishing, aggressive, early disengagement, and reluctant mid-life disengagement.

The *self-punishing response* results from the abused wife finding herself in a situation in which the payoffs of the marriage are low and the payoffs of alternatives are even lower. Factors influencing this hopeless situation include the absence of job skills that would enable her to support herself and her children, low self-esteem, a history of being raised in a dysfunctional and perhaps violent family, and the inability to trust that the husband will continue to support the family if she were to leave. The woman is in every respect a victim. The children also pay a high price for living in such an environment, as can often be seen in the psychosocial problems they present.

The *aggressive response* is characterized by the violence some women use in responding to the abuse they are experiencing. Their violent response may be due in part to the fact that the payoffs of staying in their marriage are high compared to the available alternatives. Thus, these women fight back. Violence becomes a way of life in these families. The children unwittingly are socialized to violence being a method of problem solving in interpersonal conflicts.

If the payoffs of leaving the marriage are greater than staying in the marriage, the *early disengagement response* is likely. Professional women or women with marketable job skills have viable alternatives to staying in the abusive relationship. These women, however, are under great pressure from their husbands not to leave or, if they have left, to return again to the relationship. Many of the women comprising this group never come to the attention of domestic violence agencies; rather, they appear in court seeking a divorce.

The *reluctant mid-life disengagement response* characterizes women for whom both the payoffs of the marriage and the viable alternatives are high. Generally, these women have spent many years trying to save their marriage for the sake of the children, but finally an abusive incident becomes "the straw that breaks the camel's back." Also, having resources available to them, frequently they separate from their abusive mates when their children enter college and there no longer is the need to preserve the family or when they become self-supporting. The toll is still great, however, because friendships the couple formed over the years may become strained as friends do not wish to choose sides. Frequently, the couple's children are caught in the middle of the situation, which creates problems at holidays, weddings, and other family-related events.

Ferraro and Johnson Model

In their study of 129 women who sought help from shelters, Ferraro and Johnson (1983) analyzed the victims' response to their battering from the theoretical perspective of role induction, a theory often used in conflict management (Spiegel, 1968). Role induction suggests that in a conflict one or the other parties involved in the conflict ends the disagreement by agreeing, being persuaded, or acquiescing. The behavior of the victim when battered by her partner often is analogous to one of the parties in other types of conflicts. Ferraro and Johnson suggest six rationalizations that victims use in the role induction process of responding to their abuse:

- *An appeal to the salvation ethic.* The victim places her own happiness and safety below that of her husband and feels she has the obligation to help him. The victim may verbalize that she must work to save her marriage and her husband.
- *Denial of the victimizer.* Neither the perpetrator nor the victim views the perpetrator as responsible for the abuse but, rather, projects the reason for the abuse to an external factor—for example, job stress, financial problems, or substance abuse.
- *Denial of injury.* The pain experienced by the abused partner is minimized to the extent that sometimes the abusive incident is denied as ever having occurred. The denial in part is stimulated by the fact that the victim wants to believe the battering really isn't occurring because of the implications for the future of their relationship.
- *Denial of victimization.* The victim blames herself for the abuse. Some reason is sought that excuses the abuse, such as the victim did not have dinner ready when her husband came home from work or the house was messy. In some instances, the victim may engage in self-blame by rationalizing that the conflict could have been avoided if she had not been assertive with the perpetrator at the time of the abusive incident.
- *Denial of options.* The victim believes no options are available to her other than remaining with the abuser, even though, realistically, options are available. Some victims may use this rationalization for not using services provided them by a shelter or counseling agency, choosing instead to stay with their abusive partner.

- *An appeal to higher loyalties.* Victims may appeal to traditional values or religion by ignoring the abuse and remaining in the marriage despite its cost to the victim. Religion may reinforce this rationalization by encouraging women to (a) remain in the marriage to avoid the "sin" of divorce and (b) pray for the husband's "salvation."

Walker Model

Another theoretical perspective on why women remain in abusive marriages suggests the victims are enacting the role of learned helplessness (Barnett & LaViolette, 1993; Walker, 1979). Learned helplessness, based on social learning theory, suggests that if the abused victim *feels* there is nothing she can do about her battering, that the situation is hopeless, or that she may even deserve what is happening to her she will *do nothing* about the abusive relationship, which reinforces her cognition that she is helpless. Walker (1979) writes,

> Once we believe we cannot control what happens to us, it is difficult to believe we can ever influence it, even if later we experience a favorable outcome. This concept is important in understanding why battered women do not attempt to free themselves from a battering relationship. Once the women are operating from a belief of helplessness, the perception becomes reality and they become passive, submissive, "helpless." They allow things that appear to them to be out of their control actually to get out of their control. When one listens to descriptions of battering incidents from battered women, it often seems as if these women were not actually as helpless as they perceived themselves to be. However, their behavior was determined by their negative cognitive set, or their perceptions of what they could or could not do, not by what actually existed. (pp. 47-48)

Other Research

Herbert, Silver, and Ellard (1991) studied a sample of 130 women, 35% of whom reported they were currently involved in a relationship with their abusive mate and 65% who reported having already left an abusive relationship. When comparing these two groups, the researchers found three variables that distinguished the women remaining in an abusive relationship from those who had left one. The women who stayed perceived more positive aspects in this relationship, saw little or no change in the frequency and severity of the abuse they experienced or the amount of love and affection they felt from their mate, and did not perceive their abusive relationship as being as bad as it could be. For example, these women rationalized that their husbands at least were not having affairs; the abuse was, on average, only occurring once a month or less; and the rest of the time they were "nice guys." Herbert et al. concluded that women who remain with their abusive husbands do so by cognitively structuring their situation in such a way that they view their relationship to the abusive mate in a positive manner. Also, the researchers felt that abusive spousal relationships must be viewed as a special class of close relationships and a helpful way to analyze these relationships is from the perspective of the way the victims experience and cope with stress.

Lempert (1996) studied the survival strategies of 32 women, ages 21-57, who reported experiencing repeated interpersonal violence of a physical, psychological, and/or emotional nature from their male partner. A frequently used strategy to cope with the abusive behavior was to keep the abuse hidden, thereby making the violence invisible to others. Keeping the abuse invisible was seen as a way for the abused women to maintain their sense of self.

Some theorists refer to the attachment that abused women hold for their abusive mates as the "Stockholm Syndrome," a model developed to account for the paradoxical psychological response of hostages to their captors (Graham, Rawlings, & Rimini, 1988). The model views the psychological characteristics of battered women as similar to those of hostages and emphasizes the extreme power differential between the perpetrator and his victim as similar to a captor and a hostage that can lead to strong emotional bonding. The attachment of the victim to her perpetrator is also referred to in terms of the defense mechanism "identification with the aggressor" in which the victim adopts the life view or perspective of her perpetrator rather than looking at her life situation from a reality perspective.

THE PERPETRATORS

Who are the men who abuse and batter their partners? Research has attempted to understand these perpetrators from various perspectives.

Approval of and Previous Exposure to Violence

In support of the feminist perspective on male violence, Smith (1990) found that lower-income husbands, those less educated, and husbands in relatively low-status jobs were significantly more likely than more advantaged husbands to subscribe to an ideology of familial patriarchy or male dominance in the family and were more likely to have beaten their wives. Research also shows that male batterers find support for their "macho" abusive behavior or model what they feel is appropriate sex-role behavior from friends with whom they associate. Control of the husband over the wife is a central factor in the patriarchal view of marriage. Violence is perceived as a problem-solving method that is supported by the male friendships these perpetrators hold (Williams, 1989).

Having observed violence between parents as a child may increase the likelihood that a male will model this behavior in his relationship to his partner (Rosenbaum & O'Leary, 1981b; Rouse, 1984). A predictive model of severe violence in marital relationships was tested and the result identified several significant predictors of severe violence: sex-role egalitarianism, the approval of marital violence, and having witnessed marital violence as a child. Sex-role egalitarianism is defined as an attitude that enables one to interact with others without regard to the gender of the other person. Those men who exhibited severe violence in their marriages scored low on sex-role egalitarianism or did not subscribe to an equality view of women (Stith & Farley, 1993).

Demographic Characteristics

Roberts (1987) studied a sample of 234 Indianapolis men charged with abusing their partners. In addition to information provided by the court as a result of the charges filed, secondary data were obtained from the files of the Domestic Abuse Unit of the county prosecutor's office, from motor vehicle records, and from computerized criminal histories. One limitation in this study is that the sample represents only perpetrators whose victims filed charges against them. Women who had been threatened or beaten by their perpetrator but did not file charges were not represented in the sample.

The data revealed that 75% of the batterers were between the ages of 18 and 34. The mean age was 30.2 years. There were fewer batterers found as the age level increased. The absence of more abusers in the 40-and-over age category may be due to the fact that their spouses had resigned themselves to the abuse and no longer reported the battering they experienced. Also, the large number of batterers in the 18-34 age range may reflect the use of drugs and alcohol and the resulting violence associated with this age group. Sixty percent of the battered women reported that their perpetrators were under the influence of alcohol at the time of the abuse. Nearly one third of the perpetrators were reported to use drugs, with 21% using both alcohol and drugs.

The study sample was 54% White and 44% African American. The most frequently cited relationship between the perpetrator and victim was cohabitation. Only 19% of the women who filed charges were married to the perpetrator. A reason suggested for the low number of married women filing charges against their mate is the economic and emotional dependence that married women have on their partners that may prohibit their filing charges. Approximately 48% of the batterers were unemployed, which was seven times the national unemployment rate at the time the data were collected. The majority of those who were employed worked in blue-collar positions. The researcher cautions that this does not mean that men employed in white-collar jobs do not batter but, rather, that their female partners may be less likely to report the abuse because of the threat to their mate's employment and concern that the battering not become public knowledge. Approximately 40% of the perpetrators had no previous criminal record. The 60% who did had been indicted for misdemeanors or felonies.

In summary, the profile of the battering offender was a young man who was cohabiting with rather than married to his partner, unemployed or working in a blue-collar job, and likely to be an excessive drinker and/or drug abuser who very likely had been convicted of previous charges related to the possession or use of illegal drugs or alcohol.

Caution must be raised about generalizing these findings to all such perpetrators based on 234 men who had charges filed against them. Underrepresented in this sample are more highly educated perpetrators whose abused partners did not file charges against them because of embarrassment and possible loss of the perpetrator's job but, rather, contacted a private attorney and filed for divorce. Also not included in the Roberts (1987) sample were couples where one or both partners sought counseling from a therapist in private practice. Differences between court-involved and non-court-involved perpetrators were noted in a study of 86 court-involved men and 42 non-court-involved men, all of whom abused their wives and attended a treatment program. The researchers found that the non-court-involved men had more education, were more likely to be employed full-time, and tended to earn more money (Barrerra, Palmer, Brown, & Kalaher, 1994).

Substance Abuse

Studies show a high incidence of alcohol and/or drug problems among men who abuse their wives (Carlson, 1977; Coleman, 1980; Fagan, Stewart & Hansen, 1983; Leonard & Blane, 1992; Leonard & Senchak, 1993; Powers & Kutash, 1978). These studies indicate that the abuse of alcohol or drugs often is a factor in specific abusive incidents. In some instances, the battering is most severe when the perpetrator is drinking, reflecting the perpetrator's loss of control.

Kantor and Straus (1987) examined interview data from a nationally representative sample of 5,159 families in the United States. The data revealed that excessive drinking was associated with higher wife abuse rates; however, alcohol was not an immediate antecedent of violence in the majority of the families studied. The highest rates of wife abuse were associated with a combination of drinking, blue-collar status, and the acceptance or approval of violence. The researchers concluded that the findings support the "drunken bum" theory of spouse abuse; however, alcohol is not a necessary or sufficient cause of wife battering. Reasons given by violent men for their drinking are to forget their worries, pains, and stresses (Fagan et al., 1988). Drug abuse or a dual problem with the abuse of drugs and alcohol is more likely to be associated with more severe battering incidents that often result in serious injuries to the victim (Roberts, 1988). Research also shows that female partners of abusers drink substantially more than their nonabused counterparts do. They were found frequently to drink during abusive incidents and in response to battering (Barnett & Fagan, 1993).

An implication for treatment from these studies is that intervention programs for male batterers must be closely allied with substance abuse treatment programs if the interventions are to be effective. Both types of treatment may need to be mandated by the courts. As discussed later in the evaluation of treatment programs, the use of alcohol also was a significant variable that distinguished men who complete treatment programs for spouse abuse from those who do not complete such programs (Hamberger & Hastings, 1989, 1990).

Psychological Characteristics

Studies of personality characteristics of abuse perpetrators revealed differences between groups of male abusers and nonabusers. The abusers showed evidence of marked personality disorder in that when compared to nonabusers they exhibited more depression in terms of being moody, sullen, sensitive, and overreactive to rejection. The abusers also exhibited greater conflict and confusion about identity issues. The abusers tended to show higher levels of anxiety and present more somatic complaints than the nonbatterers (Hamberger & Hastings, 1985, 1986). Alcohol problems were prevalent among the abusers.

Because no control groups were used in these studies, additional research was done comparing abusive males with and without alcohol problems with age-matched nonabusive males on measures of personality style, personality disorder, sense of well-being, and various demographic variables (Hastings & Hamberger, 1988). The nonabusive males were divided into two groups: maritally discordant and maritally satisfied. To determine the effects of alcohol abuse, the batterers were divided into two subgroups: those with and without alcohol problems.

The findings revealed that the batterers showed greater overall evidence of psychopathology on standardized personality measures when compared to the nonbatterer controls. Batterers were more dissatisfied with life and showed evidence of marked personality disorders, mood and other symptom disturbances, and cognitive and affective problems approaching psychotic proportions. The researchers felt that in a relationship the abusive male considered important, when his sense of control would be threatened, violence and intimidation were likely to occur. The personality profile of the batterers gave the impression that abusive males may tend to see situations as threatening that most individuals would not regard as such. The conflicts and stresses of the marital relationship make these individuals especially prone to violence. The research also found that batterers with alcohol problems showed more psychopathology than batterers without substance abuse problems.

The Minnesota Multiphasic Personality Inventory (MMPI) was administered to 67 men who had abused their partners on at least one occasion. The findings revealed that the men could be characterized as impulsive; showing a lack of respect for social standards; having frequent difficulties with the law and with their families; exhibiting situational depression, feelings of inadequacy or low self-esteem or both; and a tendency toward substance abuse (Hale, Zimostrad, Duckworth, & Nicholas, 1988). Research also has found, when comparing groups of male batterers with nonbatters, that the batterers were more likely to have experienced physical or emotional abuse as children (Dutton, Starzomski, & Ryan, 1996; Else, Wonderlich, Beatty, Christie, & Staton, 1993).

Bernard and Bernard (1984) studied the psychological functioning of 46 men who voluntarily entered a treatment program to control their abusive behavior. The researchers found that the men related well to each other but initially found it difficult to communicate with the female group leader. Their behavior seemed like a "Dr. Jekyll/Mr. Hyde" situation. Initially, they displayed socially desirable behaviors. However, as this facade was penetrated in the therapy group, intense feelings of social and personal (masculine) inadequacy were noted as well as frustration arising from unmet dependency needs. A common characteristic of all the group participants was their denial and minimization of the frequency and intensity of their violence toward their partners.

Finally, scores on the Fundamental Interpersonal Relations Orientation-Behavior Scale (FIRO-B) (Ryan, 1977; Schutz, 1978) of a group of 100 men who had been referred to a treatment center for physically assaulting their female partners were compared with normative samples. The batterers were more likely to be described as loners and rebels and were less outgoing, less intimate, and more cautious than the general population. The researchers felt the abusive males' designation as "loners" was indicative of their existence as "closed social systems," which prevented them from making social connections and receiving interpersonal feedback from others about their abusive behavior. The batterers demonstrated more difficulty in establishing interpersonal relationships and expressing intimacy than their nonabusive counterparts did (Allen, Carlsyn, Fehrenbach, & Benton, 1989).

When working with abusive men, mental health professionals by virtue of their education and training tend to understand perpetrators from social and psychological perspectives. However, research shows the importance of also appraising partner abuse perpetrators from a physical or biological perspective. Closed head injuries that perpetrators may have experienced at some time in their life may be a significant factor creating aggressive outbursts directed at their partners. A sample of 53 men who were abusive to their partners were compared to a sample of 45 maritally satisfied and 32 maritally discordant but nonviolent men. All were evaluated for a past history of head injury and then were examined by a physician who was not aware of the men's previous head injury or of their state of marital satisfaction. It was found that 53% of the batterers had a history of a significant, closed head injury either mild, moderate, or severe in nature compared with 25% of the nonviolent maritally discordant men and 16% of the nonviolent, married men experiencing a satisfactory relationship with their partner. Head injury remained a significant discriminating factor among the three groups when other variables, such as the use of alcohol, witnessing parental aggression, or experiencing abuse from a parent as a child, were controlled (Rosenbaum et al., 1994).

TREATMENT OF PERPETRATORS

One of the first agencies in the United States to provide services to perpetrators of partner abuse was Emerge, established in 1977 and

- Each person is responsible for his or her behavior. The victim cannot cause the violence or eliminate it.
- Provocation does not provide justification for violence.
- Violence is a behavior of choice, a dysfunctional, destructive choice with negative consequences.
- Nonviolent alternatives exist to violence as functional, appropriate choices.
- Violence is a learned behavior. Just as the perpetrator learns to be violent, so he or she can learn to be nonviolent.
- Violence impacts on all family members. Although this impact may be less obvious than on the victim, the children are learning that violence is an acceptable method of problem solving.

Figure 3.5 Basic Principles in the Treatment of Batterers

located in Boston. Since that time, numerous treatment programs for batterers have been established. General principles of treating batterers, different types of treatment programs, and several examples of programs are discussed.

Principles in Batterer Treatment

Figure 3.5 presents six basic principles on which many treatment approaches for batterers are based. These principles form the themes around which education, confrontation, and discussion occur in the treatment of abusers.

Types of Treatment Programs

Two major approaches to treatment are based on the two major theoretical perspectives for understanding partner abuse discussed earlier: the feminist perspective and the systems perspective. Although these two approaches to treatment are discussed separately, an analysis of treatment programs reveals that many programs contain elements of both approaches to treatment.

Treatment based on the feminist theoretical perspective views partner abuse as the husband's abuse of power and control over the wife physically, psychologically, sexually, and economically. The purpose of the abuse is to intimidate the victim so that the perpetrator may remain in control. The central focus of feminist-based approaches to treatment is that partner abuse is a learned behavior that has its roots in patriarchal social norms as opposed to psychopathological functioning within the perpetrator, his spouse, or problems in communication between the perpetrator and the victim.

Feminist-based treatment programs for perpetrators generally occur in a group setting, with the group leader often taking a didactic or teaching role in educating the group participants in more functional ways of perceiving the husband-wife relationship other than stereotypical male-dominant patterns in which the batterers have been socialized. Thus, this approach to treatment is often called "psychoeducational" as distinguished from "psychotherapeutic." Group discussion and interaction among the participants is encouraged as the participants work with the concept of sex-role egalitarianism and its implications in their daily living. Group members may keep logs or diaries of events that occurred during the past week in which they attempted to control their partner.

The theoretical base for the feminist treatment approach is social learning theory, which emphasizes that violence is a learned behavior that is self-reinforcing. Also, just as violence has been learned, so it can be unlearned as more effective, nonviolent methods of problem solving are learned for use in interaction with the batterer's partner or in other interpersonal relationships, such as in the workplace or socially with peers.

Although feminist-based treatment programs for male batterers generally involve only the perpetrators in the group and individual sessions, some agencies sponsoring these program may contact the victim to inform her of her rights and of resources available in the community, such as shelters and economic and legal resources. The victim may be encouraged to become involved with programs in the community that work with abused women. If the abused partner does enter therapy, the perpetrator's therapist or group leader may contact the spouse's therapist relative to the issue of the extent to which abusive behavior may still be occurring in the marital relationship but is not being reported by the perpetrator. Research indicates that male abusers report lower frequencies of violence than their female partners (Edelson & Brygger, 1986; Jourilies & O'Leary, 1985; Szinovacz, 1983). Unless such checks on their self-reporting are made, perpetrators may minimize or deny the abusive behavior in which they are engaging for fear of further prosecution.

Because male-female relationships are a critical issue in partner abuse, treatment groups for male perpetrators frequently are co-led by a male and a female therapist. This arrangement presents to the participants that males and females can have an egalitarian relationship and can relate to each other in mutually effective ways (Reese-Dukes & Reese-Dukes, 1983).

Treatment based on the systems theoretical perspective views partner abuse as a sociopolitical problem—namely, the inequality between men and women in society as well as in the marital relationship (Adams, 1988). Treatment based on this perspective is similar to psychotherapy in general or to conjoint marital counseling involving the use of individual and joint interviews of the perpetrator and his mate. One example of a systems approach to the treatment of partner abuse consists of seven phases (Cook & Cook, 1984).

Phase 1 of this treatment model focuses on an assessment of the problem occurring in the marriage as reflected in the battering and a review of the history of the marital relationship. Emphasis also is placed on examining the sequence of events before and after a battering incident to begin assessing a possible pattern. This phase usually occurs with the therapist working with the perpetrator and victim separately to expedite the information-gathering process. Also, seeing the two parties alone minimizes the risk of violence stemming from the information shared in a joint interview.

Phase 2 involves the therapist working with the female victim alone and establishing with her detailed plans for her protection if another battering incident should occur, including identifying precipitating clues, who to call for help, and where to go for assistance. The therapist also discusses with the victim that it may be necessary for her to leave the relationship for a period of time, thereby giving the couple an opportunity to reflect on their relationship and to begin to change the rules under which they have been operating.

Phase 3 focuses on the perpetrator and the necessity for him to make a commitment to be nonviolent. This may be a written commitment and may involve alternative behaviors or activities, such as physical exercise, relaxation, and time-out from the relationship. Different therapists may meet with the perpetrator and the victim in these initial stages of treatment.

Phase 4 is identified as differentiation. In this phase, which may occur separately with each partner if the couple is in a state of crisis, conjointly, or even in a group setting with other couples, the goal is that each marital partner works toward independence. The group setting can provide support in this task by individuals being able to identify with other group members. In the group sessions, members are struggling with similar issues, such as power and control, anger management, and provocation. Training in developing assertiveness skills and anger management may be included in this phase of treatment.

Identifying triangles and coalitions is the goal of Phase 5. Phases 5 through 7 generally occur with the couple together in conjoint therapy unless a violent incident has occurred. A significant component of Phase 5 is the therapist assessing if each of the couple's families is in any way undermining the progress in therapy. This assessment is based on the principle that those in battering relationships often are still tied to their families of origin, which may play significantly in the couple's violent episodes.

Phase 6 focuses on identifying sequences and themes in the couple's dysfunctional relationship. Emphasis especially is given to the purpose that violence serves in the relationship.

Phase 7 is based on the sequences and themes identified in Phase 6. In this final phase, the therapist works with the couple in identifying prosocial behaviors that can replace the aversive interactional patterns that have occurred in the marriage. The therapist works in the role of a teacher and coach as alternative ways of relating are tried by the couple (Cook & Cook, 1984).

In summary, the systems model of treatment is based on the premise that as one partner in the marital dyad makes attitudinal and behavioral changes, these changes in turn will influence the other partner and the marital relationship that consequently should lead to a cessation of violence in the relationship (McKeel & Sporakowski, 1993).

Treatment Program Examples

Each of the programs described here relies heavily on principles of feminist-based treatment approaches and involves only the perpetrator.

Changing the Perpetrator's Frame of Reference

One model for treating male batterers is based on the concept of changing a perpetrator's perception of his relationship to his partner or the frame of reference he uses in viewing his partner. A person's frame of reference may be thought of as a "die" that impresses itself on everything a person sees and does. The premise of this treatment model is that this die for male batterers—namely, that they perceive their relationship to their partner as one of intimidation and subsequent control (and which they perceive is supported by cultural norms)—must be changed if their behavior is to change. This requires a process of re-education, which can best take place in a group setting. Therapeutic change occurs as the perpetrators who comprise the group accept a new "die" or frame of reference for their spousal relationships.

Four phases comprise the intervention strategy in this treatment model: the *Yes-But Phase,* in which hostility and self-justification on the part of the members exists; the

Maybe Phase, which occurs when perpetrators begin to consider their own behavior and its consequences; the *I Will Phase,* in which group members start to take responsibility for their own actions and attempt to try out noncoercive and noncontrolling behaviors in their spousal relationships; and the *I Do Phase,* in which noncoercive and noncontrolling behaviors predominate and the group members support each other's new perceptions and resulting behaviors toward their partners. As men become involved in the group process during the course of the four phases, the group takes on a significant role for the members. The group can continue to serve as a source of support for the men as they work out problems in daily living with their new perceptions of their spousal relationship (Wood & Middleman, 1992b).

TFA Systems Treatment Model

Another treatment model for abusers involves TFA (thought, feelings, and actions) systems (Clow, Hutchins, & Vogler, 1992). This model is based on a widely accepted premise in psychotherapy that thoughts, feelings, and actions are the major dimensions of human behavior and that a person has the ability to control each of these (Ellis, 1982; Glasser, 1965; Lazarus, 1981). Behavior is conceived as dimensional or situational rather than static. An advantage of this conceptualization of behavior is the ability to organize in a relatively simple way the information a person needs to modify behavior in problem situations, such as occur in partner abuse.

This model uses a group approach involving five or more perpetrators in two 1-hour sessions for 10 weeks. Groups are conducted by one leader or sometimes by dual leaders—a male and a female. Perpetrators generally are ordered into treatment by a family court judge following an abusive spousal incident. A screening interview is conducted with the prospective group member to determine if other pathology, such as chemical dependency, is present and to consider treatment for this problem prior to the perpetrator joining the group. The screening interview also enables the group leader to assess an individual's motivation for treatment.

The initial phase of treatment focuses on client assessment. The assessment process is built on Walker's (1979) cycle of violence discussed earlier in that the thoughts and feelings of the abuser are identified during the tension-building phase prior to the battering incident. As part of the assessment, a TFA triangle is constructed for each group member. The group leader asks the perpetrator to recall what he was thinking and feeling in the minutes prior to losing control. The thoughts and feelings are identified on a large blackboard for all group members to see. Later, subsequent actions are identified. Typically, group members recall doing very little thinking prior to the abuse but were heavily into feelings and actions. They generally report negative feelings of high intensity and actions that are counterproductive, often escalating from shouting and yelling to breaking things and eventually hitting their partner. Figure 3.6 presents an example of an abuser's TFA triangle.

Following the identification of thoughts, feelings, and actions, the group leader and members determine in the moments prior to the abuse if the perpetrator was doing more feeling, more thinking, or engaging in both in equal amounts. In most instances, the abuser acts impulsively out of negative feelings without thinking. The abuser is assisted in developing awareness of his feelings prior to acting and in engaging in thinking prior to acting. Forcing group members to identify thoughts and feelings prior to an abusive incident (action) cuts through the justifications, rationalizations, and cognitive distor-

Thoughts
She cares more about the kids than me.
She doesn't keep the house clean.
She nags.
I'm not in control.
She won't have sex when I want it.

Feelings	*Actions*
Anger	Yelling
Jealousy	Swearing
Neglect	Name-calling
Disgust	Hitting

Figure 3.6 Example of a TFA Triangle
SOURCE: Clow, Hutchins, and Vogler (1992).

tions that batterers use when talking about their abusive behavior. Group members leave therapy equipped with a method of interpreting their thoughts, feelings, and actions relevant to any future potential abusive incidents so that better personal control can occur (Clow et al., 1992).

EVALUATION OF TREATMENT PROGRAMS

Evaluating the effectiveness of treatment programs for male batterers is important for the continuance or discontinuance of these programs. The literature reflects numerous examples of evaluations of groups for battered men (Bern & Bern, 1984; Dutton, 1986; Farley & Magill, 1988; Faulkner, Stoltenberg, Cogen, Nolder, & Shooter, 1992; Lindquist, Telch, & Taylor, 1983; Neidig, 1986; Petrik, Gildersleeve-High, McEllistrem, & Subotnik, 1994; Rosenbaum, 1986). As occurs in many program evaluation studies, evaluating the effectiveness of the intervention presents research methodological problems, such as documenting success in terms of actual behavioral change in the participants, the lasting effects of treatment over time, the use of comparison or control groups, and the control of intervening variables that might affect success rates of interventions (Eisikovits & Edleson, 1989). Several studies are briefly reviewed.

An evaluative study of who completed batterer treatment groups focused on three groups of participants involved in the Domestic Abuse Project in Minneapolis: men who completed treatment, those who attended some sessions, and those who attended only the initial two intake sessions. The data showed several differences between those completing treatment, who were contacted by the researchers 6 months later, and the other two groups that did not complete treatment. Those who completed the treatment program had higher educational levels, were more likely to be employed full-time, had witnessed violence in their families of origin that may have prompted them to want to change their behavior, were less likely to have been victims of child abuse, and had more children. The researchers felt that a variable that distinguished the noncompleters from the completers—namely, that the former were victims of child abuse—may have been used by the noncompleters to justify the violence they perpetrated on the basis that they themselves had experienced violence as children. A weakness in this research was the participants' self-report of any threats or occurrences of violence with their partners that may not have been as accurate as what their partners would have reported (Grusznski & Carrillo, 1988).

Three treatment programs for batterers were evaluated over a 4-year period. Both the perpetrator and his female partner were contacted at the end of the treatment groups in order to collect data on the frequency and severity of violence or threats of violence. Emphasis was placed on the female partners' input because, as stated earlier, evaluative studies of treatment programs have tended to show that perpetrators report fewer incidents of violence than their female partners (Claes & Rosenthal, 1990). Men's reports were used as an estimate of reliability of the female partners' reports. Between 59% and 67% of the men in the three studies were shown to be nonviolent at the end of their treatment. The time between the end of treatment and the follow-up interviews for those who completed it was, on average, 139.5 days, thus allowing the men time to lapse into old habits rather than measuring the effect of the treatment immediately following its completion. The researchers concluded that the treatment groups, combining educational and therapeutic procedures, were helpful to the perpetrators in assisting them to end their violent behavior together with changing their attitudes about violence (Edleson & Grusznski, 1988).

Researchers evaluated the effectiveness of a 6-month treatment program consisting of 24 weekly sessions, each lasting 2.5 hours. Eight perpetrators comprised the group. As part of the program, each group member was required to complete a "control log" (Pence & Paymar, 1992) that identified the purpose of the abusive behavior, his and his partner's feelings during and after abusive incidents, the perpetrator's belief system, whether or not he got what he wanted from the abusive behavior, and possible alternative nonabusive behaviors he could have used. The purpose of the log was to demonstrate to each group member that the purpose of his abusive behavior was to exert power and control over his mate and that this behavior has only long-term negative consequences. The research found the group participants showed significant reductions in abusiveness immediately after treatment and at 6-month and 2-year follow-ups as rated by the perpetrators and their female partners (Petrik et al., 1994).

Resistance to treatment is a common factor in perpetrator treatment programs. A frequent problem associated with male batterer groups is that men mandated by the court to participate in a treatment program do not complete the program and reoffend. In a review of 30 treatment programs for male batterers, 48% of the programs reported completion rates of under 50% (Gondolf, 1990).

In another study of treatment completion, of 526 men recommended to attend a treatment group for male batterers, 59% dropped out between the assessment and the first treatment session and 60% of those remaining went on to complete the treatment program. Thus, of the total sample recommended for treatment, only 25% completed the program. Those who dropped out tended to be young, not legally married, having low incomes, little education, unstable work histories, unstable housing arrangements, criminal histories, and consuming greater amounts of alcohol when compared to those completing treatment. The researchers concluded that "given that individuals with the above characteristics would be less likely to follow through with anything, it is not surprising that they failed to complete the treatment program" (Cadsky, Hanson, Crawford, & Lalonde, 1996, p. 60).

A significant problem in the evaluation of these treatment programs is determining if the effects of the program seen at the end of treatment or shortly thereafter continue for longer periods of time. The following evaluative study of the Duluth Domestic Abuse Prevention Project (DAPP) assessed the continuation of treatment effects 5 years following the completion of treatment. Participants in the program attended 12 weeks of counseling groups that focused on anger management skills and 10 weeks of education groups focusing on the use of abuse to maintain power and control. About one third of the men reported that they had witnessed spousal abuse in their families as they were growing up. About one fourth reported being physically abused as a child. Over a third of the participants were ordered by the court also to complete a treatment program for drug or alcohol abuse. Five years following completion of treatment, 40% of the men were identified as recidivists because they were either convicted of domestic assault, the subject of a protective order, or a police suspect for domestic assault. Several factors discriminated between recidivists and nonrecidivists. The recidivists tended to have been abused as children, previously convicted for nonassault crimes, and under court order to have a chemical dependency evaluation (Shepard, 1992).

Because drug and alcohol abuse is a significant contributing factor to spousal violence, treatment for alcoholism is a component of many treatment programs for male batterers (Conner & Ackerley, 1994). Some mental health professionals working with male batterers feel that, ideally, substance abuse treatment should precede the therapy program or, if this is not possible, should occur concurrently (Bennett, 1995). Research shows that when alcoholic batterers received treatment both for their alcoholism and their abusive behavior, the men's spousal violence rate decreased significantly (O'Farrell & Choquette, 1991).

SERVICES FOR THE VICTIM

In a review of 12 studies on the types of community and professional services that abused women most frequently contact, police, social service agencies, clergy, crisis lines, physicians, psychotherapists, women's groups, and lawyers were the main sources of assistance. Abused women tended to contact different services, depending on the type of abuse they experienced. Some services were evaluated as helpful; others were not (Gordon, 1996).

Among the services used and professionals contacted by victims of abuse are shelters, counseling services, medical services, the criminal justice system, and clergy.

Shelters

Shelters have been established throughout the United States for domestic violence victims who need temporary protection from their abusive mates. Shelters for abused women were first begun in England in 1972 under the auspices of Chiswick Women's Aid. The first shelters in the United States appeared in Minnesota in 1973, in Boston the following year, and in Cleveland in 1976. Currently, there are over 2,000 shelters for abused women in the United States. Approximately two thirds of the 3,200 counties in the United States have established shelters or victim support services (Carden, 1994; National Coalition Against Domestic Violence, 1995). Yet in less densely populated and rural areas of the country there are relatively few shelters, whereas some metropolitan area shelters cannot meet the demand for their services.

Shelters and women's support groups have been rated by those who use them as the most helpful and effective means of coping with abuse (Gordon, 1996). However, these were not the most commonly contacted resources. This could be due to the limited availability of these services or the stigma that abused women in small communities feel about discussing with someone else the abuse they are experiencing.

Although shelters differ in the services they offer, their locations, and their size, they generally fit the following description. A woman who has been the victim of abuse may contact a shelter by phone or go directly there if she knows its location. In many instances, the location of the shelter is kept confidential within a community to ensure its serving as a "safe harbor" or refuge for the victims by preventing their perpetrators from contacting them. While residing at a shelter, the victim may contact her partner by phone or see him away from the shelter, thus maintaining the confidentiality of the shelter's location. An intake worker generally meets the prospective resident and secures basic information about her and her children. The mother and her children may stay together in a single room to keep the family intact, or older children may be housed together in a dormitory arrangement. Some shelters have rules about not accommodating boys over 12 years of age.

Shelter residents generally are expected to care for themselves and their children. Food and cleaning supplies are provided by the shelter; however, each family is expected to do its own cooking and cleaning or to actively participate in group activities for meeting these tasks. Children are expected to continue in school and may be enrolled in a school district in which the shelter is located or may continue to attend their regular school, if transportation is available.

Various supportive services may be available in the shelter or through allied agencies. For example, a child care counselor at the shelter may help the mother with child care problems. A parent group may provide the mother support and guidance in her task of being a single parent while she is in the shelter and if she decides to separate from her abuser. An in-house counselor may also work with the mother, helping her examine the alternatives available to her at this time of crisis in her life. There may be support groups that a mother can attend during this critical period. In these groups, mothers can share their common experiences and learn from one another. Counselors and legal advocates may also be available in the shelter to assist the victim with a variety of problems, such as her relationship to her abusive partner and securing food stamps, housing, and employment if she decides to leave the abusive situation.

The length of stay in shelters may vary, although generally the maximum is 30 days. There may be limitations, due to shortage of space, on how often a mother and her children can use a 30-day period of refuge.

Follow-up with residents once they leave the shelter varies with different agencies that sponsor shelters. For example, an agency may remain in contact with a former resident to assist her in implementing plans to separate from her partner. A former resident may return to the shelter or agency to continue to participate in support or counseling groups.

Research documents the positive effects that shelters have on women who use them. Residency in a shelter for a group of 21 women for an average stay of approximately 10 days was found to have a significant positive effect on the women. Their belief in control by powerful others such as their abusive mates decreased, and they reported less depressive symptomatology and higher self-esteem as the length of their stay increased, thus improving their sense of personal worth

(Campbell, Sullivan, & Davidson, 1995; Orava, McLeod, & Sharpe, 1996).

A critical decision facing a woman and her children who seek the protection of a shelter is whether or not to return to the abusive mate. In a sample of 6,612 women who entered 51 Texas shelters during an 18-month period, several factors were found to be critical to a woman's decision to return to her husband (Gondolf, 1988). One significant factor was whether or not her husband was in counseling. If he was seeking counseling, she was more likely to return to him. Her economic independence, which was defined as having transportation, child care, and an income of her own, also were factors that made her more likely not to return to her abusive mate.

Similarly, in a study of 563 women who sought refuge in a shelter, researchers found that women who had some degree of financial independence apart from their husband's income, had children who were at least ambulatory, and women who had a social support system outside the family, such as friends and peers at the workplace, were more likely to leave the battering relationship than to stay in it (Wilson, Raglioni, & Downing, 1989).

Earlier in the chapter, the relationship of domestic abuse to child abuse was discussed. Child abuse is 15 times more likely to occur in families where partner abuse is present (Stacey & Shupe, 1983). Frequently, women seeking services from a shelter are reluctant to report that their children are being abused by the partner. Some fear that if this is known, their children may be removed from the home. For women who hope to return to their partners, reporting the child abuse may further alienate them from their partners, and/or they may experience reprisal from their partner for reporting the abuse. In some instances, the women themselves may be abusing the children and fear repercussions for this behavior. Although shelters were designed to meet the abused woman's needs, increasingly attention is being given to meeting the children's needs. These include working with children regarding their reactions to witnessing parental violence, the crisis of leaving their home and seeking shelter, and any parental abuse they may be experiencing (McKay, 1994).

Counseling and Other Services

Need for Services

Upon leaving the shelter, women who have been victims of abuse frequently are in need of various social services. Research indicates that often women return to the abuser following their stay in a shelter because the services they need to enable them to live independently and to parent their children are not available. In a study of 141 women who had resided for a period of time in a shelter, which was located in a medium-size, industrialized midwestern city, and were now leaving it, interviews conducted with these women regarding their immediate needs revealed that 62% needed legal assistance, over 50% needed jobs, further education, transportation, material goods, social support, health care, financial assistance, child care, and other resources for their children, and 39% needed housing. The women who planned on terminating their relationship with their partner indicated a need to work on obtaining transportation, legal assistance, financial assistance, social support and ways to further their education. Women of color were more likely than White women to identify needing health care, material goods, and resources for their children. Younger women tended to need child care, whereas for older women, it was a need for health care (Sullivan, Basta, Tan, & Davidson, 1992). The results of this research emphasize the importance of a wide range of social services that must be available to victims of domestic violence if they are to successfully be empowered to terminate the abusive relationship with their partner.

A similar study used an experimental longitudinal design to examine the impact of providing short-term advocacy services to those leaving battered women's shelters. In the study, women who received intensive, one-on-one services with trained paraprofessonal advocates for a period of 10 weeks were compared with a control group of women who received no services once they left the shelter. The women working with the advocates, who were university students trained to work in an advocacy role with the battered women, were more effective in obtaining desired resources. These included material goods and services, education, transportation, finances, legal assistance, health care, social support, employment, and dealing with issues surrounding their children (Sullivan, 1991).

Counseling Services

A model for counseling victims of partner abuse suggests that a structural approach to treatment be used involving the empowerment of abused women through recasting their perceptions, raising their consciousness, and increasing their access to opportunities and resources. Such treatment, when occurring in a group setting, provides the participants a support system (Wood & Middleman, 1992a).

The structural approach to treatment is based on the feminist perspective of partner abuse in that the abuse of women stems from the power differential between men and women in society. Thus, the plight of the battered woman is not viewed as a function of her psychological pathology but largely as a result of gender-based inequality. This approach views women as having tremendous ego strengths in that they have managed their personal lives, homes, and families despite being abused by their partner. Based on this view of the victim being powerless yet a strong individual, counseling focuses on empowering the victim by recasting perceptions of self as a person of worth having the ability to make choices for herself and her children.

A small group setting for the counseling enables a group member to realize that other women likewise have experienced abusive spousal behavior, that the abuse is not her fault, and that the group can provide her support and she can support other group members in the decisions that each is facing regarding the future. This support is provided even outside the group's formal meetings of the group. Thus the group becomes a "supportive family" for its members (Wood & Middleman, 1992a).

Another example of a counseling or treatment program for battered women that is used in individual and group settings is based on cognitive behavior therapy (Beck, 1976; Ellis & Harper, 1978; McMullin & Giles, 1981; Meichenbaum, 1977). Cognitive behavior therapy is based on the assumption there is a causal relationship between a person's thinking, feeling, and acting or behaving. A person's thoughts mediate between one's feelings and actions. Also, a basic principle in this approach to treatment is that all behaviors are learned. The following stages comprise the treatment process: engagement, assessment, goal identification, development of an action plan and treatment strategies, and evaluation (Webb, 1992).

In the *engagement phase,* a relationship is established between the counselor and battered woman. An important component here is the development of a safety plan, which may include removing all weapons from the home, identifying safe alternative places for the woman to live, and how to call the police or seek help if battering occurs.

The potential risk for the woman in leaving the partner is also appraised.

In the *assessment phase,* the battered woman's current life circumstances and emotional state are appraised. Illogical beliefs about the victim's battering and her relationship to her partner are assessed as well as her early life experiences that may contribute to her present psychosocial functioning. Standardized testing for depression, anxiety, and irrational beliefs is done.

In the *goal identification phase,* goals for treatment are identified in measurable or behavioral terms based on questions posed to the victim such as "How would you like your life to be?" and "What changes would you like to make?" The message presented in this phase of the treatment process is that the battered woman deserves a better life, that her life can be different, and that she can take responsibility for creating change based on the goals she establishes.

A specific plan for behavioral change is developed in the *action phase,* and in the *evaluation phase,* progress in achieving the goals is evaluated. Homework assignments and ongoing assessment of progress are important elements of this final phase.

Cognitive behavior therapy with battered women makes use of four techniques: modeling, thought stopping, reframing, and stress inoculation (Cormier & Cormier, 1985). Because battered women often grew up in homes in which violence was occurring and these behaviors are modeled by them in their adult lives, new behaviors are demonstrated that a woman can model. Thought stopping implies, as the words indicate, stopping worrisome thoughts a battered woman often struggles with on a daily basis related to her abusive partner. These thoughts might involve, for example, concern about her partner's mood when he returns home from work. Although the victim cannot control her husband's behavior, she is taught that worrying is a useless activity and that the safety plan she has developed in the early phase of treatment can help prevent further abuse. Through cognitive restructuring, she replaces distorted beliefs about herself and her situation with more logical and useful thoughts. This frequently helps enhance her self-esteem and gives her a sense of control over her life. Reframing involves viewing a situation from more than one perspective. Rather than engaging in self-blame over abusive incidents, the battered woman is encouraged to reframe this perspective, placing the responsibility on her husband for the abuse that occurred because of his need for power and control. Finally, she is taught problem-solving and relaxation techniques as effective ways to cope with stress (Webb, 1992).

Evaluation of Counseling Programs for Battered Women

The evaluation of counseling/support groups for victims of domestic violence reveal substantial benefits associated with group participation (Tutty, Bidgood, & Rothery, 1993). Significant improvements are noted in self-esteem, in feeling a sense of group belonging and support, and in the victims' locus of control. An important outcome of treatment programs for battered women is a change away from traditional attitudes toward marriage and the family that placed the woman in a subservient role to her mate. Group members also exhibit a reduction in stress and improvement in marital functioning. Participants who continue to live with their partners during treatment report significant decreases in both physical and emotional abuse. For women leaving their abusive mates, counseling focusing on grief resolution in which opportunities are provided to work through and mourn the loss of a significant relationship in their life and helping them adapt to the changing situation they are facing has been shown to be especially helpful (Mancoske, Standifer, & Cauley, 1994).

Ethnic, Racial, and Cultural Considerations

Counselors working with battered women must often take into account religious and cultural variables affecting the victim. For example, the position of Asian/Pacific women within their culture is strictly regulated by sex-role expectations of being subordinate to men. Strong psychological forces in the family reinforce that position. Women are expected stoically to carry out that role and when abused by a husband will take responsibility for what occurred. The perpetrator often reinforces his victim's sense of blame, causing her to feel shame for what happened. In treating African American victims of spousal violence, counselors face the need to re-educate women out of the victim role. At the community level, counselors must often advocate for job training and employment opportunities that will enable African American women to achieve financial independence apart from an abusive mate (Uzzell & Peebles-Wilkins, 1989). Therapists must be cognizant of the influence of various religious and cultural group values but simultaneously must assist women in valuing their dignity as human beings and as individuals apart from their marital relationship and the subordinate position in which their religion or culture may place them (Crites, 1991).

Medical Services

Research documents the discrepancy between the large number of women who appear at health care facilities with problems related to living in abusive relationships and the low rate of detection and intervention by the medical staff (Hilberman, 1980; McLeer, 1989; Stark, Flitcraft & Frazier, 1979). An estimated 20% to 35% of adult female patients seen in emergency rooms are victims of domestic violence (Goldberg & Tomlanovich, 1984; McLeer & Anwar, 1989; National Coalition Against Domestic Violence, 1995).

In a study of 52 cases of women seen in an urban emergency room with clear symptoms indicative of physical abuse, neither the nurses nor the doctors were willing or able to address the underlying source of the injury: abuse from a partner (Warshaw, 1989). Also, in a study of battered women in Michigan who needed emergency treatment, half of the women reported negative experiences in the hospital emergency room, such as feeling humiliated, being blamed for their abuse, having the abuse minimized, being given insufficient referrals for help, and not being identified as a battered woman (Campbell et al., 1994). Medical personnel demonstrated an awareness that the injuries could be associated with spousal violence; however, the diagnosis or disposition of the case rarely mentioned this. Nurses felt legally obligated to report some cases to the police, whereas doctors in most instances met only the patient's medical needs. The medical model that dominates the services provided by a hospital emergency room as well as the high-tech sterile environment appeared to keep nurses from acting on their compassion for the victim by referring her to local social service resources (Warshaw, 1989).

Because it was found that the majority of emergency rooms do not conduct adequate epidemiological surveillance of injuries resulting from interpersonal violence, training medical personnel to recognize symptoms of abuse in patients and how to proceed in helping these victims is important (Bell, Jenkins, Kpo, & Rhodes, 1994). Hospital emergency departments are training personnel in interviewing strategies to identify women whose injuries are the result of spousal violence and to appropriately refer them to community services (Snyder, 1994).

Some state medical societies are confronting the inability of physicians to diagnose and report spousal abuse by designing policies for reporting domestic violence, including the use of model protocols (Staff, 1994). In a study of 68 emergency departments in Massachusetts, only 18 (26%) reported having protocols in effect for dealing with victims of abuse who sought medical treatment in their emergency rooms. In January 1992, the Joint Commission on the Accreditation of Healthcare Organizations began to require hospitals to have protocols and education plans for victims of abuse, including partner abuse, in place in all emergency departments and hospital ambulatory care settings (Isaac & Sanchez, 1994).

Not only must emergency room medical personnel recognize symptoms of possible partner abuse, but private care physicians also must be alert to victims of abuse that they may see in their private practices, even though the victim might not acknowledge the source of her injuries. Family physicians have the unique opportunity to see women at various stages of their lives as well as at times when they bring their children to the physician's office for medical care. Family physicians can be alert to signs of abuse and refer patients to appropriate resources for help (Sas, Brown, & Lent, 1994). Physical indicators of possible abuse include unexplained bruises and welts on the face, lips, mouth, back, and buttocks; unexplained fractures to the skull, nose, or facial structure; injury to body areas covered by clothing, and explanations for injuries that do not fit. Psychological indicators include emotional constriction, apprehension, fearfulness, depression, and eating disturbances (Veltkamp & Miller, 1990).

Nurses' attitudes toward domestic violence are influential in the way abused women perceive their helpfulness. In studies of nursing students' attitudes toward victims of domestic violence, researchers found that a strong positive relationship existed between the students' attitudes of equality between genders and their sympathy for battered women. As the level of students' gender equality attitudes increased, their sympathy toward victims of domestic violence also increased (Coleman & Stith, 1997; Finn, 1986; Gentemann, 1984; Stith, 1990).

Nurses working in obstetrician's offices frequently encounter pregnant patients who show evidence of being physically or sexually abused by their mates. Research indicates a 17% prevalence rate of physical or sexual abuse in pregnancy when several screening questions were used with patients showing evidence of having been abused (McFarlane, Parker, Soeken, & Bullock, 1992).

Dentists are encouraged when working with women to be aware of symptoms of spousal abuse. These include lacerated, swollen faces and lips; fractured, displaced, forcibly torn away teeth; and temporomandibular joint syndrome. These symptoms may be indicative of the victim having been slapped or struck in the jaw and facial area (Stack, 1993).

Even pharmacists are advised to be alert to the symptoms of domestic abuse and to encourage the victim to seek appropriate help (Taylor, 1994). Pharmacists often work in a consultative relationship to individuals and may see women who seek medicinal advice for bruises and wounds resulting from spousal violence.

Educating medical personnel and allied health professionals to recognize and deal with spousal violence is an important step in combating this societal problem. Medical personnel are encouraged to do the following in order to empower women in a violent society (Archer, 1994):

- Stop the denial. Understand that many women are victims of domestic abuse and often present disguised symptoms.
- Respect the victim. Medical personnel's failure to respect the victim merely revictimizes her. Assure the patient of a readiness to discuss the abuse and to assist her in seeking help with the problem.
- Do not blame the victim. Under no circumstances is abuse ever acceptable.
- Seek to empower female patients. Help women take responsibility for their health and social lives.
- Be familiar with services in the community for abused women. Have available pamphlets and brochures for victims in waiting areas, examination rooms, and pharmacies.

The Criminal Justice System

The Police

Police intervention in spousal assault cases is dangerous and threatening to the lives of the police officers involved (International Association of Chiefs of Police, 1976). Straus et al. (1980), in their national study of violence in American families, reported that more police officers die answering domestic violence calls than any other single type of call. Although subsequent analyses of statistical data on the number of police deaths as well as ranking the danger that domestic assault calls pose to police officers in relation to other offenses do not support these high rates, many police officers agree that intervention in these situations often presents high risks to them. Thus, training police officers to intervene effectively in domestic violence situations is very important (Garner & Clemmer, 1986).

The assumption often is made that police are the first who are called to a home where domestic violence is occurring. Studies report, however, that battered women often do not call the police (Dobash & Dobash, 1979; Roy, 1982; Schechter, 1982). Various reasons are suggested: Battered women may first turn to family, neighbors, and friends; often they do not think the police will help them; victims fear reprisal from their perpetrators if the police become involved; victims fear social disgrace if police are involved; and victims are concerned for their children, who must witness the possible arrest of their father.

The use of police services by battered women was studied in a sample of 300 victims of domestic abuse who had sought refuge over a 10-year period in a shelter for battered women in Orlando, Florida. The results indicated that several factors related to the number of times these women called the police. The victims' education and duration of the violence were found to be significantly related to their use of the police, for 62% of the victims who had contacted the police had at least a high school education as compared to 38% who had not completed high school and did not report their abuse to the police. Also, the length of time the women had been abused was an influencing factor in their contacting the police. The data revealed that 62% of the women who had experienced physical abuse for more than 1 year contacted the police for help as compared to 37% who had been abused for less than 1 year. The data suggest that cooperative strategies be devised between the police and social service agencies working with partner abuse to encourage early intervention rather than waiting until the violence has worsened. If individuals at risk for domestic abuse (both victims and abusers) can be identified by the police, outreach can occur for education and follow-up by social service agencies that work with domestic violence (Abel & Suh, 1987).

The arrest of the abused victim by police officers is a growing concern, especially in communities where a mandatory arrest policy regarding offenders is in place. Police officers will also routinely arrest the victim on charges of disorderly conduct, especially if she argues with the officer. Many duel arrests are made because police do not want to take responsibility for identifying the party at fault in the dispute. Dual arrests frequently end in no prosecution because the victim is also a defendant in the case and prosecutors often choose to "call it a draw" and not prosecute either party (Martin, 1997).

In a study of 111 police officers who viewed vignette depictions of domestic violence, it was predicted that those officers with an inclination to arrest victims would exhibit more negative stereotypical attitudes toward abused victims as well as toward women in general. The results showed that those officers with a tendency to arrest victims in the vignettes they saw believed that domestic violence was justified in some situations, and they held stereotypical views about why women remain in abusive relationships. The others who responded in this way had not been exposed to domestic violence situations directly but were aware of this type of problem through fellow officers. These stereotypical attitudes about abuse victims and women in general may be passed through police officer ranks. This documents the importance of mental health professionals educating police about domestic abuse and how to respond properly to these situations. Such education should not merely be didactic but include role-playing, because officers participating in the research expressed discomfort about how to talk with victims of domestic violence (Saunders, 1995).

The manner in which police respond to domestic violence calls can significantly influence the outcome of the victim's cry for help as well as future incidents of violence to which the victim may be subjected. The way in which police assign responsibility for the abuse—namely, blame the husband or the wife, based on various factors such as the use of alcohol, the socioeconomic status of the abuser and the victim, alleged antagonism on the part of the wife, and the type of abuse (verbal threat, physical assault)—are important factors relative to the disposition of the case (Corenblum, 1983; Kalmus, 1979; Renzetti, 1992; Waaland & Keeley, 1985). When police project the blame for marital violence on the wife and this is perceived by the victim, there is a reluctance on her part to report further abuse to the police (Cannings, 1984). In a study of 270 abused women who contacted police for help, the women evaluated police intervention as not the most helpful and in some instances not helpful at all. This finding, however, may in part reflect the fact that at the time the data were collected some police departments had not initiated a training program for officers in dealing with domestic violence situations.

The increase in the number of women on police forces has proved helpful in domestic violence interventions. In some communities, special units are trained to intervene effectively in these situations, and especially to be aware of and sensitive to the needs of the victim. Female victims of spousal violence generally rate contact with policewomen as more favorable than contact with policemen even when the female officers do not take sides with the individuals in the domestic dispute (Yegidis & Renzy, 1994).

The Courts

Although in the past domestic violence was regarded as a private family matter rather than a crime, during the past decade a more aggressive stance has been taken in the investigation and adjudication of these cases. The nature of the abusive or violent act rather than the relationship of the individuals involved has become the focal issue, as affirmed in the 1984 report of the Attorney General's Task Force on Family Violence (1984). Ordinances passed at county and state levels throughout the country make it possible for police officers to arrest an abuser when there is evidence rather than depending on the victim to file charges against the perpetrator. This procedure is similar to the handling of nondomestic types of assaults and the processing of other crimes. When victims of domestic violence are required to file charges against the perpetrator following the assault and calling the police, frequently they do not do so but acquiesce to the cajoling and penitential maneuvers of the abuser, as reflected in the loving and contrite phase of the cycle of violence described earlier (Walker, 1979).

Pro-arrest policies are being established in police departments throughout the nation. Increasingly, states too are enacting legislation mandating arrest in spousal assault cases, including probable cause or warrantless arrest. Thus, the criminal justice system now regards domestic violence as a crime, similar to other crimes, and the responsibility for taking legal action against the perpetrator rests with the courts rather than the victim (Goolkasian, 1986).

Arrest of the perpetrator became a preferred policy for intervening in domestic violence situations following an experiment in Minneapolis in which arrest was shown to be the more effective method in deterring subsequent spousal abuse as compared to separating the couple by ordering the offender to leave for 8 hours (Sherman & Berk, 1984.) Later studies, however, pointed out methodological flaws in this study (Binder & Meeker, 1988; Dunford, Huizinga, & Elliot, 1990; Lempert, 1989). Research does not support the arrest of the perpetrator as a significant factor in reducing recidivism rates of offenders. For example, an experiment was conducted to test the relative effectiveness of three police responses to domestic abuse: advising and possibly separating the couple; issuing a citation to the offender; and arresting the offender. Cases that met the eligibility criteria were randomly assigned to one of the three responses and then tracked for at least 6 months to determine if recidivism occurred. Arrest was no more effective than the other two treatments at deterring subsequent abuse (Hirschel, Hutchison, & Dean, 1992). Several reasons are cited for these results: The offenders had previous arrests for other offenses and thus arrest was not a significant deterrent; the victims in the research had a history of chronic abuse and thus arrest may have had little impact on these relationships; and due to overcrowding in jails, the amount of time spent in jail was minimal. In many instances, a subsequent jail term was not determined for the offender following a court hearing; rather, community-based punishments and early releases from correctional institutions were used.

The dynamics of spousal violence are so complex and intertwined with historical, religious, psychological, political, and social forces that it may be unreasonable to expect any short-term action such as arrest to have a significant deterrent effect on spousal violence. However, other studies indicate that arrest had no significant impact on recidivism but did appear to decrease violence among employed men and increase it among those unemployed (Berk, Campbell, Klap, & Western, 1992; Pate & Hamilton, 1992). When the courts send a very clear message that domestic violence of any type is a crime, victims are less likely to ignore their abuse and more likely to report their assaults.

The Prosecutor

Emotional support from the prosecutor is important if the victim must confront her abuser publicly in court. Frequently, victims must reveal intimate details of their marital life to attorneys working in the prosecutorial role. Thus, advocacy and support for the victim and the establishment of special domestic violence units within the court system are factors in the successful prosecution of domestic violence cases. Victim advocates are used in some communities to provide support to the victim during the prosecution ordeal to ensure that she has adequate protection if threats are directed against her by the perpetrator, especially when the accused is released on his own recognizance prior to trial. The prosecuting attorney also can serve in a referral role to community social and legal services the victim may need. Although attendance in treatment programs for batterers is used as a diversion from trial in some communities, this practice may give the impression that partner abuse is not a crime and provide the alleged perpetrator an avenue of escape from dealing with the consequences of his behavior (National Coalition Against Domestic Violence, 1995).

The Judge

The judge hearing cases of domestic violence plays a critical role in their effective disposition. Critical issues about which judges should be informed to work effectively with these cases include knowledge about the causes of domestic violence, society's stereotypical views of this social problem, gender biases that can occur in working with perpetrators and victims, and the effects of spousal violence on the victim and other family members.

It is important that judges operate from the premise that offenders are responsible for their behavior and that society will not tolerate violent behavior toward domestic partners, as may have been sanctioned in the past. Judges also can assist in creating changes in community laws as advocates for legislation that provides victims adequate protection and proper adjudication of domestic violence cases.

Clergy

Clergy are often the first persons to whom victims, especially religious women, turn for help (Horton, Wilkins, & Wright, 1988). In a survey of clergy's perceptions and responses to domestic abuse, research data revealed that over 50% had counseled one or more female victims of spousal abuse (Martin, 1989). Religion, however, can be a "double-edged sword," for historically it has justified the subordination of women and has labeled divorce a sin.

Research evaluating victims' reactions to discussing their abuse with clergy does not always report favorable results. In a survey of 187 victims of abuse, 101 saw a minister, priest, or rabbi. Of these, 30 reported their contact as very satisfactory or satisfactory, 29 reported a dissatisfactory contact, and 42 reported a very unsatisfactory experience (Horton et al., 1988). Those indicating dissatisfied reactions reported some of the advice they were given by clergy: "Stay and work things out; God expects that," "Forgive and forget," and "Try harder not to provoke him" (Martin, 1989, p. 242). Several other studies report abused women rating the advice and counseling received from clergy as ineffective and not helpful (Bowker, 1988; Frieze, Knoble, Washburn, & Zomnir, 1980; Pagelow, 1981).

Clergy often lack awareness of and knowledge about spouse abuse and how to help the victims (Horton, 1988). The studies indicating that abused women did not feel clergy were helpful to them emphasize the importance of community spouse abuse agencies working with clergy to educate them about the nature of spouse abuse, resources available for victims, and how they can be most helpful when working with vic-

Helpful Responses

- Listened respectfully and took me seriously
- Believed my story
- Asked me directly if I was being physically hurt
- Helped me see my strengths
- Helped me see how I'd been losing self-confidence
- Helped me plan for change
- Helped me understand the effects on the children
- Directed me to someone who did help me
- Helped me to see ways to end the abuse in the future

Nonhelpful Responses

- Gave me advice I did not wish to follow
- Criticized me for staying with my partner
- Did not tell me of any other agency or professional service that could help me
- Did not listen carefully
- Suggested that my partner and I get counseling together even though he was physically abusing me
- Agreed with me when I said it wasn't that serious
- Questioned the truth of my story
- Suggested that I must have wanted the abuse
- Blamed me for what happened
- Denied the impact the abuse had on my life

Figure 3.7 Responses of Professionals That Abused Women Perceived as Helpful and Nonhelpful
SOURCE: Hamilton and Coates (1993).

tims (Martin, 1989). Increasingly, seminaries where clergy are trained are including in pastoral care courses information on how to deal with domestic violence.

Helpful and Nonhelpful Responses of Those Working With Victims of Abuse

As indicated earlier, abused women seek help from a variety of professional and community services. A sample of 270 abused women who used a variety of professional and community services evaluated the response of these agencies in terms of helpful and nonhelpful. Figure 3.7 lists the responses that this sample of abused women perceived as helpful and not helpful from the professionals and agencies they contacted for help (Hamilton & Coates, 1993).

PREVENTING PARTNER ABUSE

Although partner abuse is primarily a problem occurring between two persons, it also involves the community, which must treat the victims and perpetrators and societal institutions that sanction the subordination and powerlessness of women. Prevention of partner abuse must occur at each of these levels: personal, community, and societal.

Personal Level

Violence is not a means of problem solving, although perpetrators often resort to violence when coping with marital problems. Men must assume responsibility for their behavior, including aggressive behavior, even though society overtly and covertly supports problem resolution through the use of violence. Commonly held myths about the role of men in marital relationships are frequently used by males to excuse their aggressive behavior toward their partners—for example, a man's home is his castle and therefore he must be in control; and a wife is expected to submit to her husband's sexual demands. Education for preventing spousal violence must expose these rationalizations for violence for what they are: statements based on tradition and for the convenience of males and the suppression of females. Their eradication requires that men involve women as equal partners in relationships, including the sexual component. Changes at the personal level in male behavior will occur only as societal institutions, such as the courts and state and national legislative bodies, hold men responsible for their behavior and work toward the empowerment of all individuals regardless of gender.

Community Level

Preventive measures at the community level again involve education, which can occur in schools, clubs, and similar organizations where equality between the sexes and problem-solving skills in resolving interpersonal disagreements can be taught.

Prevention in the broadest sense of the term includes the provision of resources to help victims cope with ongoing spousal violence, lest the effects of the abuse increasingly impact on their psychosocial functioning. This includes enabling victims to effectively live independently from an abusive partner, to help children experiencing problems from witnessing parental violence, and to provide treatment resources for males who have engaged in violent spousal behavior. This requires the financial support through private and public funds at the community, state, and national levels for social service and community mental health agencies that provide these services to victims and perpetrators. Funds also must be appropriated for educating personnel working with victims and perpetrators (police, medical and allied health personnel, criminal justice system personnel, and clergy) to intervene in and prevent this social problem.

Prevention at the community level is important because partner abuse is costly to the community, as indicated earlier, in terms of victims' absenteeism from work, medical services provided by emergency rooms, and the social and psychological repercussions felt by victims and their families for which counseling and other supportive services must be provided through community social service and mental health agencies.

Societal Level

Although partner abuse is perceived as a personal problem and its impact is most severely felt by individual survivors and their families, in reality it is a societal problem. Social problems occur when the institutions that society creates to carry out its basic functions do not exist, operate ineffectively, or oppress and exploit its least powerful members.

Partner abuse reflects the failure of society to achieve its primary function: to provide opportunities for growth, development, life enhancement, and protection of all its members. Partner abuse reflects its failure to fulfill its function based on the gender of the societal member. The feminist perspective of partner abuse emphasizes the disparity of social, political, and economic power that exists between the sexes resulting from long and deep-seated social traditions.

A societal approach to preventing partner abuse calls for a correction of societal institutions and the mechanisms for carrying out basic societal functions that fail to provide equal treatment to all members of society regardless of gender. Any breakdown in society's meeting its basic function to all members, regardless of gender, requires the development and implementation of strategies for creating sociopolitical change, which is a responsibility and task of all societal members.

SUMMARY

Partner abuse can be understood from various perspectives. Feminist theory provides a theoretical perspective for understanding this social problem because the issues of power and control are central factors in partner abuse. Just as an imbalance in power occurs between the genders in society in general, so too this imbalance can be seen in the marital relationship. Abusive males ascribe to the assumption that they must be in control of their mates. When men fear they are losing their control, they often resort to physical and emotional abuse of their partners. Marital rape is seen as the epitome of this imbalance of power in that society has expected women to meet the sexual needs of men without regard to their own wishes and desires.

Although initially literature on partner abuse suggested that women stay with their abusive mates because of their psychological needs, more recent theoretical models suggest that women are often locked into remaining with an abusive mate because viable alternatives, especially relative to continued financial support of the victim and her children, are not available. Shelters in communities throughout the country provide women an opportunity to leave their abusive mates and to consider alternatives to their current situation.

Group treatment approaches for batterers generally focus on reeducating males in more effective ways of relating to their marital partners. Just as violence is a learned behavior, so too alternative nonviolent ways of coping with stress and solving problems must be learned. The provision of substance abuse treatment programs is also an important component of interventions with perpetrators, for research shows that abuse of drugs or alcohol is a significant contributing factor to partner abuse.

The prevention of partner abuse must occur at the personal, community, and societal levels. Underlying preventive efforts must be the eradication of myths supporting the dominance of men over women and using violence as a method of interpersonal problem solving.

SUGGESTED READING

Journals

Journal of Family Violence

Journal of Interpersonal Violence

Violence and Victims

Books

Bergen, R. (1996). *Wife rape: Understanding the response of survivors and service providers.* Thousand Oaks, CA: Sage.

Edleson, J., & Eisikovits, Z. (Eds.). (1996). *Future interventions with battered women and their families.* Thousand Oaks, CA: Sage.

Renzetti, C. (1992). *Violent betrayal: Partner abuse in lesbian relationship.* Newbury Park, CA: Sage.

Renzetti, C., & Miley, C. (Eds.). (1996). *Violence in gay and lesbian domestic partnerships.* New York: Haworth.

Sipe, B., & Hall, E. (1996). *I am not your victim: Anatomy of domestic violence.* Thousand Oaks, CA: Sage.

Walker, L. (1979). *The battered women.* New York: Harper & Row.

Walker, L. (1994). *Abused women and survivor therapy: A practical guide for the psychotherapist.* Washington, DC: American Psychological Association.

4

Elder Abuse

Mr. G is an 85-year-old childless widower who for 44 years was a successful salesman for a major drug firm. He has been retired for 25 years, owns his own home, has a comfortable pension, and at one time had considerable savings and investments. His large home is badly in need of repairs, the result of a lack of attention over the past 15 years due to Mr. G's failing health. The home is located in an area once considered a good neighborhood and now known for drug dealing and prostitution.

Approximately 6 years ago, a thoughtful neighbor who would look after Mr. G and do his shopping arranged for him to receive meals-on-wheels and an occasional visit from a home health aide after Mr. G developed diabetes and a heart condition that kept him homebound. The neighbor also placed an ad in the newspaper for someone to live with Mr. G and care for him, since his health was failing rapidly. A 32 year-old-woman was hired. Shortly thereafter, the neighbor moved to another part of the country because of a job transfer and lost contact with Mr. G.

During a recent visit by the home health aide, the nurse became suspicious that Mr. G's caretaker was abusing drugs. Further investigation by a social worker on the home health agency's staff revealed that the woman not only was abusing drugs and alcohol but had depleted Mr. G's savings to buy drugs and to pay off a debt of over $80,000 she had incurred

The case was reported to adult protective services.

* * *

Mr. and Mrs. Y are the parents of three teenage boys and a daughter who is living away from home at college. They live on a large farm that originally had belonged to Mr. Y's parents but that they received at the time of his father's death 5 years ago. Approximately 8 years before the father's death, Mr. Y's parents moved out of the large farmhouse into a new mobile home located on the farm. When Mr. Y's father died, his elderly mother, age 76, continued to live in the mobile home. Recently, however, Mrs. Y's mother was diagnosed as having Alzheimer's disease. At this time, the couple moved Mr. Y's mother from the mobile home into a vacant bedroom in the large farmhouse.

Moving his mother into the family home was done reluctantly because Mrs. Y and her mother-in-law never got along well. The mother-in-law was critical of her and the way she raised her children, although Mrs. Y seemed to be a good mother and had a successful marriage.

Approximately 8 months later, Mrs. Y was hospitalized for depression. She revealed to a psychologist that the burden of caring for her mother-in-law had become too great for her. Mr. Y's mother had become incontinent over the past several months, was no longer able to dress and feed herself, and would often get up during the night and wander about the house. One evening they found her in the yard in her nightgown saying she was leaving to go to church. Interviews with Mr. Y revealed that his wife's response to his mother's problems initially was that of anger. She would call his mother names and was physically and emotionally abusive to her, especially when she had become incontinent. More recently, when Mr. Y criticized his wife for her abusive behavior, she became withdrawn and depressed. He stated that his wife often verbalized that she resented having to care for her mother-in-law in light of how the latter had treated her. Mr. Y admitted that the burden of his mother's care had really fallen entirely on his wife because he was very involved in farming.

Arrangements were made by a social worker to place Mr. Y's mother in a nursing home in a nearby town.

* * *

Mr. B, age 82, lives in a high-rise condominium in a large eastern city. The condominium is beautifully furnished with antiques and oriental rugs that he and his late wife collected over the years on trips they took throughout the world. Mr. B has one son, age 56, who is an executive working in England. He sees his father approximately once a year when he travels to the United States.

Since his wife's death 4 years ago, Mr. B has largely remained to himself, venturing out of his home only to buy groceries. During the past year he has had the few groceries he needed delivered to his home, which he receives at the door, not allowing the delivery person to enter his apartment. Recently, when making a delivery to another resident in the building, the delivery person realized that he had not made any deliveries to Mr. B. for several months. He inquired about Mr. B from the doorman, who realized that he also had not seen Mr. B for a while but gave little thought to the matter, figuring that perhaps Mr. B had exited and entered the building when he was not on duty.

Several weeks later when the building's mail clerk became aware that Mr. B's mail had not been picked up for over a month, she took the mail to his apartment. Mr. B opened the door slightly to receive the mail. He was barefoot, wearing only a bathrobe. His hair was matted and his fingernails and toenails were overgrown to the point of curling under his fingers and toes. The apartment reeked of urine and feces.

The mail clerk reported this to the building superintendent who phoned Mr. B's son in England, who in turn phoned the family attorney whose offices were in the city where Mr. B lived. The attorney contacted Mr. B and later reported to the son that it appeared his father was no longer able to live alone. Mr. B's son immediately returned to the United States to arrange alternative care for his elderly father.

During the past several decades, the life expectancy of individuals has increased, resulting in many elderly persons living for a longer period of time. With the increase in the number of years people are living, health and related problems are being experienced by many of these senior citizens. Even a new category of elderly persons has developed, labeled *frail elderly,* or individuals of advanced age who have serious physical and mental problems. The increase in health and related problems that elderly persons, especially frail elderly, experience requires someone to care for them. Smaller nuclear families have resulted in a decrease in the number of family members who can serve as a helping network when an elderly family member is in need of care and support (Griffin & Williams, 1992). Also, the dispersion of nuclear family members due in some instances to having to leave the family community to find employment has resulted in the inaccessibility of family members who can provide supportive services to an elderly parent or relative.

The elderly are being encouraged to remain in their own homes rather than resorting to institutionalization. Elderly persons can effectively live in their own homes, if support services are available and used. Family care of the elderly in the homes of family members, such as adult children, also provides a way of preventing the institutionalization of the elderly.

A dark side of this picture exists however, the abuse of older persons by family members and others who serve in a caretaking role. Researchers have traced the historical development of an awareness of family violence in terms of the 1960s being the decade of sensitivity to child abuse, the 1970s to spouse abuse, and the 1980s to elder abuse (Kosberg, 1988). One of the first references to elder abuse appeared in 1975 in a letter to the editor of the *British Medical Journal* under the title "Granny Battering" (Burston, 1975). That same year, an article with the same title was published in the journal *Modern Geriatrics* documenting several cases where elderly women experienced physical damage from others (Baker, 1975).

Elder abuse became a public issue in the United States in 1978 with testimony given to a congressional subcommittee on the abuse of elderly parents (Wolf, 1988). In 1988, the National Aging Resource Center on Elder Abuse (NARCEA) conducted several national surveys that revealed problems across states relative to the reporting of elder abuse. Although authorized in 1987 but not funded until 1990, the Elder Abuse Prevention Program was established under the Older Americans Act, enacted in 1975. Approximately $2.9 million was appropriated to be divided among 600 area agencies on aging (Goldstein, 1995). During the subsequent decades, greater awareness of this social problem has developed, the result being that today public and private agencies as well as the general public are increasingly recognizing and intervening in the abuse of elderly citizens. Adult protective service divisions have been established in public social service agencies for the purpose of investigating and intervening in cases of elder abuse. Services such as meals on wheels, day care for the elderly, and home health services have been developed to enhance the elderly's quality of life.

DEFINITION OF TERMS

Although the tendency may exist to define elder abuse only in terms of physical maltreatment, elder abuse must be conceptualized more broadly. A consensus does not exist on the exact forms of abuse comprising the generic term *elder abuse* because different writers conceptualize the various forms differently (Valentine & Cash, 1986). Also, although there is some agreement regarding the major categories of elder abuse (physical, sexual, psychological), there is considerable variation in the classification of situations that might be labeled as abuse and their manifestations as seen in the variability that exists in state protective service laws regarding the elderly (American Public Welfare Association, 1988; Wolf, 1992).

Elder abuse is defined in this chapter as physical, sexual, emotional or psychological, and financial abuse. Three types of neglect are also identified.

Physical Abuse

Physical abuse of the elderly implies hitting, slapping, punching, pushing, shaking, biting, pulling hair, force-feeding, and other willful acts that may result in bruises, lacerations, fractures, or any other types of physical injury. Physical abuse in elderly marital partners, shown often to be a continuation of abuse that has occurred throughout the marital relationship or more recently occurring because of physical or mental illness, may be conceptualized also as partner abuse, discussed in Chapter 3 (Harris, 1996). In nursing homes, the improper use of restraints can constitute physical abuse, such as tying a patient or a patient's limbs to a bed or chair. The excessive drugging of an elderly person, sometimes defined separately as medical abuse, is included in the definition of elder physical abuse (Brewer, 1992).

Sexual Abuse

Although sexual abuse is not as prevalent with the elderly as it is with children, it does occur. Sexual abuse of the elderly is defined as engaging in sexual acts with an elderly person by means of force, threat of force, or without consent, including forcing an elderly person to perform sexual acts on the perpetrator (Ramsey-Klawsnik, 1995). In some instances, elderly persons may be incapable of providing consent and their unknowing involvement in sexual behavior constitutes sexual abuse. Interviewing an elderly person to assess if possible sexual abuse has occurred requires special interviewing skills because of the victim's fear of retaliation from the perpetrator, embarrassment, and concern about in some way being blamed for the abuse.

A basic component of elder sexual abuse is that the victim does not consent to the sexual activity but is forced, entrapped, tricked, threatened, or in some way coerced to participate. Sexual abuse of elders often escalates with time to more severe types of abuse. A continuum of elder sexual abuse has been developed based on victims' descriptions of the activities they typically experienced when being sexually abused. The sexual activities range from least to most severe in terms of the degree of violence and trauma to the victim. At one end of the continuum are covert forms of sexual abuse in the form of the perpetrator sexualizing the relationship with the victim by expressing interest in the victim's body, by making sexually oriented jokes or comments, or by discussing sexual activity. A pretouching phase may follow in which there is voyeurism, exhibitionism, or forcing the victim to watch pornography. At the severe end of the continuum are overt forms of elder sexual abuse including sexualized kissing and fondling, oral-genital contact, object or digital penetration of the vagina or anus, or vaginal or anal rape (Ramsey-Klawsnik, 1991).

In a review of 28 cases of suspected elder sexual abuse, several factors were noted. All the victims were female, and 71% were experiencing significant limitations in their capacity for independent functioning and self-protection. In 81% of the incidents, the perpetrators were the victims' male caregivers, with 78% of these being family members, predominantly sons and husbands. The largest category (39%) of family members were sons of the victim. Repeated vaginal rape was the most prevalent type of reported sexual assault (Ramsey-Klawsnik, 1991). Similarly, in a study of 90 cases of suspected elder sexual abuse in England, 77 of the victims were women, 85% of the women were over 75 years of age, and the majority also were widowed (Holt, 1993). The most frequently reported impediments for the victims of sexual abuse were dementia (77%), physical frailty (67%), and impaired mobility (48%).

Emotional Abuse

Emotional or psychological abuse includes name-calling; derogatory comments; the use of insults, harassment, and threats; and speaking to elderly persons in an infantilizing manner. Threats may include threatening to place an elderly person in a nursing home if the victim does not comply with the perpetrator's demands. Withholding affection, failing to provide a sense of security, and the caregiver refusing to allow an elderly person access to family members and friends may also be considered emotional abuse.

Emotional abuse includes infantilizing elderly persons by giving them dolls to care for or using "baby talk" when addressing them. Research shows that the baby-talk style of speech and intonation, although frequently used by personnel working with the elderly as a way of coveying nurturing and caring, were rated by samples of university students and older adults as conveying less respect to the elderly. The caregivers speaking in this manner were judged less competent than caregivers who spoke in a normal tone of voice. The recipients of baby talk were perceived to be less satisfied with the interaction (Ryan, Hamilton, & See, 1995; Whitbourne, Culgin, & Cassidy, 1995). The following two brief conversations contrast relating to an elderly person using baby talk and using a normal style of talking:

Baby Talk

Staff: Betsy, why aren't you getting ready for your bath? You know, sweetie, that tonight is bath night.

Resident: I just don't feel like taking a bath tonight. I've had a headache all day.

Staff: Come on now and be a good little girl. Let me give you a bath like you're supposed to get. OK, dearie?

Normal Style

Staff: Mrs. Wright, tonight is bath night. Can I help you get ready for your bath?

Resident: I just don't feel like taking a bath tonight. I've had a headache all day.

Staff: Would you rather I have the nurse talk to you about your headache and perhaps give you some medication for it? Later I can give you a bath after I finish with some of the other patients. What would you like?

Likewise, caregivers may treat an elderly person as a small child and covertly encourage residents to behave in an obedient, childlike manner by patting the person on the head or by scolding an individual for not controlling urinary or bowel functions. Emotional abuse may also include violating the rights of the elderly. An example of the latter would be the forced institutionalization of an elderly person against his or her wishes.

The various forms in which emotional abuse occurs were studied in a sample of 58 elderly persons ranging in age from 68 to 87 who were being treated for abuse (Peretti & Majecen, 1991). The most frequent forms of emotional abuse were lack of attention, lack of affection, neglect, derogatory name-calling, demeaning comments, exploitation, threats of violence, loud talking, and confinement. Those participating in the study indicated that the lack of attention and affection (failure to be kissed, hugged, or other tactile stimulation) made them feel isolated and alone in a world of others. Derogatory name-calling and comments were debasing and demeaning to the victims and implied a loss of position, worth, value, or dignity. Although some elderly tended to deny the reality of these types of remarks, they felt shame and emotional distress that they tried to keep hidden. The participants in the study also felt they often were financially taken advantage of by their caregivers and other relatives through the latter's use of their financial assets.

Financial Abuse

Because the misappropriation of elders' finances is such a common problem, financial abuse has been identified as a separate form of elder abuse. Financial abuse is defined as "the taking or misappropriation of an older person's property, possessions, or financial assets" (Wilber & Reynolds, 1996, p. 64). This may be the most permanently devastating type of elder abuse because it affects an elderly person's financial status, which in turn can affect the person's future living arrangements and level of care (Blunt, 1993). The perpetrator of financial abuse is generally a relative, friend, or caregiver in whom the elderly person has placed confidence for handling the elder's financial resources. For example, an elderly person may in good faith transfer funds to a family member, who uses the funds for personal gain rather than to meet the needs of the elderly person. Also, because an elderly person may not be able to cash checks or handle personal financial matters and therefore relies on a family member or friend to do so, the latter may deliberately deceive or cheat the elderly person.

Elderly bereaved widows are often targets for financial exploitation because of the confusion they experience in dealing with banks, creditors, brokers, and various financial institutions, especially if they have not had experience in financial management because their mates took care of these tasks (Blunt, 1993). Another form of financial exploitation involves elderly persons hoarding or squandering money, not cashing checks, and in general exhibiting confusion regarding financial management. These aspects of financial exploitation often are seen by adult protective service workers or home health aides who come into an elderly person's home and notice a disparity between the individual's income and their lifestyle (Yurkow, 1991).

The elderly are susceptible, often because of impaired cognitive functioning, to financial abuse by persons outside the family in the form of fraud (Ramsey-Klawsnik, 1995). Fraud involves the intentional deception of a person generally for the perpetrator's financial gain. Schemes to defraud the elderly include medical quackery, auto repair fraud, home improvement fraud, deceptive practices in prearranged funeral and burial plans, the fraudulent billing of services through Medicare and Medicaid, fraud related to pension plans, and excessive or duplicated insurance coverage. A recent scheme that many elderly persons have fallen victim to is the notification through official-appearing documents in the mail that they have received a large amount of money in a contest. When they call the 900 number to receive the prize, they are excessively billed for the call, are asked to deposit a large sum of money in order to receive the prize, or continue to be harassed by the promoters of the scheme to get them to comply with the deception. Financial exploitation of the elderly in nursing homes may occur when residents' personal spending allowances from Medicaid are retained by the nursing home for institutional or administrative purposes without the residents' consent.

Cultural Consideration in Assessing Financial Abuse

Mental health professionals should be sensitive to cultural considerations when screening for financial abuse in culturally diverse families (Sanchez, 1996). Figure 4.1 identifies the variables of living arrangements, financial status, systems of social support, emotional/psychological stress, and family dynamics and the way in which these variables are conceptualized in Eurocentric families as compared to the way they may be seen in minority families, especially in the screening of elder financial abuse (Sanchez, 1996, pp. 52, 56).

Discussing cultural differences that may impact on the way mental health professionals screen ethnic and minority families, Sanchez (1996) writes,

> Cultural differences in relation to living arrangements, financial status, family dynamics, systems of social support, and emotional/psychological stress should be considered when screening for financial exploitation in minority communities because there are some distinct realities in these communities. For example, Blacks have a higher incidence of extended family households than do Whites, but a lower incidence than among Hispanics. These statistics support the conviction that the significance of multi-generational households cannot be ignored. Twice as many African Americans as White elderly are in dire economic circumstances and Hispanic elderly continue to struggle with high rates of poverty that exceed poverty levels of White elderly. Native American elderly fare no better than African American elderly and His-

Indicator	*Eurocentric Families*	*Minority Families*
Living Arrangements	Property ownership; dual-headed households; monolithic or universal family structure; assumed heterogeneity	Multigenerational households; limited property ownership; female-headed households
Financial Status	Standard income levels; assets; independent resources; pensions; access to conventional resources	Cycle of poverty in minority communities/families; low levels of education; limited access to benefits (e.g., pensions, health care)
Social Support	Connected involvement in civic organizations; community service organizations; organized services	Value of reciprocal obligations; caregiving in an intergenerational context; extended family systems
Emotional/Psychological Stress	Limited trauma or turmoil; access to services to deal with stress/issues	Role of organized religion; barriers to access of formalized services; limited resources (financial) to access organized services
Family Dynamics	Nuclear in orientation; privatized	Impact of life of deprivation; immigration experiences; coerced acculturation

Figure 4.1 Common Screening Indicators of Financial Exploitation for Eurocentric and Minority Families
SOURCE: Adapted from "Distinguishing Cultural Expectations in Assessment of Financial Exploitation" by Y. Sanchez, 1996, in *Journal of Elder Abuse & Neglect,* Vol. 8, pp. 49-59. Copyright © 1996, The Haworth Press. Used with permission.

panic elderly. Low income, which often correlates with poor housing conditions, may foster relationships that inevitably will be deemed exploitative.

When these realities are considered in the assessment process, the Euro-centric screening is redirected toward a more culturally sensitive approach considerate of expectations, values, and the significance of these interactions in interrelated environments. Redefining financial exploitation will not provide a theoretical explanation for financial exploitation; however, a broader definition will assist in assessing cases and directing interventions in minority communities. It also enables us to move away from attempting to categorize people to fit neatly constructed criteria based on a limited reality. (pp. 55-56)

Neglect

Neglect is also a serious problem for the elderly and may be seen in the following forms: passive neglect, active neglect, and self-neglect. *Passive neglect* is defined as the refusal or failure to fulfill a caretaking obligation. Abandoning a person or not providing food or health-related services are examples. Passive neglect generally is not a conscious or intentional act on the part of the caregiver. Rather, it often occurs when a caregiver is not aware of community resources that may aid the elderly person in need or disputes the value of prescribed services.

Active neglect is the conscious and intentional withholding of care an elderly person needs, such as supplying proper nutrition, the meeting of toileting needs, treatment for physical conditions, and the use of restraints (Cash & Valentine, 1989; Wolf, Godkin, & Pillemer, 1986).

In *self-neglect,* which often is included in passive neglect, there are no caregivers as perpetrators; rather, elderly persons are neglecting themselves. The National Center on Elder Abuse reports that the median age of self-neglecting elders in fiscal years 1995 and 1996 was 77 (Tatara & Kuzmeskus, 1997). Self-neglect is an unfortunate label for a condition affecting the elderly because it implies willful self-degradation or destruction. Self-neglect, however, is hardly ever willful but, rather, the result of elderly persons being unable to care for themselves because of depleted physical or social resources (Longres, 1995). Self-neglect is defined by the National Association of Adult Protective Service Administrators as follows:

> Self-neglect is the result of an adult's inability, due to physical and/or mental impairments or diminished capacity, to perform essential self-care tasks including: providing essential food, clothing, shelter, and medical care; obtaining goods and services necessary to maintain physical health, mental health, emotional well-being and general safety; and/or managing financial affairs. (Duke, 1991, p. 27)

Figure 4.2 presents indicators of neglect helpful in detecting this form of elder abuse.

A significant difference between elderly who self-neglect and who experience abusive treatment from others is that the former generally live alone in their own homes. They are also likely to have some kind of impairment or to be frail or physically disabled (Longres, 1995). In a study contrasting 227 self-neglectful elderly with 421 elderly who were reportedly competent but abused or neglected by others, both groups were found to be in their mid-70s; however, the self-neglectful elderly were more likely to be males. More self-neglectful elderly as compared to the maltreated elderly had disabling characteristics, such as mental illness, substance abuse, physical disabilities, Alzheimer's disease or other related dementia, or other medical conditions. Referrals for self-neglectful elderly to a state adult protective service agency were made by community agencies as compared to the referrals for maltreated elderly that came primarily from family members (Vinton, 1991).

Although these various forms of elder abuse have been defined singularly, often they appear not in isolation but simultaneously. Also, different types of abuse (child, spouse, sibling) may have occurred at earlier times in the life of an elderly person.

ABUSE IN NURSING HOMES

Nursing homes play an important role in the long-term care of the elderly, especially the frail elderly. The number of patients in nursing homes has increased during the past 25 years from approximately 331,000 to over 1.5 million (American Health Care Association, personal communication, June 12, 1997). Patients in nursing homes may be abused by the staff or by family members.

Much of the literature on elder abuse in nursing homes is based on anecdotal data using a case-study approach. Anecdotal literature on the abuse of the elderly in nursing homes reports accounts of staff abusing elderly patients by grossly limiting their freedom, providing substandard nutrition and

- Malnourishment or dehydration
- Matted, unclean hair
- Bodily crevices caked with dirt
- Presence of odor of old urine/feces
- Oral hygiene unattended
- Overgrown finger-/toenails
- Uncut hair, unshaven
- Improperly clothed (clothing dirty, torn, inadequate)
- Untreated injuries, illnesses, other conditions
- Over- or undermedicated
- Infestation with fleas/lice
- Isolated for long periods of time
- Poor skin condition/skin breakdown (presence of rash, impetigo, eczema, urine burns, excoriation, decubiti, or pressure bedsores)
- Filthy living conditions, such as lack of heat, running water, electricity, refrigeration
- Infestation of living quarters by roaches/rodents

Figure 4.2 Indicators of Possible Elder Neglect
SOURCE: Ramsey-Klawsnik (1993b, p. 14).

living quarters, and engaging in physical and psychological abuse (Garvin & Burger, 1968; Kahana, 1973; Long, 1987). Several empirical studies; however, provide insight into the extent and nature of abuse in long-term-care facilities.

Extent and Nature of Abuse

During a 7-month period (October 1991 to April 1992), 191 incidents of elder abuse were reported to the state Long-Term Care Ombudsman Office by 534 skilled nursing, intermediate care, and residential care facilities in Orange County, California. The reported incidences represented .03 per nursing home beds per year and .008 per bed per year for the intermediate care and residential facilities in the county where the data were collected. These data are considerably less than earlier estimates that indicated that abuse occurred more frequently (Doty & Sullivan, 1983; Pillemer, 1988). This may be due to the fact that earlier studies included abusive incidents occurring but not officially reported. Assault and neglect were the most frequently cited types of abuse in the Orange County study. The average age of the victim was 81 years. Nearly twice as many women were victims as compared to men. Over 33% of the perpetrators were nursing assistants or aides. Eight of the patients during the 7-month study period died as a result of their abuse, and 31 received injuries serious enough to require major medical intervention. Again, the data reflect only abusive incidents reported and may represent only a portion of the number of the actual incidents occurring, when nonreported abusive incidents are also included (Watson, Cesario, Ziemba, & McGovern, 1993).

Another study of abuse in nursing homes focused on 57 intermediate care and skilled care nursing facilities. Intermediate care nursing homes were defined as institutions serving individuals who did not need intensive nursing care but required institutionalization because of physical or mental impairments. Skilled nursing care facilities provided care under the supervision of a physician and other therapeutic services. Participants in the research, who were interviewed by telephone, were registered nurses, licensed practical nurses, and nurse's aides. The participating intermediate care and skilled care nursing homes ranged in size from 19 to 300 beds. Among those interviewed, 36% had seen at least one incident of physical abuse in the preceding year, the most frequent form being excessive restraint of a patient. The second most frequent form of physical abuse observed was pushing, grabbing, shoving, or pinching a patient. Slapping or hitting a patient also was reported. One psychologically abusive incident had been observed by 81% of the respondents in the preceding year, the most frequent form being yelling at a patient in anger. Half of the respondents had seen a staff member insult or swear at a patient in the preceding year. The majority of those who reported seeing physical and emotional abuse of patients indicated that it had occurred more than once (Pillemer & Moore, 1989).

Staff members themselves reported engaging in abusive acts toward their elderly patients. Ten percent admitted committing one or more physically abusive acts and 40% at least one psychologically abusive act within the past year toward patients. Staff members who engaged in the physical or emotional abuse of patients reported that they frequently thought about quitting their job (a measure of job satisfaction) and viewed their patients as childlike. The researchers concluded that abuse in nursing homes toward the elderly is sufficiently extensive to merit public attention (Pillemer & Moore, 1989).

The nature of abuse of nursing home patients can be seen from reports of abusive incidents to Medicaid Fraud Control Units. Nursing homes that receive Medicaid funds fall under the jurisdiction of Medicaid Fraud Control Units that exist in 42 states and are responsible for detecting, investigating, and prosecuting Medicaid fraud and patient abuse. Reports to Medicaid Fraud Control Units from 1987 through 1992 were analyzed using standards forms of thematic and semantic content analysis. The data revealed that 411 (84%) of the 488 reported abusive acts were physical in nature. The physically abusive acts ranged from slapping a patient to causing irreparable damage. Although all types of nursing home employees were perpetrators, the largest group (302, or 62%) were nurse's aides. Although the nursing profession and nursing home employees having direct patient care responsibilities to a large extent are female, the data surprisingly suggested that males were more likely to be perpetrators, which is supported by earlier research (Godkin, Wolf, & Pillemer, 1989). In the 307 cases for which the victim's gender was identified, males were the victims in over 50% of the incidents (Payne & Cikovic, 1995).

The data from this research suggest that pressures on the job were a contributing factor to the occurrence of abuse in nursing facilities. The concept of provocation, together with inadequate staff training, may account for this finding. Perpetrators may justify their abusive actions as a response to what they interpret as provocations from uncooperative and sometimes hostile patients. The data emphasize the need for training nursing personnel, especially male staff, in effective ways to handle patient interactions without resorting to physical violence.

An additional stress factor for staff working with nursing home residents is the abuse that they experience from patients; however, this is no excuse for a staff member in turn being abusive to a patient, because there are alternative nonviolent ways to respond to violent patient behavior. In a study of nursing assistants in a Canadian 320-bed long-term-care facility for the aged, a nursing assistant, on average, could expect to be physically assaulted by residents 9.3 times per month and verbally assaulted 11.3 times per month (Goodridge, Johnston, & Thomson, 1996). In a similar study focusing on the abuse of staff that may in turn have prompted abuse toward patients, staff assistants reported that they felt supervisors or management personnel were not concerned about patients' assaultive behavior and that such assaults were simply seen as part of their job (Lanza & Campbell, 1991).

Abuse of nursing home patients can also occur at a more covert level, such a denying patients personal choices, isolating them, or negatively labeling them. In an ethnographic study of 27 aggressive and nonaggressive nursing home residents, researchers found that the staff denied personal choices to patients such as bathing times, even when patients responded nonaggressively to baths given later in the day as compared to early morning baths that provoked an aggressive response. Patients often were inappropriately isolated from others following an aggressive incident and were labeled "bad," which influenced the nature of staff-patient interactions. Prosocial behaviors that the staff displayed to nonagressive patients were replaced with aversive behaviors when dealing with aggressive patients (Meddaugh, 1993).

Factors Related to Nursing Home Patient Abuse

Three sets of variables proposed as predictive of the occurrence of physical and emotional abuse in nursing home settings are institutional, staff, and situational characteristics.

Institutional characteristics include the size of the facility, ownership, and rates charged. Research indicates that the quality of care increases with facility size in terms of number of beds (Lieberman & Tobin, 1983; Moos & Lemke, 1983; Pillemer, 1988; Pillemer & Bachman-Prehn, 1991). Although early research showed few differences related to care and possible maltreatment between for-profit and nonprofit homes, more recent studies indicate that nonprofit homes may offer superior medical and personal care. One study showed that patients in for-profit homes feared retaliation from staff members if they complained about the care they were receiving (Monk, Kaye, & Litwin, 1984). Institutions with greater expenditures per patient also have lower rates of maltreatment because they can hire more staff with better training (Pillemer & Bachman-Prehn, 1991).

Staff characteristics include the variable of education in that nurse's aides with little or no professional training are likely to express more negative attitudes toward patients. Another variable is length of time on the job. Staff members who have worked in a geriatric setting for longer periods of time express fewer negative attitudes toward patients (Pillemer & Bachman-Prehn, 1991).

One of the *situational characteristics* that affects patient care is staff burnout. Those burned-out on their jobs who experience aggression from patients are at greatest risk of engaging in physically and emotionally abusive behavior (Pillemer & Bachman-Prehn, 1991). As shown from research (Tellis-Nayak & Tellis-Nayak, 1989; Waxman, Carner, & Berkenstock, 1984), employment in a nursing home involves low wages, low prestige, and physically demanding work, often in situations of high conflict where employees are physically and emotionally assaulted. Nurse's aides express a feeling of powerlessness when working in nursing homes (Hudson, 1992). Thus not only is there a need for rigorous investigation of complaints of abuse in nursing homes, there is a serious need to upgrade nursing home staffs and to provide them training to handle the tension and stress associated with working in a nursing home facility for the elderly.

Prevention of elder abuse in nursing homes can occur through a humanistic sensitizing of the staff to the uniqueness of each individual patient beyond the patient's physical infirmities and social/psychological impairments. This is expressed in a poem (see Figure 4.3) found in the bedside drawer of a geriatric patient who had passed away in a San Diego hospital. The poem is directed to nurses in a long-term residential care facility for the aged. It exhorts her caretakers to look at her spirit, not her withered body.

Ombudsman Programs

An effective strategy for intervening in and even preventing elder abuse in nursing homes is the implementation of ombudsman programs established by the Older Americans Act of 1975. Although there are variations in the implementation of these programs across states, in general they provide nursing home residents and their families advocacy services, the goals of which are improved patient care and providing an avenue for investigating and resolving complaints (Netting, Patton, & Huber, 1992; Patton, Huber, & Netting, 1994). Grassroots citizen organizations, likewise providing advocacy and surveillance of nursing homes, often predate ombudsman programs and coexist in many communities with ombudsman programs (Filinson, 1995; Netting, Huber, Patton, & Kautz, 1995), providing supplemental manpower and assisting in circumventing political roadblocks and overcoming bureaucratic lethargy. In some instances, grass-roots citizen organizations operate on their own but nevertheless improve program performance by their scrutiny, criticism, or presence in the community (Filinson, 1995).

A sample of 166 nursing homes in Oregon was used to evaluate the effectiveness of the use of volunteer long-term-care ombudsmen in these facilities (Nelson, Huber, & Walter, 1995). The research showed that those nursing homes with an ombudsman program as compared to those without had more abuse reports and substantiated abuse complaints. Although these findings are not consistent with an earlier study (Litwin & Monk, 1987), Nelson et al. (1995) felt their research finding regarding the presence of ombudsmen making a positive influence on reports in general and substantiated reports in particular made sense because the scrutiny and presence of ombudsmen in a nursing facility would be expected to relate to heightened regulatory concern and activity. The increase in complaints may be related also to state regulatory requirements in Oregon that require mandatory reporting of elder abuse incidents by ombudsmen. Ombudsmen are also trained to follow through on reports of abuse by requesting a report of findings by the investigating agency. These reports are reviewed by volunteers and sometimes even by paid staff. If deficiencies are found in the investigation, a supplementary investigation may be requested.

Unfortunately, however, the work of ombudsmen is not always appreciated by administrators of programs and facilities for the elderly: "Depending on the relationship between long-term-care administrators, board and care home operators, and staff members of the local program, an ombudsman may be perceived as a watchdog to be avoided, a friendly visitor to be tolerated, or a resource for advice and assistance" (Netting et al., 1995, p. 355).

What do you see, nurses, what do you see?
Are you thinking when you look at me
A crabby old woman, not very wise,
Uncertain of habit, with far-away eyes,
Who dribbles her food and makes no reply
When you say in a loud voice—"I do wish you'd try."
Who seems not to notice the things that you do
And forever is losing a stocking or shoe.
Who unresisting, or not, lets you do as you will,
With bathing and feeding, the long day to fill,
Is that what you are thinking, is that what you see?
Then open your eyes, nurses. **You're not looking at me!**

I'll tell you who I am, as I sit here so still;
As I do at your bidding, as I eat at your will,
I'm a small child of 10 with a father and mother
Brothers and sisters, who love one another.
A young girl of 16 with wings on her feet,
Dreaming that soon now a lover she'll meet;
A bride soon at 20—my heart gives a leap,
Remembering the vows that I promise to keep;
At 25 now I have a young son of my own,
Who needs me to build a secure, happy home;
A woman at 30, my young now grow fast,
Bound to each other with ties that should last.

At 40, my young sons have grown and have gone,
But my man's beside me to see I don't mourn.
At 50 once more babies play round my knee,
Again we know children, my husband and me.
Dark days are upon me, my husband is dead.
I look at the future, I shudder with dread.
For my young are still rearing young of their own,
And I think of the years and love that I've known.
I'm an old woman now and nature is cruel—
'Tis her jest to make old age look like a fool.
The body it crumbles, grace and vigor depart,
There is now a stone, where once there was a heart.

But inside this old carcass a young girl still dwells,
And now and again my battered heart swells,
I remember the joys, I remember the pain,
And I'm loving and living life over again.
I think of the years all too few—gone too fast.
And accept the stark fact that nothing can last.
So open your eyes, nurses, open and see
Not a crabby old woman, look closer—**see me.**

Figure 4.3 What Do You See, Nurses?
SOURCE: Unknown.

Preventing Abuse in Nursing Homes

Staff training in working with the elderly is important to preventing abuse and neglect in nursing homes. An example of such a training program can be seen in a curriculum developed for nurses' aides by the Coalition of Advocates for the Rights of the Infirm Elderly (CARIE) and members of the Philadelphia Elder Abuse Task Force (Hudson, 1992). Three goals comprise the program: increase staff awareness of abuse, neglect, and potential abuse in long-term-care facilities; equip nurses' aides with appropriate conflict intervention strategies; and reduce abuse in long-term-care facilities, thus improving the quality of life for residents. These goals are implemented in an 8-module curriculum: I. Understanding the phenomenon of resident abuse; II. Identification and recognition of types of abuse; III. Possible causes of abuse; IV. Understanding feelings about caregiving; V. Cultural and ethnic perspectives and implications for staff-resident dynamics; VI. Abuse of staff by residents; VII. Legal and ethical issues concerning the reporting of suspected abuse; and VIII. Intervention strategies for abuse prevention. The modules are implemented through the use of videotapes, case discussions, role-play exercises, and quizzes. An evaluation of the program at several test sites revealed that participants appreciated learning about elder abuse and also the opportunity to talk about problems associated with being a nurse's aide in a nursing facility (Hudson, 1992).

INCIDENCE OF ABUSE

As with other types of family violence, statistical data cited for elder abuse represent only a fraction of the actual number of incidents. Approximately only 1 in 14 cases of elder abuse is ever reported (Pillemer & Finkelhor, 1988) resulting in the problem being "largely hidden in the shroud of family secrecy" (Tatara, 1993, p. 36).

Reports to Adult Protective Services Units

State Adult Protective Services units and state units on aging were surveyed to determine the number of reports of elder abuse they received. The data are based on 54 agencies responding to the survey, which represented the 50 states and 4 jurisdictions—the District of Columbia, Guam, Puerto Rico, and the Virgin Islands (Tatara, 1993; Tatara & Kuzmeskus, 1997). Table 4.1 presents the number of elder abuse reports received by Adult Protective Services units from 1986 to 1996.

The Prevalence of Abuse

If statistical data on elder abuse reflect only reported cases and there is a significantly greater number of unreported cases, how prevalent is the problem of elder abuse? Several studies present some answers to this question.

Researchers studied a random sample of 2,020 community-dwelling elderly persons (65 or older) in the Boston metropolitan area to learn about the prevalence of elder abuse. The study, which represented one of the first large-scale, random-sample surveys of the problem of elder abuse, measured incidents of physical abuse, neglect, and psychological abuse but not self-neglect, fraud, or exploitation (Pillemer & Finkelhor, 1988).

Based on the data collected, the researchers determined that elder abuse occurred at the rate of 32 persons per 1,000. With a 95% confidence level of this being a true figure of the extent to which elder abuse in fact occurs, it was estimated that between 8,646 and 13,487 of the 345,827 elderly persons in Boston were abused and ne-

TABLE 4.1 National Estimates of Domestic Elder Abuse Reports

Year	*Number of Reports*
1986	117,000
1987	128,000
1988	140,000
1989	*
1990	211,000
1991	213,000
1992	*
1993	227,000
1994	241,000
1995	286,000
1996	293,000

*Data not available.

glected. If this rate were similar for the entire United States, an estimated 701,000 to 1,093,560 elderly persons in the nation were being abused. Rates calculated per 1,000 persons for the various forms of abuse revealed that physical abuse was experienced by 20, chronic verbal aggression by 11, and neglect by 4. Thus, physical abuse was found to be the most prevalent form of elder abuse, with 63% of the elderly studied having been pushed, grabbed, or shoved, 43% slapped, and 10% hit with a fist, bitten, or kicked. Nearly 60% of the perpetrators were spouses, with the remainder being children (adult sons and daughters), grandchildren, siblings, and boarders (Pillemer & Finkelhor, 1988).

In a Canadian study, elders who lived in private homes were interviewed by telephone to determine if they had experienced abuse. Of those able to respond to the telephone interviews, abuse was reported by 40 per 1,000 contacted. (The use of telephone interviews did not involve those who, because of physical or mental problems, were unable to respond to the telephone but who may have experienced abuse.) Forms of abuse ranging from the most to least prevalent per 1,000 elders were financial abuse (25 cases), verbal abuse (14), physical abuse (5), and neglect (4). Rates of victimization were nearly equal for men and women. The researchers suggested that the low rate of physical abuse may have been due to lower violence rates in Canada as compared to the United States and the low number of neglect cases because of the exclusion from the sample of elderly persons unable to respond to the telephone interviews (Podnieks, Pillemer, & Nicolson cited in Wolf, 1992).

The National Center on Elder Abuse, in analyzing the 293,000 reports of elder abuse in 1996, indicated that 22.5% of these reports were from physicians and other health care professionals and 15.1% came from service providers, such as agency staff providing services to elderly persons. Family members and relatives of victims accounted for 16.3% of the reports, with the remainder coming from friends and neighbors, law enforcement personnel, clergy, banks/business institutions, and victims themselves. The majority of reports (64.2%) were substantiated. Regarding the type of maltreatment reported, neglect was the most prevalent (55%), followed by physical abuse (15%), financial/material exploitation (12%), emotional abuse (8%), and sexual abuse (.3%) (Tatara & Kuzmeskus, 1997).

Why Elder Abuse Often Is Not Reported

Elder abuse in institutional and noninstitutional settings often is not reported. Personal and structural barriers may prevent victims from seeking help (Hooyman, 1982). Consequently, these victims are not reflected in the statistics on the incidence of elder abuse. Personal barriers include feelings of embarrassment that a parent raised an abusive child, if the perpetrator is an adult child, as well as embarrassment and concern about the implications for the family's standing in the community if the abuse became known. Victims may also resign themselves to what is happening because of their dependency on others, a fear of being removed from the home and being institutionalized, a fear of reprisal from the caregiver, and a perceived lack of other available care options (Penhale, 1993). This resignation to the abuse may be viewed as powerlessness on the part of the aged. Physical weakness, isolation from family and friends, and the loss of a mate through death are additional personal barriers or limitations that prevent the elderly from exploring other options for care, even if other options are available.

Victims often deny being abused when reports of their abuse are investigated by adult protective services, thus influencing rates of substantiation of reported cases of abuse. This denial may take the form of (a) explaining the abuse as an accident or stress that the elder's caregiver is under, (b) countering the seriousness of the abuse by saying that no serious injuries were incurred, (c) assuming responsibility for provoking the abusive incident, or (d) blaming the adult protective service agency for unnecessarily intruding into their privacy (Tomita, 1990).

Structural barriers to the elderly reporting their abuse include a lack of information on available supportive services such as temporary care facilities that provide respite to a caregiver, a lack of knowledge about adult protective service agencies to which elder abuse should be reported, and a lack of awareness of an array of medical and health-related services available to assist in the care and maintenance of the elderly. Structural barriers also include the inaccessibility of some services as well as the impersonalization and fragmentation of social and medical services for the elderly.

Statistical data on elder abuse also inadequately reflect the extent of this social problem because many incidents of elder abuse never come to public attention due to the low public visibility of many elderly, especially those who are primarily homebound. Unlike the victims of child and spousal abuse who are in contact with individuals outside the home who may see their injuries or the effects of their abuse, the elderly suffering abuse frequently are isolated from contacts outside their home and hence their abuse is not noticeable to others.

The traditional view of the family with its emphasis on privacy, that what occurs behind the closed doors of the family residence is no one else's business, often deters neighbors and others from investigating whether abuse is occurring even when there are grounds for suspicion.

Finally, the inability of individuals (professionals and nonprofessionals) in contact with the elderly to recognize signs of abuse and neglect prevents many cases of elder abuse from coming to the attention of authorities. For example, medical professionals may examine patients relative to a somatic complaint or illness but fail to recognize indicators of abuse because they lack knowledge of such indicators (Bookin & Dunkle, 1985).

THEORETICAL FACTORS FOR UNDERSTANDING ELDER ABUSE

Why would someone abuse an elderly person? How can the problem of elder abuse be understood? Five theoretical perspectives that may help in understanding this social problem are psychopathology, social learning theory, social exchange theory, situational stress, and role theory. When attempting to understand individual cases of elder abuse, more than one theoretical perspective often must be taken into consideration.

Psychopathology

This theoretical perspective attempts to understand elder abuse in terms of the caregiver's problems. Repeatedly in this chapter, reference is made to the "adult child" serving as the caregiver of an elderly parent or parents. If the parent is of advanced age—for example, 80 or older—the "adult child" likely is 60 years or older. Caregivers may also be adult siblings, grandchildren, friends, neighbors, or boarders. The psychopathological perspective focuses on the caregiver's psychosocial problems that may interfere with the effective implementation of the caregiver role and might lead to abusive behavior toward an elderly person.

Because many elderly persons, especially the frail elderly, are dependent on someone else for their care, research also shows that some perpetrators are very dependent on their victim, who may be a parent or other relative. These perpetrators have been shown to exhibit severe problems in psychosocial functioning, as reflected in a high incidence of prior arrests, problems with drugs and alcohol, depression, previous hospitalizations for psychiatric illness, employment problems, and past involvement in violent behavior (Pillemer & Finkelhor, 1989).

Social Learning Theory

Social learning theory suggests that violence is a learned behavior and often is learned in the context of the family. Children raised in abusive homes where physical and emotional abuse were means of problem solving or responses to stress may in turn resort to such violence when they encounter problems in the care of their elderly parents. Perpetrators of elder abuse may also be modeling behavior seen on television or videos where the use of violence is presented as a response to interpersonal problems

Social Exchange Theory

This theoretical perspective focuses on the dependency of the elderly person and the absence of assets with which to "bargain" in a society based on the concept of distributive justice—namely, individuals with personal and social assets gain power to achieve their goals in society. Thus, what a person has to offer to others influences what that person gets in return (Meyer, 1996).

American society values youth. As people age they are not as valued or rewarded in society. Society places greater value on married persons or couples than individuals—single, widowed, or divorced. Frequently, elderly persons are alone, having lost their mate through death. Emphasis is placed in society on good health and fitness, variables that elderly persons lack (Pittaway, 1995). Independence is also valued in American society; however, the elderly's physical, psychological, and financial problems often force them to be dependent on others to meet even simple daily tasks of living. Thus, the preponderance of their needs vis-à-vis what they have to offer to others, puts the elderly in an undesirable position in society, which may result in punitive responses in the form of physical and emotional abuse from others.

Situational Stress

This theoretical perspective implies that often the duties and responsibilities of caring for an elderly person place the caregiver under a high degree of stress. This is especially true if the elderly person has physical or mental impairments. The adult child in the role of caregiver may have health, financial, emotional, and job-related problems of his or her own that may add to the stress. In some instances, the caregiver is the spouse and likewise is experiencing stress associated with aging.

A sample of 188 elderly wives was studied as to the consequences for them of caring for their elderly disabled husbands (Wilson, 1990). Disabled was defined as individuals experiencing functional limitations and incapacities resulting from illness. Although the elderly women caregivers were not abusing their mates, the study showed the consequences experienced by these women in terms of the stress of being in the role of primary caregiver and their potential risk of engaging in abusive behavior. The caregivers were confronted with unrelenting demands and pressures to provide constant care to the mate while at the same time meeting the routine needs of daily living. Those wives suffering from chronic health conditions appeared to be most negatively affected by the stress associated with their caregiving responsibilities. Some expressed fear, anger, frustration, sadness, and helplessness, and many felt overwhelmed with regard to these responsibilities. Activities the wives enjoyed such as hobbies, volunteer work, church attendance, and even just relaxing had to be given up because of the demands placed on them in caring for their husbands. Constant confinement to the house and isolation from family and friends characterized their situations. In some extreme cases, a disintegration and disruption of the marital relationship had occurred due to the stress of caregiving.

The time in life when elderly parents may be in need of care are often high stress times for adult children who are forced into the role of caregiver. The adult children may be involved with their own children and be burdened with financial pressures such as college tuition. Also, this may the period in their life when they have risen in their career to the point where their job places high demands on them, such as extensive time spent at the office or traveling. If the adult children are nearing retirement or already are retired, having to care for an elderly parent may prevent them from pursuing activities looked forward to throughout their working life. This stress may erupt in the caregiver's relationship with the elderly person in terms of physically or emotionally abusive behavior.

Role Theory

When adult children assume a caregiver role for elderly parents, a role reversal occurs. The parent, especially when there is impaired cognitive and/or physical functioning, becomes a child or one to be cared for, and the adult child takes on the role of parent to the parent. For example, loss of bowel and bladder control may require diapering the elderly parent, a function the parent performed when the adult child was a baby. The caregiver's expectations of the elderly person may be unrealistic, such as having bowel and bladder control that physiologically is no longer possible or being able to remember or to follow simple instructions regarding medication, also no longer possible. These problems may be exacerbated when the caregiver is related to the parent only through marriage and has not bonded with or was not accepted earlier on by the in-law.

Role conflict can occur when elderly parents do not view their adult children as adults but continue to relate to them as children in what is perceived as a domineering and controlling manner. Differences in lifestyles, values, religious beliefs, and morals can become significant issues and produce increased friction and stress between the aged and their adult children, especially when an elderly parent must move into the adult child's home.

THE VICTIMS

Who are the victims of elder abuse? Are there characteristics that separate them from elderly persons who are not abused? Consensus on characteristics that distinguish the abused elderly from their nonabused counterparts is lacking because of problems in the research attempting to answer this question. For example, some studies rely on professionals' reports of abuse cases rather than on interviews with the victims. Other studies use samples drawn from agencies working with the abused rather than using surveys of the general population. Finally, there has been little use of control groups in studying samples of elder abuse victims (Hudson, 1986; Pillemer & Finkelhor, 1989).

Gender and Age

A study of 60 elder abuse cases in Texas reported to a unit of Adult Protective Services were studied indicating that the victims were more likely to be over 75 years of age and female. Although the 75-and-older age group represented only 37% of the total elderly population, nearly 57% of the victims were in this age group. Sixty percent were widowed and 22% married. Nearly half had at least a major physical or mental impairment. In 80% of the cases, victims lived in their own homes. In 56% of the cases, the perpetrator lived with the victim. In 20% of the cases, the victim lived in the abuser's home and appeared to be dependent on that person. Many of the cases involved multiple forms of abuse including physical, emotional, and financial abuse. The most frequently occurring form of abuse was financial (62% of the cases), followed by emotional (55%) and physical (45%). Active neglect was found in 35% of the cases. The abuse was found to have happened more than once rather than being an isolated incident. In most instances, the abuse was reported by a third party who became aware of what was happening. There was no evidence that the perpetrators were being prosecuted (Powell & Berg, 1987).

In 1980, the Administration on Aging funded three model projects on elder abuse to demonstrate improved ways for reporting, investigating, treating, and preventing elder abuse in domestic settings. Persons 60 years of age or older who had been victimized by family members, neighbors, or other persons participated (Wolf et al., 1986). Of the 328 victims in the sample, 56% were over 75 years of age, 82% were female, 31% were married, and 77% lived with others. Half of the victims required supportive devices in ambulation or were bedridden. A greater proportion of the victims of physical and emotional abuse was considered to be in poor emotional health. Those having experienced psychological abuse were found to have problems with orientation to time, place, and person.

The National Center on Elder Abuse reported substantiated reports of abuse for fiscal years 1995 and 1996 by age (Table 4.2) and by gender (Table 4.3) (Tatara & Kuzmeskus, 1997).

TABLE 4.2 Ages of Domestic Elder Abuse Victims

	Percentage	
Age	*FY1995*	*FY1996*
60 to 64	8.0	9.2
65 to 69	11.7	11.4
70 to 74	17.7	17.2
75 to 79	17.8	18.3
80 to 84	19.5	19.1
85 and older	21.4	21.4
Unknown	3.9	3.4
Total	100.0	100.0
Number of states reporting	37	36
Median age	78	77.9

SOURCE: *Summaries of the Statistical Data on Elder Abuse in Domestic Settings for FY95 and FY96,* published by the National Center on Elder Abuse. Used with permission.

TABLE 4.3 Gender of Domestic Elder Abuse Victims

	Percentage	
Gender	*FY1995*	*FY1996*
Male	33.4	32.4
Female	66.0	67.3
Unknown	0.6	0.3
Total	100.0	100.0
Number of states reporting	38	38

SOURCE: *Summaries of the Statistical Data on Elder Abuse in Domestic Settings for FY95 and FY96,* published by the National Center on Elder Abuse. Used with permission.

In the studies cited earlier and the National Center on Elder Abuse statistics, women were more likely to be the victim (Lau & Kosberg, 1979). This is partly due to the demographics of aging in that women tend to live longer than men. However, other factors may be involved. From a feminist perspective, the power and control over women by men may be seen in the victimization of elderly women by caregivers who were husbands and sons. Women also often have fewer assets in their old age, the result of workplace discrimination in terms of their not receiving equal pay for equal work, and thus may be dependent on men for support (Aitken & Griffin, 1996; Sengstock, 1991).

Race

Certain segments of the population may be particularly vulnerable to abuse. Research shows that elderly African American women are least well off compared to other groups of elderly women (Ozawa, 1995). This lack of financial resources may necessitate their relying on family members for care when they become elderly and especially frail. Although elderly African American and Hispanic women may have worked much of their adult life, their low levels of earnings from mostly low-skilled, low-wage jobs, often without benefits, may make them dependent on public financial aid or families members for care in their later years.

Dementia

A group of elderly especially vulnerable to abuse are those who are confused and who may have Alzheimer's disease. Research shows that the occurrence of violent behaviors in families caring for a member with Alzheimer's disease is well in excess of prevalence figures for elder abuse in general (Paveza et al., 1992). A person with Alzheimer's disease is 2.25 times at greater risk to be physically abused than an older person living in the community without the disease. Caring for individuals who are cognitively incapacitated adds to the stress placed on the caregiver. As one caregiver, the adult daughter of an elderly mother with Alzheimer's disease, states,

> I haven't had a good night of sleep since I brought my mother into my house to live with me. I sleep being very conscious that my mother may call me and need help or that she might get up and fall down the stairs. I even fear that she might try to go into the kitchen to prepare a cup of tea which she no longer successfully can do by herself, although she still tries. Also, I have not entertained friends since mother has moved in. I am too tired and I am not sure what I would do with my mother while my friends are here. I have honestly been thinking of dropping out of my bridge club, but I know I shouldn't because I enjoy it so much.

Specific behaviors of confused elderly persons may put them at greater risk for abuse. A confused person's functioning may be viewed from the perspective of cognitive and social inaccessibility (Wolanin & Phillips, 1981). Cognitive inaccessibility refers to impairment in receptive functions in the form of memory, learning, and cognition and in expressive functions that prevent the elderly from interacting with their environment as caregivers would normally expect. Social inaccessibility refers to behaviors that interfere with interpersonal communication and relationships in general. Such behaviors are hostility, belligerence, suspiciousness, restlessness, wandering, agitation, and the inability to control bowel and bladder functions.

Both cognitive and social inaccessibility make an elderly person vulnerable to abuse from a caregiver. Although the caregiver may attempt cognitively to relay information to the elderly person, the former may have no assurance that the information is being received and processed, especially when the elderly person's behavior is contradictory to the information that was sent. Thus, frequent repetition of information is required, which adds to the frustration and stress experienced by the caregiver, which in turn can trigger physically or verbally abusive behaviors. Social inaccessibility in a confused elderly person also sets up a climate with a caregiver in which the elderly person may be perceived as not appreciative of the efforts of the caregiver and certainly one in which the elderly person is not able to respond with love, warmth, appreciation, and even companionship as the caregiver may expect (Beck & Phillips, 1983; Godkin et al., 1989). Again, a potentially abusive situation can occur. Finally, interpersonal problems between an adult child acting as a caregiver and an elderly parent may be expressed in provocative behavior on the part of either party, which contributes to the stress involved in the interpersonal relationship and may set up a high-risk situation for abuse (Godkin et al., 1989).

Social Isolation

Research comparing groups of abused and nonabused elders found that those abused tended to be more isolated than their nonabused counterparts. This lack of social contacts due in large part to recent losses placed them at greater risk for abuse (Godkin et al., 1989).

THE PERPETRATORS

Who are the individuals engaging in abusive behavior toward the elderly? Research provides some descriptors of these individuals.

Relationship to Victim

A random sample of persons 65 years of age and older was drawn from town lists of residents in every dwelling in Massachusetts. A sample of 2,020 persons living with spouses or adult children was formed. Screening and follow-up interviews yielded a sample of 61 elderly persons identified as abused or neglected and a control group of 215 not abused or neglected. Three types of abuse were studied: physical abuse, chronic verbal aggression, and neglect. The data revealed that spouses rather than adult children were the most frequent perpetrators of abuse.

A significant finding from this research was that items that discriminated between the abused group and those not abused pertained to the abusers and their behavior and circumstances rather than to the victim. The perpetrators, who were largely spouses, showed a high incidence of having been arrested, hospitalized for a psychiatric condition, involved in other violent behavior, or limited in their functioning because of some health problem. The perpetrators, in comparison to their nonabusive counterparts, were described as more dependent on the elderly they victimized for such things as financial assistance, household repairs, transportation, and housing. The abusers also were more likely to have suffered life stresses in the previous year such as illness or a death in their family.

The researchers also found that the abused elderly were not more ill or physically and emotionally disabled, as earlier studies suggested. Nor were the abused elderly more dependent on their perpetrators than other nonabused elderly were on their relatives. The researchers concluded that the abuse may not be related to the burden the elderly place on family members but, rather, that the victims are elders "who have responsibility for, or are at least required to interact with, ill and socioemotionally unstable relatives. The abuse appears to be a reflection of the perpetrator's problems and dependency rather than of the elderly victim's characteristics" (Pillemer & Finkelhor, 1989, p. 186).

The National Center on Elder Abuse reported the relationship of perpetrators to their victims for substantiated reports of abuse for fiscal years 1995 and 1996 (Tatara & Kuzmeskus, 1997) (see Table 4.4).

Demographic Characteristics

Reference was made earlier to the three model projects funded by the Administration on Aging in 1980 in which 328 victims and their perpetrators were studied. As

TABLE 4.4 Perpetrators of Domestic Elder Abuse

	Percentage	
Relationship of Abuser	*FY1995*	*FY1996*
Adult children	34.2	36.7
Spouse	14.1	12.6
Other relatives	12.4	10.8
Grandchildren	5.9	7.7
Service provider	4.6	3.5
Friend/neighbor	4.5	3.2
Unrelated caregiver	4.8	4.3
Sibling	2.5	2.7
Other	11.6	13.4
Unknown/missing data	5.4	5.1
Total	100.0	100.0
Number of states reporting	28	27

SOURCE: *Summaries of the Statistical Data on Elder Abuse in Domestic Settings for FY95 and FY96,* published by the National Center on Elder Abuse. Used with permission.

a group, the perpetrators were younger than their victims, with 60% being under age 60; 64% were male; and approximately 75% lived with their victims. The perpetrators were more likely to be sons of the victims than daughters, husbands than wives, and other relatives than nonrelatives. The most prevalent form of abuse occurring was psychological maltreatment or emotional abuse, which appeared in nearly 75% of the sample, followed by physical abuse, fraud or exploitation, passive neglect, and active neglect.

The victims of physical abuse were more likely to be younger and living with the perpetrator as compared to passive neglect victims who were generally older and living alone. Victims of fraud and exploitation usually lived alone. The perpetrators of physical and psychological abuse were likely to have experienced a recent decline in psychological functioning, and there were more abusers in this group who had a history of mental illness. Perpetrators of physical abuse and fraud or exploitation were more prone to alcohol abuse. Domestic partners were more likely to be perpetrators of physical and psychological abuse. In cases of fraud and exploitation, the highest proportion of perpetrators were nonrelatives (Godkin et al., 1989; Wolf et al., 1986).

Research also has found that the perpetrators often are elderly males abusing their female partners. The study concluded that this type of elder abuse is essentially a continuation of spousal abuse that has carried over into old age. A "reversal pattern" was also found in a small sample of cases in which the perpetrator was the female marital partner who had retained her health and strength as compared to her somewhat incapacitated male partner and former abuser. The burden of care in these situations became stressful, and in some instances the wife's abuse was likely in retaliation for the abuse she suffered from her husband throughout their marriage (Sengstock, 1991).

TABLE 4.5 Gender of Domestic Elder Abuse Perpetrators

	Percentage	
Gender of Perpetrator	*FY1995*	*FY1996*
Male	48.1	47.4
Female	49.9	48.9
Unknown/missing data	2.0	3.7
Total	100.0	100.0
Number of states reporting	24	23

SOURCE: *Summaries of the Statistical Data on Elder Abuse in Domestic Settings for FY95 and FY96*, published by the National Center on Elder Abuse. Used with permission.

The National Center on Elder Abuse reported for fiscal years 1995 and 1996 that slightly more females than males were perpetrators of elder abuse (see Table 4.5). However, the findings were based on such a low response rate that caution must be observed in generalizing the data nationwide (Tatara & Kuzmeskus, 1997).

Perpetrators Caring for Alzheimer's Patients

Caregivers of elderly persons with Alzheimer's disease are at risk of being physically and emotionally abusive because of the impaired cognitive functioning of the Alzheimer patient and the stress this places on the caregiver (Anetzberger, 1987; Steinmetz, 1988). Alzheimer's patient-caregiver dyads being seen at six medical sites throughout the United States were studied for incidents of abuse (Pazeva et al., 1992). The mean age of the patients was 75; for the caregivers, it was 63. Each group had twice as many females as males. Domestic partners accounted for 48% of the caregivers, adult children 37%, sons-in-law and daughters-in-law 7%, and siblings and others 8%. Patients living with adult child caregivers without a spouse present were at almost three times greater risk for violence than patients in other living arrangements, such as living alone, living with adult children with the presence of a spouse, or living with others. Also, the risk of violence toward Alzheimer's patients was greater where the caregiver was depressed.

As indicated earlier, perpetrators of sexual abuse of the elderly are males and generally are in a caregiver role to the abused elderly person (Holt, 1993; Ramsey-Klawsnik, 1991). In a study of 28 cases of elder sexual abuse, 78% of the assailants were family members, predominantly sons and husbands, who took sexual advantage of an elderly incapacitated woman in their care (Ramsey-Klawsnik, 1991).

ASSESSING AND INTERVENING IN ELDER ABUSE

Victims of elder abuse are often overlooked, due in part to the difficulty in identifying them. Physicians, nurses, physical and occupational therapists, and other allied health professionals play important roles in identifying elderly persons who may be experiencing abuse. An assessment regarding whether or not abuse is occurring should include physical and psychological evaluation of the elderly person as well as an assessment of the caregiver to determine if he or she is capable of providing care. This assessment must include the stress experienced by the caregiver in maintaining a personal life together with providing care to an elderly person (Janz, 1990).

A multidisciplinary approach to detecting and assessing elder abuse enables this social problem to be seen from various professional perspectives. The Beth Israel Elder Assessment Team (EAT) at Beth Israel Hospital in Boston, Massachusetts, is an example of a multidisciplinary approach to elder abuse assessment (Matlaw & Mayer, 1986; Matlaw & Spence, 1994). The team was organized in 1980 in response to state legislation mandating the reporting of persons age 60 and older living in long-term-care institutions who were suspected of being abused or neglected. The team is still in operation. The core team is composed of a clinical social worker, a nurse practitioner, and a physician, all of whom have professional training and additional credentials in geriatrics. The Elder Assessment Team has a two-part mission: to provide consultation and support to hospital staff regarding the clinical assessment of suspected cases of elder abuse or neglect and to educate hospital staff about the prevalence and treatment of elder abuse and neglect.

Role of Medical and Allied Health Professionals

Physicians, nurses, and allied health professionals, through their awareness that elder abuse exists and being knowledgeable about symptoms and risk factors, can play an important role in detecting and intervening in elder abuse in emergency rooms, clinics, and private physicians' offices. Specific guidelines have been created for physicians to follow in assessing and intervening in cases of elder abuse (Aravanis et al., 1993; Bloom, Ansell, & Bloom, 1989).

Some physicians may feel uncomfortable inquiring about family violence with their elderly patients when they suspect abuse. They may feel that such inquiry is not in their domain, which concentrates on the detection and treatment of illness. Also, the sociodemographic background of the family may cause the physician to feel that elder abuse is a lower socioeconomic phenomenon and would not occur in a middle- or upper-middle-class family (Lachs, 1995).

Research shows that physicians often take an inactive role when working with the elderly because of the lower level of attention given to the elderly as compared to younger patients and insufficient training in working with elderly patients. Also, frequently physicians are not aware of the general life situation of elderly patients and services available in a community to assist in helping elderly persons meet their daily needs. Finally, physicians may not be knowledgeable about laws mandating the reporting of elder abuse that they may see in patients in their practices (Blakely, Dolon, & May, 1993). Research also shows that some physicians who recognize cases of elder abuse tend to focus only on the abused individual and fail to see the abuse as an intrafamily problem. Patients showing evidence of abuse are often referred by their physician to clergy, lawyers, and other individuals outside the social service system when in fact social service agencies may be better able to provide the needed services to the abused elderly person and his or her family (Pratt, Koval, & Lloyd, 1983).

A program aimed at sensitizing physicians and medical students to the detection and treatment of elder abuse is provided by the Southeast Multi-Services Center and the Geriatric Unit of the Indiana University Department of General Internal Medicine in Indianapolis, Indiana (Blakely et al., 1993). Through the collaborative efforts of the center and the medical school, physicians are able to conduct home visits to elderly clients who are in need of medical evaluations and services. At the same time, medical students are able to gain direct exposure to the elderly within their home environments and are exposed to the work of social service providers and personnel of an adult protective service agency. The program has been shown to benefit victims of elder abuse and has sensitized physicians and medical students to the detection of, intervention in, and prevention of elder abuse.

Physical and occupational therapists employed by home health care agencies working with the elderly are in positions that enable them to detect and assess abuse of the patients they serve. If abuse is detected, these therapists may then make appropriate referrals to adult protective service agencies (Holland, Kasraian, & Leonardelli, 1987). However, physical and occupational therapists must be trained to recognize possible indicators of elder abuse.

Figure 4.4 presents indicators of physical and emotional abuse in the elderly that can help medical and allied health professionals in the detection and assessment of abuse in patients with whom they work (Bloom et al., 1989).

Physicians and other allied health professionals who have contact with elderly patients may be unaware that sexual abuse of the elderly occurs. Educating medical personnel about this problem and symptoms to watch for aids in the detection and treatment of elder sexual abuse. A list of symptoms is presented in Figure 4.5.

An important initial step in intervening in elder abuse is recognizing the problem. Mental health professionals and others who come into contact with the aged must be aware of characteristics of elderly persons, their families, and caregivers that place them at risk of being a victim or perpetrator of elder abuse. Figure 4.6 identifies such characteristics (Kosberg, 1988).

The assessment of elder abuse and subsequent interventions optimally require a multidisciplinary approach because of the diverse nature of the problems presented by the elderly and the dynamics of the setting in which the abuse occurs. For example, frequently a range of health problems is present in an abused elderly person requiring the attention of a physician and allied medical personnel including nurses, dietitians, and physical therapists. The medical problems are often overlaid with psychological problems in elderly persons who are confused, have severe memory loss, or are unable to communicate effectively. Psychosocial problems in the adult caregiver working under the stress of providing care to a dependent, confused adult may require assessment and intervention from the disciplines of psychology and social work. Effective interventions can occur only after an interdisciplinary diagnosis is made reflecting an analysis of the problems involved from a broad rather than narrow perspective. Interventions likewise may need to involve a diverse array of community agencies such as home health aides, meals-on-wheels, transportation, occasional overnight care for an elderly person to provide respite for the caregiver, and psychological counseling.

Assessment Instruments

A number of instruments are available to medical and mental health professionals for assessing elder abuse. They include Hwalek-Sengstock Elder Abuse Screening Test (Hwalek & Sengstock, 1986; Neale, Hwalek, Scott, Sengstock, & Stahl, 1991), Elder Assessment Instrument (EAI; Fulmer & Wetle, 1986), Index for Assessing the Risk of Elder Abuse in the Home (REAH;

History

1. Pattern of "physician hopping"
2. Unexplained delay in seeking treatment
3. Series of missed medical appointments
4. Previous unexplained injuries
5. Explanation of past injuries inconsistent with medical findings
6. Previous reports of similar injuries

Physical Findings

1. Injuries, which may have been inflicted on the patient by others either maliciously or through neglect
   - Fractures, dislocation
   - Burns in unusual locations or of unusual shapes
   - Bruises—bilateral on upper arms indicating holding or shaking; clustered on trunk from repeated striking; shaped similar to an object; around wrists or ankles from being tied down; inside part of thighs or arms
2. Other
   - Poor personal hygiene
   - Signs of overmedication, undermedication, misuse of medications
   - Sexually transmitted disease
   - Pain, itching, or bleeding in genital area

Observations

1. Psychological
   - Low self-esteem
   - Overly anxious or withdrawn
   - Extreme changes in mood
   - Depression
   - Suicidal ideation
   - Confusion or disorientation
2. Interaction between patient and family member/companion
   - Patient appears fearful of companion
   - Conflicting accounts of incident between patient and companion
   - Absence of assistance, attitudes of indifference, or anger toward patient exhibited by companion
   - Companion overly concerned with costs of treatment needed by patient
   - Companion denies patient the chance to interact privately with the physician

Figure 4.4 Indicators of Physical and Emotional Abuse
SOURCE: Reproduced with permission from *Geriatrics,* Vol. 44, No. 6, p. 41. Copyright © 1989 by Advanstar Communications Inc. Advanstar Communications Inc. retains all rights to the article.

- Genital or urinary irritation, injury, infection, or scarring
- Presence of sexually transmitted disease
- Intense fear reaction to an individual or to people in general
- Nightmares, night terrors, sleep disturbance
- Phobic behavior
- Mistrust of others
- Extreme upset when changed, bathed, or examined
- Regressive behaviors
- Aggressive behaviors
- Disturbed peer interactions
- Depression or blunted affect
- Poor self-esteem
- Self-destructive activity or suicidal ideation
- Coded disclosure of sexual abuse

Figure 4.5 Symptoms of Possible Elder Sexual Abuse
SOURCE: Ramsey-Klawsnik (1993a, p. 7).

Hamilton, 1989), The Elder Assessment Protocol (TEAP; Fulmer & Cahill, 1984), and H.A.L.F., an instrument that assesses an elder's *h*ealth status, a family's *a*ttitude toward aging, *l*iving arrangements, and *fi*nances (Ferguson & Beck, 1983). Two of these assessment instruments, REAH and H.A.L.F., are presented in Figures 4.7 and 4.8, respectively.

Mandatory Reporting

If the assessment reveals possible abuse, a report should be filed with adult protective service. The legal requirement for mandatory reporting of elder abuse is an essential initial step in treating as well as preventing further abuse. The specific provisions in mandatory statutes among the states differ for example in who must report elder abuse and the mandated time period for a report's investigation. Many states legally require professionals to report suspicions of elder abuse and provide immunity from civil and criminal liability for making reports in good faith (Ramsey-Klawsnik, 1993b). Mandatory reporting is primarily a case-finding device that identifies elderly persons who are possibly being abused so that an investigation by adult protective services can be implemented (Wolf, 1992).

Adult Protective Services

All 50 states have some type of adult protective services or elder abuse program, with the majority of these programs existing organizationally within state human services or social service agencies (Mixson, 1995). Similar to child protective services, adult protective services receives reports of elder abuse and screens them relative to their potential seriousness. If there is suspicion that maltreatment is occurring, an investiga-

Characteristics of Elders

- Female
- Advanced age
- Dependent upon others
- Problem drinker
- Intergenerational conflict between elder and adult child
- Internalizes blame by engaging in self-blame for the abuse
- Excessive loyalty to abusive caregiver
- Past history of abuse
- Stoical attitude
- Isolated from others
- Physical/mental impairment

Characteristics of High-Risk Family Systems

- Lack of family support
- Caregiver reluctance
- Overcrowding in family dwelling
- Isolated
- Presence of marital conflict
- Economic pressures
- Intrafamily problems
- Family members desire institutionalization of elderly person
- Disharmony in shared responsibility among relatives

Characteristics of High-Risk Caregivers

- Abuses drugs or alcohol
- Senile dementia or confusion
- Mental or emotional problems
- Lack of caregiving experience
- Economically troubled
- Abused as a child
- Experiencing extreme stress
- Isolated in home
- Blames others
- Unsympathetic
- Lacks understanding
- Unrealistic expectations
- Economically dependent
- Hypercritical

Figure 4.6 Characteristics of Elders, Caregivers, and Family Systems for Elder Abuse

REAH—An Index for Assessing the Risk of Elder Abuse in the Home

The REAH is the sum of two components, the vulnerability assessment score of the aged person (VASAP) and the stress assessment score of the caregiver (SASC). Use the tables below to calculate VASAP and SASC, then add them to find the REAH.

REAH (sum of VASAP and SASC, range 0 to 41) ___

VASAP—VULNERABILITY ASSESSMENT SCORE OF THE AGED PERSON

A. personal data section (aged person)

	2 points	*1 point*	*0 points*	*Score*
Age	85 or older	75-84	74 or younger	___
Sex		Female	Male	___
Health	Frail	Average	Robust	___
subtotal, A. personal data (sum of above, range 0 to 5)				___

B. dependency needs section (aged person)

1 point for a "yes," 0 points for a "no" or "don't know"	*Score*
Intellectual or severe mental impairment?	___
Lives in home with caregiver?	___
Needs help bathing?	___
Needs help dressing?	___
Needs help toileting? (or is incontinent or has catheter)	___
Needs help eating?	___
Depends on caregiver for all social interaction?	___
Allows caregiver to assume parental role?	___
Demanding and authoritative to caregiver?	___
Is financially dependent upon caregiver?	___
subtotal, B. dependency needs (sum of above, range 0 to 10)	___
VASAP (sum of subtotals A and B, range 0 to 15)	___

SASC—STRESS ASSESSMENT SCORE OF THE CAREGIVER

A. personal data section (caregiver)

	2 points	*1 point*	*0 points*	*Score*
Age	70 and over	45-69	Under 45	___
Physical health	Poor	Good	Excellent	___
Mental health	Poor	Good	Excellent	___
Finances	Under $7,000	$7,000-$14,000	$14,000 or more	___
Dependents (not elder)	2 or more	1	None	___
subtotal, A. personal data (sum of above, range 0 to 10)				___

B. stress factors section (caregiver)

1 point for a "yes," 0 points for a "no" or "don't know"	*Score*
Alcoholism or substance abuse?	___
Mental retardation?	___
History or observation of family violence?	___
Change in lifestyle to assume care of aged person?	___
Receives financial help from the elder?	___
Limited time for own personal activities?	___
Personal stresses (i.e., marital problems, empty nest)?	___
Mostly or always at home (unable to leave aged person)?	___
Absence of support system (family, friends, community)?	___
Shows frustrations, resentment in care of aged person?	___
Treats elder as a child?	___
Has limited knowledge of the aging process?	___
Believes any care at home is better than nursing home?	___
Minimizes or denies dependency of aged person?	___
Shows dependency toward the elder?	___
Authoritative manner with the elder?	___
subtotal, B. stress factors (sum of above, range 0 to 16)	___
SASC (sum of subtotals A and B, range 0 to 26)	___

Figure 4.7 REAH—An Index for Assessing the Risk of Elder Abuse in the Home
SOURCE: Form adapted from "Using a Prevent Elder Abuse Family Systems Approach" by G. Hamilton, 1989, in *Journal of Gerontological Nursing,* Vol. 15, pp. 21-26. Copyright © 1989 by Slack, Inc. Used with permission.

"H.A.L.F." Assessment

	ALMOST ALWAYS	*SOME OF THE TIME*	*NEVER*
HEALTH			
1. Aged Adult Risk Dynamics			
1.1 Poor health	✓		
1.2 Overly dependent on adult child	✓		
1.3 Was extremely dependent on spouse who is now deceased			
1.4 Persists in advising, admonishing, and directing the adult child on whom he/she is dependent			
2. Aged Adult Abuse Dynamics			
2.1 Has an unexplained or repeated injury			
2.2 Shows evidence of dehydration and/or malnutrition without obvious cause			
2.3 Has been given inappropriate food, drink, and/or drugs			
2.4 Shows evidence of overall poor care		✓	
2.5 Is notably passive and withdrawn	✓		
2.6 Has muscle contractures due to being restricted			
3. Adult Child/Caregiver Risk Dynamics			
3.1 Was abused or battered as a child			
3.2 Poor self-image	✓		
3.3 Limited capacity to express own needs	✓		
3.4 Alcohol or drug abuser	✓		
3.5 Psychologically unprepared to meet dependency needs of parents	✓		
3.6 Denies parent's illness			
4. Adult Child/Caregiver Abuse Dynamics			
4.1 Shows evidence of loss of control, or fear of losing control	✓		
4.2 Presents contradictory history			
4.3 Projects cause of injury onto third party			
4.4 Has delayed unduly in bringing the aged person in for care, shows detachment			
4.5 Overreacts or underreacts to the seriousness of the situation			
4.6 Complains continuously about irrelevant problems unrelated to injury			
4.7 Refuses consent for further diagnostic studies			
ATTITUDES TOWARD AGING			
5.1 Aged adult views self negatively due to aging process	✓		
5.2 Adult child views aged adult negatively due to aging process	✓		
5.3 Negative attitude toward aging	✓		
5.4 Adult child has unrealistic expectations of self or the aged adult	✓		
LIVING ARRANGEMENTS			
6.1 Aged adult insists on maintaining old patterns of independent functioning that interfere with child's needs or endanger aged adult			
6.2 Intrusive, allows adult child no privacy			
6.3 Adult child is socially isolated	✓		
6.4 Has no one to provide relief when uptight with the aged person	✓		
6.5 Aged adult is socially isolated	✓		
6.6 Has no one to provide relief when uptight with adult child	✓		
FINANCES			
7.1 Aged adult uses gift of money to control others, particularly adult children	✓		
7.2 Refuses to apply for financial aid			
7.3 Savings have been exhausted			
7.4 Adult child financially unprepared to meet dependency needs of aged adult	✓		

Figure 4.8 H.A.L.F. Assessment

SOURCE: Form adapted from "H.A.L.F.—A Tool to Assess Elder Abuse Within the Family" by D. Ferguson and C. Beck, 1983, in *Geriatric Nursing*, Vol. 4, pp. 301-304.

- Practice is to be client-focused, individualized, and based on a social work model of problem solving, as opposed to a prosecutorial or purely psychological approach.
- The vulnerable adult is the primary client, rather than the community or the family.
- The client is presumed to be mentally competent and in control of decision making until facts prove otherwise.
- The client actively participates in defining the problem and deciding the most appropriate course of action to resolve it.
- The client exercises freedom of choice and the right to refuse services as long as the individual has the capacity to understand the consequences of his or her actions.
- The service alternatives that are pursued are the least restrictive possible; more intrusive remedies, such as guardianship or institutionalization, are undertaken as a last resort.
- When legal remedies are unavoidable, the client has a right to an attorney ad litem to represent his or her interests in court.

Figure 4.9 Practice Guidelines for Adult Protective Service Workers

tion follows. A thorough investigation of reported cases of elder abuse is important to determine the validity of the report and to identify services that should be offered to the victim (Ramsey-Klawsnik, 1995). The investigation may include gathering background information by interviewing the referral source and collaterals and reviewing relevant records; interviewing the suspected victim, the suspected offender, and family members; arranging any necessary specialized diagnostic evaluations; and making a substantiation decision. Based on this investigation/assessment, a care plan is developed that may include arranging for services to be brought into the home to facilitate the continued independent living arrangements of the elderly person, moving the elderly person from the private home into a nursing home or other care facility, or referring the case to legal services (Wolf, 1992).

An important first step in the assessment of a report of possible elder abuse is providing protection to the victim if it is suspected that abuse is occurring. This may necessitate removal of the elderly person to a nursing home or other alternative living arrangement. In instances of sexual abuse, appropriate reports must be filed with law enforcement, and legal procedures prescribed by the state must be implemented. These procedures should provide the victim safety and protection from the perpetrator not only in terms of removal from the living situation in which the perpetrator has access to the victim but also preventing the perpetrator from visiting the victim where further sexual assaults may occur. Medical services for the victim must also be arranged (Ramsey-Klawsnik, 1993b).

The principles of practice that adult protective service workers follow when working with elder abuse situations is reflected in the guidelines shown in Figure 4.9.

Unfortunately, these practice principles often are not implemented because of psychosocial, cultural, economic, and other factors that may influence the adult protective service worker/client relationship. Significant problems for many adult protective service agencies include inadequate funding but extensive demand on the limited resources of funds and staff, large caseloads, a shortage of available legal assistance, and in general scarce resources that can be used when intervening in elder abuse cases. Frequently, the work of adult protective service agencies results in a triage approach, with only the most severe cases receiving service (Mixson, 1995). Also, many adult protective service workers do not have undergraduate or graduate social work degrees (Salmon & Atkinson, 1992).

Counseling and Supportive Groups

In light of research showing that the psychosocial problems of the perpetrator rather than the victim often underlie elder abuse, intervention in the form of counseling frequently is needed for adults serving in a caregiver role to an elderly person (Pillemer & Finkelhor, 1989). These services may include vocational counseling, housing placement, job placement, alcohol and drug abuse treatment, and financial support apart from dependence on the elderly person the caregiver is abusing (Wolf, 1992).

Counseling services that focus on interpersonal relationships may also be necessary when interpersonal conflicts are occurring in the caregiver-elderly person relationship. Counseling in the form of family therapy, based on systems theory, views the family as a social system and attempts to understand the family in terms of the interrelatedness and mutual interdependence among the system members. Systems theory views the abusive behavior and circumstances contributing to it as the culmination of an evolving process of interaction. Thus, the involvement of all family members, as occurs in family therapy, can be an effective intervention (Greene, 1986; Greene & Soniat, 1991). However, viewing the problem from a systems perspective, taking into account multiple factors contributing to the abuse, does not excuse the abuse or absolve perpetrators of responsibility for their abusive behavior.

Victims often resist seeking help through counseling, as most elders pride themselves on their independence and self-sufficiency, a pattern followed throughout their adult lives. However, once this resistance to seeking counseling or using supportive services is overcome, the elderly can realize the benefits derived from these resources. Elders may be less reluctant to be involved in support groups composed of elderly abused persons. One of these groups, provided by an agency and known as an empowerment group, was formed to strengthen abused seniors through

> education to identify abusive acts and seniors' rights; discussion of methods and resources for dealing with abuse; encouragement of interpersonal activity; increase of support and decrease of isolation; practice of appropriate responses to problems; and fostering of feelings of personal control. Group members identified their strengths, and worked to improve their self-esteem, using aids such as a "self-esteem tree." For each group member, each tree leaf represented a skill, strength, or achievement. The members, in this case all women, also focused on their feelings and experiences as women, the aging process, and problems of victimization. (Reis & Nahmiash, 1995, p. 669)

Counseling and supportive services to caregivers can be an effective intervention as well as aid in preventing elder abuse. Research shows that spousal caregivers of Alzheimer's patients are at greater risk of being abusive to the spousal patient than nonspousal caregivers (Pillemer & Suitor, 1992). This risk factor appears to be due to stress and a shared living arrangement. Support groups can significantly reduce the risk for abuse by giving caregivers an opportunity to share with similar individuals their concerns about their caregiving roles and to learn alternative ways of handling stressful situations that have the potential of becoming abusive (Kilburn, 1996).

Police Intervention

Police intervention in cases of elder abuse often becomes a difficult issue because of a lack of clarity or agreement on a definition of incompetence and an elderly person's right of free choice (Sengstock & Hwalek, 1986). Researchers concluded from studying two samples of elderly persons that police intervention in elder abuse cases was very appropriate; however, there was a hesitancy on the part of social agencies to use the police and a hesitancy on the part of the police to involve themselves in these cases (Sengstock & Hwalek, 1986; Sengstock & Liang, 1982).

Many incidents of elder abuse, however, fall within the scope of police intervention—for example, cases involving clear evidence of assault (broken bones, internal injuries), evidence of sexual abuse, or even death. These cases are a violation of criminal law and should result in prosecution. Criminal action may also be appropriate in cases of financial abuse and exploitation. Reluctance by the police to work on elder abuse cases often stems from the fact that clear evidence is not available; however, agencies working with elderly victims can be taught the importance of preserving evidence for subsequent police and court action. Often, though, the victims are reluctant to involve the police, but social service agency staff members can help victims see the importance of police involvement for their own future safety (Sengstock & Hwalek, 1986).

Legal Services

The provision of legal services is an important intervention, especially in cases of financial abuse. In a study of such cases seen by the Legal Aid and Defenders Association of Detroit, researchers found that clients had been financially defrauded by relatives and other adults living with them. Most of the victims were elderly but suffered no mental impairments, which may have explained their contacting Legal Aid. Reasons given for contacting Legal Aid included family members removing money from the victim's bank account without permission, placing homes and other property in other persons' names without permission, and personal property such as jewelry or furniture being stolen by relatives or landlords. Legal Aid attorneys also provided legal services to elderly victims who were being psychologically abused and whose personal rights were being violated. The research demonstrated that a legal agency can provide services to abused elders that other agencies cannot. These services include court actions, noncourt actions that require the services of a lawyer, and nonlegal actions in which an attorney can bring about action through the perceived threat of court action (Sengstock & Barrett, 1986).

Legal Guardians and Volunteers

Increasingly, legal guardians or conservators are being appointed by the court to act as trustees in managing the assets of an elderly person who is not capable of this task and who is at risk for financial abuse. A legal guardian generally is responsible for the complete care of a person who is totally incompetent and unable to manage personal and financial affairs. A conservator generally provides some assistance with business and property affairs for a person who is coherent and competent but not able to manage these affairs (Thomas, 1994). Conservators may be social workers, lawyers, clergy, and others willing to serve in this capacity.

An estimated 400,000 to 500,000 Americans have their personal decisions made by an appointed guardian, according to the American Bar Association. Individuals having legal guardians often have organic brain syndrome, senile dementia, or Alzheimer's disease, making them unable to manage their affairs (Thomas, 1994). All 50 states have mechanisms for appointing such a guardian to manage assets or make personal decisions for those unable to care for themselves, although these provisions differ from state to state (Landers, 1995). The appointment of a guardian for an elderly incapacitated person can prevent the abuse of this individual by unscrupulous caregivers and family members who might take advantage of the person.

Generally a three-step process is followed in obtaining guardianship. The first step involves a written petition that is filed in the probate court of the county where the person resides. Supportive written statements from two physicians attesting to an individual's incompetence in managing his or her affairs must accompany the petition. The second step involves the court notifying the elderly person in writing that a petition has been filed and that a hearing will be scheduled. The individual has a right to attend the hearing, to have legal counsel, and to have a trial by jury if so desired. An attorney is appointed by the court to represent the best interests of the person for whom the petition is being filed. The final step is the court procedure where the petition is heard. The judge or jury is responsible for a judgment. A later reevaluation of the person can be held.

Jewish Family Service of Worcester, Massachusetts, is one example of a legal guardianship program (Fins, 1994). This program, in existence since 1982, assumes legal guardianship of adjudicated incompetent elders. A model of social service agency guardianship has been developed that incorporates the goals of client advocacy, respect for the dignity of the elderly person, and the right of self-determination. A process for medical decision making for incapacitated elders has also been developed within the program. A team approach is used to promote "substituted judgment" and "best interests" models of decision making that also emphasize ethical considerations and elder client/family preferences (Thomas, 1994).

Volunteers have also effectively been used to provide assistance, support, and advocacy to victims in the use of social services and the criminal justice system as well as providing general social support (Filinson, 1993). The Elderly Abuse Support Project of Providence, Rhode Island, is an example of such a program. Volunteers attend an initial 8-hour training session and then monthly in-service meetings. Volunteers typically meet with clients a minimum of 2 hours per week, provide information and encouragement in pressing charges or obtaining a restraining order, provide transportation and/or accompaniment to police stations or to the court, and assist clients with the completion of any reports or forms. An evaluation of the project involving 42 abuse cases handled by the project compared with a control group of 42 cases investigated by the state's elder abuse unit but not referred to the project revealed that the volunteer advocate program, in comparison with the conventional system, led to more ambitious goal setting with the abused clients, greater achievement of these goals, and more extensive monitoring of the cases.

PREVENTING ELDER ABUSE

If elder abuse is to be prevented, the general public as well as professionals working with elderly persons must be informed about the problem of elder abuse and services made available to assist those caring for the elderly in their homes or in institutional settings.

Informing/Educating About Elder Abuse

Unlike child and domestic abuse, elder abuse is a type of family violence that has come to societal attention relatively recently. Just as professionals working with the elderly must be sensitized to those at high risk of being victims or perpetrators of elder abuse, even more so must the general public be made aware that such a problem exists and the various forms in which it appears.

In a study of what constituted elder abuse using a sample of elderly persons (average age 76) and their caregivers (average age 48), 75% of the sample defined elder abuse primarily in terms of neglect. Although recognition was also given to the physical abuse of the elderly, few elders and their caregivers included psychological, sexual, and financial abuse in their definition (Johnson, 1995).

Both professionals and the general public must be educated not only about how to recognize the various forms of elder abuse but also about their ethical and legal responsibility to report such cases to adult protective services. As stated earlier, elderly persons who are being abused often are reluctant to report it, thereby making it important that others who recognize this problem report it to the proper authorities.

The prevention of fraud and exploitation of the elderly can also occur through an educational process. Information in the media on scams through which the elderly are defrauded or exploited can assist in preventing such abusive practices. Likewise, community organizations such as the Better Business Bureau can take an active preventive role in informing the elderly and family members through media releases, talks, and workshops regarding unsavory business practices to which the elderly may be particularly vulnerable. Organizations in which elderly persons hold membership, such as the American Association of Retired Persons (AARP), community senior citizen groups, churches, lodges, and civic organizations, can effectively be used for these educational efforts. Finally, bank personnel and other individuals responsible for the management of elderly persons' finances must be made aware of how the elderly are often defrauded and should be sensitive to large withdrawals or drastic changes the elderly make in the handling of their financial matters (Blunt, 1993).

Courses are available in many communities to educate new parents in caring for a newborn child, yet adult children often have little or no preparation in caring for an elderly parent. Increasingly, communities are offering courses to assist families in their role of caring for an elderly family member at home. Courses on caring for the elderly not only provide caregivers knowledge on how to care for an elderly parent but often link the caregivers with community resources that can help make their task much easier—for example, day care for the elderly, support groups for caregivers of Alzheimer's patients, and home health services.

Various projects have been conducted over the years aimed at educating professionals as well as the elderly themselves about the problems of elder abuse, resources for intervening in the abuse, and ways to prevent it. An example is the Elder Abuse Training Project, which identified three target groups for educational programs: professionals including social workers, case managers, nurses, and doctors; community leaders including elected politicians, governmental officials, police, clergy, and officers in community civic, commerce, and fraternal/social organizations; and elderly individuals, their family members, and other concerned community members (Weiner, 1991). Although different learning objectives were determined and different programs were created flowing from the objectives for the various groups, the project's primary services were a series of educational workshops and consultation/referral assistance. Outcome objectives of this outreach educational project included increasing knowledge about elder abuse, providing information on identifying the problem, and facilitating the referral of and intervention in cases of elder abuse. A measure of its effectiveness revealed an increase in the number of calls and referrals to agencies working with the elderly from participants in the project (Weiner, 1991).

Establishing Services for the Elderly

Prevention of elder abuse can occur through the establishment of supportive services to assist adult children and others in their task of caring for the elderly, especially in noninstitutional settings, and in helping the elderly remain in their own homes. Unless supportive services (meals-on-wheels, day care for the elderly, home health aides, alternative caregivers, or respites for caregivers) are available in urban and rural communities, families are placed at risk for possibly abusing an elderly family member. For families in which elder abuse is occurring but supportive services are not available, mandatory reporting becomes a cruel hoax, for when an investigation substantiates the reported abuse, the elderly victim is likely to be revictimized by being removed from the home and unwillingly institutionalized (Ambrogi & London, 1985).

A significant problem in many communities is the coordination of existing services to elder abuse victims and their families and the identification of service gaps or needs. The Elder Abuse Resource Centre in Winnipeg, Canada, is an example of a coordinated community response to elder abuse (Wasylkewycz, 1993). This program was established after a local agency serving the elderly convened a series of meetings with government and community service agencies to exchange information and to identify existing resources available for intervening in and preventing elder abuse. One of the services developed by the Resource Centre was the establishment of a multidisciplinary team of professionals who regularly met and acted as consultants to community agency personnel regarding difficult cases of elder abuse. Another interventive service identified as a need in the community that the Centre instituted was the use of support groups for women over the age of 60 who were experiencing abuse in their marriages.

SUMMARY

Elder abuse can occur in the setting of a private home or in institutions such as homes for the aged and nursing homes. Families who bring an elderly person into their home for care are often at high risk for abuse because of the lack of training in caring for an elderly person as well as the stress this care places both on the primary caregiver and on other family members.

Social services and medical and allied health services can enable elderly persons to remain in the own homes or effectively be cared for by other family members. The provision of supportive services to family members caring for an elderly person, such as day care that allows the primary caregiver respite from the responsibilities of providing care to an elderly person, can help prevent elder abuse from occurring. The education of persons working with the elderly regarding the availability of services as well as the potential risk for abuse of an elderly person also are important steps in preventing elder abuse.

SUGGESTED READING

Journals

Geriatrics

Journal of Applied Gerontology

Journal of Elder Abuse & Neglect

Journal of Family Violence

Journal of Gerontological Social Work

Pride Institute Journal of Long Term Home Health Care

The Gerontologist

Books

Aitken, L., & Griffin, G. (1996). *Gender issues in elder abuse.* Thousand Oaks, CA: Sage.

Anetzberger, G. (1987). *The etiology of elder abuse by adult offspring.* Springfield, IL: Charles C Thomas.

Gelles, R. (1997). *Intimate violence in families.* Thousand Oaks, CA: Sage.

Pillemer, K., & Wolf, R. (Eds.). (1986). *Elder abuse: Conflict in the family.* Dover, MA: Auburn House.

5

Sibling Abuse

My memories of growing up at home focus a lot on the way my brother who was 3 years older than me treated me. He would hit, punch, and slap me continually. If I complained to my parents about it, they would say things like "You must have done something to deserve it" and "Fight your own battles and don't get us involved." After a while I started to fight back, but he was so much bigger and strong than me. I couldn't hold my own against him. Besides, then my parents had reason to excuse his actions because they saw me hitting him. This behavior continued until my brother joined the army immediately after graduation from high school. Later, I left for college and married. I have nothing to do with my brother now. I don't care if I ever see him again. He made my childhood miserable. Also, I have never forgiven my parents for allowing this to happen, but we just don't talk about it now.

* * *

When I was in grade school, I was somewhat overweight. My older sister, who was not heavy, started to tease me about my weight. She called me "Lardo." After a while my younger brother picked up on the name and began calling me this name. My weight was a frequent topic of discussion in our family. My parents would say things like "You have such a pretty face, if only you got rid of that extra weight" and "No one is going to date you when you get into high school unless you start losing weight." My parents even expected me not to have dessert when everyone in the family would eat a piece of cake my mother baked for dinner.

One time my older sister called me "Lardo" at school in front of some of my friends. Everyone laughed. I wanted to cry, but I knew I couldn't because it would only make matters worse. That evening I told my mother what had happened and her response was that I deserved it if I didn't lose weight. She told me that others also would call me that if I gained any more weight. I was very hurt by what she said. She doesn't know it, but I even thought of committing suicide.

I am now 23 years old, single, and working as a secretary in a large office. The emotional abuse I experienced from my siblings, which my mother would not stop, has made me a "loner." I go to my job, go home, and stay in my apartment. I'm thinking of joining a group for overweight people as a way to deal with my low self-esteem.

* * *

When I was about 7 years old, my brother told me he wanted to teach me something. He would baby-sit me in the evening while my mother worked a second job from which she didn't get home until after midnight. My parents were divorced, and since my Dad never paid child support my mother had to work two jobs. My brother, who was about 14 at the time, took his pants down and showed me his erect penis. He proceeded to tell me what adults do when they have sex and touched my vaginal area. Although he acted like he was doing me a big favor, he also warned me that if I ever told our mother about this he would kill me.

My sexual abuse by my brother continued until I started to menstruate. He never would penetrate me but he often would come into my bedroom when I had just gone to bed, lay on top of me, and rub back and forth simulating intercourse. Then he would masturbate or sometimes make me do it. I was too scared to tell my mother because my brother was a bully and I didn't know what he might do to me.

These are accounts of adults who as children were victims of a type of family violence that has largely gone undetected—the physical, emotional, and sexual abuse of one sibling by another.

This chapter discusses this type of family violence in terms of the various forms of sibling abuse, parental reactions to the problem, understanding sibling abuse, the victim's response to the abuse, its effect on the victims, the treatment of survivors, distinguishing sibling abuse from normal sibling rivalry, and ways this problem can be prevented.

This chapter is somewhat different from the previous chapters on child, partner, and elder abuse, for there is very little research on the subject of sibling abuse, even though this type of abuse occurs more frequently than child and domestic abuse (Straus et al., 1980). Research on sexual abuse in the form of incest studies has been done; however, many of these studies do not differentiate among the family members who were the perpetrator (parent, stepparent, cousin, sibling). Hence, the information presented here is based on my research involving 150 adult survivors of sibling abuse. These survivors responded to questionnaires sent to counseling and mental health centers throughout the United States at which they were seeking help for problems resulting from their physical, emotional, or sexual abuse by a sibling.

The data from these questionnaires were analyzed using qualitative rather than quantitative data analysis. The goal of qualitative analysis is to understand the research topic from the perspective of the participants involved—their thoughts, emotions, and firsthand experiences. Qualitative data analysis is descriptive in nature with minimal use of statistics, a characteristic of quantitative analysis (Royse, 1995). Anecdotal accounts from the survivors portray their emotions, enable learning about the problem of sibling abuse from their perspective, and impart the impact of the abuse on their lives. Thus, comments from survivors of sibling abuse who participated in the research illustrate the various themes in this chapter.

THE RESEARCH PARTICIPANTS

Who were the people seeking help from counseling and mental health centers for the effects of sibling abuse on their lives and who agreed to respond to the research questionnaire? Obviously, this was not a random sample but one biased in the direction of individuals who recognized that what they experienced from a sibling was abuse and who were experiencing problems in living resulting from their sibling's behavior toward them.

Of the 150 respondents, 89% (134) were female, average age was 37, and 85% (127) were Caucasian, 13% (20) African American, and 2% (3) other racial or ethnic backgrounds. Over one quarter (27%, or 41) were single, 47% (73) identified themselves as married, and 3% (4) indicated they were cohabiting with someone; 21% (31) were divorced. Only 1 person was widowed.

The respondents represented a well-educated group of persons: Only 16% (24) had a high school education or less, whereas 50% (75) had attended college or had completed an undergraduate degree; an additional 34% (51) held graduate degrees.

It was not possible to control for the socioeconomic status of the respondents' parents because many had no knowledge of their parents' income given the different times when the respondents were children. The educational level achieved by the parents, however, gives some indication of their social status: 57% (85) of their mothers had a high school education or less, and 43% (65) had attended college, completed college, or held graduate degree; the fathers' educational level was nearly identical, with only one more father having attended or completed college.

Although the questionnaire indicated that people could respond anonymously, 71% (107) provided their names, addresses, and phone numbers, indicating their willingness to be contacted for a possible follow-up letter or phone call.

INCIDENCE OF ABUSE

How frequently does physical abuse by a sibling occur? National statistics based on reported cases do not exist because generally cases of physical or emotional sibling abuse do not come to the attention of the authorities. Rather, abusive behavior between siblings is excused as sibling rivalry, and mandatory reporting of these incidents is not required. Intrafamilial sexual abuse statistics, which would include sibling sexual abuse, generally do not distinguish among the various family members who were the perpetrator.

Several studies in the family violence literature, however, give some indication of the extent to which sibling abuse occurs. In a survey of 57 randomly selected families, a high level of physical violence between siblings was found, as reported in families' comments and in diaries they kept for a week (Steinmetz, 1977).

Similarly, in a nationwide study of violence in 2,143 American families, the researchers found that violent acts between siblings occurred more frequently than either parent-child (child abuse) or husband-wife (partner abuse) violence in that 53 of every 100 children per year physically attack a brother or sister (Straus et al., 1980).

Likewise, a study reported by *U.S. News & World Report* found that 138,000 children, ages 3-17, used a weapon on a sibling over a 1-year period. If such attacks had occurred outside the family, they would have been considered assaults; however, because they occurred between children within a family they were basically ignored ("Battered Families," 1979).

PHYSICAL ABUSE

Forms of sibling physical abuse discussed using survivors' comments are labeled most common, unusual, and injurious or life threatening.

Most Common Forms

The most common forms of physical abuse reported by adult sibling abuse survivors consisted of hitting, slapping, shoving, punching, biting, hair pulling, scratching, and pinching. Survivors also reported having been hit with objects such as broom handles, rubber hoses, coat hangers, hairbrushes, belts, and sticks and being threatened and stabbed with broken glass, knives, razor blades, and scissors.

A 40-year-old woman described her memories of physical abuse by her brother:

> When I was three or four, my brother pushed me down some stone steps. I had approximately 30 stitches in my knee. As I grew older, my brothers typically would slug me in the arm. I was not to cry or everyone went to their rooms. My older brother would usually hit me in the stomach, push me down on the floor and hold me down while he continued to hit me in the stomach and on the arms.

A female survivor from New Mexico described the abuse she experienced from an older brother:

> He would engage me in wrestling matches daily, typically punching me in the stomach until I could not breathe, torturing my joints —wrists, knees—spitting on me, putting his knees on my arms and pinning me down and beating on my chest with his knuckles.

A male respondent described the physical abuse he received from an older brother and identified the source from which the brother learned this behavior:

> Usually the abuse would consist of getting beat up by my brother with his fists or being slapped around with the inside of his hands, a practice he learned from our parents, along with being kicked in the rear.

Unusual Form

An unusual form of sibling abuse that survivors reported was tickling. Tickling generally is not regarded as a form of abuse, but it can in fact become physically abusive under certain conditions. Tickling can be pleasant, even erotic, or it can be painful. The unpleasantness often associated with tickling is due to the fact that the nerve fibers that respond to tickling are the same ones that respond to pain (Farrell, 1985). Tickling can be pleasant when it occurs in a context of trust and mutual respect. In such a context, the victim trusts that the perpetrator will stop the behavior at the victim's request.

But tickling becomes painful and abusive if the victim has no control over the situation. When the victim requests that the tickling cease but the perpetrator continues to engage in the behavior, it is abusive. As reported by survivors in this research, some perpetrators even restrained their victims, such as pinning them to the floor. Often, there was little the victims could do because of their smaller size or weaker strength in relation to their perpetrators.

Several survivors described having serious reactions to the tickling they experienced from a sibling. An adult woman reported that a sister, 3 years older, would physically abuse her as a child by punching, slapping, and pinning her down on the floor. Most disturbing, however, was the fact that the sister would tickle her to the point that she would vomit.

Another survivor reported that

> I was ummercifully tickled by my brother who held down every limb and body part that wiggled and covered my mouth when I cried and yelled for help. He pulled my hair after I pulled his, thinking that would hurt him and he would stop.

This survivor said that her mother ignored what her brother did, calling it playing, even though she tried to convince her mother that it was not playful activity. The survivor reported that this abuse affects her even now as an adult. She does not like to be touched by other people, especially when they hug her or hold her in any way reminiscent of being restrained.

Injurious or Life-Threatening Forms

Some physical abuse between siblings had an injurious or life-threatening aspect to it. Play among siblings sometimes escalates into aggressive behavior and can result in injury. All children probably at some time or another are injured while playing, even accidentally by a sibling. Survivors described incidents where siblings shot them with BB guns, attempted to drown them, smothered them under pillows until they nearly suffocated (in one instance needing mouth-to-mouth resuscitation), and repeatedly hit them in the stomach until they lost their breath.

These incidents, however, must be distinguished from what often happens when children play and someone becomes injured. First, the experiences occurred frequently and were typical of the interactions between the siblings. Although children may at some time suffer some type of physical injury in childhood while playing with a sibling, it is generally an isolated or single incident. For the sibling abuse victims, the abuse was typical of the behavior they experienced from a sibling.

Second, the perpetrator's reaction to the injury the victim suffered must be considered. In most abusive instances, the perpetrator laughed at the victim. This reaction further "injured" the victim by giving the message that the behavior had an intentional element to it.

Finally, the experience must be understood in the context of the parents' reaction. When children are injured by a sibling when playing, parents comfort them, take care of their injuries, and punish the sibling who perpetrated the injury. At the very least, parents make an attempt to determine what happened. But when parents react to an injurious or life-threatening incident with nonchalance, denial of the suffering the victim experienced, or even blame the victim for what happened, the incident becomes abusive.

A 55-year-old woman described a physically abusive incident in childhood from a sister that resulted in injury. The scars from this injury remain today as a reminder to her of the physical abuse she experienced from this sister as a child:

> I climbed on the chicken coop and a nail penetrated my foot. It went all the way through my foot. I was literally nailed to the coop. My older sister saw me and laughed and told me that's what I deserved. She left and wouldn't help me down. After a long time my older brother came by, helped me get down and took me to the hospital for help and a tetanus shot. I was so afraid I would get lock-jaw. I still have the scar on my foot.
>
> Once my sister was ironing. She was a teen-ager. I was between four and five. I was curious as to what she was doing. I put my hands flat up on the ironing board and she immediately put the hot iron down on my hand. She laughed and told me to get lost. I still have the burn scar on my left hand.

A woman in her late 40s described the injurious abuse she suffered from an older brother as a child and her parents' response to it:

> When I was two or three, my mother went to visit my father who was in the Army and my brother and I were left in the care of my grandparents. My brother was helping my grandfather paint a fence and he painted me from head to toe with dark brown paint. I remember the paint was in my hair, face, clothing, etc. and I had to be scrubbed down with turpentine and repeated baths. Some of my hair had to be cut to get the paint out. My brother laughed and teased me about all of this. Later, during another incident my brother wrote his name on my bare back with his woodburning kit. He seemed to treat me as an object rather than as a person with any feelings. My abuse continued through high school. My brother would twist my arms or pin me down and bend my arms or legs to get me to do things he wanted me to do, such as his chores or to cover for him by lying to my parents. These incidents usually happened when my parents weren't home. When I reported them to my parents, he would say I was making it up to get him in trouble. Then we would both be punished. I knew my parents didn't know how to handle the problem, so I quit reporting to my parents. I would just arrange to go to a friend's house or have a friend over when my parents were going to be out.

Another survivor reported, "I have photographs of my brother pushing me down and trying to 'playfully' strangle me when I was an infant." This same woman remembers that as a child of 4 to 6 years old, her brother would restrain her and in a threatening but supposedly playful manner put his hands around her neck, as if to choke her to death. She indicated that as an adult she remains very frightened of men and has a phobia about anyone touching her neck. She also stated, based on her experience with her sibling, that she is not willing to have more than one child.

Respondents told of siblings smothering them with a pillow, another form of life-threatening physical abuse. This particular behavior seems to have occurred when siblings were playing together on a couch or bed. The frightening response of the victim to what initially might be described as playful activity became a clue for some perpetrators of the power and control they could exert over their sibling.

> I remember my brother putting a pillow over my head. He would hold it and laugh while I struggled to get out from under him and the pillow. I remember being *terrified.* I honestly thought he would smother me to death. This occurred frequently.

Victims' Responses to Their Physical Abuse

How did the victims who experienced physical abuse from a sibling respond to it? Several responses will be identified.

Protecting Themselves

As one would expect, the most typical response was that the victims would attempt in whatever ways possible to protect themselves from the physical assaults. A young women from New York described how she tried to protect herself from a sister who was a year older: "My sister would beat me up, and I would sit on my bed with my knees up guarding myself until she stopped."

Screaming and Crying

Another typical, natural reaction was that the victim screamed or cried out for help. Unfortunately, this reaction often provoked the perpetrator to intensify the physically abusive behavior. Following is a typical scenario: An older brother is beating on a younger sibling. If the younger sibling cries or screams for help, the beating intensifies under the warning, "Take it like you should!" or "If you cry, I'll give you more." Some children may learn or model this behavior from their parents and the way in which they have been punished by them. A parent punishes a child by spanking. After the child is spanked, the parent warns the child not to cry: "If you don't stop crying, I'll really give you something to cry about."

Separating Themselves From the Perpetrator

The position of powerlessness in which sibling abuse victims often found themselves with older and stronger siblings prompted many of them to respond in the only way they could, by separating themselves from the perpetrator and at times literally hiding in order to avoid being abused. The victims would lock themselves in their bedroom, if they were fortunate enough to have their own room, or they would spend as much time as possible away from home with friends.

Victims appeared to live in constant fear of further abuse. Attempts to scream or cry out for help often only resulted in further abuse. The only way some of the victims could cope with the abuse was always to distance themselves from the sibling. As children, life involved sensing the mood of an abusive sibling and staying as far away from the sibling as possible as a means of self-protection.

A survivor described her efforts at self-protection from an older abusive brother:

> I became a very withdrawn child. I would retreat to my room and read. If my brother was involved in a game, I wouldn't play. If he was in a particular room, I would go to a different one.

An adult woman described the abuse she experienced as a child on a daily basis from an only sibling, a brother 4 years older:

> My brother would hit me, bite me, wrestle me, etc., anytime my parents were out of sight. The times which were most frightening for me were after school or the period between the time we arrived home from school and my parents came home from work, about two to three hours. I would run to my room and lock the door or go to a friend's house so he wouldn't terrorize me.

Abusing a Younger Sibling in Turn

The response of some victims to their abuse by a sibling was to inflict the same abuse on another sibling. This behavior can be understood in two ways. One, the victim used the older sibling's behavior as a model and in turn became a perpetrator. Social learning theory states that violence or abuse is often a learned behavior. The behavior may be learned from parents—if they are abusive to each other—from an older sibling who may be abusive, from peers, or from television, movies, and videos (Huston et al., 1992; Irwin & Gross, 1995; Paik & Comstock, 1994). A continuing pattern is established, and unless the parents intervene, abuse can potentially become a normal way for older siblings to interact with younger siblings. Second, the behavior may be understood as a psychological defense. The victim assumes the characteristics of the aggressor by shifting from a passive victim role to an active aggressive role by inflicting the same behavior on another victim. The end result is that the siblings are in a constant state of conflict. A young adult woman described the process with her sibling in this way:

> The worst fights started around the time I was in third grade. I got a lot of abuse from my older brother. Then I would turn around and abuse my sister. I would get her twice as hard as what I received. As we got older, it got worse. I would have knives pulled on me. Then I would turn around and pull a gun on one of the others. I would take my anger out on my sister or younger brother. I became very violent especially toward my sister.

Telling Their Parents

Many of the victims of sibling physical abuse told their parents about the abuse, but the parents refused to help the victim. Indeed, reporting the physical abuse often resulted in the victim being further victimized. A typical parental response was to blame the victim for it. "You must have done something to deserve it," a parent would respond. Obviously, such a response provided the victim no protection from future physical assaults and discouraged the child from ever again telling the parents about the abuse.

Another common parental response was to become very angry and discipline both the perpetrator and the victim with corporal punishment. In some instances, the perpetrator would be so severely corporally punished (whipped, beaten with a belt) by a parent that the victim felt badly for having reported the abuse to the parent. These parental responses also led the victim to conclude that it did not pay to report physical abuse.

Undoubtedly, many children who are physically abused by a sibling do report the behavior to their parents, and the parents effectively intervene. The parents' intervention may involve examining the situation with the sibling, determining what provoked the abuse, perhaps identifying the contribution of each sibling to the incident that escalated to abusive behavior, and helping the siblings consider ways the altercation could have been avoided. This "problem-solving approach," discussed later, is an effective way for parents to intervene in sibling-abusive situations.

EMOTIONAL ABUSE

A frequently heard jingle states, "Sticks and stones may break my bones, but words will never hurt me." Although physical abuse may leave bruises and other evidence, there are no outwardly visible marks from emotional abuse. However, the jingle is very incorrect when it states that words, the basic component of emotional abuse, do not hurt.

Definition

The term emotional abuse or psychological maltreatment is often labeled *teasing* when it occurs among siblings (or peers). Individuals who identified themselves as victims of emotional abuse by a sibling frequently reported that they were "teased" by the sibling. The term now denotes not only a behavior that often occurs among children but is a catch-all word to denote a number of behaviors. Current synonyms for the verb *to tease* indicate the specific types of actions that constitute this behavior: *to belittle, intimidate, annoy, scorn, provoke.*

Researchers in the field of child abuse have identified emotional abuse as more prevalent and potentially even more destructive than other forms of child abuse and as often underlying physical and sexual abuse (Claussen & Crittenden, 1991; Garbarino & Vondra, 1987; Hart & Brassard, 1987). This is equally true in sibling relationships. Generally, emotional abuse among siblings includes the following behaviors: name-calling, ridicule, degradation, exacerbating a fear, the destruction of personal possessions, and the torture or destruction of a pet.

Emotional abuse is difficult to identify. Accepted legal standards are not available either for proving that emotional or behavioral problems resulted from emotional abuse or for determining the seriousness of emotional abuse (Corson & Davidson, 1987; Navarre, 1987). Also, because emotional abuse leaves no physical evidence, to an outside observer a family may appear to be operating well psychosocially, but within the family one sibling may be emotionally abusing another.

Detecting emotional abuse by a sibling is complicated by the fact that professionals and parents have tended to accept emotionally abusive behavior as a phenomenon that occurs in all children's interactions with their siblings and their peers. The teasing and verbal put-downs in which siblings engage with each other and with children in general, although disliked by parents, is often accepted as normal behavior. Between siblings this behavior is simply excused as sibling rivalry.

When parents excuse or overlook emotional abuse that occurs between siblings, the victims are given the message that this behavior is really not abusive. Different child-rearing practices and cultural values may reinforce denial that certain behaviors or styles of communication between siblings are emotionally abusive. Even victims of emotional abuse sometimes deny this form of abuse.

A similar phenomenon happened historically with the physical abuse of children by adults, as indicated in Chapter 2. This form of abuse was overlooked because children were viewed as the property of their parents and what occurred behind the closed doors of the family residence was considered the family's private business. Children who experienced severe beatings by their parents and other forms of physical assault were forced to conclude that they deserved this behavior or that these were proper forms of discipline, despite the physical and emotional suffering the victims endured. Within the past several decades, as society began recognizing adult-child physical abuse as a social problem, victims have been able to seek help for the effects of physical abuse on their lives, and society has taken steps to prevent such abuse. As long as sibling emotional abuse (as well as all forms of sibling abuse) is not recognized for what it is, victims are forced to conclude that this is normal behavior or that they deserve such treatment from their siblings.

Interaction of Emotional, Physical, and Sexual Abuse

Eleven people, or 7% of the 150-person sample, indicated that they had only been emotionally abused. Although the three forms of sibling abuse—physical, emotional, and sexual—were treated separately in the research questionnaire, the respondents indicated that one form of sibling abuse rarely occurred in isolation. (The only exception was that some survivors did not report being sexually abused by a sibling.) Generally, several forms of abuse occurred in interaction with the others. Thus, 71% (107) indicated that they had been emotionally, physically, and sexually abused. Combined with the 11 persons who indicated that they had been only emotionally abused, this means that 78% (118) of the sample had been emotionally abused.

The interaction of emotional and physical abuse is demonstrated by the following comments of a survivor of abuse from a brother 3 years older:

> I can't remember a time when my brother didn't taunt me, usually trying to get me to respond so he would be justified in hitting me. Usually he would be saying I was a crybaby or a sissy or stupid or ugly and that no one would like me, want to be around me, or whatever. Sometimes he would accuse me of doing something and if I denied it, then he would call me a liar. I usually felt overwhelmingly helpless because nothing I said or did would stop him. If no one else was around, he would start beating on me after which he would stop and go away. I felt helpless to stop any of it.

Another survivor described how her brother, 9 years older, used emotional abuse in connection with sexual abuse:

> The emotional abuse stemmed directly from the sexual abuse. The earliest memory was when I was about five years old. It is difficult for me to be specific about a single event since it is hard for me to remember many instances. I've blocked a lot out of my mind. But I always remember being afraid of being rejected by my parents. My brother was the oldest and he made me believe that my parents would always believe him over me since I was only five and he thirteen. So, you see, he always had some sort of power over me emotionally and physically. As a child and adolescent I was introverted and never really shared my inner feelings with anyone. I felt like dirt and that my needs, concerns, and opinions never mattered, only those of other people. I was always in fear of both forms of abuse (emotional and sexual). I learned to prepare myself for both. I'm so resentful that I had to do this to survive mentally in my home. My brother would always present himself in these situations as being perfect—mature, responsible, brave—a model brother. Then, I'd feel like an immature, non-credible child. He's saying things like how my parents thought he was so special, being the oldest. And, that if I told on him, I would destroy the entire family; my parents would divorce; I would be sent to a foster home. He had such emotional control over me in that sense that I "obeyed" him and never told. He had control over my self-image and my body.

Extent of the Problem

The research questionnaire asked respondents to identify how frequently emotional abuse occurred in their family while they were growing up. Their responses revealed that emotional abuse in the form of name-calling, ridicule, and degradation was a common pattern in the relationship between siblings and in some instances between the parents and the siblings. Respondents repeatedly used words like *constant* and *always* when describing the emotional abuse they experienced from a sibling. Many of the respondents spent their childhood years in a climate of name-calling, ridicule, and mockery:

> I was constantly being told I was no good, a pig, whore, slut—all sexually oriented negatives. I was constantly emotionally being degraded.

> I can't remember a time when I was growing up when my brother didn't taunt me.

> From my earliest memories, age five or so, my siblings called me names and said degrading things to me.

Forms of Emotional Abuse

Name-calling, ridicule, degradation, exacerbating a fear, destroying personal possessions, and torturing or destroying a pet are forms of emotional abuse discussed and illustrated with survivors' experiences of these forms of abuse.

Name-Calling

Nearly every individual in the sample who was emotionally abused by a sibling made reference to being called names. The perpetrator appeared to use name-calling as a way to belittle or degrade the victim. (Degradation, discussed later, also occurred without name-calling.) The name-calling generally focused on some attribute of the victims, such as their height, weight, physical characteristics, intelligence, or inability to perform a skill. The second case example that opened this chapter reflects emotional abuse focusing on a sibling's weight problem. Survivors recounted experiences with name-calling:

> When I was six, my mother realized I needed glasses. For the next several years my brothers told me I was ugly and taunted me with a lot of names referring to being unattractive.

> I was heavy as a young child, about seven or eight years old. My brother called me "Cow." He was asked to mark all the children's socks with our names so for mine he drew the face of a cow. He called me a Spanish word which I understood meant "whore."

> My sister would verbally harass me—you're ugly, stupid, fat, etc. If I did accomplish something, she would turn things around and prove that I had failed or been a fool.

Ridicule

Ridicule appeared to be a sport to some siblings and a form of emotional abuse that survivors recalled with painful emotions. Ridicule is defined here as words or actions used by the perpetrator to express contempt, often along with laughter directed against the victim. Several surviors recalled being ridiculed by siblings:

> My sister would get her friends to sing songs about how ugly I was.

> Life as a child consisted of constant taunts and ridicule on issues such as things I said, clothes I wore, my friends, etc.

> I was ridiculed by my older brothers and sisters for just being. Ridicule and put-downs were "normal" for our family.

Degradation

This form of emotional abuse deprives individuals of their sense of dignity and worth. Many survivors reported that their siblings told them that they were "worthless" and "no good." Degradation was emotionally devastating to the victims both at the time the abuse was occurring and even years later as adults. The survivors' comments indicate that the degrading messages they received as children from a sibling continued to haunt them into their adult years. It was as if the message from their abusive sibling became a self-fulfilling prophecy. This was especially true for those survivors whose parents did not intervene in the abusive behavior but ignored it, accepted it as normal behavior, or worst of all participated in it.

Children who degrade their siblings do not seem to realize how this behavior affects the victims. Those abused in this way may react by appearing as if the degrading comments have no effect. This stoical reaction perhaps is at the root of the jingle, "Sticks and stones may break my bones but words will never hurt me." By taking a defensive stance, the victim denies the emotional pain caused by the verbal assault. Unfortunately, however, this reaction often only reinforces or encourages the perpetrator to continue the emotionally abusive behavior.

Children are especially vulnerable to degrading remarks because it is during their childhood years that they are developing a positive sense of self-worth and self-esteem. Unfortunately, interactions with peers in play and at school often do not facilitate this development. Verbal put-downs between siblings (and peers) often occur so frequently that parents and others in authority tend to accept them as normal. A parent's failure to stop such behavior gives a message to the perpetrator that this is acceptable behavior. The behavior can therefore be expected to continue unless some action is taken to discontinue it.

Many sibling abuse survivors reported that their emotional abuse as a child continued into their adulthood. "Labeling theory" explains that one child in a family may be labeled the scapegoat or as outside the family circle. The nicknames they were given by their siblings as children often remained with them as adults. Similarly, the labels that children acquired that focused on a specific personality trait or physical characteristic that distinguished them from their peers continued to haunt them into adulthood:

> I was being constantly told how ugly, dumb, unwanted I was. Already about two years of age, I was told, "No one wants you around. I [my sister] wish you were dead. You aren't my real sister, your parents didn't want you, either, so they dumped you with us." I grew up feeling, if my own family doesn't like me, who will? I believed everything my sister ever told me—that I was ugly, dumb, homely, stupid, fat—even though I always was average in weight. I felt no one would ever love me. When you're little, you believe everything you're told. It can last a lifetime.

> I was told that I was no good, that no one loved me, that I was adopted (which was not true), that my parents did not really want me. My parents were always gone and emotionally unavailable, partially due to alcohol abuse, so that I was often left in the care of my two older brothers.

> My brothers loved to tease me to tears. They were ruthless in their teasing and did not let up. They teased me for being ugly. They teased me for being sloppy. They teased me for just being. This was the worst.

A young adult male who identified himself as being gay experienced degrading comments from a brother when he was growing up:

> My brother would tell me what a sissy or faggot I was; that I wasn't a man, and then would laugh. He would tell others to taunt me, to bait me. He would bring me to tears.

Survivors who experienced emotional abuse in the form of degradation reported having a pervasive feeling during childhood that they should not exist, like the survivor quoted earlier whose older brothers teased her "for just being." The transactional analysis (TA) school of psychology refers to this as "Don't Be," a "game" some parents even engage in with a child (Berne, 1967). A subtle message is given to a child in a variety of ways that life would be much better if the child were not around. The parents would have fewer financial expenses or there would be less tension in the home. This destructive and emotionally damaging "game" is also played by siblings against one another. When this "game" is analyzed from a reality perspective, its extreme psychological destructiveness can be understood. Although a child is not responsible for his or her existence, the "game" carries an underlying wish for the child's destruction.

Another form of degradation that occurred, especially by older siblings toward younger siblings and especially brothers toward their sisters, was to "use" the sibling. Sisters described their brothers as "lording it over" them. A brother would command his sister to do things on his behalf, such as household chores that he was expected to do. The failure of the victim to comply with the perpetrator's demands at times resulted in physical abuse. In essence, a brother would be exerting power and control over his sister. A survivor who was raised on a farm in the Midwest in a very religious family of eight children provides an example of this. She reported that she had to wait on her older brothers in the house, even if she had been working all day in the fields. Her parents instructed her to obey her older brothers in their absence. "It was as if my brothers could do no wrong." The older brothers took advantage of her, not only by demanding that she do tasks for them but by tricking her out of her allowance and eventually sexually abusing her.

Exacerbating a Fear

Older siblings would often exacerbate a fear that a younger sibling had, such as a fear of being lost, fear of the dark, or fear of strangers. Sibling perpetrators would use fear as a means of having power and control over the victim, thereby getting the sibling to do what they wanted. Perhaps the perpetrators were modeling this behavior after their parents because some parents coerce their children to comply with their wishes by manipulating the child through fear. The following comments by survivors illustrate the power of siblings' use of fear:

> My older siblings would take my sister and me out into the field to pick berries. When we would hear dogs barking, they would tell us they were wild dogs and then they'd run away and make us find our own way home. We were only five or six, and we didn't know our way home.

> I remember very clearly that my older sister, who was seven years older, would go to the telephone and pretend to call a man she called "Mr. Krantz." He ran an institution, she said, for "bad children" and my sister said she was going to send me there, banishing me from the family. I was terrified.

One research respondent wrote that an older sister played upon her fear of the dark to force her to do the older sister's household tasks and in general to control her. The victim was afraid of the dark, but her older sister would allow her to sleep with her as long as she did everything her older sister demanded. The victim was caught in a bind. The parents were not aware of this arrangement, but she knew that if she told her parents about it, her sister would not allow her to sleep with her and she would be alone with her fear of the dark. The survivor indicated that she acquiesced to her sister's control and repeatedly became the victim of her emotional abuse.

Destroying Personal Possessions

A child's possessions, such as a bicycle, toys, or clothing, are valued and have special meaning for the child. Everyone remembers a favorite toy, book, or blanket from their childhood. Some adults may still have these objects. These objects were often used by sibling perpetrators as a means of emotional abuse.

Yet even though the perpetrator destroys a sibling's prized object, the actual target of the abuse is the sibling. In Freudian terms, the object becomes "cathected," or invested with the emotions and feelings of the owner. Thus, harming the object is actually harming the individual who treasures the object.

One adult male participating in the research related how as a small child he experienced this form of emotional abuse from an older brother. His older brother took a pair of Mickey Mouse ears he treasured, deliberately broke them, and then laughed about it. Initially, this seems humorous. Why should an adult continue to hold on to the fact that his older brother destroyed his Mickey Mouse ears when they were children many years ago?

The destruction of the toy per se is not the point. To understand what the victim is saying and to empathize with what he is expressing in his statement, several factors must be considered. First, the destructive behavior was only one in a series of continual abusive incidents directed at the victim; this was not a one-time event. (A single abusive incident, however, may be harmful, such as sexual molestation by a sibling.)

Second, the destruction of the Mickey Mouse ears must be viewed in the context of the deliberateness of the perpetrator's action. Respondents to the research repeatedly wrote of the delight that perpetrators took in destroying something that was meaningful to them. The incident was not an accident; the deliberateness with which it occurred made it abusive.

Finally, the incident must be considered in light of its impact on the victim. The victim was deeply hurt by his brother's behavior. Again, the destruction of the Mickey Mouse ears per se was not the point, but its impact on the victim, who was the real target of the abusive behavior, is important. The statement often made when something like this happens indicates how people experience its impact: "How could someone do this to *me*!"

Survivors gave other examples of a sibling being emotionally abusive through the destruction of personal possessions:

> My sister would take my things and wreck them, cut my clothes up to fit her and blackmail me to do her housework.

> My brother would cut off the eyes, ears, mouth and fingers of my dolls and hand them to me.

Torturing or Destroying a Pet

Although the torture or destruction of a pet may resemble the destruction of prized possessions, it involves the abuse of life, an animal's life. This implies an even greater degree of cruelty toward the object, although the emotional pain the sibling experienced may be the same.

Survivors reported the torture and destruction of their pets by a sibling as examples of emotional abuse:

> My second-oldest brother shot my little dog that I loved dearly. It loved me, only me. I cried by its grave for several days. Twenty years passed before I could care for another dog.

> My older brother would come to my room and tear up my toys. He would beat my dog after tying his legs together and wrapping a cloth around its mouth to tie it shut. My brother would tell me I was stupid and say, "Why me, why me? Why did I get a sister so stupid and dumb?" My brother also would tell me he hated me and wished I were dead.

> My brother took my pet frog and stabbed it to death in front of me while I begged him not to. Then he just laughed!

Victims' Responses

Earlier, victims of physical abuse indicated that they responded to their siblings' abuse by protecting themselves, screaming and crying, separating themselves from the perpetrator, abusing a younger sibling, and telling their parents. Victims of emotional abuse responded to their abuse in these ways and also by fighting back and internalizing the abusive message.

Fighting Back

Unlike survivors of physical abuse, sibling survivors of emotional abuse reported that they fought back and in turn emotionally abused the perpetrator by name-calling, ridicule, and degrading comments. Victims of physical abuse did not respond this way because generally they were younger than their abusers and did not have the strength to effectively fight back.

A survivor wrote that an older sister would "yell swear words and names" at her as one aspect of her verbal abuse. At the age of 8 or 9, she was shocked by her sister's language but she soon "gave as good as I got, swear-word-wise." Another respondent reported, "I retaliated with equally mean words."

An adult woman wrote about how she handled her sister's emotionally abusive comments:

> I would turn the emotional abuse around on my sister. I would make her cry and go into hysterics. She would just go crazy. The more I got from my older brother, the more and more I would give my sister.

This survivor's comment may explain why some parents view emotional abuse among their children as "normal sibling rivalry." Parents conclude that since all the siblings are engaging in emotionally abusive behavior it must be normal. Survivors reported that in some instances their parents even joined in by calling them names or making fun of them as their siblings were doing. Emotional abuse in these families became a normal way of interacting—normal, yet pathological in its destructiveness to the individuals involved.

Internalizing the Abusive Message

A response unique to victims of emotional abuse was to accept and internalize the abusive messages they were receiving. The victims accepted the name-calling, ridicule, and especially the degrading comments as if what was being said were true. The perpetrator's abuse became a self-fulfilling prophecy for the victim. Accepting the message as reality confirmed the victims in their role as victims into which the perpetrators had initially put them.

One survivor reported that "I believed *everything* my sister ever told me. I was dumb, homely, stupid, fat. No one would ever love me." This survivor stated that now at age 41, as a reasonably bright adult woman, she still believes most of her abusive sister's comments, that she is no good, dumb, and ugly. She still feels that her worth as a person is only as good as what she does. As she describes it, in her adult life she is constantly trying to prove with her actions that she is worth something.

SEXUAL ABUSE

Sibling sexual abuse was defined in this research as inappropriate sexual contact, such as touching, fondling, indecent exposure, attempted penetration, intercourse, rape, or sodomy, between siblings.

Research on Sibling Incest

The term *incest* is generally thought of as referring to sexual relations between fathers and daughters. Most of the literature on incest focuses on the parent-child relationship, even though researchers feel that sibling incest is more common (Finkelhor, 1979; Justice & Justice, 1979; Meiselman, 1978). The lack of attention to this type of sexual abuse may be due to the reluctance of families to report to authorities the occurrence of sibling incest, minimization of the problem by parents, the threat under which victims are placed when it occurs, and the perception that sexual contact between siblings is within the normal range of acceptable sexual play or exploration between siblings (Adler & Schutz, 1995; Doyle, 1996).

Studies on sibling incest have been hampered by (a) their small sample size, which makes it difficult to generalize the data from the sample to the general population and (b) the absence of comparison groups. For example, Adler and Schutz (1995) studied 12 males who were sibling incest offenders referred for evaluation and treatment to a hospital-based outpatient clinic. The sample came from middle- to upper-middle-class, suburban, primarily Caucasian families where the majority had parents married to each other and living in the home. The offenders had no previous records with juvenile justice authorities. Other studies on sibling incest, however, report previous offender contact with the juvenile system, the physical absence of a parent and low socioeconomic status (Becker, Kaplan, Cunningham-Rathner, & Kavoussi, 1986; Finkelhor, 1979; O'Brien, 1991). Although no one in Adler and Schutz's (1995) sample reported having been sexually abused, a history of intrafamilial physical abuse by one or both parents was present. Other studies of sibling sexual abuse, however, report that rates of prior sexual victimization on the part of the perpetrators ranged from approximately 25% to 50% of the sample (Becker et al., 1986; Smith & Israel, 1987; O'Brien, 1991). Although the perpetrators denied using verbal threats to intimidate their victims, 75% of the victims reported that they had been verbally threatened to maintain silence about the sexual abuse.

O'Brien (1991) studied the characteristics of 170 adolescent male sexual offenders who had been referred for evaluation and/or treatment to an outpatient mental health clinic. The offenders were subdivided into three groups: sibling sexual abusers, child molesters, and nonchild offenders. Compared with the child molesters and nonchild offenders, the sibling sexual abusers admitted committing more sexual crimes, had longer offending careers, and generally engaged in more intrusive sexual behavior, such as vaginal penetration. O'Brien concluded that this was because the sibling victim is easily available to the perpetrator and the context of secrecy in which the sexual abuse occurs in the family prevents early disclosure.

Cole (1990) studied a volunteer sample of 122 adult women from 28 states who had been sexually abused by a brother and 148 women sexually abused by their father. The mean age of the onset of the sexual abuse for the brother-sister survivors was 8.2 years compared to 5.2 years for the father-daughter survivors. Approximately one third of both groups experienced the sexual abuse for 4 to 10 years and did not disclose the abuse for 20 years or more. The sibling sexual abuse survivors reported feeling more responsible for their abuse as compared to their father-daughter survivor counterparts.

Finally, Doyle (1996) studied 12 women who during individual or group therapy revealed sexual abuse by a brother. Although sibling sexual abuse is generally thought to be perpetrated by an older brother, Doyle found that 4 of the 12 perpetrators were younger brothers abusing older sisters.

Incidence of Abuse

Adults are generally assumed to be the perpetrators of child sexual abuse and most likely are closely known by the victim. However, an early study on incest reported that brother-sister sexual relationships may be five times more common as father-daughter incest (Gebhard, Gagnon, Pomeroy, & Christenson, 1965).

Several studies on the extent of sexual abuse in general give some indication of the extent to which sibling sexual abuse occurs. Finkelhor (1984a) reported that the incidence of sexual abuse in general is basically unknown. Estimates are that 35% of all girls by the time they reach adulthood have been sexually abused. This includes incidents where the perpetrators are siblings. A survey of 796 undergraduates attending six New England colleges found that 15% of the females and 10% of the males reported some type of sexual experience involving a sibling (Finkelhor, 1980). Fondling and touching the genitals were the most common activities in all age categories. Twenty-five percent of the incidents could be regarded as exploitive because force was used and because of the large age disparity between the individuals involved. Forty percent of the students reported that they had been less than 8 years old at the time of the sexual experience. However, 73% of the experiences occurred when at least one partner was older than 8, and 35% occurred when one partner was more than 12 years of age.

These studies probably grossly underestimate the extent of sibling sexual abuse because feelings of embarrassment and shame connected with the event prevent both perpetrators and victims from talking about it. Many adults also may no longer remember childhood sexual incidents with a sibling. The information on sibling sexual abuse frequently comes from reports filed in court against a perpetrator. However, these cases barely represent the extent to which this problem occurs because most incidents of sexual abuse by siblings go not only unreported but undetected by parents.

Studies on the incidence of child sexual abuse by adults indicate that most incidents are never disclosed. The cases that come to the attention of the courts, mental health clinics, and support groups for sexual abuse survivors appear to be the exception rather than the norm. As the comments by respondents in the present research reveal, the same is true for victims of sexual abuse by a sibling.

Of the 150 respondents in this research, 67% (100) indicated that they had been sexually abused by a sibling while growing up, compared with 33% (50) who had been physically and/or emotionally abused.

Why were so many more of the respondents survivors of sexual abuse as compared to survivors of physical and emotional abuse? One reason may be that many of the individuals participating in the research were already in treatment for their abuse at counseling centers or were affiliated with support groups for people who experienced abuse. Survivors of sexual abuse may seek treatment for their abuse more readily than survivors of physical or emotional abuse. Even between siblings, sexual abuse is recognized by society as *abuse*, unlike physical and emotional abuse, which are often ignored and overlooked. For example, the meaning of the term *incest* is commonly understood to mean illicit sexual activity between family members, including that between brothers and sisters. But the meaning of the terms *emotional abuse* and *physical abuse* between siblings is not commonly understood. Thus, it may be easier for persons who have been sexually abused to acknowledge their victimization than it is for those who have been physically and emotionally abused. Also, the trauma from sexual abuse may be more severe than that from physical or emotional abuse and thus may cause victims to more readily seek treatment for its impact on their lives.

Sexual abuse did not occur in isolation for those survivors responding to this research. Three percent (5) indicated that they had been both physically and sexually abused, 11% (16) had been both emotionally and sexually abused, and 37% (55) had been physically, emotionally, and sexually abused. Other research has found similar results in that victims were not only sexually abused but also physically and emotionally abused (Brassard & Galardo, 1987; Claussen & Crittenden, 1991). Goodwin (1982) found that in 50% of incest cases reported to a protective service agency there was also evidence of physical abuse or neglect.

The interaction of sexual and physical abuse can be seen in the survivors' comments. Some were threatened with physical harm and even death by their sibling perpetrator if they reported the sexual abuse to their parents. The interaction of sexual and emotional abuse is exemplified by the comment of one respondent whose sexual molestation by a brother 10 years older, including forceful vaginal penetration, began when she was 3 or 4 years old: "Later, when I was about seven or eight years old, he would tease me by asking me if I was a virgin and laughing when I said no. It was humiliating."

Although far more females than males reported having experienced sexual abuse from a sibling, males also are sexually abused (Rosencrans, 1997). In their review of eight random-sample community surveys that had interviewed both men and women regarding sexual abuse during childhood, Finkelhor and Baron (1986) found a much higher percentage of males who had been sexually abused than the present study found. Approximately 2.5 women were sexually abused for every man. Among all victims of sexual abuse, 71% were females and 29% were males. A study of boys and girls who were sexually abused revealed that, although the majority of all victims were sexually abused within the family, boys were more likely than girls to be victimized by someone outside the home (36.7% vs. 10.9%) (Faller, 1989). Researchers found in a sample of 375 individuals who had been physically or sexually abused before age 18 that females were almost 3 times more likely than males to experience any type of abuse and over 11 times more likely than males to report sexual abuse (Silverman, Reinherz, & Giaconia, 1996). Clinicians generally agree that the sexual abuse of boys is underreported due to stereotypical expectations regarding masculinity and the fear that disclosure on the part of the victims may give them the appearance of being homosexual.

Earliest Memories

Survivors reported that, as best as they can remember, the earliest incident of sexual abuse by a sibling occurred when they were 5 to 7 years old. This may be merely the earliest incident that survivors could recall; their sexual abuse may actually have begun at a much earlier age. Some survivors reported being aware that they were sexually abused as infants, but they did not indicate how they became aware of this. For example, one survivor recalled, "Sexual abuse was a part of my life from the time I was an infant. The age of three months is the earliest memory I have."

Parents often think of children as beginning to engage in sexual activity when they reach adolescence or become sexually mature—not at age 4 or 5. Parents may rationalize that their children are not interested in or knowledgeable about sex at such an early age. Even though a child is not yet sexually mature and does not exhibit any interest in sex, the child still can become a victim of sexual abuse.

In most incidents of sibling sexual abuse reported in this research, the perpetrator was an older brother or sister, generally 3 to 10 years older than the victim. The sexual abuse of the younger sibling may have been prevented if the victim's parents had provided the child information about preventing sexual abuse, such as forcefully to say no and to report the incident immediately to them.

The following comments describe survivors' earliest memories of their abuse:

> I was four years old and my older brother told me that he wanted to show me something that Mom and Dad did. I refused. Then he offered to pay me a quarter and said that I would like it. If I turned him down, it was clear that he would hurt me. So I gave in and he made me perform oral sex with him.

> My brother threatened to kill me if I told our parents about him molesting me. I was three or four years of age at the time; he was about eighteen. He showed me the butcher block we kept in the cellar with the ax and blood. He said he'd kill me there if I told.

> My earliest memory is of my brother sneaking into my bed while we were on vacation and were sharing one bedroom. This happened while my parents were still out on the town. I pretended I was asleep, and it was very difficult to determine what to do about it because of the physical pleasure but inappropriate and selfish behavior on his part.

Typical Experiences

Only a few survivors participating in this research reported that their sexual abuse by a sibling was a one-time event. In most instances, the abuse continued and proceeded to other and different kinds of sexual abuse, often accompanied by physical and emotional abuse. The repetitious nature of the sexual abuse for siblings resembles that of children who are victims of sexual assault by an adult male, such as their father or another family member. The sexual assault is generally repeated and continues until the child is old enough forcibly to prohibit the behavior or until the sexually abusive behavior is discovered and appropriate interventions occur.

The sexual abuse that siblings experienced generally was accompanied by physical threats of harm or even death voiced by the perpetrator if they told their parents. This is a significant way in which sibling sexual abuse differs from adult-child sexual abuse. Adult sexual abuse of children generally occurs in the context of the perpetrator telling the victim that he or she is special and that the sexual activity will be a secret they alone share. Threats of harm may occur; however, through enticement, the child victim becomes entrapped in the perpetrator's web of abuse (Gonzalez et al., 1993; Petronio et al., 1996; Summit, 1983).

Several respondents described how their sexual abuse by an older sibling progressed during their childhood:

> I can't remember exactly how the sexual abuse started but when I was smaller there was a lot of experimenting. He would do things to me like putting his finger in my vagina. Then, as I got older, he would perform oral sex on me.

> Initially I was forced to masturbate him one night, but from then on it moved quickly to oral sex on him and eventually rape.

Clarification should be made about the use of the term *rape.* In most states, rape is legally defined as the penetration of the penis into the vagina under force or the threat of force. Based on a growing understanding of sexual abuse and its effect on victims, rape is now being defined more broadly, consistent with feminist thought (Russell, 1986). Thus, rape may refer to any sexual activity between a perpetrator and a victim in which force, the threat of force, or threats in general are used. (An example of a threat in general is the perpetrator warning the victim not to tell anyone about their sexual activity because he might be sent to jail.)

The more inclusive meaning of the term has important implications for both the prosecution of perpetrators and the treatment of the victims. In terms of prosecuting the perpetrator, his use of aggression, force, or threats brings his behavior into the realm of rape, regardless of the nature of the activity. For example, fondling a victim's genitals can no longer be labeled less harmful than sexual intercourse because the consequences are the same: The victim's right to privacy has been abused by means of an aggressive act. In other words, the victim has been raped. Likewise, the implication for the treatment of the victim is that regardless of the nature of the activity a victim of sexual abuse is a victim of an aggressive act. The respondent quoted earlier used the word rape in the legal sense: sexual intercourse under the threat of force. Actually, she had already been a victim of rape when she was forced to engage in masturbation and oral sex against her wishes.

The following survivors' comments describe their typical experiences of sexual abuse by a sibling.

> It began as games and grew to "look and feel." As I became older, he played with my breasts and then fondled my genitals, always wanting but never achieving intercourse. He showed me with his fingers how it would feel.

> I would try to put off going to bed. I would try to cover up tight with my blankets. My brother would come into my room and touch me all over. I would pretend that I was asleep. After he left, I would cry and cry.

Sibling sexual abuse is a phenomenon that can occur in families regardless of their socioeconomic status. The following comment is by a survivor whose mother had completed several years of college and whose father held a graduate degree from a university:

> It became much more frequent as he got older. It mostly happened when I was in sixth to ninth grade, ages eleven to fifteen. I knew he would try, so I would lock myself in my room. He would pick the lock and force me to the ground or bed. I can remember yelling at him, or crying, or begging, or throwing myself down and saying, "Go ahead," which he did, or saying I would tell. His response was, "Well, if you're going to tell, I might as well go ahead." I tried everything I could think of, for example, appealing to his morals as a brother. One time I remember holding a knife to myself. He got it away, always laughing. He'd force off my clothes, rub and suck my breasts, put his penis between them, and rub. He would perform oral sex on me often. I remember sucking his penis once. He did not come in my mouth. He would rub his penis all over my vulva and press against my vagina. He never inserted it, just pressed against it. I kept a calendar during his senior year of high school. I had made it a "countdown" of when he'd move out upon graduation with the numbers going down.

A common tactic of perpetrators was to isolate the victim in order for the sexual abuse to occur. One respondent described how her older brother would know when to attack her:

He would always seem to know when I was alone and when no one could hear. I would always know when he entered a room when it would happen. He would make me terrified. I would think, "Oh, no, not again!" He'd try to compliment me in a sexual way. Complimenting a 4- to 6-year-old on her "great breasts" was not what I'd call a turn-on. He'd either undress me or make me undress myself. He would undress and make me touch his erection. I hated that because he'd force me to do it and would hold my hand against it to almost masturbate him. He never orgasmed, though. He'd touch me, almost like he was examining me. A few times he had oral sex on me. He attempted intercourse but that was difficult. He'd force my legs apart. I was always so scared because my muscles were so tight and my opening was so small. He never really could enter without severe pain. I would say he was hurting me, which he was, and I'd cry in hopes he'd stop. Sometimes he did. Other times he would force himself inside of me so that I would hurt for days.

Although most of the survivors were females, the following comment is from an adult male survivor:

My brother caught me masturbating once. That's when the sexual abuse began. At night he would have me fondle him, masturbate him and fellate him, depending on what he wanted. He threatened to tell Mom about catching me masturbating if I didn't go along. The abuse went on about a year or two. It was always at night. He would lay on his back. A street light would shine across his body through the curtains, and he would call me to come "do" him. I felt like I was on stage with the street light and trapped in a bad part. I hated him immensely. Finally, after a year or so I told him he could tell whomever he wanted but I wouldn't do it anymore. The abuse stopped, but the damage was done. My feelings would haunt me into high school, college, and my marriage.

SURVIVORS' RESPONSES TO THEIR SEXUAL ABUSE

Survivors' responses to sexual abuse by a sibling differed from their responses to emotional and physical abuse. In cases of emotional abuse, for example, a typical response was to fight back verbally and in turn to ridicule and call the perpetrator names. Generally, this was not effective and only served to further victimize the victim because the perpetrator intensified the abuse or shifted to other tactics. Victims of sibling physical abuse were often unable to fight back due to limitations in size and strength compared to their perpetrators. Thus, they resorted to hiding or withdrawing into themselves to get away from the perpetrator and the physical abuse.

In cases of sexual abuse, none of the survivors reported that they fought back. Undoubtedly, some siblings do fight back against sexual abuse by another sibling. Those who do are demonstrating their empowerment by their ability to say no, which may distinguish them from the sexual abuse survivors who comprised the sample discussed here. An assertive verbal response can be an effective way for a child to prevent sexual abuse.

A common response of female victims of sibling sexual assault was to feign sleep. This response was also frequently reported by child victims of sexual assault by adult males within their household. These children often "play possum" as a way of coping with the assault, lacking the ability to use force to ward off their assailant (Summit, 1983). This behavior may also be a psychological defense against the emotional pain and suffering the victim experiences. It was as if she were saying, "If I am asleep, I won't be aware of what is happening. It won't hurt me as much." This response, however, often works against the victim later if she attempts to prosecute the perpetrator. Unfortunately, children are frequently attacked by attorneys and discredited by juries in the prosecution of sexual abuse cases because they made no protest or outcry. Such accusations only add to their guilt and self-blame. Thus, the entire sexual assault, the traumatic incident as well as the investigation that follows it, can be psychologically devastating for a child victim.

A more frequent response was to acquiesce or to submit to the sexual abuse. This response must be seen within the context of the abuse. First, the victims, especially young siblings, often were not aware of what they were doing when an older sibling engaged them in sexual play. Only after the event, sometimes many years later, when they began to experience shame and guilt for their involvement in the behavior did they begin to feel like a victim. They frequently coped with their feelings of shame and guilt by blaming themselves for participating in the behavior, but in reality they may have had no other option, considering their lack of information about or empowerment over sexual assault.

Second, as stated earlier, sibling sexual abuse often occurred within the context of threats. An older sibling would threaten a younger sibling that if the parents were told the victim would be harmed or both would be punished. The latter tactic left the victim feeling partly responsible for the sexual activity. Thus, the victim was frequently set up to pretend as if nothing had happened lest the victim experience retaliation from the perpetrator and from their parents for reporting the incident. One survivor wrote,

> Once my mother was suspicious [about my being sexually abused by my brothers]. She confronted my brothers and they denied it. She told them she would ask me. Then she waited several days. During that time they told me I'd better not tell her or they'd get me into trouble.

Although the victim is pressured into remaining silent, this does not alleviate the emotional trauma associated with the sexual abuse. Rather, it forces the victim silently to bear the anxiety, shame, guilt, and other emotions. The only visible sign of this situation on the part of the victim may be a tendency to withdraw, to want to be alone. Thus, withdrawn behavior is an important clue for parents, teachers, and other adults who are in contact with children that something is bothering the child about which he or she is not able to or dare not talk. The withdrawn behavior may indicate that the child is attempting to repress the emotions surrounding a painful experience.

One survivor described how she handled her victimization from a brother for many years:

> I had no recollection of the sexual abuse from my brother until I was pregnant with my daughter. I then started having very graphic nightmares about my brother raping me. I was about three or four years old in the dreams. He was on top of me, holding me down and forcing himself into me. I was crying and screaming at him to stop. He would say, "You know you like it." I thought I was a pervert to have those dreams, so I didn't tell anyone about them until when my daughter was about a year old. I was physically abusing her, and I went to Parents Anonymous for help. The sponsor asked me if I had been sexually abused. I said I hadn't, but I told her about the nightmares. She said she thought it had really

> happened. With her support and encouragement, I asked my sisters first. They said he had abused them, but there was no penetration. Then I confronted him. I told him just exactly what was in the dreams, down to the last detail. There was a silence; then he said, "You are right. I did that."

SEXUAL CURIOSITY

Is any contact of a sexual nature between siblings sexual abuse? Some contacts may be described as sexual curiosity. All children explore their bodies and to some extent and at some time may engage in visual or even manual exploration of a sibling's body. This is one way that children discover sexual differences or verify what they have been told by their parents about the differences between boys and girls. Two small children exploring each other's bodies does not predestine them to a life of emotional chaos and suffering. For example, 4-year-old Tim was observed by a nursery school attendant showing his penis to Sue, who was the same age. When the children became aware that the attendant had seen their behavior, Tim's reaction was to blame Sue, saying she had asked him to do this. Sue denied it. The nursery school attendant reported the activity to the teacher who took the children aside and talked with them about their sexuality at a level that they could understand and reviewed with them an earlier discussion in which all the children had participated on the subject of good touches and secret touches.

Sexual activity may be viewed relative to the age and psychosocial developmental level of a child. Among preschool-age children (ages 0-5), patterns of activity include intense curiosity, seen in taking advantage of opportunities to explore their universe. This may be expressed in the sexual behaviors of masturbation and looking at others' bodies. Among primary-school-age children (ages 6-10), activities include game playing with peers and continuing to seize opportunities to explore their universe. Sexual behaviors for this age group may include masturbation, looking at others' bodies, sexual exposure of themselves to others, and even sexual fondling of peers or younger children in a play or gamelike atmosphere. Among preadolescent children (ages 10-12) and adolescents (ages 13-18), behaviors focus on individuation including separation from parents and family and developing relationships with peers. Among adolescents, this includes practicing intimacy with peers of the same or opposite sex. Sexual behaviors for these developmental stages includes masturbation, an intense interest in voyeuristic activities involving viewing others' bodies through pictures, films, or videos (some of which may be pornographic), or attempts at "peeking" in opposite-sex locker/dressing rooms. Open-mouth kissing, sexual fondling, simulated intercourse, and intercourse involving penetration are sexual activities engaged in at these developmental stages (Sgroi, Bunk, & Wabrek, 1988).

Sexual activity among consenting participants probably presents the least risk of unfavorable consequences. But often young children appear to consent but actually do not because they cannot anticipate unfavorable consequences from their behavior. In many instances, what appears to be consent may actually be only passive consent, or the inability to make a rational decision because of limited cognitive skills and life experiences.

One factor affecting children's psychosexual development is societal attitudes toward sexuality demonstrated by parents. Some adults are very uncomfortable with sexual issues and thus attempt to handle them with their children by pretending this area of life does not exist. At the other end of the continuum, some advocate open sexual activity in the presence of children and even encourage children to engage in sexual activity. But neither approach guarantees healthy psychosexual development.

Because of the impact of sexual abuse by an adult, a peer, or sibling on a child's later adult psychosocial functioning, it is important for parents to take a proactive approach to sexuality with their children by providing them information about sex that is appropriate to their age and psychosocial development, empowering them with the knowledge and ability to discriminate between good touches and secret touches, and providing an atmosphere at home where their sexual concerns and problems can be discussed.

PARENTAL AWARENESS OF SIBLING ABUSE

Prior to discussing parental reactions to sibling abuse, the question should be asked if the parents were even aware that abuse was occurring between or among the siblings in their family. Among the 150 participants in the study discussed here, 71% (70) of those surviving sibling physical abuse and 69% (81) of those surviving sibling emotional abuse felt their parents were aware of what was happening, which is understandable because it is difficult to hide these types of abuse. However, regarding sexual abuse, only 18% (18) of the survivors felt their parents were aware of this behavior, which finding is also understandable because the sexual abuse occurred only when the parents were away from home or during the night when parents were asleep.

The parents' lack of awareness of siblings' sexual abuse was also often due to the inability of the victims to inform their parents about what was happening. One would think that children could surely tell their parents, but the data indicate the contrary. Many victims could not tell their parents for several reasons, one of which is that at the time the sexual abuse was occurring the victim often did not perceive it as abuse. The victim was not cognitively or emotionally mature enough to understand that it was indeed abuse. This was especially true of young children. However, the way the survivors in this research perceive the sexual activity now as adults, looking back on their childhood, is very different from the way they perceived it when they were children. For example, this is true of a survivor who was 7 years old during her first sexual incident with her older brother. He took her into the woods while their mother was working and he "played dirty" with her by touching her on her breasts and genitals and making her do likewise to him. Afterward, he threatened to kill her if she told anyone. The survivor, now as an adult, recalled her reaction to the sexual abuse at the time: "I didn't even realize what he was doing. To me it was like brushing my hair." As an adult, however, this survivor's reaction to the abuse is very different. She is aware that this was an abusive incident, the first of many. Looking back on these experiences, she is very angry that as a small child she was used by her brother. As a result, she experiences feelings of low self-esteem.

A second reason why children frequently did not tell their parents about sibling sexual abuse is that the abuse often occurred in the context of abuse of authority. Some of the perpetrators, older brothers of the victims, were acting as baby-sitters for their younger sisters when they abused them sexually. The younger sibling had been instructed by the parents to obey the older brother. Siblings wrote,

> I remember a vague feeling that my brother was more important than me and I should keep quiet and do what he wanted.

> I was taught to do as people told me.

A third reason why children did not tell their parents was that the perpetrator threatened the victim with retaliation if he or she told, like the survivor who recounted being abused in the woods by her brother. In the context of a physical threat, the victim was fearful that if the abuse were reported to the parents, the sibling perpetrator might act on the threat. Moreover, if the abuse occurred while the perpetrator was baby-sitting the victim, the victim feared that if left in the care of the perpetrator at a later time the perpetrator would punish the victim for reporting the abuse (Gonzalez et al., 1993; Petronio et al., 1996).

Note the comments of survivors of sibling sexual abuse that occurred in the context of a threat, such as this male survivor who recalled how his older brother threatened him:

> He would lay me down, put his big fist by my face and he would say, "If you scream, this is what you'll get." Then he would masturbate me.

And from this female survivor:

> I would be in my bed asleep. He would jump in the bed with me. I would try and push him out. I was just not strong enough and he would always keep a baseball bat or knife with him.

A fourth reason why victims did not tell their parents about the abuse is that they blamed themselves for what happened. Some survivors in this research spoke of experiencing pleasurable physical feelings during the sexual encounters with a sibling. Because they derived sexual pleasure from the experience, often of an autonomic nature, the survivors blamed themselves for contributing to the abuse. They were afraid to report the activity to their parents lest their abusive sibling in self-defense would tell their parents of this participation. Moreover, to keep the victim from telling the parents, the perpetrator often blamed the victim for not resisting the sexual advances. "You could have stopped it [sexual abuse], if you had wanted," perpetrators defensively would say as they attempted to shift the blame for the abuse from themselves to the victim. Generally, the survivors participating in this research had not been empowered by their parents by being informed about good touches and secret touches so as to resist sexual advances effectively.

A final reason why the victims did not tell their parents is that the climate in the home made it impossible for them to report it. One survivor did the best she could to communicate with her parents about the sexual abuse:

> I remember every time my parents went out, I'd sit in my parents' room while they got ready and I'd ask them, "Do you really have to go out tonight? Can't you stay home?" That's as close as I could get to telling them or asking for their protection.

Another victim felt the climate in the home was such that she could not tell her parents what was happening:

> Somehow they should have provided a family atmosphere in which their children—me at this point—could have approached them with

the situation without being fearful of getting into trouble.

PARENTAL REACTIONS TO SIBLING ABUSE

How did the parents who were aware of the abuse occurring in their homes between the siblings respond? Six different parental responses are identified and discussed.

Ignoring or Minimizing the Abuse

A typical parental response to sibling physical and emotional abuse was to ignore or minimize it. Parents often excused the behavior on the basis that it was merely sibling rivalry. "Boys will be boys; children will be children," victims were told by their parents. While it is true that certain behaviors are accepted as appropriate for children because of their level of maturity, the *abuse* of one sibling by another should not be. Nothing excuses or justifies the abuse of one person by another.

Several survivors provided comments regarding this parental response:

> They ignored or minimized the abuse. They told me, "Boys were boys and needed to clear their system."

> I told them once and they didn't believe me and they would leave me alone with him again. Then I really suffered for telling on him. I soon learned not to tell.

> My parents saw my brother's physical abuse of me as normal sibling rivalry and did not correct any of what he did. If they were around when it was occurring, they would just say we had to learn to get along better.

Blaming the Victim

Other parents responded to the abuse that was occurring by acknowledging it when it was reported to them but then blaming the victim for it occurrence. This parental response was reported frequently by sibling abuse survivors in this research and by survivors in other studies of sibling abuse (Laviola, 1992; Loredo, 1982). When parents blamed the victim, the victim became a victim a second time; this is known as "revictimization." The unfortunate outcome of this parental response is that perpetrators are absolved of responsibility for their actions and are given the implicit message that the behavior was appropriate or that the victim deserved what the perpetrator did. The perpetrator in essence is given license to continue the behavior. Survivors wrote,

> My parents would usually break it up when my brother was abusing me but with me being the oldest, I'd always get accused of causing the problem and be told that I should set a better example and I wouldn't get hurt.

> I was hurt by the abuse I received from a younger sister, but my sister was not blamed or it was turned around that I had done something to cause it. She was never wrong.

> My parents didn't know [often about the abuse] but they would have blamed me or at least made excuses for my brother. My mother would say, "Men are hunters, don't trust any, not even your own brother." But she meant it in general, not for her son, the "King."

Inappropriately Responding to the Behavior

The manner in which some parents responded to the abusive behavior occurring between or among siblings was ineffective and in some instances exacerbated the abuse. For example, survivors reported that their parents used severe corporal punishment on the perpetrator in an attempt to stop the physically or emotionally abusive behavior against a sibling. One survivor reported that when she told her parents about the physical abuse she was receiving from her older brother, her father beat the brother so badly that she resolved never to tell her father again. A two-stage process of self-blame resulted from her father's action. First, the victim blamed herself for her brother's severe beating because she had reported his behavior to her father. Second, she blamed herself for the abuse, feeling that perhaps she may in some way have caused him to treat her this way.

Another survivor described a similar situation:

> My older brothers received a severe beating when I told my parents how they were abusing me. The severity of the beating, however, discouraged me from ever reporting again what happened because I wanted to avoid a more violent outcome.

Yet another inappropriate response to sibling abuse was for the parents to abuse the perpetrator. For example, if the perpetrator was hitting or calling the victim names, the parents would do the same to the perpetrator. This approach appears to be based on the myth that giving perpetrators a dose of their own medicine will teach them to stop the behavior. Some parents use this form of behavioral control with small children. They may bite a child who has bitten them or encourage a child who has been slapped to slap back. Unfortunately, this form of discipline establishes no new behavioral patterns for the child. Rather, mimicking the perpetrator's aversive or abusive behavior reinforces this behavior in the child. Just as violence sometimes begets more violence, the violence in this form of punishment encourages continued violence. The perpetrator may become angrier as a result of this form of discipline and likely ventilate this anger once again on the victim or on someone else, as occurred for this survivor:

> My parents would yell at her and pinch and bite her to "teach" her how it felt so she'd stop doing it. It only made it worse for me though. They'd clean my wounds and tell me a story to tell my teacher to explain my bandages and markings.

Some survivors reported that when they told their parents about the abuse they experienced from a sibling, all the children were indiscriminately punished, which only further victimized the victim and did not protect the victim from additional abuse.

> Dad would yell at us and threaten us with a belt if we didn't shut up. Anger was not directed at my brother who abused me but at all the kids. I learned to cry silently because of my Dad. The belt was worse than my brother's abuse.

Research on the effects of parental punishment of sibling aggression or fighting indicates that parents are more likely to punish the older sibling rather than the younger (Felson & Russo, 1988). This tendency to punish the older or more powerful sibling, the researchers found, generally results in more frequent aggression because the younger siblings do not hesitate to be verbally or physically aggressive, knowing the parents will identify with them and punish the older sibling. A more effective approach, the researchers found, is for parents to intervene in the fighting but not to engage in punishment.

Joining in the Abuse

Perhaps the saddest parental response, especially to emotional abuse such as name-calling and ridicule, was to join the perpetrator in abusing the victim. The effect on the victims was devastating, for they were further victimized by the very parents from whom they sought protection. Victims could turn for protection to no one else. The crying and the sadness these victims felt is understandable:

> My mother would pick up on it [the abuse] and also make fun of me.

> When I was six and started school, the girls took me into the bathroom and put me in the toilet to wash me. Then they called me "Stinkweed." I was crushed. When I got home, I talked about it. Even my whole family laughed at me and called me that daily. It still hurts. It's something I'll never forget. They still remind me of it.

Disbelieving the Abuse Was Occurring

When some victims of sibling abuse, especially sexual abuse, reported the abuse to their parents, the parental response was disbelief. Again, the effect of this response was further victimization. Not only were they victims of their parents' disbelief and failure to protect them, but they were victims of the perpetrator's continuing behavior. Two survivors recalled the effect of being disbelieved by their parents:

> When I tried to tell my father about it, he called my mother and brother into the room, told them my accusations, and asked my brother if it was true. Naturally, he said I was lying, and my mother stood there supporting him. Nothing happened, except that I got beaten later by my mother for daring to say anything and for "lying." My brother knew that from then on there was nothing he couldn't do to me. He was immune from punishment. Never again did I say a word since to do so would only have meant more abuse from them both. I concluded it was better to keep my mouth shut.

> When I tried to tell them about the beatings I was taking, they didn't believe me and they would leave me alone with him again. So when it came to the sexual abuse, I didn't think they would believe me.

Indifference

Another parental response to sibling abuse in the family was indifference. Some parents may simply not have known what to do; others' indifference may have stemmed from their own overwhelming problems or from being under so much stress that they did not have the energy to look beyond their own problems. One survivor commented on this parental response:

> I told my mother about my older brother molesting me about two years after it happened and she asked me what I expected her to do about it. I never bothered to tell her about other things that happened because obviously she didn't care.

UNDERSTANDING SIBLING ABUSE

How can we understand why one sibling would physically, emotionally, or sexually abuse another? Following are reasons drawn from the survivors' accounts of their abuse that help us to understand why sibling abuse occurs.

The Abuse of Power and Control Over Others

A commonality in all forms of sibling abuse, whether it be physical, emotional, or sexual, as well as of all types of family violence—child, partner, and elder abuse—is the abuse of power and the pathological need of the perpetrator to control another person. The abuse of power focuses on a more powerful individual abusing a less powerful one. In sibling abuse, as the comments of respondents indicated, this often was an older sibling abusing a younger sibling. In most instances, power was related to the gender of the perpetrator, with a male sibling abusing his sister. The need for power and control on the part of males at the individual, family, and societal levels was discussed in Chapter 1.

Female survivors of sibling abuse reported what appeared to be an underlying assumption of their brothers; namely, that the latter had a right to assert their will over their sisters. Physical force and verbal abuse were seen as appropriate ways to achieve this goal. In instances of sexual abuse, brothers tended to view their sisters as sexual objects rather than as individuals.

Inappropriate Expectations

The most frequently cited reason for sibling abuse, generally of a younger sibling by an older sibling, was that the older sibling was in charge of the younger at the time the abuse was occurring. The older sibling was baby-sitting the younger when the parents were away from home at night or immediately after school before the parents returned home from work. The parents had inappropriate expectations of the older sibling in that this child was not capable of handling the responsibility of caring for a younger sibling. Several survivors described what happened to them when an older sibling baby-sat them:

> When my parents went out dancing or to my aunt's home on a Saturday night, my two older brothers baby-sat us six children. Not long after they left, my brothers would tell us to go to bed. It was too early, so we didn't want to go to bed. When we resisted, we were hit. I was punched and slapped by my oldest brother. If I defended myself by hitting back, my oldest brother would grab my wrists in the air as he screamed at me that he would hit me more. He would be telling me what to do and to go to bed. I would be crying hard even more and would go to bed.

> My mother would go to bingo leaving my sister (three years older) in charge with specific chores to be done. She would make us do the work. If it didn't get done when she said, she would hit us with a belt. Leaving her in charge gave her every right to do whatever she wanted.

Modeling Parental Behavior

Respondents reported that the physically and emotionally abusive behavior they experienced from their sibling was no different from the way their parents treated each other. One survivor wrote,

> How could I expect my brother to treat me differently other than being physically and emotionally abusive when this is the kind of behavior we as kids saw our parents continually engage in toward each other?

A review of research on parents who are abusive toward each other reveals a high likelihood that the parents also will abuse their children (O'Keefe, 1995; Ross, 1996; Saunders, 1994). In domestic violence studies, about 50% of the men who batter their partners are also reported to abuse their children. Slightly more than a third of the battered women, on average, reported having abused their children. To these findings, based on the current research, should be added the fact that in families where there is spousal and child abuse it is highly likely that sibling abuse also is occurring. This can be explained in two ways. First, the children may be modeling their behavior toward each other after their parents' behavior. Second, research shows that children who witness parental violence tend to have more behavioral problems than children not exposed to parental violence (Hughes et al., 1989; Jouriles, Barling, & O'Leary, 1987; O'Keefe, 1995; Suh & Abel, 1990). Sibling abuse may be one manifestation of such behavioral problems.

Parents Overwhelmed by Their Own Problems

Another reason for sibling abuse is that parents are often so overwhelmed by their own problems that they are unaware of what is happening between or among siblings. The parents may not have the energy or the ability to handle the situation. Some of the parents of survivors in the research were coping with alcohol problems, mental illness, financial difficulties, and marital problems, as these comments indicate:

> My family was very chaotic. My father was an alcoholic. My mother died when I was eleven years old. My father had many lovers and was gone a lot of the time.

> I don't think my mother knew how badly I was being hurt by an older sister and I was afraid to tell her for fear of retaliation. She was busy trying to survive on practically nothing and deal with her own emotional problems, and probably she had systemic lupus then, even though it wasn't diagnosed for another fifteen years or so. But I think she didn't want to know how bad things were because she was powerless to change her circumstances.

Research suggests that adolescent sibling sexual abuse perpetrators often come from discordant families. Worling (1995) compared 32 adolescent male sex offenders who assaulted younger siblings with 28 males who offended against nonsibling children. Adolescent sibling-incest offenders reported significantly more marital discord, parental rejection, use of physical punishment, a more negative and argumentative family atmosphere, and general dissatisfaction with family relationships than did their nonsibling sexual offender counterparts. The researcher suggests several possible explanations for the relationship between discordant families and sibling-incest perpetrators. First, children who live with abusive and rejecting parents may turn to each other for comfort, nurturance, and support. As these children enter adolescence, a risk of sexualizing these relationships may occur. Second, intrafamilial offenders may be seeking some form of retribution within their families for the abuse and rejection they have suffered. Third, the adolescents may be modeling their aggressive behavior toward their siblings after what they observe in their parents' relationship to each other as well as to their children. Fourth, although the research data did not suggest this, the sibling-incest offenders may be exposed to more sexualized behaviors in the home, such as family nudity, pornography, or witnessing parental sexual acts.

Although parents' inability to intervene effectively in sibling abuse may be a reflection of their psychological problems, the problem is better viewed from a broader perspective, such as from an ecological or social-situational perspective (Garbarino, 1977; Parke & Collmer, 1975; Wiehe, 1989) that views the family as a system within the larger social system of which it is a part. A mutual dependence exists between a family and its social environment, and interdependent interactions occur between the two systems. The psychosocial development of individual family members, as well as that of the family as a whole, occurs in the context of the physical, social, political, and economic characteristics of society. Thus, parenting cannot be viewed only from the perspective of psychological functioning. Rather, external social forces impacting on each parent also must be considered. For example, inadequate opportunities for vocational training may require parents to work two or more unskilled jobs. Inadequate housing may prevent siblings of age and gender differences from having adequate privacy. Psychiatric hospitalization, outpatient mental health treatment, or substance abuse treatment programs may not be available or a person may be unable to pay for such treatment. Latchkey programs for children who return home from school before their parents return home from work may not be available, thus forcing an older sibling to care for younger siblings. Under these difficult social circumstances, problems arise that can affect the children in terms of their relationships with their parents and toward each other as siblings.

Contribution of the Victim

Another causal factor associated with sibling abuse is the victim's own contribution to the abuse, particularly to physical and emotional abuse. This causal factor is known in the literature on child abuse as the interactional theory (Parke & Collmer, 1975).

When an adult abuses a child, the adult does not necessarily abuse all the children in a family. Frequently, the abuse is selective and directed at one specific child. Certain physical characteristics may make a child more prone to abuse. Some children also may exhibit behaviors that make them targets for abuse. In these cases, abuse often becomes cyclical and escalates. This in turn reinforces the child's behavior, which may prompt more emotional and physical abuse of that child. Research supports the hypothesis that some behavioral patterns of abused children tend to invite further abuse (Bakan, 1971; Patterson, 1982).

It is important to note that the interactional theory of child abuse *does not blame the child for the abuse.* Blaming the child implies that in some way the child deserves what occurred, but no one deserves to be abused. Rather, the interactional theory identifies and analyzes factors contributing to the abuse for the purpose of helping prevent and treat the abuse.

The interactional theory, generally applied to the abuse of children by adults, also applies to sibling abuse. Some siblings may be more prone to abuse by another sibling because of physical characteristics. In name-calling and ridicule, as noted in survivors' comments, physical characteristics such as height or weight frequently become the targets of a sibling's emotional abuse. Likewise, the behavior of some siblings may set up situations in which abuse is more likely to occur. For example, when a younger sibling makes excessive demands on an older sibling for attention or repeatedly uses another sibling's possessions without permission, incidents of abuse may occur. Again, this is not to blame the younger sibling for the abuse; rather, it is to place responsibility on the parents to be aware of such interactions and to effectively intervene. Using the problem-solving approach, discussed later, may help determine ways the siblings are expected to relate to each other.

Ineffective Interventions

As has been previously mentioned, the inability of parents to intervene and effectively stop sibling abuse because they do not know how is a factor relating to sibling abuse. This does not mean the parents in the research sample were not interested in or concerned about the abuse; rather, the way they tried to stop it was ineffective. Consequently, the abuse continued and in some instances escalated out of control. Behaviors such as verbal put-downs, name-calling, hitting, and slapping occur to some extent between siblings in all families. This is not abnormal, and effective parental intervention generally stops the behavior. Parents may take the problem-solving approach with their children, which conveys the message that the behavior should be avoided and will not be tolerated in the family. The parents' intervention also prevents the behavior from escalating into a pattern of abuse.

Ineffective interventions by contrast do not give this message. The children are not instructed on how to avoid the abusive behavior. When severe corporal punishment is used, such as giving the perpetrator a beating, the abuse may even escalate. The perpetrator becomes angry at the victim for reporting what happened and in retaliation escalates the abuse. The victim may be forced to not report abuse in the future for fear of retaliation. Survivors wrote,

> My older brothers received a severe beating when I told my parents how they were abusing me. The severity of the beating, however, discouraged me from ever reporting again what happened because I wanted to avoid a more violent outcome.

> My parents were so busy abusing themselves and each other and us that it was only natural that as siblings we would abuse each other.

Some respondents described the atmosphere in their home as a "battleground." A culture of violence developed for all family members living in this atmosphere. Verbal and physical assaults become a typical pattern of interaction—between husband and wife and between parents and children. Researchers are becoming aware that often more than one type of violence occurs in a family, such as spousal abuse and child abuse (Sutphen, Wiehe, & Leukefeld, 1996; Wiehe, 1997a). In families where both of these types of violence are occurring, drug and alcohol abuse generally are prominent. These families have been identified as "multiple abuse families." Based on survivors' comments, sibling abuse also is prevalent in these families.

Sibling Abuse Viewed as Normal

Some parents accepted physical abuse between siblings as normal because they felt that the sibling perpetrator was "going through a phase." They excused the behavior as appropriate for males, or they accepted the behavior as "normal sibling rivalry":

> The abuse was considered normal behavior by my parents, who had no idea what normal might be. I might add that the physical abuse by my siblings was much less than the emotional and sexual abuse by them.

Sibling rivalry has been around for as long as there have been brothers and sisters. Literature is filled with examples of siblings attacking one another. The biblical story of Cain and Abel is just one example. The fact that sibling rivalry is so universal suggests to some parents that sibling abuse is normal. Sibling rivalry is normal; sibling abuse is not.

Why does rivalry between siblings occur? According to Adele Faber and Elaine Mazlish (1988) in *Siblings Without Rivalry: How to Help Your Children Live Together So You Can Live Too,* the presence of another sibling in the home casts a shadow upon the life and well-being of the firstborn. A sibling implies there will be *less*—less attention from the parents, less time with the parents, less energy for meeting the firstborn's needs. The first child may even think that the parents love the second child more. Thus, the new sibling implies a threat. Psychologist Alfred Adler referred to the birth of a second child as a "dethroning" of the first-born.

EFFECTS OF ABUSE ON THE SURVIVOR

How does sibling abuse in childhood affect the survivors as adults? "Time heals all wounds" runs an old adage; however, the number of individuals seeking help from mental health professionals and joining support groups for the abused disapproves this statement. Physical, emotional, or sexual abuse by a sibling can have devastating effects on survivors, whether the perpetrator of the abuse was an adult or a sibling, as research documents (Bagley & Ramsay, 1986; Beitchman et al., 1992; Briere & Runtz, 1990; Meuenzenmaier, Meyer, Struening, & Ferber, 1993; Moeller et al., 1993; Mullen, Martin, Anderson, Romans, & Herbison, 1996). The emotional pain the abuse causes never seems to go completely away, even when the survivor seeks psychotherapy. Survivors simply learn to cope with the pain, but the memory of the abuse does not disappear: "I get so angry just thinking about how humiliating, degrading this was. And my brother has been dead for twenty years."

Prior to discussing the effects that being physically, emotionally, or sexually abused by a sibling as a child had on the survivors as adults, some comments should be made about the effects of the abuse on the victims at the time the abuse was occurring or shortly thereafter. Several studies provide a description of the immediate effects of abuse by an adult on a child victim that may also be applicable to victims of sibling abuse. The behavior of 93 prepubertal children evaluated for sexual abuse and 80 nonabused children was examined using the Child Behavior Checklist approximately 4 months after the sexually abused children had been clinically seen for their abuse (Dubowitz et al., 1993). The sexually abused children had significantly more behavior problems than their nonabused counterparts, including depression, aggression, sleep and somatic complaints, hyperactivity, and sexual problems.

Similarly, in a study of school-age children who had been physically abused as compared to a nonabused sample, the abused children displayed pervasive and severe academic and social/emotional problems (Kurtz et al., 1993). They performed poorly on standardized tests of language and math skills, received low performance assessments by teachers, and were more likely than their nonabused counterparts to have repeated one or more grades. A number of the children who were age 14 and up already had dropped out of school. The research concluded that, because physically abused children are often angry, distractible, anxious, and lack self-control, it is extremely difficult for these children to learn.

The abuse can affect victims in the years immediately following the abuse rather than waiting until adulthood, as the survivors in the present research reported. For example, in a 17-year longitudinal study of 375 people who had been physically and sexually abused before age 18 by a family member (mother, father, sibling, stepparent, uncle, cousin), those who were abused, as compared to their nonabused counterparts, demonstrated significant impairments in functioning at both ages 15 and 21, including depression, anxiety, psychiatric disorders, emotional-behavioral problems, suicidal ideation, and suicide attempts (Silverman et al., 1996).

Poor Self-Esteem

Nearly every respondent to the research, whether a victim of physical, emotional, or sexual abuse from a sibling, referred to poor self-esteem. From their responses, it would appear that low self-esteem is a universal effect of sibling abuse.

Low self-esteem appears to be an effect of all types of abuse whether by an adult or a sibling. Research on the effects of parents' psychological maltreatment of their children found that the children tended to feel unwanted, inferior, unloved, and inadequate—symptoms that can affect a person's psychological development (Garbarino, Guttman, & Seeley, 1986). Similarly, survivors reported that the abuse they experienced as children from a sibling left them feeling they were in some way inferior, inadequate, and worthless:

> I lack self-esteem and self-confidence. I cling to my husband and am afraid of a lot of things.

> The abuse contributed to my low self-esteem and self-confidence. I still have difficulty accepting credit for successes. I have a continuing sense of being worthless and unlovable, despite evidence to the contrary.

> I feel unwanted, unloved. I feel like no one could love me. I feel no one needs or wants me. I feel like no one cares!

Problems in Relationships With the Opposite Sex

Women who were physically, emotionally, or sexually abused by a brother reported that the abuse affected their attitude toward males. The survivors' attitudes may be described as distrustful, suspicious, fearful, and even hateful. The emotions the women experienced stemming from their abuse by a brother are in turn transferred to all men. This disgust and distrust of men has significantly affected their ability to relate to and especially to form intimate relationships with them. The abuse that some respondents experienced from a brother while growing up even influenced their decision not to marry.

An underlying fear and suspicion of men pervades the female survivors. Their fear of entrapment by men, which the survivors reported, may stem from the restraints their brothers placed on them while physically abusing them, such as pinning them to the floor. It may also stem from the entrapment they felt in their family when they pleaded in vain for protection from the abuse. As has been seen, when victims reported their sexual abuse by a brother to their parents, they often were not provided protection but were blamed for what happened, which may have heightened their feeling of entrapment.

Several survivors described how their childhood abuse has affected their relationships with the opposite sex:

> I am uncertain of men's real intentions. I see them as a source of pain.

> I have a lot of fear of men and tend to use my mind and intellect to push men away and intimidate them the same way I was intimidated. I have a lot of difficulties in my relationships with men. I tend to disagree a lot and to be very afraid and contemptuous of a man's need for me.

Difficulty With Interpersonal Relationships

Some survivors have difficulty relating not only to members of the opposite sex but to anyone, regardless of gender. Difficulties in interpersonal relationships impair these survivors' ability, say, to hold a job. Others reported compensating for their poor feelings of self-worth by trying too hard to please others.

The survivors commented about their inability to handle anger appropriately in interpersonal relationships. They frequently used the words *rage* and *anger* when describing their reactions to their childhood abuse by a sibling. Some survivors spoke of this anger being with them constantly and having a need to suppress these feelings. Other research shows that one outcome frequently experienced by incest survivors is the suppression of anger, which creates more symptoms for them as compared to survivors who appropriately express their angry feelings (Scott & Day, 1996). Survivors mentioned their fear of (a) expressing any anger, (b) others' anger, and (c) what they described as their own uncontrollable outbursts of anger. The victims related their present anger to that felt in three phases of their life: the anger they felt as a child but were not able to express because of their parents' inappropriate response to their abuse by a sibling; a continual festering of this anger throughout their adult years, the source of which they often did not know until they sought professional help; and the anger toward their sibling that they still experience today for the abuse they suffered. Although many of the survivors have sought professional help, their anger is still a factor with which they must continually cope:

> I'm afraid that everyone is going to abuse me in some way. I don't trust anyone. I feel in everything people say or do that they want to hurt me. I always want to take the blame for any mistake made, or I feel that everyone is blaming me.

> It has made me very cynical and untrusting of those who attempt to get close quickly. I grew up feeling if your own family doesn't like or want you, who will?

Repeating the Victim Role in Other Relationships

A significant effect of sibling abuse is that the survivors as adults enter into relationships in which they are revictimized. Many survivors choose friends and mates that place them in situations where they again become victims of abuse. This phenomenon relates to the survivors' feelings of low self-esteem and worthlessness. Their behavior gives the message to others that they are worthless and deserve to be used and abused.

Research on adult-child sexual abuse indicates that the victims are likely to continue being abused as adults (Faller, 1989; Herman & Hirschman, 1977; McGuire & Wagner, 1978; Summit & Kryso, 1978). Child sexual abuse survivors may internalize their victimization to the extent that they regard the abuse as something they deserved. Thus, they unconsciously choose mates who continue to abuse them. A similar phenomenon occurs among women who have been battered by their husbands. They frequently leave one abusive relationship and enter into another, thereby continuing their role of victim (Walker, 1994). The following comments confirm this behavior:

> I now know that my brother hurt me because he needed something desperately from me that he felt he didn't have himself. He felt weaker than me. I tend to pick men now who are weaker than me and need a lot. Then I push them away. I also pick men who have a covert sadistic streak.

> It took me into my thirties before I began to see a pattern from the abuse I experienced from an older sister. I chose a first husband who abused me. Also, I tend to constantly be doing too much as if to make me feel better.

Continued Self-Blame

Survivors who blame themselves for the sexual abuse often continue this pattern into adulthood. Intellectually, they know that such thinking is absurd, but emotionally they cannot accept the fact they did not stop the sexual abuse (Agosta & Loring, 1988). Survivors find themselves repeatedly thinking that they allowed themselves to be sexually abused, even though in reality there probably was little at the time that they could have done to prevent it. One survivor wrote about her self-blame for the sexual abuse she experienced from an older brother:

> I was told by several women and especially by my older sister that it was *my* fault because of the way I dressed and carried myself. I am very self-conscious now as an adult of how I dress. I do not like or wear short skirts. I prefer turtleneck sweaters and high-necked blouses. I do not accept compliments very well from men, other than my husband.

One respondent at the age of 4 was paid a quarter by her older brother to perform oral sex. She complied largely out of fear that if she didn't he would hurt her. She commented, "I have punished myself for 22 years for taking that quarter from him. I don't like myself."

Sexual Dysfunction

Survivors of sexual abuse by a sibling in particular noted that the abuse has affected their sexual functioning. Two extreme reactions were reported: One was avoidance of all sexual contact, and the other was sexual compulsivity. Some female survivors reported that because of their sexual abuse by an older brother they have an aversion to sex, sometimes even in marriage:

> I have been deeply affected by the sexual abuse from my brother. Even after years of therapy, it's hard for me to be truly open sexually with a man. I often experience shame and disgust around sex and tend to focus on the man's experience and pleasure rather than on my own. I have a hard time initiating sex. I often experience myself as a sexual object to be used and contemptuously discarded by men.

Others use sex as a weapon:

> I became very sexually active after leaving home at age 20. I did not want to have meaningful or strong relationships with anyone but to have sex with many men and never see them again, so that they might have a feeling of being used and hurt.

The findings of several studies on adults who were sexually abused as children support the comments of survivors of sibling sexual abuse in this research about sexual problems (Bagley & Ramsey, 1986; Briere & Runtz, 1988; Kinzl et al., 1995). Briere (1984) and Meiselman (1978), using samples of adults who had been sexually abused as children and control groups of persons who had not been sexually abused, found that the sexual abuse survivors had a higher percentage of sexual problems than the control group. Sarwer and Durlak (1996) investigated 359 married adult women who sought sex therapy with their partners. A high percentage of these women had experienced sexual abuse as a child. The study also found that childhood sexual abuse involving physical force and penetration were predictive of an increased likelihood of sexual dysfunction. Studies also indicate that an unusually high percentage of both male and female prostitutes report being sexually abused as children (Blume, 1986; Janus, 1984; Silbert & Pines, 1983).

Eating Disorders, Alcoholism, and Drug Abuse

Survivors reported that sibling abuse has affected their adult lives in the form of eating disorders:

> I have an eating disorder in the form of bulimia and am at times anorexic. These problems have to do with the denial of needs and the shame and hate I have regarding taking things into my body.

Research shows a relationship between sexual abuse as a child and bulimia nervosa in adult women. For example, 38 women who were receiving treatment for incest abuse were compared with a control group of 27 women also in treatment but denied having been sexually abused. The incest victims were significantly more likely to binge, vomit, experience a loss of control over their eating habits, and report dissatisfaction with their bodies as compared to those in the control group. The incest victims also more frequently engaged in other maladaptive behaviors such as the abuse of alcohol, suicidal gestures, self-mutilation and smoking (Wonderlich et al., 1996). Similarly, 72 women suffering from bulimia nervosa were compared with a matched control group of 72 women not displaying bulimic symptoms (Miller & McCluskey-Fawcett, 1993). Rates of self-reported sexual abuse were significantly greater in the women diagnosed as bulimic. The researchers suggested that the eating disorder may have developed in an attempt to cope with sexual victimization.

Other survivors reported problems with alcohol and drugs. One wrote, "I still tend to blunt my feelings or drown them in booze. I am in Alcoholics Anonymous."

Numerous studies show a relationship between being sexually abused as a child and later drug abuse (Boyd et al., 1993; Boyd et al., 1994; Covington & Kohen, 1984; Harrison et al., 1997; Widom et al., 1995). For example, in a sample of recovering chemically dependent women, researchers found that 68% of the 60 respondents had been recipients of unwanted sexual contacts from family and nonfamily members (Teets, 1995).

Depression

Survivors repeatedly referred to experiencing depression as adults that they directly associate with their childhood abuse from a sibling. Researchers have found a similar relationship between childhood sexual abuse and adult depression in adult survivors of childhood sexual abuse by adults known to the victim. In a nonclinical sample of 278 university women, 15% had sexual contacts with a significantly older person before the age of 15. Those who had a sexual abuse history showed greater depressive symptomatology than those who had not experienced sexual abuse. Their depression appeared to relate to a sense of powerlessness they felt at the time of the abuse and that they continued to experience in adulthood (Briere & Runtz, 1988).

When the 150 participants in the research discussed here were asked if they had ever been hospitalized for depression, 26% (39) responded affirmatively. Because so large a proportion had been hospitalized for depression, it may be assumed that even more had sought help for depression on an outpatient basis.

Some survivors' depression was so severe that it led to suicide attempts. Over 33% of the sexual abuse survivors reported having attempted suicide. Research reports even higher suicide-attempt rates for victims of sexual abuse by adults (Briere, Evans, Runtz, & Wall, 1988; DeYoung, 1982). When asked how her sexual abuse by a sibling affects her as an adult, a 42-year-old woman responded, "Terribly! I have seriously considered suicide. I experience severe depression requiring medication."

Posttraumatic Stress Disorder

Survivors reported that they experience anxiety attacks and flashbacks of their abuse by a sibling, which are symptoms of posttraumatic stress disorder (PTSD), a psychosocial dysfunctioning experienced by individuals who have been traumatized. Anxiety attacks were reported by survivors when they were in situations with someone wanting to be intimate with them or in more general interpersonal relationships with peers and bosses. The anxiety seemed to be reminiscent of encounters the survivors had with their sibling perpetrator where they felt they could not escape from the physical or sexual abuse that was about to occur. Survivors described flashbacks of their sexual abuse by a brother occurring especially when they were engaged in sexual activity:

> Until recently sexual intercourse was not very enjoyable. Well, I would enjoy it but could never achieve an orgasm. Sometimes sex would become so emotionally upsetting that in the middle of it I would remember the past and the moment would be destroyed and I'd usually cry.

> Sometimes I will be thinking about what my brother did to me and when my husband approaches me for sex, I will push him away. I find myself daydreaming about the whole nightmare of my sexual abuse. It's like it's still happening and never going to stop.

Other research shows that a high number of individuals who experienced child sexual abuse also show the symptomatology of PTSD. In one study that assessed 117 help-seeking adult survivors of childhood sexual abuse to determine the relationship between their sexual abuse and PTSD, 72% met full *DSM-III* criteria for current and 85% for lifetime posttraumatic stress disorder, based on PTSD intensity scores (Rodriguez et al., 1996). Other studies have reported a similar relationship between child sexual abuse and posttraumatic stress disorder with in some instances even higher rates (Beitchman, et al., 1992; O'Neill & Gupta, 1991; Saunders, 1991).

DISTINGUISHING ABUSIVE BEHAVIOR FROM NORMAL BEHAVIOR

This chapter has focused on the abusive behavior of one sibling toward another, including behaviors that involved physical, emotional, and sexual abuse. The question may appropriately be asked whether these behaviors were really abuse or normal sibling interactions or even, in the case of sexual abuse, are some of the actions merely sexual curiosity between siblings?

Some siblings hit, slap, and punch each other. Siblings at times may call each other names. The critical question then is how can one distinguish between normal sibling interactions and sibling abusive behaviors? Four criteria will be presented to answer this question.

A word of caution is in order regarding these criteria. The criteria should not be applied in an "either/or" or absolute manner. Human behavior is very complex and does not lend itself to easy scrutiny. Many shades of gray can be found in sibling interactions, and questions as to whether a specific behavior is abusive will remain. Based on the physical pain and emotional suffering survivors of sibling abuse experienced, it would be wise to err in the direction of protecting the victim in cases of uncertainty.

Before trying to distinguish between normal and abusive behavior, the specific behavior must be identified. The specific behavior may be identified by isolating what is occurring from the emotions surrounding the behavior, such as anger, hurt, or shame. The following are three examples of sibling interactions, each of which illustrates a specific behavior.

Example 1: Two siblings, 2 and 4 years old, are constantly fighting over toys. When the 4-year-old chooses a toy with which to play, the 2-year-old wants the same toy. A struggle ensues and one of them, generally the 2-year-old, ends up crying.

Example 2. Sue is 14 years old. She is very angry at her parents about the limits they have set on her dating. Her parents require that she do no individual dating but go out with boys only in mixed groups. Also, they have established a weekend evening curfew of 10 p.m. But Mitzi, Sue's 17-year-old sister, is allowed to go on dates alone with a boy to a movie or a school activity. Her weekend curfew is 11 p.m. Sue is very jealous of Mitzi's privileges, and every weekend she reminds her parents about how unfairly they are treating her. Furthermore, the two girls wage a constant battle over this issue. Recently, the parents overheard Sue calling Mitzi "an ugly bitch" after a heated discussion of their different dating privileges.

Example 3. A mother notices that her 4-year-old son is fascinated by his new baby sister when her diaper is being changed. He seems very curious about the baby's genital area and is always present when diapers are changed.

What specific behavior is occurring in each of the above examples? In the first example, the behavior is *fighting,* in the second, *name-calling,* and, in the third, *observation,* and although the example does not state this, the 4-year-old boy probably also is *questioning* the mother about the differences in genitalia that he is observing.

Criterion 1: Is the Behavior Age-Appropriate?

The first criterion for distinguishing abusive behavior from nonabusive behavior is the behavior's age-appropriateness. Consider the first example: Is it appropriate for a 2-year-old and a 4-year-old to be struggling over toys? Yes, it is. The 2-year-old is probably simply mimicking his older sibling in play. With whatever toy his older sibling plays, he too wants to play. It is easier to do what "big brother" is doing, and it is probably more fun, even though "big brother" doesn't feel this way.

Consider the second example. Jealousy and fighting over differences in privileges are quite age-appropriate between adolescents. They are both struggling with their own identities and attempting to try their wings outside the safe nest of their home. Sue, at age 14, does not view herself as less mature than Mitzi and sees no reason why she shouldn't have the same privileges. But name-calling is hardly an appropriate way for Sue to handle her anger, although it is not uncommon.

A word of caution at this point: Even though fighting and jealously between siblings can be expected to occur, they should not be ignored. Nonabusive behavior can escalate into abusive behavior if effective parental intervention does not occur. Ignoring the behavior will not make it go away. Moreover, constant fighting between siblings is unpleasant not only for those involved but for those around the behavior.

The critical question is how to intervene. For parents who are having difficulty handling dysfunctional sibling interactions, various avenues of assistance are available. Parent education courses are available through community mental health agencies, churches, and other educational resources. Books that focus on sibling relationships are available at bookstores or public libraries. Examples of such books are *Siblings Without Rivalry* (Faber & Mazlish, 1988), *How to Talk So Kids Will Listen & Listen So Kids Will Talk* (Faber & Mazlish, 1982), and *Help! The Kids Are at It Again: Using Kids' Quarrels to Teach People Skills* (Crary, 1997).

Consider the third example: Observation and questioning on the part of a 4-year-old are normal, as is sexual curiosity. The child who has never seen a clitoris may be expected to ask why his sister is different. If the 4-year-old child wants to touch his baby sister's clitoris, an effective parental response may be to differentiate for the child appropriate and inappropriate touches. This example highlights the importance of children having sexual information regarding appropriate and inappropriate touching relevant to their psychosocial development.

Age-appropriate behavior can be determined by professionals with a knowledge of child development and by books on child development (Vander Zanden, 1993; Zastrow & Kirst-Ashman, 1997). Determining what is age-appropriate behavior can also occur through parents talking to other parents and sharing information on their children's behavior. The parents of a mentally retarded child, for example, told their friends that their 4-year-old would sometimes crawl on the floor and bark like a dog or meow like a cat. The parents saw this as an example of his retardation. The friends, however, pointed out that their 4-year-old child, who was not mentally retarded, frequently did the same thing. As a matter of fact, they said he had once asked if he could try eating out of a bowl on the floor like the family pets. Thus, the first set of parents learned that this was age-appropriate behavior for their 4-year-old.

However, some behavioral interactions between siblings are not age-appropriate and should be considered abusive. Consider the following examples. A 10-year-old brother destroys his 3-year-old sister's dolls by pulling out their hair, tearing off a leg or arm, or stabbing them with a knife. An 8-year-old sister composes a song about her younger brother who is overweight. The words make fun of him and call him "tubby." She sings it whenever she is around him and in front of his friends. A 14-year-old boy fondles the genitals of his 3-year-old sister behind a shed in the backyard.

These examples portray three behaviors: the destruction of toys, ridicule through name-calling, and sexual fondling. In light of the age of the participants, especially the perpetrators, these are not age-appropriate behaviors. A 10-year-old boy should have learned to respect the toys of other children and not destroy them. Likewise, an 8-year-old girl may delight in some teasing, but in this instance the teasing is vicious in nature as it is done before her brother's peers. And a boy fondling the genitals of his younger sister is not appropriate behavior at any age. By the age of 14, a boy should be aware of sexual differences between boys and girls and between good touches and secret touches. Moreover, the fact that the behavior is occurring in a clandestine setting implies that the perpetrator has some awareness that the behavior is inappropriate. Also, the younger child is not mature enough to decide whether she wishes to participate.

Criterion 2: How Often and How Long Has the Behavior Been Occurring?

Fighting, name-calling, teasing, and even some sexual exploration occur between siblings at some time or another and may be considered normal sibling rivalry or simple sexual curiosity. But frequency and duration of the behavior may turn a nonabusive behavior into an abusive one. When fighting, name-calling, teasing, and sexual exploration occur frequently over a long period of time, the behavior becomes abusive, especially if the perpetrator is admonished to stop but doesn't.

This does not mean that a single occurrence of a potentially abusive behavior between siblings, such as sexual activity, should be minimized. In some instances, sexual abuse by a sibling is only a single occurrence, but its effects on the survivor are serious and can affect the individual into adulthood. Recall the survivor who at the age of four was paid a quarter by her older brother for performing oral sex and who complied largely out of fear of retaliation: "I have punished myself for 22 years for taking that quarter from him. I don't like myself." Thus, frequency and duration should not be used as the *only* criteria in determining whether a behavior is abusive.

How long is too long, and how frequently is too frequently? A definite period of time or number of occurrences would be helpful, but such a pat answer is not available. When a child complains on more than one occasion about the behavior of a sibling, the parents should explore the complaint. Likewise, when parents begin to feel uncomfortable about a behavior in which a child is engaging toward a sibling, the time has come to intervene. A critical element in both of these situations is the observation of a *pattern* of behavior that is occurring over a period of time. Ignoring dysfunctional sibling behaviors will not necessarily make them disappear.

Criterion 3: Is There an Aspect of Victimization in the Behavior?

A *victim* is someone who is an unwilling, nonconsenting object of abusive behavior and is hurt or injured by the action or actions of another. The research respondents who were abused by a sibling think of themselves as *victims* of their sibling's actions. They vividly recalled what they had experienced many years before. They were the targets of their sibling's physical assaults, the butt of their ridicule, or the object of their sexual abuse.

An individual in the victim role may be a dupe or may have been placed in a gullible position by the other person. Many of the respondents, especially those sexually abused by a sibling, had been placed in the victim role because of their powerlessness. They were duped or enticed to participate in sexual activity, were threatened, or were taken advantage of because of their age. These victims often had little choice but to acquiesce to their sibling's sexual demands because they felt there was nothing else they could do or were not mature enough to realize what was happening.

A victim, an unwilling participant, may not even be able to give or withhold consent. The fact that a victim participates in an activity does not mean that the participation was voluntary. A child may be unable to consent verbally to an older sibling's sexual advances because he or she is simply too young. For example, a 2-year-old child is not able to protest her older brother's sexual explorations. Likewise, a mentally retarded or emotionally disturbed adolescent who is the continual object of jokes and ridicule by a sibling may not be able to fend off these verbal assaults.

The question of whether an individual is being victimized can often be determined by assessing how the perpetrator gained access to the individual. If access was gained through game playing, trickery, deceit, bribery, or force, the person who is the object of the behavior is a victim. For example, a 4-year-old girl is bribed with candy to go to a tree house that her brother and his friends have built in the backyard; when she gets there, she is asked to remove her panties and expose herself. An older brother constantly acquires money from a younger sibling on the pretense that the coin size determines its value. In both instances, the sibling is a victim and the behavior is abusive.

Another indication of victimization is the emotions surrounding a behavior that the sibling feels. A sibling called a name by another sibling may experience embarrassment or hurt, yet others who are the targets of name-calling may not be offended by the terms used. A husband and wife, for example, may call each other names that out of context would be offensive but in context are terms of endearment. The emotional reaction of the person who is being called the name may be an important clue as to whether he or she is being put into a victim role.

Individuals who have been targets of abusive behavior may not realize their victimization until long after the act. A prepubertal young girl who is sexually abused by an older sibling may not realize the consequences of the activity in which she is involved. She may become aware of her victimization only after she experiences sexual dysfunctioning in her relationships with the opposite sex or in other problems in living.

Victims commonly blame themselves for their victimization. Many of the respondents to the research not only blamed themselves for what happened but were blamed by the perpetrator or their parents. A parallel may be drawn to wives abused by their husbands. A wife may excuse and thereby tolerate her husband's abusive behavior by telling herself that she deserved his anger because she did not have dinner ready on time or was insensitive to his wishes. That she is a victim may not become clear to her until later when she joins a group for abused women and realizes that she cannot always please her husband, that his expectations are unrealistic, and that his actions are abusive. Sibling abuse victims, too, may have difficulty realizing their victimization if their parents blame them and do not protect them.

Criterion 4: What Is the Purpose of the Behavior?

The motivation of one sibling to engage in a behavior with another sibling is tied to the purpose the behavior serves.

In most instances of emotional abuse by a sibling, the purpose is to belittle the victim with name-calling or ridicule. This is destructive behavior and therefore abusive. If the victim provoked the perpetrator, both individuals are engaging in abusive behavior and are placing themselves in their roles of victim and perpetrator. Obviously, there are more appropriate ways for siblings to settle differences between themselves. For example, taking a problem-solving approach is an effective way to break abusive behavior between siblings.

When an older sibling, generally a male, sexually abuses a sibling for the purpose of achieving sexual gratification, the purpose of the behavior is not observation but sexual pleasure. Survivors of childhood sexual abuse by a sibling reported that the perpetrator received sexual satisfaction, such as through masturbation, by viewing or touching a younger sibling's genitals. In most instances of sexual abuse reported by these research respondents, the individual who was the target of the behavior was victimized and the behavior was age-inappropriate. Such behavior must be regarded as abuse.

Sexual exploration with the intent of sadism or suffering is also abusive behavior. An older sibling may insert objects into the anus or vagina of a younger sibling with the intention of seeing the sibling suffer. The perpetrator may or may not masturbate. Again, the activity sets one sibling up as a victim.

In some incidents of sexual abuse, an additional person besides the sibling perpetrator may be involved. Children may be requested or forced to engage in sexual activity because it gives a third party sexual gratification. An older sibling, for example, may encourage two younger siblings to engage in sexual play while the older sibling watches. Or one sibling may encourage another to abuse a third sibling physically or emotionally. In these instances, the behavior is abusive because of the purpose the behavior served for the dual perpetrators.

A word of caution on the purpose the behavior serves for the perpetrator: Children are frequently not able to conceptualize the purpose of behaviors in which they engage. When parents ask a young child who has done something with serious consequences "Why did you do that?" the child often responds, "I don't know." Although partially defensive, the response may also indicate that cognitive limitations prevent the child from identifying why he or she did something. Children may not yet perceive cause and effect; rather, they engage in behavior at an impulsive level with little thought for the consequences. Nor have children had the range of experiences that enable them to anticipate consequences, especially undesirable ones. In other words, they lack the maturity to look beyond their own behavior to the consequences.

Supplementary Questions

The following questions may also help in distinguishing abusive behavior from normal behavior:

- In what context did the behavior occur?
- What preceded the behavior?
- What was the victim's contribution to what occurred?
- Was the perpetrator imitating something he or she had seen?
- Was the behavior planned or spontaneous?
- Has the behavior ever occurred before?
- How did the victim feel about what occurred?
- What was the perpetrator's reaction to what occurred?
- Has the perpetrator been confronted in the past about this behavior?

PROBLEM SOLVING AS AN INTERVENTION IN SIBLING ABUSE

The acronym SAFE provides a guide for parents to intervene effectively in sibling interactions that have the potential of becoming abusive. Each letter represents a step in the problem-solving process.

"S" stands for *s*top the action and *s*et a climate for problem solving. When two siblings are engaged in hitting, slapping, pushing, name-calling, and other potentially abusive behaviors, it may be necessary for a parent to stop the behavior. Separating the children by having them go to their own rooms or engage in activities by themselves for a period of time may prevent the behavior from escalating into abuse. A climate for problem solving can be set by assuring the siblings that, based on the frequency with which this behavior has occurred, there is a need to discuss their actions toward one another. After dinner or before the family begins to watch TV in the evening may be an appropriate time to sit down together to talk about the behavior and to consider alternatives to resolving the problems that occur between or among the siblings.

"A" stands for *a*ssess what is happening. An assessment should occur in the family meeting of the facts and feelings regarding what happens prior to the siblings becoming embroiled in a conflict and engaging in aversive verbal or physical behavior. All siblings involved in the conflict should talk about what happens as well as how they were feeling at the time and after the conflict.

"F" represents *f*ind out what will work. This is the core of the problem-solving process. The central question is "What can you do to avoid the negative physical and verbal interactions that occur?" Although parents may be tempted to present simple solutions to the problem, they should skillfully involve the children in analyzing the conflicts and what they can do to avoid them. A recent conflict can serve as the basis for this discussion.

In this aspect of the problem-solving process, the family may wish to determine some basic rules that all must follow. For example, no one borrows toys, clothing, or other possessions from another sibling without expressed permission from that person. When the door to a bedroom or bathroom is closed, no one enters without permission from the person in the room. Frequently, conflicts develop around the completion of household chores assigned to siblings such as taking out the trash, setting the table, and washing the dishes. Mounting a chart on the refrigerator clearly identifying who is responsible for what task on what day and establishing consequences for not fulfilling responsibilities often help reduce these conflicts.

"E" stands for *e*valuating a few days or a week later whether or not what was determined in the family problem-solving conference is being implemented. Evaluation is important and may provide clues as to how to fine-tune the outcomes determined in the problem-solving process so as to make them a viable means of preventing sibling rivalry from becoming sibling abuse.

The problem-solving process is not a one-time event for a family; it may need to be used frequently as siblings and parents confront problems in living together. The participation of all family members in the process makes all responsible for their behavior and assists them to function as a family unit with minimal conflict.

TREATING SURVIVORS

Although the treatment of survivors of sibling physical, emotional, and sexual abuse in essence does not differ from the treatment of survivors of adult-child physical, emotional, and sexual abuse, several factors are relevant for mental health professionals working with sibling abuse survivors.

Uncovering Sibling Abuse

Numerous sibling abuse survivors who read my first book on the subject (Wiehe, 1997b) have written expressing appreciation that my research has brought the problem of sibling abuse out into the open. Two words that many survivors used when expressing their appreciation for the research on sibling abuse were that the research *validated* or *affirmed* for them that what they experienced from a sibling as they were growing up was not sibling rivalry but sibling abuse. A survivor from Montana wrote,

> I am a sibling abuse survivor and can now say that after having found your book in the library and having read it. I have looked for years in the literature for something written about the way my older brother treated me and even today as an adult continues to do so. Even a therapist I went to for a short period of time denied what I experienced was really abuse but "just a bad case of sibling rivalry." Your book affirms for me that I am an abuse survivor and I am now in meaningful therapy with a group of other survivors.

I include these comments so that mental health professionals can become aware of the confusion that exists over the differences between sibling rivalry and sibling abuse, and even worse, the denial that sibling abuse does occur. This sense of confusion and denial is found not only among parents of victims but even among mental health professionals to whom some survivors turn for treatment for the effects of their abuse by a sibling.

Perhaps what these comments most importantly demonstrate is the need for mental health professionals to be aware that sibling abuse does exist. Evidence of sibling abuse may occur, for example, in family therapy sessions where a therapist, focusing on problems affecting the family as a whole, may overlook and fail to explore the aversive behaviors that are occurring between the siblings. Also, in cases of spousal and child abuse, based on the theory that violence is a learned behavior, exploration of the relationship of the siblings toward each other should occur because the children may be modeling in their relationship to their siblings the behavior that the parents are engaging in with each other and with the children.

Therapists should keep in mind when assessing clients' problems that sibling abuse can be an etiologic factor affecting the problems in living some adults may be experiencing and for which help is being sought. How should an assessment to determine if sibling abuse occurred in childhood be done? A therapist might be tempted to directly ask "Were you ever physically, emotionally, or sexually abused by a sibling?" Experience shows, however, that such a direct question in many instances provokes a defensive denial. Individuals are reluctant to state they are victims of abuse unless the abuse has been very blatant. Also, as the comments of survivors indicate, survivors often do not identify the aversive treatment they experienced from a sibling as abuse, and some survivors blame themselves for the abuse they experienced, thus making them reluctant to say that they were victimized by a sibling.

A more indirect but effective way to assess whether or not sibling abuse occurred is for a therapist to ask a client first to describe pleasant memories they have of their childhood associations with their siblings. Following a discussion of these memories, the therapist should ask the client to describe unpleasant memories of childhood associations with their siblings. The unpleasant memories provide the therapist the opportunity to explore selected memories in depth and to assess whether or not these memories are indicative of abuse. The latter assessment can be made using the criteria previously discussed for distinguishing sibling rivalry from sibling abuse: Were the behaviors age-appropriate? How long and how often did the behavior occur? Was the client a victim of the sibling engaging in the behavior? What purpose did the behavior serve? Such an assessment allows the therapist to determine if physical, emotional, or sexual sibling abuse occurred and if there may be an association between these abusive behaviors experienced by the client and the problems in living that the client is currently experiencing. The identification of effects of sibling abuse discussed earlier may also assist the therapist in the latter task.

A Differential Effect of Sibling Abuse

Numerous effects of sibling sexual abuse reported by survivors have been identified earlier. However, a significant difference in the context in which sibling sexual abuse occurs as compared to adult-child sexual abuse may create a differential effect in adult survivors. The context in which sibling sexual occurs is usually that of a threat. Recall the comments of survivors in earlier chapters who reported that their older brothers threatened to harm them in various ways or to make their sexual victimization look as if it were their fault if the victimization became known to the parents. Yet, because most perpetrators of adult-child sexual abuse, whether intra- or extrafamilial, are known to the victim, the context in which the sexual abuse occurs usually involves the victim implicitly trusting the perpetrator because of the loving relationship between the two persons, such as a grandfather and his granddaughter, or because of the authority role of the perpetrator, such as the scout leader and a scout. The loving relationship context may be reinforced by the perpetrator giving the victim gifts, such as candy, special favors, or privileges. This violation of trust that occurs in adult-child sexual abuse significantly affects the survivor's ability to trust others (Agosta & Loring, 1988).

Because sibling sexual abuse generally occurs in the context of a threat, the victim becomes entrapped in the desire to please the perpetrator or feels that she must comply for the sake of her own safety (Summit, 1983). The outcome of this scenario for adult survivors of sibling sexual abuse frequently is self-blame for allowing oneself to become entrapped. There initially may be denial that sexual abuse occurred or a reluctance to discuss the victimization because the survivor is embarrassed that she allowed the abuse to occur. (Thus, the manner in which sibling abuse is assessed, as discussed earlier, is important to the information the therapist can gather.) Regarding the survivor's self-blame for the sexual abuse, in reality she may have had no choice but to comply because, developmentally speaking, she cognitively did not understand what was happening, was operating under a threat, or had not been empowered by her parents to prevent sexual victimization.

One effect of this context of fear in which sibling sexual abuse occurs is that the adult survivor expresses a fear of others, especially individuals who represent power or authority, such as teachers and employment supervisors. One adult survivor of sexual abuse reported that she changed jobs, and in some instances even cities where she lived, over six times in the space of a few years. Her fear of authority and her need to please her superiors at work were so intense that she misinterpreted any criticism as failure and reacted with fear, with the result that she would defensively take flight and seek other employment and even residency. She reported that until she sought therapy for the effects of the abuse, she was not aware of the intense fear that she was living under that pervaded many of her adult interpersonal relationships.

Substance Abuse

Numerous survivors of sibling abuse reported that they were experiencing problems with drugs and alcohol as an effect of their abuse. Although the participants in this research were adults (average age 37), the problem of substance abuse may have started much earlier in life, considering the participants experienced their abuse as young children. Other research also reports a significant relationship between adolescent chemical dependency and a history of abuse. For example, a review of 250 cases at a rural midwestern chemical dependency treatment center revealed that 70% of the patients had some history of abuse, with 27% having experienced child/adolescent physical abuse and 9% sexual abuse (Potter-Efron & Potter-Efron, 1985). Other studies have likewise found high rates of abuse in chemically dependent adolescents (e.g., Cavaiola & Schiff, 1989).

Therapists treating chemically dependent adolescents may wish to pay close attention in their assessment to the possibility of abuse perpetrated by a parent, another adult, or even a sibling. Cavaiola and Schiff (1989), based on their study of chemically dependent adolescents who were abused, provide insight for mental health professionals treating such clients:

> While alcohol and drugs may play a self-enhancing role in chemical dependence, it appears that for the abused chemically dependent adolescent, the self-enhancement or self-medicating role of these chemicals is short-lived. In these adolescents the chemical

> dependence is the first layer of defense; it must be removed before an attempt can be made to work through the repetitive trauma of abuse. This work is similar to working with a burn victim or multiple surgical case because of difficult scarring and adhesions. The therapeutic work is long-term and enduring in nature. (p. 333)

Cavaiola and Schiff also caution that chemically dependent adolescents do not readily reveal having been abused. The researchers report that, on average, the abused adolescents did not disclose the specifics of their abuse trauma until approximately the fourth week of residential chemical dependence treatment. The abuse and chemical dependency wreaked havoc on the adolescents' self-esteem. The struggle for appropriate self-esteem, sobriety, and recovery from victimization can be a lifelong process for these adolescents (Cavaiola & Schiff, 1989).

Stages of Therapy

The stages that survivors go through in therapy for the sexual abuse they experienced from an adult as a child (Sgroi, 1989a) are very similar to those for sibling abuse survivors, with slight modifications due to the context in which the abuse occurs, as discussed earlier. These stages are acknowledging the reality of the abuse, overcoming secondary responses to the abuse, forgiving oneself (ending self-blame and punishment), adopting positive coping behaviors, and relinquishing survivor identity. They do not necessarily occur in an orderly fashion with one following the other but may occur in a cyclical manner with repetitions or with survivors reworking aspects of an earlier stage later in therapy.

Acknowledging the Reality of the Abuse

As discussed earlier, this is perhaps the most critical aspect of sibling abuse because of the denial from significant other persons in the survivor's life that the aversive behaviors experienced from a sibling as a child was really abuse. Following exploration of these behaviors, the therapist's validation or affirmation of them by labeling them abusive can free up the survivor's emotional energy to begin coping with the effects of the abuse.

Various protective coping mechanisms are used by survivors in order to deny the reality of the abuse they experienced (Sgroi & Bunk, 1988). These mechanisms consume enormous amounts of emotional energy. Protective coping mechanisms include distancing oneself from emotions associated with the abuse, such as fear, shame, or anger; continually giving to and caring for others but not allowing oneself to accept nurturance, as often seen in a constant activity or "busyness" in life; denying the seriousness of the abuse experienced or even denying that the events occurred; and self-blame for what happened.

Overcoming Secondary Responses to the Abuse

In this stage of recovery, denial of abuse at the time of the event is distinguished from *contemporary denial* occurring in therapy. In contemporary denial, the survivor continues to deny or excuse what happened as abuse. Support for this denial may come from family members when told the survivor is seeking therapy for childhood abuse, or it comes from the perpetrator when asked to apologize and assume responsibility for his or her behavior. Group therapy is helpful to survivors in this recovery stage, for they can confront each other about the defensive mechanisms they are engaging in based on their own personal experiences in going through this therapeutic stage (Sgroi, 1989c).

Forgiving Oneself

In this stage of the therapeutic process, if survivors are able to forgive themselves for the abuse that occurred and relinquish self-blame, a freeing-up process occurs. Sgroi (1989c) identifies specifically how this process occurs in the context of group therapy:

- The survivor receives acceptance of the validity of one's childhood victimization and current responses to it.
- Caring from others is also received, coupled with a message that the survivor is viewed by other members of the group as good and not blameworthy or deserving of punishment for the abuse experienced.
- The survivor receives feedback from group members regarding their self-blaming and self-punishing behaviors.
- Concrete suggestions for substituting self-blaming behaviors with self-affirming behaviors are also received by the survivor in the context of the group members' wishes that the survivor will choose to stop practicing self-punishment.
- Group members extend forgiveness to the survivor for the childhood sexual victimization and current secondary responses to it. This stage in the therapeutic process represents a recognition that the survivor has become a self-abuser and now is ready to move away from that emotional state.

Adopting Positive Coping Behaviors

Exploration focuses on alternative ways to handle the effects of the abuse. This may include acknowledging the futility of getting family members and especially the perpetrator to recognize that what the survivor experienced was abuse. Those who participated in the research reported here experienced frustration in trying to get their perpetrator to acknowledge responsibility for his or her sexual abuse of them and finally concluding that distancing themselves from the perpetrator and even other family members who were supportive of the perpetrator's denial was a more effective way of coping with the abuse.

Relinquishing Survivor Identify

Sgroi (1989c) states this stage can be summarized in the following comment a survivor may make who has successfully completed the therapeutic process:

> I am a human being, a person with strengths and weaknesses, good qualities and faults; a person who makes mistakes but also has useful and positive accomplishments. I was sexually abused when I was a child and that is an important part of my history. But that was then; this is now, and I no longer need to identify myself as a survivor. Instead it is more accurate for me simply to identify myself as a person and a self—no more and no less." (p. 128)

PREVENTING SIBLING ABUSE

How can sibling abuse be prevented? Survivors suggested several ways in which this can occur.

Building Awareness of the Problem

Nearly every survivor commented that people must be made aware that sibling abuse does occur and that all interactions between or among siblings do not fall under the category of normal sibling rivalry. Respondents also emphasized that sibling abuse can occur in any family regardless of socioeconomic status, race, or religion. Sibling abuse is more likely to occur in multiproblem or dysfunctional families; however, no family with more than one child is entirely exempt from the problem. Although it was not possible to determine the socioeconomic background of the survivors participating in this research at the time they were abused by a sibling, the respondents appeared to have come from middle-income families because their parents were quite well educated, with 43% having attended college or graduate school. The survivors also rated their families as moderately religious, as evident in this comment: "My problem and others is that we come from religious, 'looking good' families on the outside but where there was a lot of pain and dysfunctioning on the inside."

Listening to Children and Believing Them

The sibling abuse survivors participating in the research frequently lamented their parents' reaction to the abuse, as the following comments reflect:

> If only my parents had listened to me. If only they had believed me when I told them what was happening.

> I would tell my mother about the way my brothers were treating me, but she always brushed it off. I really don't think she cared what they did. At least that's the message I got from her. It didn't pay for me to tell her my troubles.

Research on reports of children being sexually abused by adults has found that an overwhelming majority of the reports are true. Actually, very few reports that children make about being sexually abused by an adult are false. For example, when the cases of 287 children who alleged they had been sexually abused were reviewed, only 28 (less than 9%) could not be substantiated (Cantrell, 1981). Children may report their sexual abuse rather tentatively and over a period of time, but parents should not regard that the report is not true (Gonzalez et al., 1993).

Providing Good Supervision to Children in the Absence of Parents

Sibling abuse occurred most frequently when an older sibling was baby-sitting a younger sibling after school before the parents arrived home from work or in the evening when the parents went away. One survivor stated,

> Parents should wake up and realize that just because a child is the oldest doesn't mean they can take care of the younger children. My folks would always leave us with my older sister. This is when I and my other brothers and sisters suffered. My sister felt she could do anything she wanted to us. She did.

It may be appropriate for an older brother or sister to act as a baby-sitter when the parents go away for an evening, but the parents must provide an environment in which this sibling can appropriately and effectively act as a substitute parent. Optimally, parents should discuss with the sibling in charge as well as with other siblings the rights and responsibilities of each—for example, the appliances they may use, their bedtime, and whether or not friends are allowed to visit. Equally important, parents should evaluate how effectively the older sibling handled his or her responsibilities while they were gone. This evaluation should not occur in the presence of all the siblings because sibling sexual abuse often occurs in the context of a threat. A younger sibling, when asked by her parents how an older sibling functioned as a baby-sitter, may not be able to reveal what happened for fear of retaliation from the older sibling.

Communities can provide parents who must work latchkey programs after school, thereby avoiding placing siblings in charge of each other. These programs are often government subsidized or operated by parent organizations and may be located in a school or a neighborhood church. Latchkey programs provide children a snack after school, supervised recreation, and assistance with homework. Often, these programs are free to low-income parents or have a sliding-scale fee to make them affordable. Parents can find out about them from their local child care resource and referral agency. Some communities have established telephone support services for children who are home alone after school. Staffed by volunteers, the services can handle a wide range of children's problems, including those with siblings.

Giving Children Appropriate Sex Instruction

Information about sexuality appropriate to a child's age and developmental stage is important in preventing sibling abuse. Providing information about sexuality is not a one-time event but must be imparted at different times in a child's life, appropriate to the age of the child and the age of the siblings with whom the child interacts. Such instruction empowers children to be in control of their sexuality and decreases the chance for sexual victimization.

A positive attitude about sex also implies that individuals have a right to privacy or times and places where they can be alone. Parents, for example, must set rules or expectations about privacy in the use of a bathroom, a setting for sexual abuse mentioned by several research respondents.

A healthy attitude about sex also implies that parents respond appropriately when sexuality is debased in films, videos, and TV programs, in sexually slanted innuendoes that one sibling may make toward another, and in sexually oriented jokes. The survivors of sexual abuse indicated that their parents' failure to confront these factors, especially the sexual innuendoes of a sibling, established a climate in the family in which sexual abuse would be tolerated. The survivors appeared to be saying that because their parents allowed these unhealthy aspects of sexuality to exist in the family, the perpetrator perceived that the sexual abuse of another sibling might also be tolerated.

Giving Children Permission to Own Their Own Bodies

Children have a right to own their own bodies. They have the right to be hugged, kissed, and touched in appropriate places on their bodies in an appropriate manner by appropriate people. The converse is equally true. Children have the right *not* to be hugged, kissed, or touched in inappropriate places on their bodies in an inappropriate manner by inapproppropriate people. Thus, children must be given permission to say no to inappropriate and especially secret touches. Programs with these goals in mind are being effectively conducted in many schools throughout the country.

Violence-Proofing the Home

Society is very violent, as seen daily on television, movies, and videos and in newspapers and magazines. Just as a room can be made soundproof or a building waterproof, so can parents strive to violence-proof the home. Obviously, a family cannot keep out every mention of violence; however, parents can develop a sensitivity to the violence that enters the home, such as through television or videos. Violence begets violence, and a constant exposure to violence not only desensitizes children to violence but may even act as a stimulus to engage in violent (abusive) behavior toward siblings.

Another important way that parents can help reduce violence is to be sensitive to how siblings treat each other. Verbal put-downs of one sibling by another (emotional abuse) are often a prelude to physical abuse. Put-downs that are gender associated can be a prelude to sexual abuse in which a brother inappropriately assumes the right and power to dominate and abuse a sister.

Nor should pushing, shoving, hitting, or other acts of violence go unnoticed or tolerated. Children can be given the message, in a nurturing context, that physical abuse is an unacceptable form of behavior and that when differences occur, problem solving is the appropriate way to handle disagreements.

SUMMARY

Research has shown that violence between siblings occurs more frequently than that between spouses and between parents and children. Yet this type of family violence, termed sibling abuse, has largely gone unnoticed. Adult survivors of childhood abuse by a sibling report that the abuse has adversely affected their lives, for they often experience low self-esteem, depression, problems with drugs and alcohol, and problems in interpersonal relationships. Parents can effectively intervene in sibling abuse by first being aware that not all interactions are simply attributable to sibling rivalry. A problem-solving approach can help siblings resolve differences that normally occur in any family, thus reducing the chances of normal sibling rivalry escalating into sibling abuse.

SUGGESTED READING

Wiehe, V. (1997). *Sibling abuse: The hidden physical, emotional, and sexual trauma* (2nd ed.). Thousand Oaks, CA: Sage.

References

Abel, E., & Suh, E. (1987). Use of police services by battered women. *Social Work, 32,* 526-528.

Ackley, D. (1977). A brief overview of child abuse. *Social Casework, 58,* 21-24.

Adams, C. (1993). I just raped my wife! What are you going to do about it, pastor? In E. Buchwald, P. Fletcher, & M. Rother (Eds.), *Transforming a rape culture* (pp. 57-86). Minneapolis, MN: Milkweed.

Adams, O. (1988). Feminist-based interventions for battering men. In L. Caesar & K. Hamberger (Eds.), *Therapeutic interventions with batterers: Theory and practice* (pp. 3-23). New York: Springer.

Adler, N., & Schutz, J. (1995). Sibling incest offenders. *Child Abuse & Neglect, 19,* 811-819.

Adshead, G., Howett, M., & Mason, F. (1994). Women who sexually abuse children: The undiscovered country. *Journal of Sexual Aggression, 1,* 45-56.

Agosta, C., & Loring, M. (1988). Understanding and treating the adult retrospective victim of child abuse. In S. Sgroi (Ed.), *Vulnerable populations* (Vol. 1, pp. 115-135). Lexington, MA: Lexington Books.

Aguilar, R., & Nightingale, N. (1994). The impact of specific battering experiences on the self-esteem of abused women. *Journal of Family Violence, 9,* 35-45.

Ainsworth, M., Blehar, M., Waters, E., & Wall, S. (1978). *Patterns of attachment: A psychological study of the strange situation.* Hillsdale, NJ: Lawrence Erlbaum.

Aitken, L., & Griffin, G. (1996). *Gender issues in elder abuse.* Thousand Oaks, CA: Sage.

Alexander, P., Neimeyer, R., & Follette, V. (1991). Group therapy for women sexually abused as children. *Journal of Interpersonal Violence, 6,* 218-231.

Allen, K., Carlsyn, D., Fehrenbach, P., & Benton, G. (1989). A study of the interpersonal behaviors of male batterers. *Journal of Interpersonal Violence, 4,* 79-89.

Alston, R., & Lenhoff, K. (1995). Chronic pain and childhood sexual abuse: Implications for rehabilitation education. *Rehabilitation Education, 9,* 37-49.

Ambrogi, D., & London, C. (1985). Elder abuse laws. *Generations, 13,* 37-41.

American Psychiatric Association. (1994). *Diagnostic and statistical manual of mental disorders* (4th ed.). Washington, DC: Author.

American Public Welfare Association, National Association of State Units on Aging. (1988). *A comprehensive analysis of state policy and practice related to elder abuse.* Washington, DC: Author.

Anderson, C. (1989). Temperature and aggression: Ubiquitous effects of heat on occurrences of human violence. *Psychological Bulletin, 106,* 74-96.

Anderson, C., Anderson, K., & Deuser, W. (1996). Examining an affective aggression framework: Weapon and temperature effects on aggressive thoughts, affect, and attitudes. *Personality & Social Psychology Bulletin, 21,* 366-376.

Anderson, C., Deuser, W., & DeNeve, K. (1995). Hot temperatures, hostile affect, hostile cognition, and arousal: Tests of a general model of affective aggression. *Personality & Social Psychology Bulletin, 21,* 434-448.

Anetzberger, G. (1987). *The etiology of elder abuse by adult offspring.* Springfield, IL: Charles C Thomas.

Anetzberger, G., Korbin, J., & Austin, C. (1994). Alcoholism and elder abuse. *Journal of Interpersonal Violence, 9,* 184-193.

Apt, C., & Hulbert, D. (1993). The sexuality of women in physically abused marriages: A comparative study. *Journal of Family Violence, 8,* 57-70.

Aravanis, S., Adelman, R., Breckman, R., Fulmer, T., Holder, E., Lach, M., O'Brien, J., & Sanders, A. (1993). Diagnostic and treatment guidelines on elder abuse and neglect. *Archives of Family Medicine, 2,* 371-388.

Archer, L. (1994). Empowering women in a violent society. *Canadian Family Physician, 40,* 974-985.

Aronson, J., Thornewell, C., & Williams, K. (1995). Wife assault in old age: Coming out of obscurity. *Canadian Journal of Aging, 14,* 72-88.

Attias, R., & Goodwin, J. (1985). Knowledge and management strategies in incest cases: A survey of physicians, psychologists, and family counselors. *Child Abuse & Neglect, 9,* 527-533.

Attorney General's Task Force on Family Violence. (1984, September). *Final report.* Washington, DC: Author.

Augustine, R. (1990-1991). The safe haven for rapists. *Journal of Family Law, 29,* 559-591.

Ayalon, O., & Van Tassel, I. (1987). Living in dangerous environments. In M. Brassard, R. Germain, & S. Hart (Eds.), *Psychological maltreatment of children and youth* (pp. 171-184). Elmsford, NY: Pergamon.

Azar, S., Robinson, D., Hekimian, E., & Twentyman, C. (1984). Unrealistic expectations and problem-solving ability in maltreating and comparison mothers. *Journal of Consulting and Clinical Psychology, 52,* 687-691.

Bagley, C., & Ramsay, R. (1986). Sexual abuse in childhood: Psychosocial outcomes and implications for social work practice. *Journal of Social Work and Human Sexuality, 4,* 33-47.

Bagley, C., Wood, M., & Young, L. (1994). Victim to abuser: Mental health and behavioral sequels of child sexual abuse in a community survey of young adult males. *Child Abuse & Neglect, 18,* 683-697.

Bakan, D. (1971). *Slaughter of the innocents.* San Francisco: Jossey-Bass.

Baker, A. (1975). Granny battering. *Modern Geriatrics, 5,* 20-24.

Baldwin, J., & Oliver, J. (1975). Epidemiology and family characteristics of severely abused children. *British Journal of Preventive Social Medicine, 29,* 205-221.

Bandura, A. (1965). Influence of model's reinforcement contingencies on the acquisition of imitative responses. *Journal of Personality and Social Psychology, 1,* 589-595.

Bandura, A. (1973). *Aggression: A social learning analysis.* New York: Prentice Hall.

Bandura, A. (1977). *Social learning theory.* Englewood, Cliffs, NJ: Prentice Hall.

Bandura, A., Ross, D., & Ross, S. (1963). Vicarious reinforcement and imitative learning. *Journal of Abnormal and Social Psychology, 63,* 575-582.

Barker, R., Dembo, T., & Lewin, K. (1941). Frustration and aggression: An experiment with young children. *University of Iowa Studies in Child Welfare, 18*(1), 1-64.

Barnard, C. (1990). Alcoholism and sex abuse in the family: Incest and marital rape. *Journal of Chemical Dependency Treatment, 3,* 131-144.

Barnett, O., & Fagan, R. (1993). Alcohol use in male spouse abusers and their female partners. *Journal of Family Violence, 8,* 1-25.

Barnett, O., & LaViolette, A. (1993). *It could happen to anyone: Why battered women stay.* Newbury Park, CA: Sage.

Baron, R., & Ransberger, V. (1978). Ambient temperature and the occurrence of collective violence: The "long, hot summer" revisited. *Journal of Personality and Social Psychology, 36,* 351-360.

Barongan, C., & Hall, G. (1995). The influence of misogynous rap music on sexual aggression against women. *Psychology of Women Quarterly, 19,* 195-207.

Barrera, M., Palmer, S., Brown, R., & Kalaher, S. (1994). Characteristics of court-involved men and non-court-involved men who abuse their wives. *Journal of Family Violence, 9,* 333-345.

Barshis, V. (1983). The question of marital rape. *Women's Studies International Forum, 6,* 383-393.

Barth, R., Blythe, B., Schinke, S., & Shilling, R. (1983). Self-control training with maltreating parents. *Child Welfare, 62,* 314-324.

Bateson, G. (1972). *Steps to an ecology of mind.* New York: Chandler.

Bath, H., & Haapala, D. (1993). Intensive family preservation services with abused and neglected children: An examination of group differences. *Child Abuse & Neglect, 17,* 213-225.

Batson, C., Turk, C., Shaw, L., & Klein, T. (1995). Information function of empathy emotion: Learning that we value the other's welfare. *Journal of Personality and Social Psychology, 68,* 300-313.

Battered families: A growing nightmare. (1979, January). *U.S. News & World Report,* pp. 60, 61.

Bavolek, S. (1984). *Handbook for the Adult-Adolescent Parenting Inventory (AAPI).* Park City, UT: Family Development Resources, Inc.

Bavolek, S. (1989). Assessing and treating high-risk parenting attitudes. In J. Pardeck (Ed.), *Child abuse and neglect: Theory, research and practice* (pp. 97-110). New York: Gordon & Breach.

Bear, E., & Dimock, P. (1988). *Adults molested as children: A survivor's manual for women and men.* Orwell, VT: Safer Society Press.

Beck, A. (1976). *Cognitive therapy and emotional disorders.* New York: International Universities Press.

Beck, C., & Phillips, L. (1983). Abuse of the elderly. *Journal of Gerontological Nursing, 9,* 97-101.

Becker, J., Kaplan, M., Cunningham-Rathner, B., & Kavoussi, R. (1986). Characteristics of adolescent incest sexual perpetrators. *Journal of Family Violence, 1,* 85-97.

Becker, J., & Quinsey, V. (1993). Assessing suspected child molesters. *Child Abuse & Neglect, 17,* 169-174.

Behling, W. (1979). Alcohol abuse as encountered in 51 instances of reported child abuse. *Clinical Pediatrics, 18,* 87-91.

Beitchman, J., Zucker, K., Hood, J., DaCosta, G., Akman, D., & Cassavia, E. (1992). A review of the long-term effects of child sexual abuse. *Child Abuse & Neglect, 16,* 101-118.

Bell, C., Jenkins, E., Kpo, W., & Rhodes, H. (1994). Response of emergency rooms to victims of interpersonal violence. *Hospital and Community Psychiatry, 45,* 142-146.

Bellak, A. (1982, June). Comparable worth: A practitioner's view. In *Comparable worth: Issue for the 80's. A consultation for the U.S. Commission on Civil Rights* (pp. 75-82). Washington, DC: U.S. Commission on Civil Rights.

Belsky, J., Rovine, M., & Taylor, D. (1984). The Pennsylvania Infant and Family Development Project, III. The origins of individual differences in infant-mother attachment: Maternal and infant contributions. *Child Development, 55,* 718-728.

Bennett, L. (1995). Substance abuse and the domestic assault of women. *Social Work, 40,* 760-771.

Berg, P. (1976). Parental expectations and attitudes in child-abusing families (Doctoral dissertation, University of Southern California). *Dissertation Abstracts International, 37,* 1889B.

Bergen, R. (1996). *Wife rape: Understanding the response of survivors and service providers.* Thousand Oaks, CA: Sage.

Berk, R., Campbell, A., Klap, R., & Western, B. (1992). The deterrent effect of arrest in incidents of domestic violence: A Bayesian analysis of four field experiments. *American Sociological Review, 57,* 698-708.

Berkowitz, C. (1987). Sexual abuse of children and adolescents. *Advances in Pediatrics, 34,* 274-312.

Berkowitz, L. (1965). Some aspects of observed aggression. *Journal of Personality and Social Psychology, 2,* 359-369.

Berkowitz, L. (1969). *Roots of aggression: A re-examination of the frustration-aggression hypothesis.* New York: Atherton.

Berkowitz, L. (1978). Whatever happened to the frustration-aggression hypothesis? *American Behavioral Scientist, 21,* 691-708.

Berkowitz, L. (1990). On the formation and regulation of anger and aggression: A cognitive-neoassociationistic analysis. *American Psychologist, 45,* 494-503.

Berkowitz, L., & Geen, R. (1966). Film violence and the cue properties of available targets. *Journal of Personality and Social Psychology, 3,* 525-530.

Berkowitz, L., & Green, J. (1962). The stimulus qualities of the scapegoat. *Journal of Abnormal and Social Psychology, 64,* 293-301.

Berkowitz, L., & LePage, A. (1967). Weapons as aggression-eliciting stimuli. *Journal of Personality and Social Psychology, 7,* 202-207.

Berliner, L., & Ernst, E. (1984). Group work with preadolescent sexual assault victims. In I. Stuart & J. Greer (Eds.), *Victims of sexual aggression* (pp. 105-123). New York: Van Nostrand Reinhold.

Bern, E., & Bern, L. (1984). A group program for men who commit violence toward their wives. *Social Work, 7,* 63-77.

Bernard, J., & Bernard, M. (1984). The abusive male seeking treatment: Jekyll and Hyde. *Family Relations, 33,* 543-547.

Berne, E. (1967). *Games people play.* New York: Grove.

Bernstein, A. (1995, November/December). Should you be told that your neighbor is a sex offender? *Ms. Magazine,* pp. 24-26.

Berzon, B. (1989). *Permanent partners: Building gay and lesbian relationships that last.* New York: Plume.

Best, J. (1990). *Threatened children: Rhetoric and concern about child victims.* Chicago: University of Chicago Press.

Bidwell, L., & White, P. (1986). The family context of marital rape. *Journal of Family Violence, 1,* 277-287.

Binder, A., & Meeker, J. (1988). Experiments as reforms. *Journal of Criminal Justice and Behavior, 16,* 347-358.

Birns, B., & Meyer, S. (1993). Mothers' role in incest: Dysfunctional women or dysfunctional theories? *Journal of Child Sexual Abuse, 2,* 127-135.

Bjorkqvist, K., & Osterman, K. (1992). Parental influence on children's self-estimated aggressiveness. *Aggressive Behavior, 18,* 411-423.

Blake-White, J., & Kline, C. (1985). Treating the dissociative process in adult victims of childhood incest. *Social Casework, 66,* 394-402.

Blakely, B., Dolon, R., & May, D. (1993). Improving the responses of physicians to elder abuse and neglect: Contributions of a model program. *Journal of Gerontological Social Work, 19,* 35-47.

Blanchard, G. (1995). *The difficult connection: The therapeutic relationship in sex offender treatment.* Brandon, VT: Safer Society Press.

Bloom, J., Ansell, P., & Bloom, M. (1989). Detecting elder abuse: A guide for physicians. *Geriatrics, 44,* 40-44.

Bloom, M. (1995). Primary prevention overview. In R. Edwards (Ed.), *Encyclopedia of social work* (19th ed., Vol. 3, pp. 1895-1905). Washington, DC: National Association of Social Work Press.

Blume, E. (1986, September). The walking wounded: Post-incest syndrome. *SIECUS Report XV, 1,* 5-7.

Blunt, A. (1993). Financial exploitation of the incapacitated: Investigation and remedies. *Journal of Elder Abuse & Neglect, 5,* 19-32.

Bograd, M. (1994). Battering, competing clinical models, and paucity of research: Notes to those in the trenches. *The Consulting Psychologist, 22,* 593-597.

Bookin, D., & Dunkle, R. (1985). Elder abuse: Issues for the practitioner. *Social Casework: The Journal of Contemporary Social Work, 66,* 3-12.

Bornman, L., & Lieber, L. (1984). *Self-help and the treatment of child abuse.* Chicago: National Committee for Prevention of Child Abuse.

Bowker, L. (1988). Religious victims and their religious leaders: Services delivered to one thousand battered women by the clergy. In A. Horton & J. Williamson (Eds.), *Abuse and religion: When praying isn't enough* (pp. 229-234). Lexington, MA: Lexington Books.

Boyd, C., Blow, F., & Orgain, L. (1993). Gender differences among African-American women substance abusers. *Journal of Psychoactive Drugs, 25,* 301-305.

Boyd, C., Guthrie, B., Pohl, J., Whitmarsh, J., & Henderson, D. (1994). African-American women who smoke crack cocaine: Sexual trauma and the mother-daughter relationship. *Journal of Psychoactive Drugs, 26,* 243-247.

Boyd-Franklin, N. (1989). *Black families in therapy.* New York: Guilford.

Brassard, M., & Galardo, M. (1987). Psychological maltreatment: The unifying construct in child abuse and neglect. *School Psychology Review, 16,* 127-136.

Brewer, H. (1992). Physical restraints: A potential form of abuse. *Journal of Elder Abuse & Neglect, 4,* 47-58.

Briere, J. (1984, May). *The effects of childhood sexual abuse on later psychological functioning: Defining a post-sexual abuse syndrome.* Paper presented at the National Conference on Sexual Victimization of Children, Washington, DC.

Briere, J., Evans, D., Runtz, M., & Wall, T. (1988). Symptomatology in men who were molested as children: A comparison study. *American Journal of Orthopsychiatry, 58,* 457-461.

Briere, J., Henschel, D., & Smiljanich, K. (1992). Attitudes toward sexual abuse: Sex differences and construct validity. *Journal of Research in Personality, 26,* 398-406.

Briere, J., & Runtz, M. (1987). Post-sexual abuse trauma: Data and implications for clinical practice. *Journal of Interpersonal Violence, 2,* 367-379.

Briere, J., & Runtz, M. (1988). Symptomatology associated with prior sexual abuse in a nonclinical sample. *Child Abuse & Neglect, 12,* 51-59.

Briere, J., & Runtz, M. (1989a). The Trauma Symptom Checklist (TSC-33). *Journal of Interpersonal Violence, 4,* 151-153.

Briere, J., & Runtz, M. (1989b). University males' sexual interest in children. Predicting potential indices of "pedophilia" in a nonforensic sample. *Child Abuse & Neglect, 13,* 65-75.

Briere, J., & Runtz, M. (1990). Differential adult symptomatologies associated with three types of child abuse histories. *Child Abuse & Neglect, 14,* 357-364.

Browne, A. (1987). *When battered women kill.* New York: Free Press.

Browne, A. (1993). *Report of the Council on Scientific Affairs* (Rep. No. I-91). Washington, DC: Council on Scientific Affairs.

Browne, A., & Finkelhor, D. (1986). Impact of childhood sexual abuse: A review of the research. *Psychological Bulletin, 99,* 66-77.

Bureau of Justice Statistics. (1984, April). *Family violence.* Washington, DC: U.S. Department of Justice.

Bureau of Justice Statistics. (1995, August). *Violence against women: Estimates from the redesigned survey.* Washington, DC: U.S. Department of Justice.

Burgess, A., & Hartman, C. (1993). Children's drawings. *Child Abuse & Neglect, 17,* 161-168.

Burgess, R., & Conger, R. (1977). Family interaction patterns related to child abuse and neglect: Some preliminary findings. *Child Abuse & Neglect, 1,* 269-277.

Burrell, B., Thompson, B., & Sexton, D. (1994). Predicting child abuse potential across family types. *Child Abuse & Neglect, 18,* 1039-1049.

Burston, G. (1975). Granny battering. *British Medical Journal, 3,* 592.

Busby, D., Glenn, E., Steggell, G., & Adamson, D. (1993). Treatment issues for survivors of physical and sexual abuse. *Journal of Marital and Family Therapy, 19,* 377-392.

Bushman, B. (1993). Human aggression while under the influence of alcohol and other drugs: An integrative research review. *Current Directions in Psychological Science, 2,* 148-152.

Buss, A. (1971). Aggression pays. In J. Singer (Ed.), *The control of aggression and violence: Cognitive and physiological factors* (pp. 7-18). New York: Academic Press.

Byer, C., & Shainberg, L. (1994). *Dimensions of human sexuality.* Madison, WI: Brown & Benchmark.

Cadsky, O., Hanson, R., Crawford, M., & Lalonde, C. (1996). Attrition from a male batterer treatment program: Client-treatment congruence and lifestyle instability. *Violence and Victims, 11,* 51-64.

Caffey, J. (1946). Multiple fracture in the long bones of infants suffering from chronic subdural hematoma. *American Journal of Roentgenology, Radium Therapy and Nuclear Medicine, 56,* 163-173.

Cameron, C. (1994). Women survivors confronting their abusers: Issues, decisions, and outcomes. *Journal of Child Sexual Abuse, 3,* 7-35.

Campbell, J. (1989). Women's responses to sexual abuse in intimate relationships. *Health Care for Women International, 8,* 335-347.

Campbell, J., Pliska, M., Taylor, W., & Sheridan, D. (1994). Battered women's experiences in the emergency department. *Journal of Emergency Nursing, 20,* 280-288.

Campbell, N., & Sutton, J. (1983). Impact of parent education groups on family environment. *Journal of Specialists in Group Work, 8,* 126-132.

Campbell, R., Sullivan, C., & Davidson, W. (1995). Women who use domestic violence shelters: Changes in depression over time. *Psychology of Women Quarterly, 19,* 237-255.

Cannings, M. (1984). Myths and stereotypes: Obstacles to effective police intervention in domestic disputes involving a battered woman. *Police Journal, 57,* 43-56.

Cantrell, H. (1981). Sexual abuse of children in Denver, 1979: Reviewed with implications for pediatric intervention and possible prevention. *Child Abuse & Neglect, 5,* 75-85.

Carden, A. (1994). Wife abuse and the wife abusers: Review and recommendations. *The Counseling Psychologist, 22,* 539-582.

Carey, T. (1994). Spare the rod and spoil the child: Is this a sensible justification for the use of punishment in child rearing? *Child Abuse & Neglect, 18,* 1005-1010.

Carlsmith, J., & Anderson, C. (1979). Ambient temperature and the occurrence of collective violence: A new analysis. *Journal of Personality and Social Psychology, 37,* 337-344.

Carlson, B. (1977). Battered women and their assailants. *Social Work, 22,* 455-460.

Carlson, M., Marcus-Newhall, A., & Miller, N. (1990). Effects of situational aggression cues: A quantitative review. *Journal of Personality and Social Psychology, 58,* 622-633.

Carroll, J., & Wolpe, P. (1996). *Sexuality and gender in society.* New York: HarperCollins.

Cascardi, M., & O'Leary, K. D. (1992). Depressive symptomatology, self-esteem, and self-blame in battered women. *Journal of Family Violence, 7,* 249-259.

Cascardi, M., & Vivian, D. (1995). Context for specific episodes of marital violence: Gender and severity of violence differences. *Journal of Family Violence, 10,* 265-293.

Cash, T., & Valentine, D. (1989). A decade of adult protective services: Case characteristics. *Journal of Gerontological Social Work, 15,* 21-26.

Cavoila, A., & Schiff, M. (1989). Self-esteem in abused chemically dependent adolescents. *Child Abuse & Neglect, 13,* 327-334.

Cerezo, M. A., & Frias, D. (1994). Emotional and cognitive adjustment in abused children. *Child Abuse & Neglect, 18,* 923-932.

Chaffin, M., Kelleher, K., & Hollenberg, J. (1996). Onset of physical abuse and neglect: Psychiatric, substance abuse, and social risk factors from prospective community data. *Child Abuse & Neglect, 20,* 191-203.

Chan, Y. (1994). Parenting stress and social support of mothers who physically abuse their children in Hong Kong. *Child Abuse & Neglect, 18,* 261-269.

Chauncey, S. (1994). Emotional concerns and treatment of male partners of female sexual abuse survivors. *Social Work, 39,* 669-676.

Claes, J., & Rosenthal, D. (1990). Men who batter women: A study in power. *Journal of Family Violence, 5,* 215-224.

Clark, K. (1975). Knowledge of child development and behavior interaction patterns of mothers who abuse their children (Doctoral dissertation, Wayne State University). *Dissertation Abstracts International, 36,* 5784B.

Claussen, A., & Crittenden, P. (1991). Physical and psychological maltreatment: Relations among types of maltreatment. *Child Abuse & Neglect, 15,* 5-18.

Close, E. (1994, August 8). Truths about spouse abuse. *Newsweek,* p. 49.

Clow, D., Hutchins, D., & Vogler, D. (1992). TFA systems: A unique group treatment of spouse abusers. *Journal for Specialists in Group Work, 17,* 74-83.

Cohn, A. (1983). *An approach to preventing child abuse.* Chicago: National Committee for Prevention of Child Abuse.

Cohn, D. (1991). Anatomical doll play of preschoolers referred for sexual abuse and those not referred. *Child Abuse & Neglect, 15,* 455-466.

Cole, A. (1990). *Brother-sister sexual abuse: Experiences, feeling reactions, and a comparison to father-daughter sexual abuse.* Unpublished doctoral dissertation, Union Institute, Cincinnati, OH.

Cole, P., Woolger, C., Power, T., & Smith, K. (1992). Parenting difficulties among adult survivors of father-daughter incest. *Child Abuse & Neglect, 16,* 239-249.

Coleman, J., & Stith, S. (1997). Nursing students' attitudes toward victims of domestic violence as predicted by selected individual and relationship variables. *Journal of Family Violence, 12,* 113-138.

Coleman, K. (1980). Conjugal violence: What 33 men report. *Journal of Marital and Family Therapy, 6,* 207-213.

Collins, L., & Collins, R. (1989). *The SAY book: A personal workbook for socially aware youth.* Boys Town, NE: Father Flanagan's Boys' Home.

Conger, R., Burgess, R., & Barrett, C. (1979). Child abuse related to life change and perceptions of illness: Some preliminary findings. *Family Coordinator, 58,* 73-77.

Conlin, M. (1995). Silent suffering: A case study of elder abuse and neglect. *Journal of the American Geriatrics Society, 43,* 1303-1308.

Connelly, C., & Straus, M. (1992). Mother's age and risk for physical abuse. *Child Abuse & Neglect, 16,* 709-718.

Conner, K., & Ackerley, G. (1994). Alcohol-related battering: Developing treatment strategies. *Journal of Family Violence, 9,* 143-155.

Conroy, R. (1993). Low cholesterol and violent death: The evidence, the gaps, the theory, and the practical implications. *Irish Journal of Psychological Medicine, 10,* 67-70.

Coohey, C. (1996). Child maltreatment: Testing the social isolation hypothesis. *Child Abuse & Neglect, 20,* 241-254.

Cook, D., & Cook, A. (1984). A systemic treatment approach to wife battering. *Journal of Marital and Family Therapy, 10,* 83-93.

Corder, B., Haizlip, T., & DeBoer, P. (1990). A pilot study for a structured, time-limited therapy group for sexually abused preadolescent children. *Child Abuse & Neglect, 14,* 243-251.

Corenblum, H. (1983). Reactions to alcohol-related marital violence. *Journal of Studies in Alcohol, 44,* 665-674.

Cormier, W., & Cormier, S. (1985). *Interviewing strategies for helpers.* Pacific Grove, CA: Brooks/Cole.

Corson, J., & Davidson, H. (1987). Emotional abuse and the law. In M. Brassard, R. Germain, & S. Hart (Eds.), *Psychological maltreatment* (pp. 185-202). Elmsford, NY: Pergamon.

Costin, L. (1991). Unraveling the Mary Ellen legend: Origins of the "cruelty movement." *Social Service Review, 65,* 203-223.

Coulton, C., Korbin, J., Su, M., & Chow, J. (1995). Community-level factors and child maltreatment rates. *Child Development, 66,* 1262-1276.

Courter, G. (1996). *I speak for this child.* New York: Crown.

Covington, S., & Kohen, J. (1984). Women, alcohol, and sexuality. *Advances in Alcohol and Substance Abuse, 4,* 41-56.

Crain, W. (1992). *Theories of development: Concepts and applications* (3rd ed.). Englewood Cliffs, NJ: Prentice Hall.

Crary, E. (1997). *Help! The kids are at it again: Using kids' quarrels to teach people skills.* Seattle: Parenting Press.

Crenshaw, W., Bartell, P., & Lichtenberg, J. (1994). Proposed revisions to mandatory reporting laws: An exploratory survey of child protective service agencies. *Child Welfare, 73,* 15-27.

Crites, L. (1991). Cross-cultural counseling in wife-beating cases. *Response, 13,* 8-12.

Cronin, C. (1995). Adolescents' reports of parental spousal violence in military and civilian families. *Journal of Interpersonal Violence, 10,* 117-122.

DaGloria, J., & DeRidder, R. (1979). Sex differences in aggression: Are current notions misleading? *European Journal of Social Psychology, 9,* 49-66.

Dattalo, P. (1995). A typology of child protective services cases based on client-presenting problems. *Journal of Social Service Research, 21,* 55-79.

Davis, P. (1996, July 28). The sex offender next door. *New York Times Magazine,* pp. 20-27, 39-43.

Day, P. (1996). *A new history of social welfare* (2nd ed.). Englewood Cliffs, NJ: Prentice Hall.

Deaux, K. (1976). *The behavior of women and men.* Monterey, CA: Brooks/Cole.

Deblinger, E., McLeer, S., Atkins, M., Ralphe, D., & Foa, E. (1989). Posttraumatic stress in sexually abused, physically abused, and nonabused children. *Child Abuse & Neglect, 18,* 403-408.

DeMause, L. (1976). *The history of childhood.* London: Souvenir.

DeMause, L. (1991). The universality of incest. *Journal of Psychohistory, 19,* 123-164.

Dembo, M., Sweitzer, M., & Lauritzen, P. (1985). An evaluation of group parent education: Behavioral, PET, and Adlerian programs. *Review of Educational Research, 55,* 155-200.

Demos, J. (1986). *Past, present and personal.* New York: Oxford University Press.

Deschner, J. (1984). *The hitting habit.* New York: Free Press.

DeYoung, M. (1982). *The sexual victimization of children.* Jefferson, NC: McFarland.

Dhooper, S., & Schneider, P. (1995). Evaluation of a school-based child abuse prevention program. *Research on Social Work Practice, 5,* 36-46.

DiLalla, L., & Gottesman, I. (1991). Biological and genetic contributors to violence: Widom's untold tale. *Psychological Bulletin, 109,* 125-129.

Dill, J., & Anderson, C. (1995). Effects of frustration justification on hostile aggression. *Aggressive Behavior, 21,* 359-369.

Dobash, R. E., & Dobash, R. P. (1979). *Violence against wives.* New York: Free Press.

Dobash, R. E., & Dobash, R. P. (1992). *Women, violence and social change.* London: Routledge & Kegan Paul.

Dobash, R. P., Dobash, R. E., Wilson, M., & Daly, M. (1992). The myth of sexual symmetry in marital violence. *Social Problems, 39,* 71-91.

Dollard, J., Doob, L., Miller, N., Mowere, O., & Sears, R. (1939). *Frustration and aggression.* New Haven, CT: Yale University Press.

Donnerstein, E., & Wilson, D. (1976). The effects of noise and perceived control upon ongoing and subsequent aggressive behavior. *Journal of Personality and Social Psychology, 36,* 1270-1277.

Doty, P., & Sullivan, E. (1983). Abuse, neglect, and mistreatment in nursing homes. *Millbank Memorial Fund Quarterly/Health and Society, 61,* 222-251.

Downs, A., & Gowan, D. (1980). Sex differences in reinforcement and punishment on prime-time television. *Sex Roles, 6,* 683-694.

Downs, E., & Jenkins, S. (1993). The relationship between empathic response and scores on the California Psychological Inventory. *Perceptual and Motor Skills, 77,* 680-682.

Doyle, C. (1996). Sexual abuse by siblings: The victims' perspectives. *Journal of Sexual Aggression, 2,* 17-32.

Drake, B. (1996). Unraveling "unsubstantiated." *Child Maltreatment, 1,* 261-271.

Drake, B., & Pandey, S. (1996). Understanding the relationship between neighborhood poverty and specific types of child maltreatment. *Child Abuse & Neglect, 20,* 1003-1018.

Driver, E. (1989). An introduction. In E. Driver & A. Droisen (Eds.), *Child sexual abuse: A feminist reader* (pp. 1-68). New York: New York University Press.

Dubowitz, H., Black, M., Harrington, D., & Verschoore, A. (1993). A follow-up study of behavior problems associated with child sexual abuse. *Child Abuse & Neglect, 17,* 743-754.

Duke, J. (1991). A national study of self-neglecting adult protective services clients. In T. Tatara & M. Rittman (Eds.) & K. Kaufer-Flores (Coordinator), *Findings of five elder abuse studies* (pp. 23-53). Washington, DC: National Aging Resource Center on Elder Abuse.

Dukewich, T., Borkowski, J., & Whitman, T. (1996). Adolescent mothers and child abuse potential: An evaluation of risk factors. *Child Abuse & Neglect, 20,* 1031-1047.

Dunford, F., Huizinga, D., & Elliot, D. (1990). The role of arrest in domestic assault: The Omaha police experiment. *Criminology, 28,* 183-206.

Duquette, D., & Ramsey, S. (1986). Using lay volunteers to represent children in child protection court proceedings. *Child Abuse & Neglect, 10,* 293-308.

Dutton, D. (1986). The outcomes of court-mandated treatment for wife assault: A quasi-experimental evaluation. *Violence and Victims, 1,* 163-175.

Dutton, D. (1995). *The batterer: A psychological profile.* New York: Basic Books.

Dutton, D., Starzomski, A., & Ryan, L. (1996). Antecedents of abusive personality and abusive behavior in wife assaulters. *Journal of Family Violence, 11,* 113-132.

Dyck, R., & Rule, B. (1978). Effect on retaliation of causal attributions concerning attack. *Journal of Personality and Social Psychology, 36,* 521-529.

Ebbesen, E., Duncan, B., & Konecni, V. (1975). Effects of content of verbal aggression on future verbal aggression: A field experiment. *Journal of Experimental Social Psychology, 11,* 192-204.

Edelson, J., & Brygger, M. (1986). Gender differences in reporting of battering incidences. *Family Relations, 35,* 377-382.

Edelson, J., & Grusznski, R. (1988). Treating men who batter: Four years of outcome data from the domestic abuse project. *Journal of Social Service Research, 12,* 3-22.

Edmunds, S. B. (1997). The personal impact of working with sex offenders. In S. B. Edmunds (Ed.), *Impact: Working with sexual abusers* (pp. 11-26). Brandon, VT: Safer Society Press.

Egeland, B., & Farber, E. (1984). Infant-mother attachment: Factors related to its development and changes over time. *Child Development, 55,* 753-771.

Egeland, B., & Susman-Stillman, A. (1996). Dissociation as a mediator of child abuse across generations. *Child Abuse & Neglect, 20,* 1123-1132.

Eibl-Eibesfeldt, I. (1979). *The biology of peace and war: Men, animals, and aggression.* New York: Viking.

Eisikovits, Z., & Edleson, J. (1989). Intervening with men who batter: A critical review of the literature. *Social Service Review, 63,* 384-414.

Elliot, P. (1996). Shattering illusions: Same-sex domestic violence. In C. Renzetti & C. Miley (Eds.), *Violence in gay and lesbian domestic partnerships* (pp. 1-8). New York: Haworth.

Ellis, A. (1982). Rational-emotive family therapy. In A. Horne & M. Ohisen (Eds.), *Family counseling and therapy* (pp. 302-328). Itasca, IL: Peacock.

Ellis, A., & Harper, R. (1978). *A new guide to rational living.* North Hollywood, CA: Wilshire Press.

Ellis, D., & Dekeseredy, W. (1989). Marital status and woman abuse: The DAD model. *International Journal of Sociology of the Family, 19,* 67-87.

Elmer, E. (1960). Abused children seen in hospitals. *Social Work, 5,* 98-102.

Elrod, J., & Rubin, R. (1993). Parental involvement in sexual abuse prevention education. *Child Abuse & Neglect, 17,* 527-538.

Else, L., Wonderlich, S., Beatty, W., Christie, D., & Staton, R. (1993). Personality characteristics of men who physically abuse women. *Hospital and Community Psychiatry, 44,* 54-58.

Eron, L. (1980a). Adolescent aggression and television. *Annals of the New York Academy of Sciences, 347,* 319-331.

Eron, L. (1980b). Prescription for reduction of aggression. *American Psychologist, 35,* 244-252.

Eron, L., & Huesmann, L. (1985). The role of television in the development of prosocial and antisocial behavior. In D. Olweus, M. Radke-Yarrow, & J. Block (Eds.), *Development of antisocial and prosocial behavior* (pp. 285-314). Orlando, FL: Academic Press.

Everson, M., & Boat, B. (1994). Putting the anatomical doll controversy in perspective: An examination of the major uses and criticisms of the dolls in child sexual abuse evaluations. *Child Abuse & Neglect, 18,* 113-129.

Faber, A., & Mazlish, E. (1982). *How to talk so kids will listen & listen so kids will talk.* New York: Avon.

Faber, A., & Mazlish, E. (1988). *Siblings without rivalry: How to help your children live together so you can live too.* New York: Avon.

Fagan, J., Barnett, O., & Patton, J. (1988). Reasons for alcohol use in maritally violent men. *American Journal of Drug & Alcohol Abuse, 14,* 371-392.

Fagan, J., Stewart, D., & Hansen, K. (1983). Violent men or violent husbands. In D. Finkelhor, R. Gelles, G. Hotaling, & M. Straus (Eds.), *The dark side of families: Current family violence research* (pp. 49-67). Beverly Hills, CA: Sage.

Faller, K. (1989). Characteristics of a clinical sample of sexually abused children: How boy and girl victims differ. *Child Abuse & Neglect, 13,* 281-291.

Famularo, R., Kinscherff, R., & Fenton, T. (1992). Parental substance abuse and the nature of child maltreatment. *Child Abuse & Neglect, 16,* 475-483.

Famularo, R., Stone, K., Barnum, R., & Wharton, R. (1986). Alcoholism and severe child maltreatment. *American Journal of Orthopsychiatry, 56,* 481-485.

Farley, D., & Magill, J. (1988). An evaluation of a group program for men who batter. *Social Work With Groups, 11,* 53-65.

Farley, N. (1996). A survey of factors contributing to gay and lesbian domestic violence. In C. Renzetti & C. Miley (Eds.), *Violence in gay and lesbian domestic partnerships* (pp. 35-42). New York: Haworth.

Farrell, L. (1985, April). The touching truth about tickling. *Mademoiselle,* pp. 54, 56.

Faulkner, K., Stoltenberg, C., Cogen, R., Nolder, M., & Shooter, E. (1992). Cognitive-behavioral group treatment for male spouse abusers. *Journal of Family Violence, 7,* 37-55.

Feinauer, L., Callahan, E., & Hilton, H. (1996). Positive intimate relationships decrease depression in sexually abused women. *American Journal of Family Therapy, 24,* 99-106.

Felson, R. (1992). "Kick 'em when they're down": Explanation of the relationship between stress and interpersonal aggression and violence. *Sociological Quarterly, 33,* 1-16.

Felson, R., & Russo, N. (1988). Parental punishment and sibling aggression. *Social Psychology Quarterly, 51,* 11-18.

Ferguson, D., & Beck, C. (1983). H.A.L.F.—A tool to assess elder abuse within the family. *Geriatric Nursing, 4,* 301-304.

Ferraro, K., & Johnson, J. (1983). How women experience battering: The process of victimization. *Social Problems, 30,* 325-339.

Feshbach, N., & Feshbach, S. (1969). The relationship between empathy and aggression in two age groups. *Developmental Psychology, 1,* 102-107.

Feshbach, S. (1964). The function of aggression and the regulation of aggressive drive. *Psychological Review, 71,* 257-272.

Filinson, R. (1993). An evaluation of a program of volunteer advocates for elder abuse victims. *Journal of Elder Abuse & Neglect, 5,* 77-93.

Filinson, R. (1995). A survey of grass-roots advocacy organizations for nursing home residents. *Journal of Elder Abuse & Neglect, 7,* 75-91.

Finkelhor, D. (1979). *Sexually victimized children.* New York: Free Press.

Finkelhor, D. (1980). Sex among siblings: A survey of prevalence, variety, and effects. *Achives of Sexual Behavior, 9,* 171-193.

Finkelhor, D. (1984a). *Child sexual abuse: New theory and research.* New York: Free Press.

Finkelhor, D. (1984b). The prevention of child sexual abuse: An overview of needs and problems. *SIECUS Report, 13,* 1-5.

Finkelhor, D. (1993). Epidemiological factors in the clinical identification of child sexual abuse. *Child Abuse & Neglect, 17,* 67-70.

Finkelhor, D., & Baron, L. (1986). Risk factors for child sexual abuse. *Journal of Interpersonal Violence, 1,* 43-71.

Finkelhor, D., & Dziuba-Leatherman, J. (1994). Victimization of children. *American Psychologist, 49,* 173-183.

Finkelhor, D., & Dziuba-Leatherman, J. (1995). Victimization prevention programs: A national survey of children's exposure and reactions. *Child Abuse & Neglect, 19,* 129-139.

Finkelhor, D., Hotaling, G., Lewis, I., & Smith, C. (1990). Sexual abuse in a national survey of adult men and women: Prevalence, characteristics, and risk factors. *Child Abuse & Neglect, 14,* 14-28.

Finkelhor, D., & Yllö, K. (1985). *License to rape: Sexual abuse and wives.* New York: Holt, Rinehart & Winston.

Finkelhor, D., & Zellman, G. (1991). Flexible reporting options for skilled child abuse professionals. *Child Abuse & Neglect, 15,* 335-341.

Finn, J. (1986). The relationship between sex-role attitudes and attitudes supporting marital violence. *Sex Roles, 14,* 235-243.

Fins, D. (1994). Health care decision-making for incapacitated elders: An innovative social service agency model. *Journal of Elder Abuse & Neglect, 6,* 39-51.

Flanzer, J. (1993). Alcohol and other drugs are key causal agents of violence. In R. Gelles & D. Loseke (Eds.), *Current controversies on family violence* (pp. 171-181). Newbury Park, CA: Sage.

Fleming, J., Mullen, P., & Bammer, G. (1997). A study of potential risk factors for sexual abuse in childhood. *Child Abuse & Neglect, 21,* 49-58.

Flynn, C. (1994). Regional differences in attitudes toward corporal punishment. *Journal of Marriage and the Family, 56,* 314-324.

Forehand, R., & Kotchick, B. (1996). Cultural diversity: A wake-up call for parent training. *Behavior Therapy, 27,* 187-206.

Fowler, C., Burns, S., & Roehl, J. (1983). The role of group therapy in incest counseling. *International Journal of Family Therapy, 5,* 127-135.

Freedman, J., Sears, D., & Carlsmith, J. (1981). *Social psychology* (4th ed.). Englewood Cliffs, NJ: Prentice Hall.

Freeman, J. (Ed.). (1995). *Women: A feminist perspective* (5th ed.). Mountain View, CA: Mayfield.

Freud, A. (1946). *The ego and the mechanisms of defense.* London: Hogarth.

Frey-Angel, J. (1989). Treating children of violent families: A sibling group approach. *Social Work With Groups, 12,* 95-107.

Friedrich, W. (1990). *Psychotherapy of sexually abused children and their families.* New York: Norton.

Friedrich, W. (1995). *Psychotherapy with sexually abused boys: An integrated approach.* Thousand Oaks, CA: Sage.

Friedrich, W., Berliner, L., Urquiza, A., & Beilke, R. (1988). Brief diagnostic group treatment of sexually abused boys. *Journal of Interpersonal Violence, 3,* 331-343.

Frieze, I. (1983). Investigating the causes and consequences of marital rape. *Signs: Journal of Women in Culture and Society, 8,* 532-553.

Frieze, I., Knoble, J., Washburn, C., & Zomnir, G. (1980). *Characteristics of battered women and their marriages* (NIMH Grant No. R01 MH 30913 final rep.). Pittsburgh, PA: University of Pittsburgh Press.

Fritz, M. (1989). Commentary: Full circle or forward. *Child Abuse & Neglect, 13,* 313-318.

Frodi, A. (1975). The effect of exposure to weapons on aggressive behavior from across-cultural perspective. *International Journal of Psychology, 10,* 283-292.

Frodi, A. (1981). Contribution of infant characteristics to child abuse. *American Journal of Mental Deficiency, 85,* 341-349.

Frodi, A., & Lamb, M. (1980). Child abusers' responses to infant smiles. *Child Development, 51,* 238-241.

Fryer, G., & Miyoshi, T. (1994). A survival analysis of the revictimization of children: The case of Colorado. *Child Abuse & Neglect, 18,* 1063-1071.

Fulmer, T., & Cahill, V. (1984). Assessing elder abuse: A study. *Journal of Gerontological Nursing, 10,* 16-20.

Fulmer, T., & Wetle, T. (1986). Elder abuse: Screening and intervention. *Nurse Practitioner, 11,* 33-38.

Garbarino, J. (1976). A preliminary study of some ecological correlates of child abuse: The impact of socioeconomic stress on mothers. *Child Development, 47,* 178-185.

Garbarino, J. (1977). The human ecology of child maltreatment: A conceptual model for research. *Journal of Marriage and the Family, 39,* 721-735.

Garbarino, J., & Ebata, A. (1983). The significance of ethnic and cultural differences in child maltreatment. *Journal of Marriage and the Family, 45,* 773-783.

Garbarino, J., Guttman, E., & Seeley, J. (1986). *The psychologically battered child.* San Francisco: Jossey-Bass.

Garbarino, J., & Kostelny, K. (1992). Child maltreatment as a community problem. *Child Abuse & Neglect, 16,* 455-464.

Garbarino, J., & Vondra, J. (1987). Psychological maltreatment: Issues and perspectives. In M. Brassard, R. Germain, & S. Hart (Eds.), *The psychological maltreatment of children and youth* (pp. 25-44). Elmsford, NY: Pergamon.

Garner, J., & Clemmer, E. (1986, November). *Danger to police in domestic disturbances: A new look.* Washington, DC: U.S. Department of Justice, National Institute of Justice.

Garvin, R., & Burger, R. (1968). *Where they go to die: The tragedy of America's aged.* New York: Delacorte.

Gebhard, P., Gagnon, J., Pomeroy, W., & Christenson, C. (1965). *Sex offenders: An analysis of types.* New York: Harper & Row.

Geen, R., & Berkowitz, L. (1966). Name-mediated aggressive cue properties. *Jour-*

nal of Personality and Social Psychology, 11, 389-392.

Geen, R., & O'Neal, E. (1969). Activation of cue-elicited aggression by general arousal. *Journal of Personality and Social Psychology, 11,* 389-392.

Gelinas, D. (1983). The persisting negative effects of incest. *Psychiatry, 46,* 312-329.

Gellert, G., Maxwell, R., Durfee, M., & Wagner, G. (1995). Fatalities assessed by the Orange County Child Death Review Team, 1989-1991. *Child Abuse & Neglect, 19,* 875-883.

Gelles, R. (1974). *The violent home.* Beverly Hills, CA: Sage.

Gelles, R. (1993). Through a sociological lens: Social structure and family violence. In R. Gelles & D. Loseke (Eds.), *Current controversies on family violence* (pp. 31-46). Newbury Park, CA: Sage.

Gelles, R. (1996). *The book of David.* New York: Basic Books.

Gentemann, K. (1984). Wife-beating: Attitudes of a nonclinical population. *Victimology, 9,* 109-119.

George, M. (1994). Riding the donkey backwards: Men as the unacceptable victims of marital violence. *Journal of Men's Studies, 3,* 137-159.

Gibson, R., & Hartshorne, T. (1996). Childhood sexual abuse and adult loneliness and network orientation. *Child Abuse & Neglect, 20,* 1087-1093.

Gil, E. (1996). *Systemic treatment of families who abuse.* San Francisco: Jossey-Bass.

Giles-Sims, J. (1983). *Wife battering: A systems theory approach.* New York: Guilford.

Gilgun, J. (1986). Sexually abused girls' knowledge about sexual abuse and sexuality. *Journal of Interpersonal Violence, 1,* 309-325.

Glasser, W. (1965). *Reality therapy: A new approach to psychiatry.* New York: Harper & Row.

Godkin, M., Wolf, R., & Pillemer, K. (1989). A case-comparison analysis of elder abuse and neglect. *International Journal of Aging and Human Development, 28,* 207-225.

Goldberg, W., & Tomlanovich, M. (1984). Domestic violence victims in the emergency department. *Journal of the American Medical Association, 251,* 3259-3264.

Golden, G., & Frank, P. (1994). When 50-50 isn't fair: The case against couple counseling in domestic abuse. *Social Work, 39,* 636-637.

Goldman, J., Graves, L., Ward, M., Albanese, I., Sorensen, E., & Chamberlain, C. (1993). Self-report of guardians ad litem: Provision of information to judges in child abuse cases and neglect cases. *Child Abuse & Neglect, 17,* 227-232.

Goldstein, A., Keller, H., & Erne, D. (1985). *Changing the abusive parent.* Champaign, IL: Research Press.

Goldstein, M. (1995). Maltreatment of elderly persons. *Psychiatric Services, 46,* 1219-1221, 1225.

Gondolf, E. (1988). The effect of batterer counseling on shelter outcome. *Journal of Interpersonal Violence, 5,* 275-289.

Gondolf, E. (1990). An exploratory survey of court-mandated batterer programs. *Response, 13,* 7-11.

Gonzalez, L., Waterman, J., Kelly, R., McCord, J., & Oliveri, M. (1993). Children's patterns of disclosures and recantations of sexual and ritualistic abuse allegations in psychotherapy. *Child Abuse & Neglect, 17,* 281-289.

Goodridge, D., Johnston, P., & Thomson, M. (1996). Conflict and aggression as stressors in the work environment of nursing assistants: Implications for institutional elder abuse. *Journal of Elder Abuse & Neglect, 8,* 49-67.

Goodwin, J. (1981). Suicide attempts in sexual abuse victims and their mothers. *Child Abuse & Neglect, 5,* 217-221.

Goodwin, J. (1982). *Sexual abuse: Incest victims and their families.* Boston: John W. Wright.

Goodwin, J. (1985). Posttraumatic symptoms in incest victims. In S. Eth & R. Pynoos (Eds.), *Posttraumatic stress disorder in children* (pp. 155-168). Washington, DC: American Psychiatric Press.

Goodwin, J., Sahd, D., & Rada, R. (1982). False accusations and false denials of incest: Clinical myths and clinical realities. In J. Goodwin (Ed.), *Sexual abuse: Incest victims and their families* (pp. 17-26). Boston: John Wright.

Goolkasian, F. (1986). *Confronting domestic violence: The role of criminal court judges.* Washington, DC: U.S. Department of Justice.

Gordon, J. (1996). Community services for abused women: A review of perceived usefulness and efficacy. *Journal of Interpersonal Violence, 11,* 315-329.

Gottman, J., & Katz, L. (1989). Effects of marital discord on young children's peer interaction and health. *Developmental Psychology, 25,* 373-381.

Grafman, J., Schwab, K., Warden, D., & Pridget, A. (1996). Frontal lobe injuries, violence, and aggression: A report of the Vietnam Head Injury Study. *Neurology, 46,* 1231-1238.

Graham, D., Rawlings, E., & Rimini, N. (1988). Survivors of terror: Battered women, hostages, and the Stockholm Syndrome. In K. Yllö & K. Bogard (Eds.), *Feminist perspectives on wife abuse* (pp. 217-233). Newbury Park, CA: Sage.

Graziano, A., & Mills, J. (1992). Treatment for abused children: When is a partial solution acceptable? *Child Abuse & Neglect, 16,* 217-228.

Green, A., Gaines, R., & Sandgrund, A. (1974). Child abuse: Pathological syndrome of family interaction. *American Journal of Psychiatry, 131,* 882-886.

Greene, R. (1986). *Social work with the aged and their families.* Hawthorne, NY: Aldine de Gruyter.

Greene, R., & Soniat, B. (1991). Clinical interventions with older adults in need of protection: A family systems perspective. *Journal of Family Psychotherapy, 2,* 1-15.

Greenwald, E., & Leitenberg, H. (1990). Posttraumatic stress disorder in a nonclinical and nonstudent sample of adult women sexually abused as children. *Journal of Interpersonal Violence, 5,* 691-703.

Greven, P. (1977). *The Protestant temperament.* New York: Knopf.

Griffin, L., & Williams, O. (1992). Abuse among African-American elderly. *Journal of Family Violence, 7,* 19-35.

Gross, A. (1978). The male role and heterosexual behavior. *Journal of Social Issues, 34,* 87-107.

Groth, N. (1979). *Men who rape.* New York: Plenum.

Groth, N., Hobson, W., & Gary, T. (1982). The child molester: Clinical observation. In J. Conte & D. Shore (Eds.), *Social work and child sexual abuse* (pp. 129-144). New York: Haworth.

Groth, N., & Oliveri, F. (1989). Understanding sexual offense behavior and differentiating among sexual abusers: Basic conceptual issues. In S. Sgroi (Ed.), *Vulnerable populations* (Vol. 2, pp. 309-327). Lexington, MA: Lexington Books.

Grusznski, R., Brink, J., & Edleson, J. (1988). Support and education groups for children of battered women. *Child Welfare, 67,* 431-444.

Grusznski, R., & Carrillo, T. (1988). Who completes batterers' treatment groups? An empirical investigation. *Journal of Family Violence, 3,* 141-150.

Gustafson, R. (1994). Alcohol and aggression. *Journal of Offender Services, Counseling and Rehabilitation, 21,* 1-80.

Hall, G., & Hirschman, R. (1991). Toward a theory of sexual aggression: A quadripartite model. *Journal of Consulting and Clinical Psychology, 59,* 662-669.

Hale, G., Zimostrad, S., Duckworth, J., & Nicholas, D. (1988). Abusive partners: MMPI profiles of male batterers. *Journal of Mental Health Counseling, 10,* 214-224.

Hale, M. (1991). *History of the pleas of the crown.* London: Professional Books. (Original work published 1736)

Hamberger, L. (1996). Intervention in gay male intimate violence requires coordinated efforts on multiple levels. In C. Renzetti & C. Miley (Eds.), *Violence in gay and lesbian domestic partnerships* (pp. 83-91). New York: Haworth.

Hamberger, L., & Hastings, J. (1985, March). *Personality correlates of men who abuse their partners: Some preliminary data.* Paper presented at the annual meeting of the Society of Personality Assessment, Berkeley, CA.

Hamberger, L., & Hastings, J. (1986). Personality correlates of men who abuse their partners: A cross-validation study. *Journal of Family Violence, 1,* 323-341.

Hamberger, L., & Hastings, J. (1989). Counseling male spouse abusers: Characteristics of treatment completers and dropouts. *Violence and Victims, 4,* 275-286.

Hamberger, L., & Hastings, J. (1990). Recidivism following spouse abuse abatement counseling: Treatment program implications. *Violence and Victims, 5,* 157-170.

Hamilton, B., & Coates, J. (1993). Perceived helpfulness and use of professional services by abused women. *Journal of Family Violence, 8,* 313-324.

Hamilton, G. (1989). Using a prevent-elder-abuse family systems approach. *Journal of Gerontological Nursing, 15,* 21-26.

Hankoff, L. (1990). The neuroscience of violence. *International Journal of Offender Therapy and Comparative Criminology, 34,* 3-6.

Hansen, N. (1994). A critique of Carden's integrative model for treatment of batterers: One clinician's perspective. *The Counseling Psychologist, 22,* 583-586.

Harper, J. (1993). Prepuberal male victims of incest: A clinical study. *Child Abuse & Neglect, 17,* 419-421.

Harris, M. (1974). Mediators between frustration and aggression in a field experiment. *Journal of Experimental and Social Psychology, 10,* 96-115.

Harris, S. (1996). For better or for worse: Spouse abuse grown old. *Journal of Elder Abuse & Neglect, 8,* 1-30.

Harrison, P., Fulkerson, J., & Beebe, T. (1997). Multiple substance use among adolescent physical and sexual abuse victims. *Child Abuse & Neglect, 21,* 529-539.

Hart, B. (1988). Beyond the "duty to warn": A therapist's "duty to protect" battered women and children. In K. Yllö & M. Bograd (Eds.), *Feminist perspectives on wife abuse* (pp. 234-248). Newbury Park, CA: Sage.

Hart, S., & Brassard, M. (1987). A major threat to children's mental health—psychological maltreatment. *American Psychologist, 42,* 160-165.

Hastings, J., & Hamberger, L. (1988). Personality characteristics of spouse abusers: A controlled comparison. *Violence and Victims, 3,* 31-48.

Hawkins, W., & Duncan, D. (1985). Perpetrator and family characteristics related to child abuse and neglect: Comparison of substantiated and unsubstantiated reports. *Psychological Reports, 56,* 407-410.

Henning, K., Leitenberg, H., Coffey, P., Bennett, R., & Jankowski, M. (1997). Long-term psychological adjustment to witnessing interparental physical conflict during childhood. *Child Abuse & Neglect, 21,* 501-515.

Henning, K., Leitenberg, H., Coffey, P., Turner, T., & Bennett, R. (1996). Long-term psychological and social impact of witnessing physical conflict between parents. *Journal of Interpersonal Violence, 11,* 35-51.

Herbert, T., Silver, R., & Ellard, J. (1991). Coping with an abusive relationships: I. How and why do women stay? *Journal of Marriage and the Family, 53,* 311-325.

Heriot, J. (1996). Maternal protectiveness following the disclosure of intrafamilial child sexual abuse. *Journal of Interpersonal Violence, 11,* 181-194.

Herman, J. (1981). *Father-daughter incest.* Cambridge, MA: Harvard University Press.

Herman, J., & Hirschman, L. (1977). Father-daughter incest. *Signs: Journal of Women in Culture and Society, 4,* 735-756.

Herman, J., Russell, D., & Trocki, K. (1986). Long-term effects of incestuous abuse in childhood. *American Journal of Psychiatry, 143,* 1293-1296.

Hernandez, J. (1995). The concurrence of eating disorders with histories of child abuse among adolescents. *Journal of Sexual Abuse, 4,* 73-85.

Hester, M., Kelly, L., & Radford, J. (Eds.). (1996). *Women, violence and male power: Feminist activism, research and practice.* Philadelphia: Open University Press.

Hibbard, R., & Hartman, G. (1993). Components of child and parent interviews in cases of alleged sexual abuse. *Child Abuse & Neglect, 17,* 495-500.

Hilberman, E. (1980). Overview: The wife-beater's wife reconsidered. *American Journal of Psychiatry, 137,* 1336-1347.

Hilberman, E., & Munson, K. (1978). Sixty battered women. *Victimology, 2,* 460-470.

Hilton, Z. (1992). Battered women's concerns about their children witnessing wife assault. *Journal of Interpersonal Violence, 7,* 77-86.

Hinds, M. (1993, October 19). Not like the movie: A dare leads to death. *New York Times,* pp. A1, A22.

Hirschel, J., Hutchison, I., & Dean, C. (1992). The failure of arrest to deter spouse abuse. *Journal of Research in Crime and Delinquency, 29,* 7-33.

Hoffman, M. (1978). Empathy: Its development and prosocial implications. In C. B. Keasey (Ed.), *Nebraska Symposium on Motivation* (Vol. 25, pp. 169-217). Lincoln: University of Nebraska Press.

Hogan, R. (1979). Moral conduct and moral character: A psychological perspective. *Psychological Bulletin, 79,* 217-232.

Holland, L., Kasraian, K., & Leonardelli, C. (1987). Elder abuse: An analysis of the current problem and potential role of the rehabilitation professional. *Physical & Occupational Therapy in Geriatrics, 5,* 41-50.

Hollingshead, A. (1975). *Four Factor Index of Social Status.* New Haven, CT: Author.

Holmes, S., & Robins, L. (1988). The role of parental disciplinary practices in the development of depression and alcoholism. *Psychiatry, 51,* 24-35.

Holt, M. (1993). Elder sexual abuse in Britain: Preliminary findings. *Journal of Elder Abuse & Neglect, 5,* 63-71.

Holtzworth-Munroe, A. (1988). Causal attributions in marital violence: Theoretical and methodological issues. *Clinical Psychology Review, 8,* 331-334.

Homstead, K., & Werthamer, L. (1989). Time-limited group therapy for adolescent victims of child sexual abuse. In S. Sgroi (Ed.), *Vulnerable populations* (Vol. 2, pp. 65-84). Lexington, MA: Lexington Books.

Hooyman, N. (1982). Mobilizing social networks to prevent elderly abuse. *Physical & Occupational Therapy in Geriatrics, 2,* 21-35.

Hornstein, H. (1976). *Cruelty and kindness.* Englewood Cliffs, NJ: Prentice Hall.

Horton, A. (1988). Practical guidelines for professionals working with religious spouse abuse victims. In A. Horton & J. Williamson (Eds.), *Abuse and religion: When praying isn't enough* (pp. 89-99). Lexington, MA: Lexington Books.

Horton, A., Wilkins, M., & Wright, W. (1988). Women who ended abuse: What religious leaders and religion did for these victims.

In A. Horton & J. Williamson (Eds.), *Abuse and religion: When praying isn't enough* (pp. 235-246). Lexington, MA: Lexington Books.

Houskamp, B., & Foy, D. (1991). The assessment of posttraumatic stress disorder in battered women. *Journal of Interpersonal Violence, 6,* 367-375.

Hovland, C., & Sears, R. (1940). Minor studies in aggression: VI. Correlation of lynchings with economic indices. *Journal of Personality, 9,* 301-310.

Hudson, B. (1992). Ensuring an abuse-free environment: A learning program for nursing home staff. *Journal of Elder Abuse & Neglect, 4,* 25-36.

Hudson, M. (1986). Elder mistreatment: Current research. In K. Pillemer & R. Wolf (Eds.), *Elder abuse: Conflict in the family* (pp. 240-269). Dover, MA: Auburn House.

Hudson, S., & Ward, T. (1997). Intimacy, loneliness, and attachment style in sexual offenders. *Journal of Interpersonal Violence, 12,* 323-339.

Hughes, H., & Barad, S. (1983). Psychological functioning of children in a battered women's shelter: A preliminary investigation. *American Journal of Orthopsychiatry, 53,* 525-531.

Hughes, H., Parkinson, D., & Vargo, M. (1989). Witnessing spouse abuse and experiencing physical abuse: A "double whammy"? *Journal of Family Violence, 4,* 197-209.

Huston, A., Donnerstein, E., Fairchild, H., Feshbach, N., Katz, P., Murray, J., Rubenstein, E., Wilcox, B., & Zuckerman, D. (1992). *Big world, small screen: The role of television in American society.* Lincoln: University of Nebraska Press.

Hutchison, I., Hirschel, J., & Pesackis, C. (1994). Family violence and police utilization. *Violence and Victims, 9,* 299-313.

Hwalek, M., & Sengstock, M. (1986). Assessing the probability of abuse of the elderly: Toward development of a clinical screening instrument. *Journal of Applied Gerontology, 5,* 153-173.

Hyde, J. (1994). *Understanding human sexuality* (5th ed.). New York: McGraw-Hill.

International Association of Chiefs of Police. (1976). *Investigation of wife beating* (Training Key No. 246). Gaithersburg, MD: Author.

Irwin, A., & Gross, A. (1995). Cognitive tempo, violent video games, and aggressive behavior in young boys. *Journal of Family Violence, 10,* 337-350.

Isaac, N., & Sanchez, R. (1994). Emergency department response to battered women in Massachusetts. *Annals of Emergency Medicine, 23,* 855-858.

Island, D., & Letellier, P. (1991). *Men who beat the men who love them.* New York: Harrington Park.

Jackson, K., Holzman, C., Barnard, T., & Paradis, C. (1997). Working with sex offenders: The impact on practitioners. In S. B. Edmunds (Ed.), *Impact: Working with sexual abusers* (pp. 61-73). Brandon, VT: Safer Society Press.

Jacobson, N. (1994). Rewards and dangers in researching domestic violence. *Family Process, 33,* 81-86.

Jaffe, P., Wilson, S., & Wolfe, D. (1986). Promoting changes in attitudes and understanding of conflict resolution among child witnesses of family violence. *Canadian Journal of Behavioral Science, 18,* 357-366.

Jansson, B. (1997). *The reluctant welfare state* (3rd ed.). New York: Brooks/Cole.

Janus, M. (1984, September). On early victimization and adolescent male prostitution. *SIECUS Report XII, 1,* 8-9.

Janz, M. (1990). Clues to elder abuse. *Geriatric Nursing, 10,* 220-221.

Jaudes, P., Ekwo, E., & Voorhis, J. (1995). Association of drug abuse and child abuse. *Child Abuse & Neglect, 19,* 1065-1075.

Jeffords, C. (1984). The impact of sex-role and religious attitudes upon forced marital intercourse norms. *Sex Roles, 11,* 543-552.

Jeffords, C., & Dull, R. (1982). Demographic variations in attitudes towards marital rapc immunity. *Journal of Marriage and the Family, 44,* 755-762.

Johanek, M. (1988). Treatment of male victims of child sexual abuse in military service. In S. Sgroi (Ed.), *Vulnerable populations* (Vol. 1, pp. 103-113). Lexington, MA: Lexington Books.

Johnson, B., & Morse, H. (1968). Injured children and their parents. *Children, 15,* 147-152.

Johnson, I. (1995). Family members' perceptions of and attitudes toward elder abuse. *Families in Society: The Journal of Contemporary Human Services, 1,* 220-229.

Johnson, R., & Shrier, D. (1987). Past sexual victimization by females of male patients in an adolescent medicine clinic population. *American Journal of Psychiatry, 144,* 650-652.

Johnson, S., & Lobitz, C. (1974). The personal and marital adjustment of parents as related to observed child deviance and parenting behavior. *Journal of Abnormal and Child Psychology, 2,* 193-207.

Jones, A., & Schechter, S. (1992). *When love goes wrong.* New York: HarperCollins.

Jones, D., & McGraw, J. (1987). Reliable and fictitious accounts of sexual abuse to children. *Journal of Interpersonal Violence, 2,* 27-45.

Jones, R., & Jones, J. (1987). Racism as psychological maltreatment. In M. Brassard, R. Germain, & S. Hart (Eds.), *Psychological maltreatment of children and youth* (pp. 146-158). Elmsford, NY: Pergamon.

Jouriles, E., Barling, J., & O'Leary, K. (1987). Predicting child behavior problems in maritally violent families. *Journal of Abnormal Child Psychology, 15,* 165-173.

Jouriles, E., & O'Leary, K. (1985). Interspousal reliability of reports of marital violence. *Journal of Consulting and Counseling Psychology, 53,* 419-421.

Justice, B., & Justice, R. (1979). *The broken taboo: Sex in the family.* New York: Human Sciences Press.

Kadushin, A., & Martin, J. (1988). *Child welfare services.* New York: Macmillan.

Kahana, E. (1973). The humane treatment of old people in institutions. *The Gerontologist, 13,* 282-288.

Kalichman, S., Brosig, C., & Kalichman, M. (1994). Mandatory child abuse reporting laws: Issues and implications for treating offenders. *Journal of Offender Rehabilitation, 21,* 27-43.

Kalichman, S., & Craig, M. (1991). Professional psychologists' decisions to report suspected child abuse: Clinician and situation influences. *Professional Psychology: Research and Practice, 22,* 84-89.

Kalichman, S., Craig, M., & Follingstad, D. (1989). Factors influencing the reporting of father-child sexual abuse: A study of licensed psychologists. *Professional Psychology: Research and Practice, 20,* 84-89.

Kalmus, O. (1979). The attribution of responsibility in a wife abuse context. *Victimology, 4,* 284-291.

Kantor, G., & Straus, M. (1987). The "drunken bum" theory of wife beating. *Social Problems, 34,* 213-230.

Kaufman, I., Peck, A., & Tagiuri, L. (1954). The family constellation and overt incestuous relations between father and daughter. *American Journal of Orthopsychiatry, 24,* 266-279.

Kaufman, J., & Zigler, E. (1987). Do abused children become abusive parents? *American Journal of Orthopsychiatry, 57,* 186-192.

Kaufman, K., Wallace, A., Johnson, C., & Reeder, M. (1996). Comparing female and male perpetrators' modus operandi. *Journal of Interpersonal Violence, 10,* 322-333.

Keilitz, S. (1994). Legal report: Civil protection orders: A viable justice system tool for deterring domestic violence. *Violence and Victims, 9,* 79-84.

Kemp, A., Green, B., Hovanitz, C., & Rawlings, E. (1995). Incidence and correlates of posttraumatic stress disorder in battered women: Shelter and community samples. *Journal of Interpersonal Violence, 10,* 43-55.

Kempe, H., Silverman, F., Steele, H., Droegemueller, W., & Silver, H. (1962). The battered-child syndrome. *Journal of the American Medical Association, 181,* 17-24.

Kendall-Tackett, K. (1992). Beyond anatomical dolls: Professionals' use of other play therapy techniques. *Child Abuse & Neglect, 16,* 139-142.

Kern, J., & Hastings, T. (1995). Differential family environments of bulimics and victims of childhood sexual abuse: Achievement orientation. *Journal of Clinical Psychology, 51,* 499-506.

Kilburn, J. (1996). Network effects in caregiver to care-recipient violence: A study of caregivers to those diagnosed with Alzheimer's disease. *Journal of Elder Abuse & Neglect, 8,* 69-80.

Kinzl, J., Traweger, C., & Biebl, W. (1995). Sexual dsyfunctions: Relationship to childhood sexual abuse and early family experiences in a nonclinical sample. *Child Abuse & Neglect, 19,* 785-792.

Kleck, G., & Patterson, E. (1993). The impact of gun control and gun ownership levels on violence rates. *Journal of Quantitative Criminology, 9,* 249-287.

Knopp, F. (1984). *Retraining adult sex offenders: Methods and models.* Syracuse, NY: Safer Society Press.

Kosberg, J. (1988). Preventing elder abuse: Identification of high-risk factors prior to placement decisions. *The Gerontologist, 28,* 43-50.

Koss, M. (1992). The underdetection of rape: Methodological choices influence incidence estimates. *Journal of Social Issues 48,* 61-75.

Koverola, C., Pound, J., Heger, A., & Lytle, C. (1993). Relationship of child sexual abuse to depression. *Child Abuse & Neglect, 17,* 393-400.

Kravitz, R., & Driscoll, J. (1983). Expectations for childhood development among child-abusing and nonabusing parents. *American Journal of Orthopsychiatry, 53,* 336-344.

Krestan, J., & Bepko, C. (1980). The problem of fusion in the lesbian relationship. *Family Process, 19,* 277-289.

Krishnan, V., & Morrison, K. (1995). An ecological model of child maltreatment in a Canadian province. *Child Abuse & Neglect, 19,* 101-113.

Kruttschnitt, C., McLeod, J., & Dornfeld, M. (1994). The economic environment of child abuse. *Social Problems, 41,* 299-315.

Kulik, J. & Brown, R. (1979). Frustration, attribution of blame, and aggression. *Journal of Experimental Social Psychology, 15,* 183-194.

Kunz, J., & Bahr, S. (1996). A profile of parental homicide against children. *Journal of Family Violence, 11,* 347-362.

Kurdek, L. (1994). Areas of conflict for gay, lesbian, and heterosexual couples: What couples argue about influences relationship satisfaction. *Journal of Marriage and the Family, 56,* 923-934.

Kurtz, P., Gaudin, J., Wodarski, J., & Howing, P. (1993). Maltreatment and the school-aged child: School performance consequences. *Child Abuse & Neglect, 17,* 581-589.

Kurz, D. (1993). Physical assaults by husbands: A major social problem. In R. Gelles & D. Loseke (Eds.), *Current controversies on family violence* (pp. 88-103). Newbury Park, CA: Sage.

Lacey, J. (1990). Incest, incestuous fantasy and indecency: A clinical catchment area study of normal-weight bulimic women. *British Journal of Psychiatry, 157,* 399-403.

Lachs, M. (1995). Preaching to the unconverted: Educating physicians about elder abuse. *Journal of Elder Abuse & Neglect, 7,* 1-12.

Landers, S. (1995, May). Guardianship grows in elder care. *NASW News,* p. 3.

Langhinrichsen-Rohling, J., Smutzler, N., & Vivian, D. (1994). Positivity in marriage: The role of discord and physical aggression against wives. *Journal of Marriage and the Family, 56,* 69-79.

Langley, R., & Levy, R. (1977). *Wife beating: The silent crisis.* New York: E. P. Dutton.

Lanktree, C., & Briere, J. (1995). Outcome of therapy for sexually abused children: A repeated measures study. *Child Abuse & Neglect, 19,* 1145-1155.

Lanza, M., & Campbell, D. (1991). Patient assault: A comparison study of reporting methods. *Journal of Nursing Quality Assurance, 5,* 60-68.

Lau, E., & Kosberg, J. (1979, September-October). Abuse of the elderly by informal care providers. *Aging,* pp. 10-15.

Laviola, M. (1992). Effects of older brother-younger sister incest: A study of the dynamics of 17 cases. *Child Abuse & Neglect, 16,* 409-421.

Lawrence, K., & Foy, D. (1993). Posttraumatic stress disorder among battered women: Risk and resiliency factors. *Violence and Victims, 8,* 17-28.

Lawson, C. (1993). Mother-son sexual abuse: Rare or underreported? A critique of the research. *Child Abuse & Neglect, 17,* 261-269.

Lawson, L., & Chaffin, M. (1992). False negatives in sexual abuse disclosure interviews. *Journal of Interpersonal Violence, 7,* 532-542.

Lazarus, A. (1981). *The practice of multimodal therapy.* New York: McGraw-Hill.

Lazoritz, S., & Shelman, E. (1996). Before Mary Ellen. *Child Abuse & Neglect, 20,* 235-237.

Leitenberg, J., Greewald, E., & Cado, S. (1992). A retrospective study of long-term methods of coping with having been sexually abused during childhood. *Child Abuse & Neglect, 16,* 399-407.

Lempert, L. (1996). Women's strategies for survival: Developing agency in abusive relationships. *Journal of Family Violence, 11,* 269-289.

Lempert, R. (1989). Humility is a virtue: On the publicization of policy-relevant research. *Law and Society Review, 23,* 145-161.

Leonard, K., & Blane, H. (1992). Alcohol and marital aggression in a national sample of young men. *Journal of Interpersonal Violence, 7,* 19-30.

Leonard, K., & Senchak, M. (1993). Alcohol and premarital aggression among newlywed couples. *Journal of Studies on Alcohol, 11,* 96-108.

Letellier, P. (1996). Twin epidemics: Domestic violence and HIV infection among gay and bisexual men. In C. Renzetti & C. Miley (Eds.), *Violence in gay and lesbian domestic partnerships* (pp. 69-81). New York: Haworth.

LeTourneau, C. (1981). Empathy and stress: How they affect parental aggression. *Social Work, 26,* 529-538.

Levine, M. (1975). Interparental violence and its effects on the children: A study of 50 families in general practice. *Medicine, Science, and Law, 15,* 172-176.

Leyens, J., Camino, L., Parke, R., & Berkowitz, L. (1975). Effects of movie violence on aggression in a field setting as a function of group dominance and cohesion. *Journal of Personality and Social Psychology, 32,* 346-360.

Leyens, J., & Fraczek, A. (1984). Aggression as an interpersonal phenomenon. In H. Tajfel (Ed.), *The social dimension: European development in social psychology* (Vol. 1, pp. 184-203). Cambridge, England: Cambridge University Press.

Leyens, J., & Parke, R. (1975). Aggressive slides can induce a weapons effect. *European Journal of Social Psychology, 5,* 229-236.

Lie, G., Schlitt, R., Bush, J., Montagne, M., & Reyes, L. (1991). Lesbians in currently aggressive relationships: How frequently do they report aggressive past relationships? *Violence and Victims, 6,* 121-135.

Lieber, L. (1983). The self-help approach: Parents Anonymous. *Journal of Clinical Child Psychology, 12,* 288-291.

Lieberman, M., & Tobin, S. (1983). *The experience of old age: Stress, coping, and survival.* New York: Basic Books.

Lindenbaum, J. (1985). The shattering of an illusion: The problem of competition in lesbian relationships. *Violence and Victims, 6,* 121-135.

Lindon, J., & Norse, C. (1994). A multidimensional model of groupwork for adolescent girls who have been sexually abused. *Child Abuse & Neglect, 18,* 341-348.

Lindquist, C., Telch, C., & Taylor, J. (1983). Evaluation of a conjugal violence treatment program: A pilot study. *Behavioral Counseling and Community Intervention, 3,* 76-90.

Linnoila, M., & Virkkunen, M. (1992). Aggression, suicidality, and serotonin. *Journal of Clinical Psychiatry, 53,* 46-51.

Linnoila, M., Virkkunen, M., George, T., & Higley, D. (1993). Impulse control disorders. *International Clinical Psychopharmacology, 8,* 53-56.

Lisak, D., & Ivan, C. (1995). Deficits in intimacy and empathy in sexually aggressive men. *Journal of Interpersonal Violence, 10,* 296-308.

Litwin, H., & Monk, A. (1987). Do nursing home patient ombudsmen make a difference? *Journal of Gerontological Social Work, 2,* 95-104.

Litzelfelner, P., & Petr, C. (1997). Case advocacy in child welfare. *Social Work, 42,* 392-402.

Lockhart, L., White, B., Causby, V., & Isaac, A. (1994). Letting out the secret: Violence in lesbian relationships. *Journal of Interpersonal Violence, 9,* 469-492.

Loftin, C., McDowall, D., Wiersema, B., & Cottey, T. (1991). Effects of restrictive licensing of handguns on homicide and suicide in the District of Columbia. *New England Journal of Medicine, 325,* 1615-1620.

Logan, S., Freeman, E., & McRoy, R. (Eds.). (1990). *Social work practice with Black families: A culturally specific perspective.* White Plains, NY: Longman.

Long, S. (1987). *Death without dignity.* Austin: Texas Monthly Press.

Longres, J. (1995). Self-neglect among the elderly. *Journal of Elder Abuse & Neglect, 7,* 69-86.

Lorber, R., Felton, D., & Reid, J. (1984). A social learning approach to the reduction of coercive processes in child abusive families: A molecular analysis. *Advanced Behavior Research Therapy, 6,* 29-45.

Loredo, C. (1982). Sibling incest. In S. Sgroi (Ed.), *Handbook of clinical intervention in child sexual abuse* (pp. 177-188). Lexington, MA: D. C. Heath.

Lorenz, K. (1966). *On aggression.* New York: Harcourt Brace Jovanovich.

Lott, B. (1994). *Women's lives: Themes and variations in gender learning* (2nd ed.). Pacific Grove, CA: Brooks/Cole.

Loulan, J. (1987). *Lesbian passion.* San Francisco: Spinsters/Aunt Lute.

Lowery, M. (1987). Adult survivors of childhood incest. *Journal of Psychosocial Nursing, 25,* 27-31.

Lucal, B. (1995). The problem with "battered husbands." *Deviant Behavior, 16,* 95-112.

Lukianowicz, N. (1972). Incest. *British Journal of Psychiatry, 120,* 301-313.

Lung, C., & Daro, D. (1996). *Current trends in child abuse reporting and fatalities: The results of the 1995 Annual Fifty-State Survey.* Chicago: National Committee to Prevent Child Abuse.

Lystad, M. (1975). Violence in the home: A review of the literature. *American Journal of Orthopsychiatry, 45,* 328-345.

Maccoby, E., & Jacklin, C. (1974). *The psychology of sex differences.* Stanford, CA: Stanford University Press.

Maccoby, E., & Martin, J. (1983). Socialization in the context of the family: Parent-child interaction. In P. H. Mussen (Ed.), *Handbook of child psychology* (4th ed., pp. 1-101). New York: John Wiley.

Maisch, R. (1973). *Incest.* London: André Deutsch.

Mamay, P., & Simpson, R. (1981). Three female roles in television commercials. *Sex Roles, 7,* 1223-1232.

Mancoske, R., Standifer, D., & Cauley, C. (1994). The effectiveness of brief counseling services for battered women. *Research on Social Work Practice, 4,* 53-63.

Mandell, J., & Damon, L. (1989). *Group treatment for sexually abused children.* New York: Guilford.

Manion, I., McIntyre, J., Firestone, P., Ligenzinska, M., Ensom, R., & Wells, G. (1996). Secondary traumatization in parents following the disclosure of extrafamilial child sexual abuse: Initial effects. *Child Abuse & Neglect, 20,* 1095-1109.

Margolin, L. (1992). Child abuse by mothers' boyfriends: Why the overrepresentation? *Child Abuse & Neglect, 16,* 541-551.

Marino, M. (1992). Empathy levels and depression in physically-abusive adolescent mothers and non-physically-abusive adolescent mothers. *Dissertation Abstracts International, 53*(09), 3378A.

Marshall, L. (1996). Psychological abuse of women: Six distinct clusters. *Journal of Family Violence, 11,* 379-409.

Marshall, P., & Norgard, K. (1983). *Child abuse and neglect: Sharing responsibility.* New York: John Wiley.

Martin, D. (1981). *Battered wives.* San Francisco: Volcano Press.

Martin, M. (1997). Double your trouble: Dual arrest in family violence. *Journal of Family Violence, 12,* 139-157.

Martin, S. (1989). Research note: The response of clergy to spouse abuse in a suburban county. *Violence and Victims, 4,* 217-225.

Marvasti, J. (1989). Play therapy with sexually abused children. In S. Sgroi (Ed.), *Vulnerable populations* (Vol. 2, pp. 1-42). Lexington, MA: Lexington Books.

Massat, C. (1995). Is older better? Adolescent parenthood and maltreatment. *Child Welfare, 74,* 325-336.

Matlaw, J., & Mayer, J. (1986). Elder abuse: Ethical and practical dilemmas for social work. *Social Work, 31,* 85-94.

Matlaw, J., & Spence, D. (1994). The hospital elder assessment team: A protocol for suspected cases of elder abuse and neglect. *Journal of Elder Abuse & Neglect, 6,* 23-37.

McCammon, S., Knox, D., & Schacht, C. (1993). *Choices in sexuality.* Minneapolis, MN: West.

McCandlish, B. (1982). Therapeutic issues with lesbian couples. *Journal of Homosexuality, 7,* 71-78.

McCann, J., Voris, J., Simon, M., & Wells, R. (1990). Comparison of genital examination techniques in prepubertal girls. *Pediatrics, 85,* 182-187.

McCloskey, L., Figueredo, A., & Koss, M. (1995). The effects of systemic family violence on children's mental health. *Child Development, 66,* 1239-1261.

McFarlane, J., Parker, B., Soeken, K., & Bullock, L. (1992). Assessing for abuse during pregnancy: Severity and frequency of injuries and associated entry into prenatal care.

Journal of the American Medical Association, 267, 3176-3178.

MacFarlane, K., Waterman, J., Conerly, S., Damon, L., Durfee, M., & Long, S. (1986). *Sexual abuse of young children.* New York: Guilford.

McGain, B., & McKinzey, R. (1995). The efficacy of group treatment in sexually abused girls. *Child Abuse & Neglect, 19,* 1157-1169.

McGoldrick, M., Giordano, J., & Pearce, J. (1996). *Ethnicity and family therapy.* New York: Guilford.

McGuire, L., & Wagner, N. (1978). Sexual dysfunction in women who were molested as children: One response pattern and suggestions for treatment. *Journal of Sex and Marital Therapy, 1,* 11-15.

McKay, M. (1994). The link between domestic violence and child abuse: Assessment and treatment considerations. *Child Welfare, 73,* 29-39.

McKeel, A., & Sporakowski, M. (1993). How shelter counselors' views about responsibility for wife abuse relate to services they provide to battered women. *Journal of Family Violence, 8,* 101-112.

McLaughlin, I., Leonard, K., & Senchak, M. (1992). Prevalence and distribution of premarital aggression among couples applying for a marriage license. *Journal of Family Violence, 7,* 309-319.

McLeer, S. (1989). Education is not enough: A systems failure in protecting battered women. *Annals of Emergency Medicine, 18,* 651-653.

McLeer, S., & Anwar, R. (1989). A study of battered women presenting in an emergency department. *American Journal of Public Health, 79,* 65-66.

McMullin, R., & Giles, T. (1981). *Cognitive behavior therapy: A restructuring approach.* New York: Grune & Stratton.

McNeely, R., & Robinson-Simpson, G. (1987). The truth about domestic violence: A falsely framed issue. *Social Work, 32,* 485-490.

McNew, J., & Abell, N. (1995). Posttraumatic stress symptomatology: Similarities and differences between Vietnam veterans and adult survivors of childhood sexual abuse. *Social Work, 40,* 115-126.

McNulty, C., & Wardle, J. (1995). Adult disclosure of sexual abuse: A primary cause of psychological distress? *Child Abuse & Neglect, 19,* 549-555.

Meddaugh, D. (1993). Covert elder abuse in the nursing home. *Journal of Elder Abuse & Neglect, 5,* 21-37.

"Megan's Laws" face legal challenges by sex offenders. (1996). *News, Media, and the Law, 20,* 21-22.

Mehrabian, A., & Epstein, N. (1972). A measure of emotional empathy. *Journal of Personality, 40,* 525-543.

Meichenbaum, D. (1977). *Cognitive behavior modification: An integrative approach.* New York: Plenum.

Meiselman, L. (1978). *Incest: A psychological study of causes and effects with treatment recommendations.* San Francisco: Jossey-Bass.

Meuenzenmaier, K., Meyer, I., Struening, E., & Ferber, J. (1993). Childhood abuse and neglect among women outpatients with chronic mental illness. *Hospital and Community Psychiatry, 44,* 666-670.

Meyer, D. (1996). *Social psychology* (5th ed.). New York: McGraw-Hill.

Meyer, W., Walker, P., Emory, L., & Smith, E. (1985). Physical, metabolic and hormonal effects on men of long-term therapy with medroxyprogesterone acetate. *Fertility and Sterility, 43,* 102-109.

Miletski, H. (1995). *Mother-son incest: The unthinkable broken taboo.* Brandon, VT: Safer Society Press.

Miller, D. (1983). *For your own good: Hidden cruelty in child-rearing and the roots of violence.* New York: Free Press.

Miller, D., McCluskey-Fawcett, K., & Irving, L. (1993). The relationship between childhood sexual abuse and subsequent onset of bulimia nervosa. *Child Abuse & Neglect, 17,* 305-314.

Miller, D., & Porter, C. (1983). Self-blame in victims of violence. *Journal of Social Issues, 39,* 139-152.

Miller, L. (1994). Traumatic brain injury and aggression. *Journal of Offender Services, Counseling, and Rehabilitation, 21,* 91-103.

Mills, L. (1996). Empowering battered women transnationally: The case for postmodern interventions. *Social Work, 41,* 261-268.

Mills, T. (1985). The assault on the self: Stages in coping with a battering husband. *Qualitative Sociology, 8,* 103-123.

Milner, J. (1993). Social information processing and physical child abuse. *Clinical Psychology Review, 143,* 275-294.

Milner, J., Halsey, L., & Fultz, J. (1995). Empathic responsiveness and affective reactivity to infant stimuli in high- and low-risk for physical child abuse mothers. *Child Abuse & Neglect, 19,* 767-780.

Miltenberger, R., & Thiesse-Duffy, E. (1988). Evaluation of home-based programs for teaching personal safety skills to children. *Journal of Applied Behavior Analysis, 21,* 81-87.

Mintz, A. (1946). A reexamination of correlations between lynchings and economic indices. *Journal of Abnormal and Social Psychology, 46,* 154-160.

Mixson, P. (1995). An adult protective service perspective. *Journal of Elder Abuse & Neglect, 7,* 69-87.

Moeller, T., Bachmann, G., & Moeller, J. (1993). The combined effects of physical, sexual, and emotional abuse during childhood: Long-term health consequences for women. *Child Abuse & Neglect, 17,* 623-640.

Moisan, P., Sanders-Phillips, K., & Moisan, P. (1997). Ethnic differences in circumstances of abuse and symptoms of depression and anger among sexually abused Black and Latino boys. *Child Abuse & Neglect, 21,* 473-488.

Monk, A., Kaye, L., & Litwin, H. (1984). *Resolving grievances in the nursing home: A study of the ombudsman program.* New York: Columbia University Press.

Moos, R., & Lemke, S. (1983). Assessing and improving social-ecological settings. In E. Seidman (Ed.), *Handbook of social intervention* (pp. 143-162). Beverly Hills, CA: Sage.

Mullen, P., Martin, J., Anderson, J., Romans, S., & Herbison, G. (1996). The long-term impact of the physical, emotional, and sexual abuse of children: A community study. *Child Abuse & Neglect, 20,* 7-21.

Murphy, J., Jellinek, M., Quinn, D., Smith, G., Poitrast, F., & Goshko, M. (1991). Substance abuse and serious child mistreatment: Prevalence, risk, and outcome in a court sample. *Child Abuse & Neglect, 15,* 197-211.

Nance, J. (1975). *The gentle Tasaday: A stone age people in the Philippine rain forest.* New York: Harcourt Brace Jovanovich.

National Center on Child Abuse and Neglect. (1988a). *Study findings: Study of national incidence and prevalence of child abuse and neglect, 1988* (DHHS Publication No. 20-01093). Washington, DC: Government Printing Office.

National Center on Child Abuse and Neglect. (1988b). *Executive summary: Study of national incidence and prevalence of child abuse and neglect, 1988* (DHHS Publication No. 20-01095). Washington, DC: Government Printing Office.

National Coalition Against Domestic Violence. (1995). [Membership and other information available from the coalition at P.O. Box 18749, Denver, CO 80218-0749.]

National Institute of Mental Health. (1982). *Television and behavior: Ten years of sci-*

entific progress and implications for the eighties (Vols. 1-2). Rockville, MD: Author.

National Resource Center on Child Abuse and Neglect. (1995). *Childhood fatalities due to child abuse and neglect: Information sheet.* Englewood, CO: Author.

Navarre, E. (1987). Psychological maltreatment: The core component of child abuse. In M. Brassard, R. Germain, & S. Hart (Eds.), *Psychological maltreatment* (pp. 45-56). Elmsford, NY: Pergamon.

Neale, A., Hwalek, M., Scott, R., Sengstock, M., & Stahl, C. (1991). Validation of the Hwalek-Sengstock Elder Abuse Screening Test. *Journal of Applied Gerontology, 10,* 406-418.

Needleman, H. (1996). Bone lead levels and delinquent behavior. *Journal of the American Medical Association, 275*(5), 363-369.

Neidig, P. (1986). The development and evaluation of a spouse abuse treatment program in a military setting. *Evaluation and Program Planning, 9,* 275-280.

Neidig, P., & Friedman, D. (1984). *Spouse abuse: A treatment program for couples.* Champaign, IL: Research Press.

Nelki, J., & Watters, J. (1989). A group for sexually abused young children: Unraveling the web. *Child Abuse & Neglect, 13,* 369-377.

Nelson, H., Huber, R., & Walter, K. (1995). The relationship between volunteer long-term care ombudsmen and regulatory nursing home actions. *The Gerontologist, 15,* 509-514.

Netting, F., Huber, R., Patton, R., & Kautz, J. (1995). Elder rights and the long-term care ombudsman program. *Social Work, 40,* 351-357.

Netting, F., Patton, R., & Huber, R. (1992). The long-term care ombudsman program: What does the complaint reporting system tell us? *The Gerontologist, 32,* 843-848.

Ney, P., Fung, T., & Wickett, A. (1994). The worst combination of child abuse and neglect. *Child Abuse & Neglect, 18,* 705-714.

Nibert, D., Cooper, S., & Ford, J. (1989). Parents' observations of the effect of a sexual-abuse prevention program on preschool children. *Child Welfare, 68,* 539-546.

Nurse, S. (1964). Familial patterns of parents who abuse their children. *Smith College Studies in Social Work, 35,* 11-25.

O'Brien, J. (1971). Violence in divorce-prone families. *Journal of Marriage and the Family, 33,* 692-698.

O'Brien, M. (1991). Taking sibling incest seriously. In M. Patton (Ed.), *Family sexual abuse: Frontline research and evaluation* (pp. 75-92). Newbury Park, CA: Sage.

O'Farrell, T., & Choquette, K. (1991). Marital violence in the year before and after spouse-involved alcoholism treatment. *Family Dynamics of Addiction Quarterly, 1,* 32-40.

O'Keefe, M. (1995). Predictors of child abuse in maritally violent families. *Journal of Interpersonal Violence, 10,* 3-25.

O'Leary, M., & Dengerink, H. (1973). Aggression as a function of intensity and pattern of attack. *Journal of Experimental Research in Personality, 7,* 61-70.

O'Neill, K., & Gupta, K. (1991). Posttraumatic stress disorder in women who were victims of childhood sexual abuse. *Irish Journal of Psychological Medicine, 8,* 124-127.

Olafson, E., Corwin, D., & Summit, R. (1993). Modern history of child sexual abuse awareness: Cycles of discovery and suppression. *Child Abuse & Neglect, 17,* 7-24.

Oliver, J., & Taylor, A. (1971). Five generations of ill-treated children in one family pedigree. *British Journal of Psychiatry, 119,* 473-480.

Oltmanns, T., Broderick, J., & O'Leary, K. (1977). Marital adjustment and the efficacy of behavior therapy with children. *Journal of Consulting and Clinical Psychology, 45,* 724-729.

Orava, T., McLeod, P., & Sharpe, D. (1996). Perceptions of control, depressive symptomatology, and self-esteem of women in transition from abusive relationships. *Journal of Family Violence, 11,* 167-186.

Ozawa, M. (1995). The economic status of vulnerable older women. *Social Work, 40,* 323-331.

Page, M., & Scheidt, R. (1971). The elusive weapons effect: Demand awareness, evaluation apprehension, and slightly sophisticated subjects. *Journal of Personality and Social Psychology, 20,* 304-318.

Pagelow, M. (1981). *Women battering: Victims and their experiences.* Beverly Hills, CA: Sage.

Paik, H., & Comstock, G. (1994). The effects of television violence on antisocial behavior: A meta-analysis. *Communication Research, 21,* 516-546.

Parke, R., & Collmer, C. (1975). Child abuse: An interdisciplinary analysis. In E. Hetherington (Ed.), *Child development research* (pp. 509-590). Chicago: University of Chicago Press.

Parker, R. (1993). The effects of context on alcohol and violence. *Alcohol, Health & Research World, 17,* 117-122.

Pate, A., & Hamilton, E. (1992). Formal and informal deterrents to domestic violence: The Dade County spouse assault experiment. *American Sociological Review, 57,* 691-697.

Patterson, G. (1979). A performance theory for coercive family interaction. In R. Cairns (Ed.), *The analysis of social interactions: Methods, issues, and illustrations* (pp. 119-162). Hillsdale, NJ: Lawrence Erlbaum.

Patterson, G. (1982). *Coercive family process.* Eugene, OR: Castalia.

Patton, R., Huber, R., & Netting, F. (1994). The long-term care ombudsman program and complaints of abuse and neglect: What have we learned? *Journal of Elder Abuse & Neglect, 6,* 97-115.

Paulson, M., & Chaleff, A. (1973). Parent surrogate roles: A dynamic concept in understanding and treating abusive parents. *Journal of Clinical and Consulting Child Psychology, 38,* 129-134.

Payne, B., & Cikovic, R. (1995). An empirical examination of the characteristics, consequences, and causes of elder abuse in nursing homes. *Journal of Elder Abuse & Neglect, 7,* 61-74.

Pazeva, G., Cohen, D., Eisdorfer, C., Freels, S., Semla, T., Ashford, J. W., Gorelick, P., Hirschman, R., Luchins, D., & Levy, P. (1992). Severe family violence and Alzheimer's disease: Prevalence and risk factors. *The Gerontologist, 32,* 493-497.

Pearlman, S. (1989). Distancing and connectedness: Impact on couple formation in lesbian relationships. *Women and Therapy, 8,* 77-88.

Pence, E., & Paymar, M. (1992). *Power and control tactics of men who batter.* New York: Springer.

Penhale, B. (1993). The abuse of elderly people: Considerations for practice. *British Journal of Social Work, 23,* 95-112.

Penrod, S. (1986). *Social psychology.* Englewood Cliffs, NJ: Prentice Hall.

Peretti, P., & Majecen, K. (1991). Emotional abuse among the elderly: Affecting behavior variables. *Social Behavior and Personality, 19,* 255-261.

Perez, C., & Widom, C. (1994). Childhood victimization and long-term intellectual and academic outcomes. *Child Abuse & Neglect, 18,* 617-633.

Peters, D., & Range, L. (1995). Childhood sexual abuse and current suicidality in college women and men. *Child Abuse & Neglect, 19,* 335-341.

Peters, J. (1976). Children who are victims of sexual assault and the psychology of offenders. *American Journal of Psychotherapy, 30,* 598-642.

Peterson, L., Gable, S., & Saldana, L. (1996). Treatment of maternal addiction to prevent child abuse and neglect. *Addictive Behaviors, 21,* 789-801.

Petrik, N., Gildersleeve-High, L., McEllistrem, J., & Subotnik, L. (1994). The reduction of male abusiveness as a result of treatment: Reality or myth? *Journal of Family Violence, 9,* 307-316.

Petrik, N., Petrik, R., & Subotnik, L. (1994). Powerlessness and the need to control. *Journal of Interpersonal Violence, 9,* 278-285.

Petronio, S., Reeder, H., Hecht, M., & Ros-Mendoza, T. (1996). Disclosure of sexual abuse by children and adolescents. *Journal of Applied Communication Research, 24,* 181-199.

Pfouts, J. (1978). Violent families: Coping responses of abused wives. *Child Welfare, 57,* 101-111.

Phillips, D. (1974). Suicide, motor vehicle fatalities, and the mass media: Evidence toward a theory of suggestion. *American Sociological Review, 39,* 340-354.

Phillips, D. (1983). The impact of mass media violence on U.S. homicides. *American Sociological Review, 48,* 560-568.

Phillips, D., & Hensley, J. (1984). When violence is rewarded or punished: The impact of mass media stories on homicide. *Journal of Communication, 34,* 101-116.

Pillemer, K. (1988). Maltreatment of patients in nursing homes: Overview and research agenda. *Journal of Health and Social Behavior, 29,* 227-238.

Pillemer, K., & Bachman-Prehn, R. (1991). Helping and hurting: Predictors of maltreatment of patients in nursing homes. *Research on Aging, 13,* 74-95.

Pillemer, K., & Finkelhor, D. (1988). The prevalence of elder abuse: A random sample survey. *The Gerontologist, 28,* 51-57.

Pillemer, K., & Finkelhor, D. (1989). Causes of elder abuse: Caregiver stress versus problem relatives. *Journal of Orthopsychiatry, 59,* 179-187.

Pillemer, K., & Moore, D. (1989). Abuse of patients in nursing homes: Findings from a survey of staff. *The Gerontologist, 29,* 314-320.

Pillemer, K., & Suitor, J. (1992). Violence and violent feelings: What causes them among family caregivers? *Journal of Gerontology: Social Sciences, 47,* S165-S172.

Pittaway, E. (1995). Risk factors for abuse and neglect among older adults. *Canadian Journal on Aging, 14,* 20-44.

Pittaway, E., Westhues, A., & Peressini, T. (1995). Risk factors for abuse and neglect among older adults. *Canadian Journal on Aging, 14,* 20-44.

Popple, P., & Leighninger, L. (1996). *Social work, social welfare, and American society* (3rd ed.). Boston: Allyn & Bacon.

Porter, B., & O'Leary, K. D. (1980). Marital discord and childhood behavior problems. *Journal of Abnormal Child Psychology, 8,* 287-295.

Potter-Efron, R., & Potter-Efron, P. (1985). Family violence as a treatment issue with chemically dependent adolescents. *Alcoholism Treatment Quarterly, 2,* 1-5.

Powell, S., & Berg, R. (1987). When the elderly are abused: Characteristics and intervention. *Educational Gerontology, 13,* 71-83.

Powers, R., & Kutash, I. (1978). Substance-induced aggression. In I. Kutash, S. Kutash, & L. Schlesinger (Eds.), *Violence perspectives on murder and aggression* (pp. 317-342). San Francisco: Jossey-Bass.

Pratt, C., Koval, J., & Lloyd, S. (1983). Service workers' responses to abuse of the elderly. *Social Casework: The Journal of Contemporary Social Work, 64,* 147-153.

Proctor, E., & Davis, L. (1994). The challenge of racial difference: Skills for clinical practice. *Social Work, 39,* 314-323.

Ragg, D. (1991). Differential group programming for children exposed to spouse abuse. *Journal of Child and Youth Care, 5,* 59-75.

Ragg, D., & Webb, C. (1992). Group treatment for the preschool child witness of spouse abuse. *Journal of Child and Youth Care, 7,* 1-19.

Raleigh, M., McGuire, M., Brammer, G., & Pollack, D. (1991). Serotonergic mechanisms promote dominance acquisitions in adult male vervet monkeys. *Brain Research, 559,* 181-190.

Ramsey-Klawsnik, H. (1991). Elder sexual abuse: Preliminary findings. *Journal of Elder Abuse & Neglect, 3,* 73-90.

Ramsey-Klawsnik, H. (1993a). Interviewing elders for suspected sexual abuse: Guidelines and techniques. *Journal of Elder Abuse & Neglect, 5,* 5-18.

Ramsey-Klawsnik, H. (1993b). Recognizing and responding to elder maltreatment. *Pride Institute Journal of Long Term Home Health Care, 12,* 12-20.

Ramsey-Klawsnik, H. (1995). Investigating suspected elder maltreatment. *Journal of Elder Abuse & Neglect, 7,* 41-67.

Raven, B., & Rubin, J. (1983). *Social psychology* (2nd ed.). New York: John Wiley.

Reese-Dukes, J., & Reese-Dukes, C. (1983). Pairs for pairs: A theoretical base for cotherapy as a nonsexist process in couples counseling. *Personnel and Guidance Journal, 62,* 99-101.

Reid, J., Taplin, P., & Lorber, R. (1981). A social interactional approach to the treatment of abusive families. In R. Stuart (Ed.), *Violent behavior: Social learning approaches to prediction, management and treatment* (pp. 83-101). New York: Brunner/Mazel.

Reid, K., Mathews, G., & Liss, P. (1995). My partner is hurting: Group work with male partners and adult survivors of sexual abuse. *Social Work With Groups, 18,* 81-87.

Reis, M., & Nahmiash, D. (1995). When seniors are abused: An intervention model. *The Gerontologist, 35,* 666-671.

Renzetti, C. (1992). *Violent betrayal: Partner abuse in lesbian relationships.* Newbury Park, CA: Sage.

Reschly, D., & Graham-Clay, S. (1987). Psychological abuse from prejudice and cultural bias. In M. Brassard, R. Germain, & S. Hart (Eds.), *Psychological maltreatment of children and youth* (pp. 137-145). Elmsford, NY: Pergamon.

Ridley, M. (Ed.). (1987). *The Darwin reader.* New York: Norton.

Rivers, P. (1994). *Alcohol and human behavior.* Englewood Cliffs, NJ: Prentice Hall.

Roberts, A. (1987). Psychosocial characteristics of batterers: A study of 234 men charged with domestic violence offenses. *Journal of Family Violence, 2,* 81-93.

Roberts, A. (1988). Substance abuse among men who batter their mates: The dangerous mix. *Journal of Substance Abuse Treatment, 5,* 83-87.

Roberts, A. (1996a). Battered women who kill: A comparative study of incarcerated participants with a community sample of battered women. *Journal of Family Violence, 11,* 291-304.

Roberts, A. (Ed.). (1996b). *Helping battered women: New perspectives and remedies.* New York: Oxford University Press.

Robinson, J. (1989). Clinical treatment of Black families: Issues and strategies. *Social Work, 33,* 323-329.

Rodriguez, C., & Green, A. (1997). Parenting stress and anger expression as predictors of child abuse potential. *Child Abuse & Neglect, 21,* 367-377.

Rodriguez, N., Kemp, H., Ryan, S., & Foy, D. (1997). Posttraumatic stress disorder in adult female survivors of childhood sexual abuse: A comparison study. *Journal of Consulting and Clinical Psychology, 65,* 53-59.

Rodriguez, N., Ryan, S., Rowan, A., & Foy, D. (1996). Posttraumatic stress disorder in a clinical sample of adult survivors of childhood sexual abuse. *Child Abuse & Neglect, 20,* 943-952.

Rosenbaum, A. (1986). Group treatment for abusive men: Process and outcome. *Psychotherapy, 23,* 607-612.

Rosenbaum, A., & O'Leary, K. D. (1981a). Children: The unintended victims of marital violence. *American Journal of Orthopsychiatry, 51,* 692-699.

Rosenbaum, A., & O'Leary, K. D. (1981b). Marital violence: Characteristics of abusive couples. *Journal of Consulting and Clinical Psychology, 49,* 63-71.

Rosenbaum, A., Hoge, S., Adelman, S., Warnken, W., Fletcher, K., & Kane, R. (1994). Head injury in partner-abusive men. *Journal of Clinical & Consulting Psychology, 62,* 1187-1193.

Rosencrans, B. (1997). *The last secret: Daughters sexually abused by mothers.* Brandon, VT: Safer Society Press.

Rosenstein, P. (1995). Parental levels of empathy as related to risk assessment in child protective services. *Child Abuse & Neglect, 19,* 1349-1360.

Ross, S. (1996). Risk of physical abuse to children of spouse-abusing parents. *Child Abuse & Neglect, 20,* 589-598.

Rouse, L. (1984). Models, self-esteem, and locus of control as factors contributing to spouse abuse. *Victimology, 9,* 130-141.

Rowan, A., Foy, D., Rodriquez, N., & Ryan, S. (1994). Posttraumatic stress disorder in a clinical sample of adults sexually abused as children. *Child Abuse & Neglect, 18,* 51-61.

Roy, A., & Linnoila, M. (1989). CSF studies on alcoholism and related behaviors. *Progress in Neuro Psychopharmacology and Biological Psychiatry, 13,* 505-511.

Roy, M. (1982). *The abusive partner: An analysis of domestic battering.* New York: Van Nostrand.

Roys, D., & Timms, R. (1995). Personality profiles of adult males sexually molested by their maternal caregivers: Preliminary findings. *Journal of Child Sexual Abuse, 4,* 63-77.

Royse, D. (1995). *Research methods in social work.* Chicago: Nelson-Hall.

Rudin, M., Zalewski, C., & Bodmer-Turner, J. (1995). Characteristics of child sexual abuse victims according to perpetrator gender. *Child Abuse & Neglect, 19,* 963-973.

Rush, F. (1980). *The best kept secret.* New York: Prentice Hall.

Rushton, J., Fulker, D., Neale, M., Nias, D., & Eysenck, H. (1986). Altruism and aggression: The heritability of individual differences. *Journal of Personality and Social Psychology, 50,* 1192-1198.

Russell, D. (1986). *The secret trauma.* New York: Basic Books.

Russell, D. (1990). *Rape in marriage.* Bloomington: Indiana University Press.

Ruth, S. (1995). *Issues in feminism* (3rd ed.). Mountain View, CA: Mayfield.

Rutter, M. (1978). Family, area, and school influences in the genesis of conduct disorders. In L. Hersov & D. Schaffer (Eds.), *Aggression and antisocial behavior in childhood and adolescence* (pp. 95-114). Oxford, England: Pergamon.

Rutter, M. (1980). Protective factors in children's responses to stress and disadvantage. In M. Kent & J. Rolf (Eds.), *Primary prevention of psychopathology: Vol. 3. Promoting social competence and coping in children* (pp. 49-74). Hanover, NH: University Press of New England.

Ryan, E., Hamilton, J., & See, S. (1995). Patronizing the old: How do younger and older adults respond to baby talk in the nursing home? *International Journal of Aging and Human Development, 39,* 21-32.

Ryan, K. (1995). Do courtship-violent men have characteristics associated with a "battering personality"? *Journal of Family Violence, 10,* 99-120.

Ryan, L. (1977). *Clinical interpretation of the FIRO-B.* Palo Alto, CA: Consulting Psychologists Press.

Sabotta, E., & Davis, R. (1992). Fatality after report to a child abuse registry in Washington state, 1973-1986. *Child Abuse & Neglect, 16,* 627-635.

Salmon, M., & Atkinson, V. (1992). Characteristics of adult protective services social workers. *Journal of Elder Abuse & Neglect, 4,* 101-121.

Sampson, E. (1991). *Social worlds, personal lives: An introduction to social psychology.* New York: Harcourt Brace Jovanovich.

Sanchez, Y. (1996). Distinguishing cultural expectations in assessment of financial exploitation. *Journal of Elder Abuse & Neglect, 8,* 49-59.

Sarwar, D., & Durlak, J. (1996). Childhood sexual abuse as a predictor of adult female sexual dysfunction: A study of couples seeking sex therapy. *Child Abuse & Neglect, 20,* 963-972.

Sas, G., Brown, J., & Lent, B. (1994). Detecting woman abuse in family practice. *Canadian Family Physician, 40,* 861-864.

Sato, R., & Heiby, E. (1992). Correlates of depressive symptoms among battered women. *Journal of Family Violence, 7,* 229-245.

Saul, L. (1972). Personal and social psychopathology and the primary prevention of violence. *American Journal of Psychiatry, 128,* 1578-1581.

Saunders, D. (1988). Wife abuse, husband abuse, or mutual combat? A feminist perspective on the empirical findings. In K. Yllö & M. Bograd (Eds.), *Feminist perspectives on wife abuse* (pp. 90-113). Newbury Park, CA: Sage.

Saunders, D. (1994). Child custody decisions in families experiencing woman abuse. *Social Work, 39,* 51-59.

Saunders, D. (1995). The tendency to arrest victims of domestic violence: A preliminary analysis of officer characteristics. *Journal of Interpersonal Violence, 10,* 147-158.

Saunders, E. (1991). Rorschach indicators of chronic childhood sexual abuse in female borderline patients. *Bulletin of the Menninger Clinic, 55,* 48-71.

Schechter, S. (1982). *Women and male violence: The visions and the struggles of the battered women's movement.* Boston: South End Press.

Schiffer, M. (1984). *Children's group therapy: Methods and case histories.* New York: Free Press.

Schulman, J., Lorion, R., Kupst, M., & Schwarcz, L. (1991). A prevention approach to enhancing positive parenting: Preliminary steps in program development. *Journal of Community Psychology, 19,* 254-265.

Schutz, W. (1978). *The FIRO awareness scales manual.* Palo Alto, CA: Consulting Psychologists Press.

Scott, R., & Day, H. (1996). Association of abuse-related symptoms and style of anger expression for female survivors of childhood incest. *Journal of Interpersonal Violence, 11,* 208-220.

Seaver, C. (1996). Muted lives: Older battered women. *Journal of Elder Abuse & Neglect, 8,* 3-21.

Sengstock, M. (1991). Sex and gender implications in cases of elder abuse. *Journal of Women & Aging, 3,* 25-43.

Sengstock, M., & Barrett, S. (1986). Elderly victims of family abuse, neglect, and maltreatment: Can legal assistance help? *Journal of Gerontological Social Work, 9,* 43-61.

Sengstock, M., & Hwalek, M. (1986). Domestic abuse of the elderly: Which cases involve the police? *Journal of Interpersonal Violence, 1,* 335-349.

Sengstock, M., & Liang, J. (1982). *Identifying and characterizing elder abuse.* Detroit, MI: Wayne State University, Institute of Gerontology.

Sermabeikian, P., & Martinez, D. (1994). Treatment of adolescent sexual offenders: Theory-based practice. *Child Abuse & Neglect, 18,* 969-976.

Sgroi, S. (1989a). Community-based treatment for sexual offenders against children. In S. Sgroi (Ed.), *Vulnerable populations* (Vol. 2, pp. 351-393). Lexington, MA: Lexington Books.

Sgroi, S. (1989b). Healing together: Peer group therapy for adult survivors of child sexual abuse. In S. Sgroi (Ed.), *Vulnerable populations* (Vol. 2, pp. 131-166). Lexington, MA: Lexington Books.

Sgroi, S. (1989c). Stages of recovery for adult survivors of child sexual abuse. In S. Sgroi (Ed.), *Vulnerable populations* (Vol. 2, pp. 111-130). Lexington, MA: Lexington Books.

Sgroi, S., & Bunk, B. (1988). A clinical approach to adult survivors of child sexual abuse. In S. Sgroi (Ed.), *Vulnerable populations* (Vol. 1, pp. 137-186). Lexington, MA: Lexington, Books.

Sgroi, S., Bunk, B., & Wabrek, C. (1988). Children's sexual behaviors and their relationship to sexual abuse. In S. Sgroi (Ed.), *Vulnerable populations* (Vol. 1, pp. 137-186). Lexington, MA: Lexington Books.

Shen, F. (1995, March 10). Battered women find insurers shun them. *Lexington Herald Leader,* pp. 1, 9.

Shepard, M. (1992). Predicting batterer recidivism five years after community intervention. *Journal of Family Violence, 7,* 167-178.

Shepard, M., & Pence, E. (1988). The effect of battering on the employment status of women. *Affilia, 3,* 55-61.

Sherman, L., & Berk, R. (1984). The specific deterrent effects of arrest for domestic assault. *American Sociological Review, 49,* 261-272.

Shields, N., & Hanneke, C. (1992). Comparing the psychological impact of battering, marital rape and stranger rape. *Clinical Sociology Review, 10,* 151-169.

Showers, J. (1992). "Don't shake the baby": The effectiveness of a prevention program. *Child Abuse & Neglect, 16,* 11-18.

Silbert, M., & Pines, A. (1983). Early sexual exploitation as an influence in prostitution. *Social Work, 2,* 285-289.

Silver, L., Dublin, C., & Lourie, R. (1969). Does violence breed violence? Contributions from a study of the child abuse syndrome. *American Journal of Psychiatry, 126,* 404-407.

Silverman, A., Reinherz, H., & Giaconia, R. (1996). The long-term sequelae of child and adolescent abuse: A longitudinal community study. *Child Abuse & Neglect, 20,* 709-723.

Silvern, L., & Kaersvang, L. (1989). The traumatized children of violent marriages. *Child Welfare, 4,* 421-436.

Simmons, K., Sack, T., & Miller, G. (1996). Sexual abuse and chemical dependency: Implications for women in recovery. *Women & Therapy, 19,* 17-30.

Simon, L., Sales, B., Kaszniak, A., & Kahn, M. (1992). Characteristics of child molesters: Implications for the fixated-regressed dichotomy. *Journal of Interpersonal Violence, 7,* 211-225.

Simpson, A. (1988). Vulnerability and the age of female consent: Legal innovation and its effect on prosecutions for rape in eighteenth-century London. In G. Rousseau & R. Porter (Eds.), *Sexual underworlds of the Enlightenment* (pp. 181-205). Chapel Hill: University of North Carolina Press.

Sinclair, J., Larzelere, R., Paine, M., Jones, P., Graham, K., & Jones, M. (1995). Outcome of group treatment for sexually abused adolescent females living in a group home setting. *Journal of Interpersonal Violence, 10,* 533-542.

Sirles, E., & Franke, P. (1989). Factors influencing mothers' reactions to intrafamily sexual abuse. *Child Abuse & Neglect, 13,* 131-140.

Smiljanich, K., & Briere, J. (1996). Self-reported sexual interest in children: Sex differences and psychosocial correlates in a university sample. *Violence and Victims, 11,* 39-50.

Smith, H., & Israel, E. (1987). Sibling incest: A study of the dynamics of 25 cases. *Child Abuse & Neglect, 11,* 101-108.

Smith, M. (1990). Patriarchal ideology and wife beating: A test of a feminist hypothesis. *Violence and Victims, 5,* 257-273.

Smith, R. (1995, September). What to do with the serial abuse? *NASW News,* p. 3.

Smith, S., & Meyer, R. (1984). Child abuse reporting laws and psychotherapy. *American Journal of Law and Psychiatry, 7,* 351-366.

Smucker, M., Craighead, W., Craighead, L., & Green, B. (1986). Normative and reliability data for the Children's Depression Inventory. *Journal of Abnormal Child Psychology, 14,* 25-39.

Snell, J., Rosenwald, R., & Robey, A. (1964). The wifebeater's wife. *Archives of General Psychiatry, 11,* 107-112.

Snyder, J. (1994). Emergency department protocols for domestic violence. *Journal of Emergency Nursing, 20,* 65-68.

Sorensen, T., & Snow, B. (1991). How children tell: The process of disclosure in child sexual abuse. *Child Welfare, 70,* 3-15.

Spaccarelli, S., Sandler, I., & Roosa, M. (1994). History of spouse violence against mother: Correlated risks and unique effects in child mental health. *Journal of Family Violence, 9,* 79-95.

Spiegel, J. (1968). The resolution of role conflict within the family. In N. Bell & E. Vogel (Eds.), *A modern introduction to the family* (pp. 391-411). New York: Free Press.

Sprenkle, D. (1994). Wife abuse through the lens of "systems theory." *The Counseling Psychologist, 22,* 598-602.

Stacey, W., & Shupe, A. (1983). *The family secret.* Boston: Beacon.

Stack, A. (1993). Dentistry and family violence. *Journal of the Massachusetts Dental Society, 42,* 41-46.

Staff. (1994, April). SMS Board of Directors approves policy on reporting of domestic violence. The assessment and treatment of victims of domestic abuse: Model protocol. *Wisconsin Medical Journal,* pp. 178-181.

Stark, E., & Flitcraft, A. (1988). Women and children at risk: A feminist perspective on child abuse. *International Journal of Health Services, 18,* 97-118.

Stark, E., Flitcraft, A., & Frazier, W. (1979). Medicine and patriarchal violence: The social construction of a private event. *International Journal of Health Services, 9,* 461-492.

Steele, B. (1975). Working with abusive parents: A psychiatrist's view. *Children Today, 4,* 3.

Steinberg, L., Catalano, R., & Dooley, D. (1981). Economic antecedents of child abuse and neglect. *Child Development, 52,* 975-985.

Steinmetz, S. (1977). *The cycle of violence: Assertive, aggressive and abusive family interaction.* New York: Praeger.

Steinmetz, S. (1977-1978). The battered husband syndrome. *Victimology, 2,* 499-509.

Steinmetz, S. (1988). *Duty bound: Elder abuse and family care.* Newbury Park, CA: Sage.

Stets, J., & Straus, M. (1989). The marriage license as a hitting license: A comparison of assaults in dating, cohabiting, and married couples. *Journal of Family Violence, 4,* 161-180.

Stevens, M. (1994). Stopping domestic violence: More answers and more questions needed. *The Counseling Psychologist, 22,* 587-592.

Steward, M., Farquhar, L., Dicharry, D., Glick, D., & Martin, P. (1986). Group therapy: A treatment of choice for young victims of child abuse. *International Journal of Group Psychotherapy, 36,* 261-277.

Stith, S. (1990). Police response to domestic violence: The influence of individuals and familial factors. *Victims and Violence, 5,* 37-49.

Stith, S., & Farley, S. (1993). A predictive model of male spousal violence. *Journal of Family Violence, 8,* 183-201.

Stout, K. (1991). Intimate femicide: A national demographic overview. *Journal of Interpersonal Violence, 6,* 476-485.

Straus, M. (1980). Victims and aggressors in marital violence. *American Behavioral Scientist, 23,* 681-704.

Straus, M. (1990). Injury and frequency of assault and the "representative sample fallacy" in measuring wife beating and child abuse. In M. Straus & R. Gelles (Eds.), *Physical violence in American families: Risk factors and adaptations to violence in 8,145 families* (pp. 75-91). New Brunswick, NJ: Transaction Books.

Straus, M. (1993). Physical assaults by wives: A major social problem. In R. Gelles & D. Loseke (Eds.), *Current controversies on family violence* (pp. 67-87). Newbury Park, CA: Sage.

Straus, M. (1994). *Beating the devil out of them: Corporal punishment in American families and its effect on children.* Boston: Lexington Press.

Straus, M., & Kaufman-Kantor, G. (1994). Corporal punishment by parents of adolescents: A risk factor in the epidemiology of depression, suicide, alcohol abuse, and wife beating. *Adolescence, 29,* 543-562.

Straus, M., Gelles, R., & Steinmetz, S. (1980). *Behind closed doors: Violence in the American family.* Garden City, NY: Anchor.

Suh, E., & Abel, E. (1990). The impact of spousal violence on the children of the abused. *Journal of Independent Social Work, 4,* 27-34.

Sullivan, C. (1991). The provision of advocacy services to women leaving abusive partners. *Journal of Interpersonal Violence, 6,* 41-54.

Sullivan, C., Basta, J., Tan, C., & Davidson, W. (1992). After the crisis: A needs assessment of women leaving a domestic violence shelter. *Violence and Victims, 7,* 267-275.

Sullivan, J., & Mosher, D. (1990). Acceptance of guided imagery of marital rape as a function of macho personality. *Violence and Victims, 5,* 275-286.

Summit, R. (1983). Child sexual abuse accommodation syndrome. *Child Abuse & Neglect, 7,* 177-193.

Summit, R., & Kryso, J. (1978). Sexual abuse of children: A clinical spectrum. *American Journal of Orthopsychiatry, 48,* 237-251.

Sutphen, R., Wiehe, V., & Leukefeld, C. (1996, September). *Dual violence families: The relationship between spouse abuse, child abuse and substance abuse.* Paper presented at the National Conference on Child Abuse and Neglect, Washington, DC.

Swoboda, J., Elwork, A., Sales, B., & Levine, D. (1978). Knowledge of and compliance with privileged communication and child abuse reporting laws. *Professional Psychology, 9,* 449-457.

Szinovacz, M. (1983). Using couple data as a methodological tool: The case of marital violence. *Journal of Marriage and the Family, 45,* 633-644.

Tanner, D. (1978). *The lesbian couple.* Lexington, MA: D. C. Heath.

Tatara, T. (1993). Understanding the nature and scope of domestic elder abuse with the use of state aggregate data: Summaries of the key findings of a national survey of state APS and aging agencies. *Journal of Elder Abuse & Neglect, 5,* 35-57.

Tatara, T., & Kuzmeskus, L. (1997). *Summaries of the statistical data on elder abuse in domestic settings for FY 95 and FY 96.* Washington, DC: National Center on Elder Abuse.

Taylor, H. G. (1994). Family violence and the community pharmacist. *American Pharmacy, NS34,* 41-44.

Taylor, S. (1967). Aggressive behavior and physiological arousal as a function of provocation and the tendency to inhibit aggression. *Journal of Personality and Social Psychology, 36,* 778-793.

Taylor, S., & Pisano, R. (1971). Physical aggression as a function of frustration and physical attack. *Journal of Social Psychology, 84,* 261-267.

Teets, J. (1995). Childhood sexual trauma of chemically dependent women. *Journal of Psychoactive Drugs, 27,* 231-238.

Tellis-Nayak, V., & Tellis-Nayak, M. (1989). Quality of care and the burden of two cultures: When the world of the nurse's aide enters the world of the nursing home. *The Gerontologist, 29,* 307-313.

Telzrow, C. (1987). Influence by negative and limiting models. In M. Brassard, R. Germain, & S. Hart (Eds.), *Psychological maltreatment of children and youth* (pp. 121-136). Elmsford, NY: Pergamon.

Thibaut, J., & Kelley, H. (1959). *The social psychology of groups.* New York: John Wiley.

Thomas, A., & Chess, S. (1977). *Temperament and development.* New York: Brunner/Mazel.

Thomas, B. (1994). Research considerations: Guardianship and the vulnerable elderly. *Journal of Gerontological Nursing, 20,* 10-16.

Thorn-Finch, R. (1992). *Ending the silence: The origins and treatment of male violence against women.* Toronto: University of Toronto Press.

Tierney, K., & Corwin, D. (1983). Exploring intrafamilial child sexual abuse: A systems approach. In D. Finkelhor, R. Gelles, G. Hotaling, & M. Straus (Eds.), *The dark side of families: Current family violence research* (pp. 102-116). Beverly Hills, CA: Sage.

Todres, R., & Bunston, T. (1993). Parent education program evaluation: A review of the literature. *Canadian Journal of Community Mental Health, 12,* 225-257.

Tomita, S. (1990). The denial of elder mistreatment by victims and abusers: The application of neutralization theory. *Violence and Victims, 5,* 171-184.

Trafford, A. (1991, February 26). Why battered women kill: Self-defense, not revenge is often the motive. *Washington Post,* p. 2.

Tsai, M., & Wagner, N. (1978). Therapy groups for women sexually molested as children. *Archives of Sexual Behavior, 7,* 417-427.

Turner, C., Layton, J., & Simons, L. (1975). Naturalistic studies of aggressive behavior: Aggressive stimuli, victim visibility, and horn honking. *Journal of Personality and Social Psychology, 31,* 1098-1107.

Turner, C., Simons, L., Berkowitz, L., & Frodi, A. (1977). The stimulating and inhibiting effects of weapons on aggressive behavior. *Aggressive Behavior, 3,* 355-378.

Turner, H., & Finkelhor, D. (1996). Corporal punishment as a stressor among youth. *Journal of Marriage and the Family, 58,* 155-166.

Tutty, L. (1992). The ability of elementary school children to learn child sexual abuse prevention concepts. *Child Abuse & Neglect, 16,* 369-384.

Tutty, L., Bidgood, B., & Rothery, M. (1993). Support groups for battered women: Research on their efficacy. *Journal of Family Violence, 8,* 325-343.

Tyson, P., & Sobschak, K. (1994). Perceptual responses to infant crying after EEG biofeedback assisted stress management training: Implications for physical child abuse. *Child Abuse & Neglect, 18,* 933-943.

Uzzell, O., & Peebles-Wilkins, W. (1989). Black spouse abuse: A focus on relational factors and intervention strategies. *Western Journal of Black Studies, 13,* 10-16.

Valentine, D., & Cash, T. (1986). A definitional discussion of elder maltreatment. *Journal of Gerontological Social Work, 9,* 17-28.

Vander Zanden, J. (1993). *Human development.* New York: Knopf.

Veltkamp, L., & Miller, T. (1990). Clinical strategies in recognizing spouse abuse. *Psychiatric Quarterly, 61,* 179-187.

Vinton, L. (1991). An exploratory study of self-neglectful elderly. *Journal of Gerontological Social Work, 18,* 55-67.

Virkkunen, M., & Linnoila, M. (1990). Serotonin in early onset, male alcoholics with violent behavior. *Annals of Medicine, 22,* 327-331.

Vissing, Y., Straus, M., Gelles, R., & Harrop, J. (1991). Verbal aggression by parents and psychosocial problems of children. *Child Abuse & Neglect, 15,* 223-238.

Waaland, P., & Keeley, S. (1985). Police decision-making in wife abuse: The impact of legal and extralegal factors. *Law and Human Behavior, 9,* 355-366.

Wager, J., & Rodway, M. (1995). An evaluation of a group treatment approach for children who have witnessed wife abuse. *Journal of Family Violence, 10,* 295-306.

Waldby, C., Clancy, A., Emetchi, J., & Summerfield, C. (1989). Theoretical perspectives on father-daughter incest. In E. Driver & A. Droisen (Eds.), *Child sexual abuse: A feminist reader* (pp. 88-106). New York: New York University Press.

Walker, E., Katon, W., Hansom, J., Harrop-Griffiths, J., Holm, L., Jones, M., Hickok, L., & Russo, J. (1995). Psychiatric diagnoses and sexual victimization in women with chronic pelvic pain. *Psychosomatics, 36,* 531-540.

Walker, L. (1979). *The battered woman.* New York: Harper & Row.

Walker, L. (1984). *The battered woman syndrome.* New York: Springer.

Walker, L. (1994). *Abused women and survivor therapy: A practical guide for the psychotherapist.* Washington, DC: American Psychological Association.

Waller, G. (1994). Childhood sexual abuse and borderline personality disorder in the eating disorders. *Child Abuse & Neglect, 18,* 97-101.

Walters, R., & Willows, D. (1968). Imitation behavior of disturbed children following exposure to aggressive and nonaggressive models. *Child Development, 39,* 79-91.

Wang, C., & Daro, D. (1997). *Current trends in child abuse reporting and fatalities: The results of the 1996 Annual Fifty-State Survey.* Chicago: National Committee to Prevent Child Abuse.

Warner, J., & Hansen, D. (1994). The identification and reporting of physical abuse by physicians: A review and implications for research. *Child Abuse & Neglect, 18,* 11-25.

Warnken, W., Rosenbaum, A., Fletcher, K., Hoge, S., & Adelman, S. (1994). Head-injured males: A population at risk for relationship aggression? *Violence and Victims, 9,* 153-166.

Warshaw, C. (1989). Limitations of the medical model in the care of battered women. *Gender & Society, 3,* 506-517.

Wasik, B., & Roberts, R. (1994). Survey of home visiting programs for abused and neglected children and their families. *Child Abuse & Neglect, 18,* 271-283.

Wasylkewycz, M. (1993). The Elder Abuse Resource Centre, a coordinated community response to elder abuse: One Canadian perspective. *Journal of Elder Abuse & Neglect, 5,* 21-33.

Watkins, C., Terrell, F., Miller, F., & Terrell, S. (1989). Cultural mistrust and its effects on expectational variables in Black client-White counselor relationships. *Journal of Counseling Psychology, 36,* 447-450.

Watkins, S. (1990). The Mary Ellen myth: Correcting child welfare history. *Social Work, 35,* 500-503.

Watson, M., Cesario, T., Ziemba, S., & McGovern, P. (1993). Elder abuse in long-term care environments: A pilot study using information from long-term care ombudsman reports in one California county. *Journal of Elder Abuse & Neglect, 5,* 95-111.

Waxman, H., Carner, E., & Berkenstock, G. (1984). Job turnover and job satisfaction among nursing home aides. *The Gerontologist, 24,* 503-509.

Webb, W. (1992). Treatment issues and cognitive behavior technique with battered women. *Journal of Family Violence, 7,* 205-217.

Weiner, A. (1991). A community-based education model for identification and prevention of elder abuse. *Journal of Gerontological Social Work, 16,* 107-119.

Weiss, B., Dodge, K., Bates, J., & Pettit, G. (1992). Some consequences of early harsh discipline: Child aggression and a maladaptive social information processing style. *Child Development, 63,* 1321-1335.

Wells, S., Stein, T., Fluke, J., & Downing, J. (1989). Screening in child protection services. *Social Service Research, 9,* 17-30.

Whatley, M. (1993). For better or worse: The case of marital rape. *Violence and Victims, 8,* 29-39.

Whipple, E., & Webster-Stratton, C. (1991). The role of parental stress in physically abusive families. *Child Abuse & Neglect, 15,* 279-291.

Whitbourne, S., Culgin, S., & Cassidy, E. (1995). Evaluation of infantilizing intonation and content of speech directed at the aged. *International Journal of Aging and Human Development, 41,* 109-116.

White, G., Katz, J., & Scarborough, K. (1992). The impact of professional football games upon violent assaults on women. *Violence and Victims, 7,* 157-171.

White, H., Brick, J., & Hansell, S. (1993). A longitudinal investigation of alcohol use and aggression in adolescence. *Journal of Studies on Alcohol,* Suppl. No. 11, 62-77.

Widom, C., Ireland, T., & Glynn, P. (1995). Alcohol abuse in abused and neglected children followed up: Are they at increased risk? *Journal of Studies on Alcohol, 56,* 207-217.

Wiehe, V. (1987). Empathy and locus of control in child abusers. *Journal of Social Service Research, 9,* 17-30.

Wiehe, V. (1989). Child abuse: An ecological perspective. In R. Pardeck (Ed.), *Child abuse and neglect: Theory, research and practice* (pp. 139-147). New York: Gordon & Breach.

Wiehe, V. (1990). Religious influence on parental attitudes toward the use of corporal punishment. *Journal of Family Violence, 5,* 173-186.

Wiehe, V. (1992). Abusive and nonabusive parents: How they were parented. *Journal of Social Service Research, 15,* 81-93.

Wiehe, V. (1996). *Working with child abuse and neglect: A primer.* Thousand Oaks, CA: Sage.

Wiehe, V. (1997a, April). *Multiple-violence families.* Paper presented at the Conference on Vulnerable Families, Seattle.

Wiehe, V. (1997b). *Sibling abuse: The hidden physical, emotional, and sexual trauma* (2nd ed.). Thousand Oaks, CA: Sage.

Wiehe, V., & Richards, A. (1995). *Intimate betrayal: The trauma of acquaintance rape.* Thousand Oaks, CA: Sage.

Wilber, K., & Reynolds, S. (1996). Introducing a framework for defining financial abuse of the elderly. *Journal of Elder Abuse & Neglect, 8,* 61-80.

Williams, H. (1997, March 26). End the domestic arms race. *Washington Post,* p. A19.

Williams, O. (1989). Spouse abuse: Social learning, attribution and interventions. *Journal of Health and Social Policy, 1,* 91-107.

Wilson, M., Raglioni, A., & Downing, D. (1989). Analyzing factors influencing readmission to a battered women's shelter. *Journal of Family Violence, 4,* 275-284.

Wilson, V. (1990). The consequences of elderly wives caring for disabled husbands: Implications for practice. *Social Work, 35,* 417-421.

Wind, T., & Silvern, L. (1994). Parenting and family stress as mediators of the long-term effects of child abuse. *Child Abuse & Neglect, 18,* 439-453.

Wodarski, J., Kurtz, P., Gaudin, J., & Howing, P. (1990). Maltreatment and the school-age child: Major academic, socioemotional and adaptive outcomes. *Social Work, 35,* 506-513.

Wolanin, M., & Phillips, L. (1981). *Confusion: Prevention and care.* St. Louis, MO: C. V. Mosby.

Wolf, R. (1988). Elder abuse: Ten years later. *Journal of the American Geriatrics Society, 36,* 758-762.

Wolf, R. (1992). Victimization of the elderly: Elder abuse and neglect. *Reviews in Clinical Gerontology, 2,* 269-276.

Wolf, R., Godkin, M., & Pillemer, K. (1986). Maltreatment of the elderly: A comparative analysis. *Pride Institute Journal of Long Term Home Health Care, 5,* 10-17.

Wolfner, G., & Gelles, R. (1993). A profile of violence toward children: A national study. *Child Abuse & Neglect, 17,* 197-212.

Wolock, I., & Magura, S. (1996). Parental substance abuse as a predictor of child maltreatment re-reports. *Child Abuse & Neglect, 20,* 1183-1193.

Wonderlich, S., Donaldson, M., Carson, D., Staton, D., Gertz, L., Leach, L., & Johnson, M. (1996). Eating disturbance and incest. *Journal of Interpersonal Violence, 11,* 195-207.

Wood, G., & Middleman, R. (1992a). Groups to empower battered women. *Affilia, 7,* 82-95.

Wood, G., & Middleman, R. (1992b). Re-casting the die: A small group approach to giving batterers a chance to change. *Social Work With Groups, 15,* 5-18.

Woodling, B., & Heger, A. (1986). The use of the colposcope in the diagnosis of sexual abuse in the pediatric age group. *Child Abuse & Neglect, 10,* 111-114.

Worling, J. (1995). Adolescent sibling-incest offenders: Differences in family and individual functioning when compared to adolescent nonsibling sex offenders. *Child Abuse & Neglect, 19,* 633-643.

Wozencraft, T., Wagner, W., & Pellegrin, A. (1991). Depression and suicidal ideation in sexually abused children. *Child Abuse & Neglect, 15,* 505-511.

Wright, R. (1995, March 13). The biology of violence. *New Yorker,* pp. 68-77.

Wurtele, S., & Miller-Perrin, C. (1992). *Preventing child sexual abuse: Sharing the responsibility.* Lincoln: University of Nebraska Press.

Yegidis, B. (1988). Wife abuse and marital rape among women who seek help. *Affilia, 3,* 62-68.

Yegidis, B. (1992). Family violence: Contemporary research findings and practice issues. *Community Mental Health Journal, 28,* 519-529.

Yegidis, B., & Renzy, R. (1994). Battered women's experiences with a preferred arrest policy. *Affilia, 9,* 60-70.

Yllö, K., & LeClerc, D. (1988). Marital rape. In A. Horton & J. Williamson (Eds.), *Abuse and religion: When praying isn't enough* (pp. 48-57). Lexington, MA: Lexington Books.

Yokley, J. (Ed.). (1990). *The use of victim-offender communication in the treatment of sexual abuse: Three intervention models.* Orwell, VT: Safer Society Press.

Yokley, J., & McGuire, D. (1990). Introduction to the therapeutic use of victim-offender communication. In J. Yokley (Ed.), *The use of victim-offender communication in the treatment of sexual abuse: Three intervention models* (pp. 7-22). Orwell, VT: Safer Society Press.

Young, L. (1992). Sexual abuse and the problem of embodiment. *Child Abuse & Neglect, 16,* 89-100.

Yurkow, J. (1991). Abuse and neglect of the frail elderly. *Pride Institute Journal of Long Term Home Health Care, 10,* 36-39.

Zastrow, C., & Kirst-Ashman, K. (1997). *Understanding human behavior and the social environment* (4th ed.). Chicago: Nelson-Hall.

Zorza, J. (1994). Woman battering: High costs and the state of the law [Special issue]. *Clearinghouse Review, 28,* 383-395.

Zuckerman, D. (1996). Media violence, gun control, and public policy. *American Journal of Orthopsychiatry, 66,* 378-389.

Index

About the Author

Vernon R. Wiehe is Professor in the College of Social Work at the University of Kentucky in Lexington. After receiving a master's degree from the University of Chicago, he did postgraduate work in the Program of Advanced Studies in Social Work at Smith College and received his Ph.D. from Washington University in St. Louis.

His research and writing are primarily in the field of family violence. His books include *Sibling Abuse: The Hidden Physical, Emotional and Sexual Trauma; Perilous Rivalry: When Siblings Become Abusive; Working With Child Abuse and Neglect; A Primer; Brother/Sister Hurt: Recognizing the Effects of Sibling Abuse*; and *Intimate Betrayal: The Trauma of Acquaintance Rape.* He is also author of over 45 articles in professional journals.

He is a frequently cited author and lecturer who has lectured extensively on the subject of family violence both in the United States and abroad and has appeared as a guest on numerous U.S. radio and TV talk shows.